Using Micro
Word 5

CW00621336

IBM® Version

Bryan Pfaffenberger

CORPORATION

LEADING COMPUTER KNOWLEDGE

Using Microsoft® Word 5

IBM® Version

Library of Congress Catalog No.: 89-60240
ISBN 0-88022-409-6

92 91 90 89   8 7 6 5 4 3

Interpretation of the printing code: the rightmost double-digit number is the year of the book's printing; the rightmost single-digit number, the number of the book's printing. For example, a printing code of 89-1 shows that the first printing of the book occurred in 1989.

Using Microsoft Word 5: IBM Version is based on Versions 4 and 5.

DEDICATION

To Julia

Publishing Manager

Lloyd J. Short

Production Editor

Gregory Robertson

Editors

Sara Allaei
Kelly Currie
Kelly D. Dobbs
Jeannine Freudenberger
Alice Martina Smith
Richard Turner

Technical Editor

Frank Jones

Indexer

Sherry Massey

Book Design and Production

Dan Armstrong
Brad Chinn
Cheryl English
David Kline
Lori A. Lyons
Jennifer Matthews
Dennis Sheehan
Mae Louise Shinault
Peter Tocco

Composed in Helvetica and Excellent No. 47
by Que Corporation

ABOUT THE AUTHOR

Bryan Pfaffenberger

A nationally known writer on computer-related topics, Bryan Pfaffenberger, Ph.D., teaches in the School of Engineering and Applied Science at the University of Virginia, where he is Assistant Professor of Humanities. He is contributing editor of the *Research in Word Processing Newsletter* and the author of more than a dozen books, including *Microsoft Word Techniques and Applications*, *Microsoft Word 5 Tips, Tricks, and Traps: IBM Version*, *Using Microsoft Word 4: Macintosh Version*, and *Using Sprint*, all published by Que Corporation, and *Microcomputer Applications in Qualitative Research*, published by Sage. Dr. Pfaffenberger's interests include the social history and sociology of technology, international studies (he is the Associate Director of the University of Virginia's Center for South Asian Studies), and the anthropology of science and engineering. Dr. Pfaffenberger also enjoys spending time with his children. He lives in Charlottesville, Virginia.

CONTENTS AT A GLANCE

TABLE OF CONTENTS

I   Word 5 Fundamentals

4   Word 5 Formatting Strategies: Characters and Paragraphs

II Word 5's Features and Applications

15   Enhancing Group Productivity: Using Annotations and Redlining...................... 373

16   Creating Form Letters 389

III   Desktop Publishing with Microsoft Word

ACKNOWLEDGMENTS

A project like this one requires help from many people. Even though I alone take responsibility for this book's shortcomings, I would like to thank Lloyd Short, publishing manager; Greg Robertson, production editor; Frank Jones, technical editor; the other editors, and production personnel.

TRADEMARK
ACKNOWLEDGMENTS

Que Corporation has made every effort to supply trademark information about company names, products, and services mentioned in this book. Trademarks indicated below were derived from various sources. Que Corporation cannot attest to the accuracy of this information.

DIAGRAM-MASTER is a trademark of Decision Resources.

Harvard Graphics is trademark of Software Publishing Corporation.

Hercules Graphics Card is a trademark of Hercules Computer Technology.

Hewlett-Packard is a registered trademark of Hewlett-Packard Co.

IBM is a registered trademark of International Business Machines, Inc.

Lotus, Symphony, and 1-2-3 are registered trademarks of Lotus Development Corporation.

Microsoft is a registered trademark of Microsoft Corporation.

PageMaker is a registered trademark of Aldus Corporation.

PC Paintbrush is a registered trademark of ZSoft Corporation.

PostScript is a registered trademark of Adobe Systems Incorporated.

ProKey is a trademark of RoseSoft, Inc.

Que is a registered trademark of Que Corporation.

SideKick and Quattro are registered trademarks of Borland International.

SuperCalc is a registered trademark of Computer Associates International, Inc.

Ventura Publisher is a registered trademark of Ventura Software, Inc.

VP-Planner is a registered trademark of Paperback Software International.

WordPerfect is a registered trademark of WordPerfect Corporation.

CONVENTIONS USED
IN THIS BOOK

The conventions used in this book have been established to help you learn to use the program quickly and easily. As much as possible, the conventions correspond with those used in the Microsoft Word documentation.

The letters you press to make choices on menus are capitalized and in boldface type (**C**opy). Field names are in boldface type (**font color**). Material you are to type either is in *italic* type or is in normal type and set on a line by itself. Messages that appear on-screen are in a special typeface. Menu names are in upper- and lowercase, rather than as they appear on-screen (all uppercase).

Procedures for mouse users are indicated by a mouse icon in the margin. Features and commands new to Microsoft Word 5 are indicated by a Word 5 icon in the margin. Keyboard shortcuts also are indicated by margin icons.

Power user tips are set off from the text by lines above and below the tip. Cautions are set off by heavier lines above and below the text, and begin with the word **Caution**.

Introduction

Microsoft® Word is one of the top packages for professional word processing in the world of IBM®-format personal computing. Like its chief competitor, WordPerfect®, Word comes equipped with an impressive array of features, and serves a wide variety of users. Word's package includes features such as versatile printer support, outlining, automatically generated tables of contents and indexes, footnotes, macros, a macro editor, style sheets, a 220,000-word thesaurus, spell checking, form-letter generation from mailing lists, and much more. And with the remarkable new version of Word, Version 5, the list includes the graphics features demanded by today's marketplace, like on-screen integration of text and graphics.

Presenting Microsoft Word 5

In a competitive marketplace, even a program like Word will always have rivals when it comes to lists of features. But features alone do not necessarily add up to quality. What makes Word special in the IBM PC and compatible marketplace is not just that the program offers so many features, but that Word does the best job of bringing the Macintosh® style of word processing to the IBM-compatible world. Because of all the feature-by-feature comparisons, however, this fact and its significance have become lost.

The Macintosh word processing style emphasizes "what-you-see-is-what-you-get" (WYSIWYG) screen displays; ideally, you should see the results of text-formatting commands right on-screen. (Formatting commands control the appearance of your document when printed.) The point of WYSIWYG formatting is that it makes formatting

1

transparent to the user. You don't have to spend mental energy trying to predict the effects of a command, because you see these effects immediately. With Version 5, Word's WYSIWYG features have reached full fruition. The following new features enable you to view nearly every format before printing:

❑ The Show Layout option on the Options menu displays multiple columns on-screen even while you're editing.

❑ Print preView, a new option on the Print command menu, displays all document formats—including running heads, graphics, page numbers, margins, and footnotes—just the way they will print.

❑ You can incorporate graphics into Word documents and you can size, box, position, and anchor a graphic so that text "floats" around the picture.

❑ The Show Line Breaks option on the Options menu displays accurately how many letters of a certain font can fit in a printed inch, which greatly simplifies the task of aligning proportionally spaced text. The tab ruler adjusts to different font sizes, too.

❑ Page breaks appear automatically as you type, showing you precisely where Word intends to start printing a new page. And the page breaks are active: if you insert or delete text, Word automatically repositions the page breaks.

Word excels in another facet of the Macintosh philosophy: namely, the use of the mouse for editing and issuing commands. (A *mouse* is a small, hand-held control device that you move around on your desk. A pointer on the screen echoes the mouse's movements. As you point at something on the screen and click the button, the program responds.)

Human physiology provides good grounds for using the mouse. Evolution equipped human beings with extraordinary hand-eye coordination—so much so, in fact, that a big portion of the brain is devoted to controlling hand-eye coordination while the rest of the brain is doing something else. What this fact means for you is simple: You can use your hand to point at something without having to think about what you're doing. Performing an editing or command operation with the keyboard requires that you frame the operation in letters and words that you can type at the keyboard. The part of your brain that's devoted to thinking thus gets interrupted. With the mouse, however, you simply point at the sentence you want to move, and click the correct mouse button. The train of thought that goes into quality writing isn't broken.

You don't *have* to use the mouse with Word, because a keyboard counterpart exists for almost every mouse function. But if you want to experience the ease of use that makes the Macintosh so attractive to so many people, you should give the mouse a try.

If you have used Word before, you're already familiar with the program's style, and you will be pleased to discover that Version 5 genuinely fulfills Word's WYSIWYG promise. But perhaps the most significant fact about Version 5 is that Microsoft has responded to the constructive suggestions users have been making about ways to improve Word. For an experienced Word user, the following list of Word 5 characteristics is like a dream come true:

❏ Setting tabs is much easier with Version 5. Fewer keystrokes are required, and as you set each tab, you see the effect on-screen even before you press Enter.

❏ You can mix single-column and multiple-column formats on a single page. No more trickery with running heads to create a newsletter banner.

❏ A timed backup and autosave feature ensures that you never lose your work, even if the power fails. And if the power does fail, a special program reconstructs your work, right up to the last keystroke.

❏ The Options menu contains the Window Options settings. You can set all your options with just one command.

❏ Spell has been improved so that it's up to the world-class standards set by the rest of the program.

❏ Running heads now align at the margin rather than the edge of the page.

❏ A new feature called *annotation*, which allows you to enter personalized notes on a draft, enhances the usefulness of Word's redlining feature (the Format revision-Marks command). In previous versions, the redlining feature allowed collaborative writers to propose and approve text insertions, deletions, and moves, but provided no convenient way to attach explanatory notes.

❏ You can save a file in pure ASCII format (with line breaks at the end of every line) in just one step.

❏ You can set new default margins without creating a style sheet.

❑ When you're loading files with Word, you don't have to remember the names of subdirectories on your hard disk.

Thanks to these major improvements, this powerful program is now truly a joy to use. The changes listed above are best appreciated by experienced users; if you're just starting with Word and word processing, you probably will not know anything about most of these features. But don't let that concern you now. The key point is that Word has finally realized its potential. If you have chosen Word 5, you have made an excellent choice indeed.

Using Microsoft Word 5 is your guide to this new version of an already outstanding program. The text is not a rehash of an existing book with a few chapters tacked on to bring it up to date. Every word of this book was written with Word 5, about Word 5, and while keeping Word 5's special features in mind. Whether you're new to Word or an experienced Word user, this book has been designed to provide precisely the information and skills you need in order to master the Word 5 style of word processing.

Preparing for High-Productivity Word Processing

When a new technology comes along, it usually takes time for people to grasp its potential. Early in the telephone's history, for instance, a common belief was that people would use the telephone to listen to distant musical concerts! When word processing software first became available, however, people saw right away that it was vastly superior to the old type-and-retype cycle of mechanical writing. With the text kept in the computer's memory, you can change the text all you want before printing it. And even if further changes are necessary, printing another draft is a cinch.

What is truly amazing about contemporary word processing, however, is the way people are using intermediate and advanced program features, not just the basic ones, to realize huge productivity gains. The following are some examples of what just a few users are doing with Word 5:

❑ A legal secretary must make absolutely sure that he uses the latest version of standard clauses for wills, leases, and other legal documents. He therefore creates and names standard clauses using Word 5's new *bookmarks*, which are like named ranges in a spreadsheet. Now, when he types a will, he inserts the bookmark with the Library Link Document command, and Word uses the text contained in the bookmark.

❑ A novelist uses Word's on-line *thesaurus*, an impressive compilation of 220,000 English synonyms, to find just the right word to express a mood or to describe a scene. This method is far faster (and much more convenient) than consulting a printed thesaurus, and because she uses the electronic version frequently, her writing has acquired a new vividness.

❑ A professional grant proposal writer uses Word's *outlining* feature to sketch the structure of a proposal before writing it. And after the first draft is written, he switches to the outline view to rearrange the proposal's structure in seconds, just by moving headings on the outline.

❑ An attorney uses Word to generate a *table of legal authorities* cited in the briefs she writes. The whole process is automatic and takes only two minutes.

❑ The chairperson of a small community organization uses Word's *multiple-column* and *laser-printing* features to produce a simple but handsome newsletter. He also uses Word's list-sorting feature to maintain a database of newsletter subscribers, and the program's print-merging features to print mailing labels. With these features, he can put out a new issue of the newsletter—including printing the mailing labels—in one afternoon.

❑ A departmental supervisor uses Word's *macro* and *form-creation* features to fill out more than a dozen forms she must complete each month. The macro, a list of instructions that tells Word how to follow a procedure automatically, prompts her for specific information needed to complete the form. After she provides the information, Word performs the necessary calculations automatically and prints the form precisely the way management wants it.

❑ A free-lance computer programmer uses Word to produce handsomely printed documentation for her programs. After structuring the document with Word's outlining feature, she gives Word commands that automatically generate a *table of contents*. She uses additional commands that generate a list of figures, a list of tables, and an automatically compiled index. The whole table-generating and indexing operation takes only a few minutes.

❑ A high school English teacher uses Word's *glossaries*—storage places for commonly used (boilerplate) text—to store extensive comments on common writing problems, such as dangling modifiers and comma splices. His students prepare their essays on disk, and he reads them on-screen (with a printed copy on hand). When he encounters an error, he enters the relevant boilerplate into the student's paper with one keystroke, adding personalized comments as needed. The result? Students receive extensive, high-quality comments on their writing, and the teacher has more time to spend interacting with students.

❑ A business manager uses Word to write reports that automatically incorporate Lotus® 1-2-3® spreadsheets and graphs. The text floats around the tables and graphs, which are seamlessly integrated with the report and beautifully printed, complete with informative captions.

Even if you have never used Word before, or if you have used it only for basic word processing, you can learn to take advantage of these and other high-productivity techniques. This book isn't just about Word 5; it's also about helping you learn the program well enough that these techniques are within your grasp.

Why a Book about Word 5?

Microsoft Word 5 comes with an outstanding manual and an even better computer-based training program. So why a book about Word 5?

Word's documentation, good as it is, suffers from the drawback of all computer program documentation: its purpose is to survey every Word feature, even the ones that people seldom use. Even if you're experienced with word processing programs, unwrapping all those thick manuals filled with page after page of computer commands is a daunting experience. And aside from a few tutorials, the manuals are encyclopedic; they strive to tell you *everything* about a feature. That is the manual's job, but the effect is dismaying. You get a great deal of complexity thrown at you all at once.

Word's documentation leaves little room for telling you what you want to know most: "How do I put all this information to work on daily writing tasks?" As a Word 5 user, you want to produce documents, such as business forms, business reports, newsletters, form letters, legal briefs, alphabetized price lists, and others. But Word's documentation often doesn't make the connection between the detailed information it presents and the specific challenges of producing specific documents. In other words, the manuals show you how to do something, but they often fail to explain just what it is you're doing—and why.

Using Microsoft Word 5 is intended to remedy these deficiencies in the following three ways:

❑ First, this book seeks to describe Word 5 in the way the best corporate training programs do: by introducing information in small, manageable units and building knowledge one step at a time. Menu techniques for accomplishing a task are always introduced first, because these techniques help you develop knowledge of the program's command structure. (If a keyboard shortcut is available, it's mentioned right after the menu technique and is highlighted by a special icon in the margin.)

❑ Second, the book focuses on specific applications, such as creating lists, tables, newsletters, footnotes, and indexes. Throughout the book, the goal is to clarify the concepts that underlie the application of Word 5 and to teach you the specific skills you need in order to use the program effectively.

❑ Third, this book develops an approach to Word gained from long experience in using and teaching others how to use the program. When you see the Power User Tip icon (see "Conventions Used in This Book"), you will learn how Word's power users approach daily writing, editing, formatting, and printing tasks. (A *power user* is a professional or business user who depends on the program for high performance on the job and in consequence has attained knowledge of the program far beyond the average level.)

Using Microsoft Word 5, in sum, isn't concerned so much with providing an encyclopedic reference as it is with teaching you how to apply this amazing program. Still, you will find plenty of detailed information for reference purposes, because all of Word's functions and commands receive treatment in the book. But with this text, you take the program one step at a time, and each step takes you closer to mastery.

How This Book Is Organized— and How To Use It

If you haven't yet installed Word on your computer, begin by reading the Appendix, "Word 5 Installation, Setup, and Start-Up Options." If you have a hard disk, be sure to read the Appendix even if you have already installed the program; you will find some important tips about how to set up your hard disk for optimal performance with Word.

Mastering the Basics

If you're new to Word, begin with Part I. And even if you have some previous experience with Word, you will still find Part I worth skimming. Even though the material is introductory and elementary, you will learn how power users approach day-to-day tasks with Word. You should read (or skim) in order the chapters in Part I. They introduce key terms, techniques, and strategies in a sequence designed to teach Word skills and concepts.

Part I, "Word 5 Fundamentals," assumes that you have no previous knowledge of Word or any other word processing program. This section does assume, however, that you know how to turn on your computer, format disks, and perform other basic personal computer operations.

Chapter 1, "Preparing To Use Word 5," introduces the information you need in order to use Word 5, including starting the program, understanding the Word 5 keyboard and the screen display, using command menus, moving the cursor and scrolling, and managing files.

Chapter 2, "Your First Word 5 Document—Quickly!," walks you through the creation, formatting, editing, and printing of a business letter. You learn important fundamentals of Word, such as how to center text, change paragraph alignment, delete and insert text, perform block moves, split and join paragraphs, and print your work. You learn, too, how to edit and format your text as you're writing with Word.

Chapter 3, "Word 5 Editing Strategies," expands your knowledge of the editing concepts introduced in Chapter 2. You learn how to open files you have already created; when to use the overtype mode; how to move around in a large document; and how to select, copy, delete, and move text. In addition, you learn how to use Word's powerful search-and-replace features and how to make the best use of the Undo command.

Chapter 4, "Word 5 Formatting Strategies: Characters and Paragraphs," expands your knowledge of the formatting concepts introduced in Chapter 2. You learn how to understand and use Word's measurement options, how to attach emphasis (such as boldface or italic) to characters, and how to format paragraphs (using formats such as double line spacing, right margin justification, and hanging indents). In addition, you learn how to format paragraphs side-by-side and how to use Word's search-and-replace command to replace character or paragraph styles throughout a document.

Chapter 5, "Word 5 Formatting Strategies: Page Formatting," shows you how to alter Word's default page formatting settings. You learn how to set margins and page sizes, add page numbers and line numbers, and create running heads (short versions of a document's title that appear at the top or bottom of each page). You learn also how to divide your document into sections, each with its own distinctive page format.

Chapter 6, "Using the Thesaurus, Checking Spelling, and Controlling Hyphenation," introduces Word's excellent thesaurus, which opens a 220,000-word synonym dictionary right on your screen. After you highlight the word you want, Word inserts it in your text. This chapter also shows you how to use the much-improved Word 5 version of Spell and how to hyphenate your document automatically so that words are broken correctly at the ends of lines.

Chapter 7, "Printing Your Work," shows you how to print your work attractively and correctly. You learn how to preview page breaks and formatting before you print and how to use Word 5's large variety of print options, which give you precise control over the printing process. You learn how to print a single page of a document or a range of pages, multiple copies, drafts, and document summary sheets.

Using Advanced Techniques and Applications

Part II, "Word 5's Features and Applications," builds on the knowledge you have acquired in Part I. This part of the book focuses on advanced techniques and applications, such as using windows, creating running heads, using annotations, creating newsletters, outlining, using glossaries, linking documents with spreadsheets, and creating form letters.

You need not read every chapter in Part II, and you need not read them in order. Each chapter addresses a single topic, which is explored in depth. Most readers, however, can profit from reading Chapter 8 ("Finding and Managing Documents"), Chapter 9 ("Customizing the Screen and Using Windows"), and Chapter 10 ("Organizing Your Document with Outlining"), which present advanced Word features everyone can use. Choose from the remaining chapters according to the nature of the work you plan to do with Word.

Chapter 8, "Finding and Managing Documents," builds on the knowledge you already have about the basics of saving and loading documents. You learn how to save all active documents in one step, how to save documents as ASCII files, and how to manage disk space and memory. And if you're using a hard disk (and who isn't, these days?), you learn how to take advantage of Word's remarkable document-retrieval feature, which lets you search an entire hard disk for documents based on matching key words, authors' names, dates of creation, and other criteria. The chapter also explains how to automate file backup and archiving procedures.

Chapter 9, "Customizing the Screen and Using Windows," shows you how to shape Word's screen to your needs. You learn how to hide the command menu and the window border and how to display the ruler, show line breaks as they will appear when printed, and reveal special characters. The chapter shows you how, as you explore Word's windows, you can open new windows on the same or different documents, change window size and zoom windows, and remove windows from the screen. You will see how easily you can copy and move text from one window to another.

Chapter 10, "Organizing Your Document with Outlining," covers one of Word's best features: its powerful and flexible outline mode. You can use outlining to organize your thoughts before writing, as you would any outlining utility. But what makes Word's outline mode so powerful is its seamless integration with your document. As you learn in this chapter, you can create an outline so that the outline's headings correspond to section titles in your document. This feature demonstrates Word 5's power: Simply by rearranging the headings in your outline, you can completely restructure your document. It's far and away the most powerful editing technique ever devised.

Chapter 11, "Creating Tables and Lists with Tabs, Autosort, and Math," is the first chapter to focus specifically on advanced formatting techniques. You learn how to gain full control over Word's tab features, and you apply this knowledge to the creation and formatting of tables and lists. You also learn how to use Autosort to sort data alphabetically or numerically and how to use Word's math features to add up columns of data (and perform more sophisticated operations).

Chapter 12, "Using Glossaries and Bookmarks," thoroughly explores Word's glossaries, which are storage places for commonly used passages of text called "boilerplate." You learn how to create and insert boilerplate passages and how to save, load, and manage glossary files. This chapter also introduces a new Word 5 feature called *bookmarks*, which you use to assign names to units of text. You can use bookmarks to move around your document speedily, to create automatic cross-references, and to retrieve boilerplate text.

Chapter 13, "Creating Indexes and Tables of Contents," shows you how to use Word so that the program automatically generates an index, a table of contents, and (if you want) additional tables when you print your document. If your job responsibilities include the writing of reports, proposals, or documentation, you will find this chapter invaluable.

Chapter 14, "The Legal and Scholarly Word," introduces the use of Word for attorneys and scholars. You learn how to create, edit, and print attractive footnotes or endnotes. You learn, too, how to use Word's advanced features to generate a bibliography of works you have cited and how to use one of the macros supplied with Word to generate a table of legal authorities. Don't think for a minute that Word is inferior to any other program in this area!

Chapter 15, "Enhancing Group Productivity: Using Annotations and Redlining," covers the use of Word in collaborative writing situations. You learn how to retrieve standardized, authoritative versions of text automatically, how to insert comments in a draft, and how to propose and approve editorial changes.

Chapter 16, "Creating Form Letters," is for anyone who must send the same letter to many people. Word's form-letter and mailing-list features are extremely flexible and powerful. You can even create a letter that will include special text for just those people who meet criteria you specify.

Applying Word to Desktop Publishing

Part III, "Desktop Publishing with Microsoft Word," shows you how new Version 5 features can make short work of many business and professional applications in desktop publishing, such as creating business forms, departmental newsletters, and illustrated reports.

Chapter 17, "Creating Forms and Illustrations," introduces the Word features that help you design, print, and even fill out business forms. If you have ever had to pay a printer to design and print a business form, you will find that this chapter can save you money as well as time.

Chapter 18, "Integrating Text and Graphics," fully explores Version 5's exciting new graphics features. You will learn how to incorporate graphics into Word documents and "anchor" their position so that text flows around them.

Chapter 19, "Creating Multiple-Column Text and Newsletters," is for anyone who is currently producing a newsletter—or thinking of starting one. You learn how to use new Word 5 features that display multiple columns of text on-screen even while you're editing, and how to show precisely the way columns, running heads, and all other formatting features will appear when printed. And you learn how you can mix single- and multiple-column text on one page.

Customizing the Program

Part IV, "Word 5's Style Sheets and Macros," shows you how to customize and automate Word so that the program works precisely the way you want.

Chapter 20, "Using Style Sheets," introduces one of Word's most powerful—and least understood—features. In this chapter, you learn how to customize Word's keyboard so that with a single keystroke you can enter precisely the formats you want. You learn how to create a style sheet, which is a list of your own formatting instructions linked to an Alt-key formatting command. You learn, too, how you can set up Word to take full advantage of your printer's fonts, making a special font such as Helvetica the default font for all your documents. Style sheets may seem like an advanced feature, but after reading this chapter, you will undoubtedly agree that everyone should use them. You will be amazed at how easily you can create and use Word 5's style sheets.

Chapter 21, "Creating and Using Word 5 Macros," shows you how to automate Word 5's operations with macros—lists of instructions that tell Word to perform a complex series of actions automatically. With Word's elegant and powerful macro programming language, you can write macros that enter text and give commands just as if someone were typing them at the keyboard. Using the language's looping and conditional branch statements, you can write macros that perform such operations over and over, or perform them only if a condition is met. Word's macro programming language is a real jewel: It's simple and easy to learn, yet powerful enough for professional applications.

The material in Part IV is advanced, but these chapters are important. In them, you find the road to professional productivity. If you want Word to jump through hoops for you, you need to learn to use style sheets and macros and work them into everything you do with Word. And even if you have never even programmed your telephone to dial numbers automatically, you will find that these chapters can teach you to write highly effective style sheets and macros immediately. You learn quickly because the chapters are keyed to, and draw on, skills and concepts that you have developed by reading Part I and selected chapters in Part II.

The appendix shows you how to install Word.

Required Equipment for Word 5

Microsoft's goal in creating Word 5 was to develop a powerful new version of this program but keep it small enough so that it could run on almost any IBM-format computer with DOS 2.0 or later. You can thus run Word on a dual floppy, 8088-based computer—and you can also run it on the most sophisticated new PS/2™ models that use the OS/2® operating system.

At the minimum, however, you need 360K of free memory (RAM—random access memory) when you start Word. RAM is your computer's internal memory, which stores programs and data so that they are accessible for processing. (You can use the CHKDSK program on your DOS disk to find out how much RAM is available.) Because DOS consumes some RAM, you need at least 512K of RAM in your computer to be on the safe side. Having 640K is better, because more room is then available for memory-intensive operations like sorting and searching.

Although you can run Word 5 on a dual floppy system, using the program with a hard disk is highly recommended. With a hard disk, you can create a single Word directory that contains Spell, Thesaurus, Help, and Learning Word.

You can use Word with nearly any video adapter and monitor designed for IBM-format computing, including the Hercules Graphics Card, the Hercules Graphics Card Plus, the Genius adapter and full-page monitor, the IBM Enhanced Graphics Adapter (EGA) and video graphics array (VGA) adapters and monitors, and the Hewlett-Packard Vectra® adapter and monitor. The program is at its best, however, with high-resolution graphics or color systems.

Word takes full advantage of the mouse, and although it's optional, you should try it. People who use a mouse say that they would never go back to editing with the keyboard alone. But rest assured: You *can* use only the keyboard without sacrificing any of the program's functions or versatility.

Conventions Used in This Book

As you read *Using Microsoft Word 5*, watch for special icons in the margins. These icons are your key to special features of this book.

Keyboard Shortcut icon. This icon alerts you to keyboard shortcuts you can substitute for menu command techniques. Look for the key combination in the margin (Ctrl-F7, for example). To facilitate learning, the menu technique is always presented first and then the keyboard shortcut—if one is available. Try the keyboard shortcuts. You probably will find that some or most of them deserve to be part of your everyday working repertoire of Word techniques.

Word 5 icon. This icon highlights features new to Word 5 and old features that have been revised to make them easier to use. If you're already familiar with a previous version of Word, these icons will alert you to new material.

Mouse icon. This icon calls your attention to mouse techniques you can substitute for the keyboard methods described in the text. If you're using the mouse, you will find these icons helpful. If you're not using the mouse, you can skip over the sections highlighted by these icons.

❑ *Cautions.* Though not an icon, this material is set off with a rule above and below it and the word **Caution** in the text. These sections warn you of problems people frequently encounter when they're learning Word, and chart a course around those problems.

❑ *Power User Tips.* These tips highlight techniques or approaches that power users of Microsoft Word have developed through experience. Power user tips are separated from regular text by rules above and below them. These tips show you the road to Word mastery.

You will notice some special typefaces in this book. They provide more clues to the learning process.

❑ When command names are mentioned, the letters that you type to select the command are boldfaced (**F**ormat **T**ab **Se**t). In the command mode, you can choose these commands simply by typing the command's capitalized letter. You need not type an uppercase letter, however; Word recognizes lowercase letters. For more information on choosing commands, see Chapter 1.

❑ On-screen messages are printed in a special "computer" typeface (the Enter page number field).

❑ The names of command fields are boldfaced (the **line spacing** field).

❑ Material that *you* type is either set off on a line by itself or printed in italic. For example, if you see the instruction "Enter *2 li* in the **line spacing** field," type the italicized material exactly as it appears.

Learning Word

As you develop your knowledge of Word 5, you will surely experience some frustrations, mistakes, and setbacks along the way. But that's how you learn. You are not a failure at personal computing if you make a mistake or give a command incorrectly! As you will see, Word is a forgiving program. In most cases, you can cancel the ill effects of an incorrect command if you choose the Undo command before doing anything else. (For more information, see the section in Chapter 1 on "Using the Undo Command.") Keep your eyes open for the caution icons, which highlight problems many people experience when learning Word.

Microsoft Word 5 is an extensive, wonderful program for professional writing, and you cannot learn it in a day. The fact that the programming wizards at Microsoft could stuff all these functions into a program you can use on a 512K machine is nothing short of astounding. But you can learn Word in small, manageable chunks, and this book is designed to present Word in precisely that way. Just remember: Even if you have lived at sea level all your life, you can walk over a mountain pass. All you have to do is put one foot in front of the other and take one step at a time.

Word 5
Fundamentals

Includes

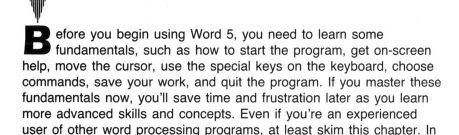

Preparing To Use
Word 5

Before you begin using Word 5, you need to learn some
fundamentals, such as how to start the program, get on-screen
help, move the cursor, use the special keys on the keyboard, choose
commands, save your work, and quit the program. If you master these
fundamentals now, you'll save time and frustration later as you learn
more advanced skills and concepts. Even if you're an experienced
user of other word processing programs, at least skim this chapter. In
it, you will learn how to do the following:

- ❑ Master Word fundamentals by using Learning Word, a
  computer-based training program

- ❑ Start Word at the beginning of a writing or editing session

- ❑ Understand the features of the Word 5 display screen

- ❑ Discern the difference between the edit mode and the
  command mode and understand how to move between them

- ❑ Use the special keys on your computer's keyboard, such as
  Esc, Ctrl, Alt, and the function keys

- ❑ Discern the difference between the text mode and the graphics
  mode

- ❑ Move the cursor and scroll the screen

- ❑ Choose commands, whether you use the keyboard, the mouse,
  or both

❏ Obtain, with a keystroke, on-screen help that explains commands or program functions and that even offers tutorials you can take while you're editing

❏ Save your work to disk and make the best use of Word 5's new autosave feature

❏ Quit Word at the end of a writing session

Even if you're new to word processing, you should already know a few computer fundamentals, and this chapter assumes that you have this knowledge. You should know how to turn on the power and obtain the DOS prompt, which is an on-screen letter (such as A or C) followed by a greater-than symbol (>). You should know how to format disks, switch from one drive to another, display a directory of a disk's contents, copy files from one disk to another, and erase unwanted files. If you have a hard disk, you should know how to create directories and how to switch from one directory to another.

If you don't know how to accomplish these tasks, take some time now to learn them. Read your computer's manual and, above all, get help from someone who has experience using an IBM PC or a compatible computer. *MS-DOS User's Guide*, 3rd Edition, and *Using PC DOS*, 2nd Edition (both published by Que® Corporation), are excellent guides for anyone who uses DOS, whether at the novice or advanced level. The better you understand these basic computer tasks, the less chance you have of destroying your work accidentally.

If you haven't yet installed Word 5 on your system, skip now to the appendix, "Word and Your Computer: Configuring Your System for Word 5 and Using SETUP."

If you're eager to start a test document and you already have some experience with Word and word processing, you may want to skim this chapter or skip directly to Chapter 2, "Your First Word 5 Document—Quickly!"

Using the Learning Word Program

The program called Learning Word is an excellent example of computer-based training software. It uses short lessons to teach you the fundamentals of Microsoft Word, right on the screen. Word Essentials, the set of introductory lessons, is for anyone who has never used Word before. If you have no previous experience with Microsoft Word, you may want to explore the Word Essentials lessons before you start Word for the first time. Later, you can explore the intermediate and advanced lessons to get an introduction to such features as glossaries, style sheets, and macros.

The Word Essentials Disk comes in two versions, a mouse version and a keyboard version. To use the introductory lessons in Learning Word, follow these instructions:

1. After obtaining the A› prompt, place the Word Essentials Disk in drive A.

2. Type *learn* and press Enter.

3. Follow the instructions on the screen.

Starting Word

Word gives you many start-up options. You can start Word, for instance, to take full advantage of special monitors and video cards. If you have a Hercules Graphics Card™ or an EGA video card and monitor, you can display up to 43 lines of text on the screen. You can also start Word and load the last document on which you were working, and Word takes you to the exact place you stopped writing or editing. This section discusses only the simplest of these start-up options. For a survey of all the start-up options, see the appendix.

Starting Word on a Dual Floppy System

Before starting Word, use your DOS start-up disk, the one that SETUP modified, to boot your system. (For information on using SETUP, see the appendix.) Then take these steps:

1. After you see the DOS prompt (A›) displayed on the screen, remove the DOS disk.

2. Place in drive A the Word 5 program disk that SETUP created.

3. Insert a blank, formatted disk in drive B.

4. Type *word* and press Enter.

Word starts and displays a new, unnamed document.

Starting Word on a Hard Disk System

To start Word on a hard disk system, follow these steps:

1. Make sure that the DOS prompt (for most systems, C›) is displayed on-screen.

2. Type *cd*, press the space bar, and type a backslash (\) and the name of the directory in which you stored the Word program. If you stored Word in a directory called WORD, for instance, type *cd \word*, and press Enter.

3. When the DOS prompt reappears, type *word* and press Enter.

Word starts and displays a new, unnamed document.

If you used SETUP and allowed it to name the Word program directory WORD—and doing so is a good idea—you can start Word from any directory on your hard disk. Word always saves your document to the currently logged directory unless you specifically instruct the program otherwise. If you start Word from a directory called DOCS, for example, Word saves your work to that directory, not Word's. For this reason, your Word program directory won't become cluttered with your document files, and less chance exists that you'll accidentally delete a program file when you're disposing of unwanted documents.

Caution: If you didn't use SETUP or if you accidentally erase the AUTOEXEC.BAT file that SETUP creates, you won't be able to start Word unless you have made Word's directory the default directory in such cases. You must create a new AUTOEXEC.BAT file that includes a PATH statement. For more information on AUTOEXEC.BAT and PATH, see the appendix.

If Word Doesn't Start

If you see the message Bad command or file name when you try to start Word, run SETUP again or see the appendix for instructions on how to include a PATH instruction in your AUTOEXEC.BAT file.

If you haven't run the SETUP program, you may have trouble starting Word. When you run SETUP, it automatically modifies your DOS start-up disk so that the disk contains a file called CONFIG.SYS, which includes the instruction

FILES = 20

The minimum number of files is 20, but you can specify up to 99 files in this instruction, at the cost of some free memory in RAM. If you want to use a mouse, the CONFIG.SYS file must also contain the instruction

DEVICE = MOUSE.SYS

Word cannot run unless you have started your computer with the CONFIG.SYS file present on the DOS start-up disk. If you accidentally delete this file, or if you start your computer with a DOS disk that does not contain it, Word may not run, or some features may not be available.

To make sure that CONFIG.SYS is on your DOS start-up disk, follow these steps:

1. If you're using a dual floppy system, place your DOS start-up disk in drive A and log on to that drive. If you're using a hard disk, log on to the hard disk's root directory (usually C:\).

2. Type *type config.sys* and press Enter.

3. You should see on-screen this text:

   ```
   FILES=20
   DEVICE=MOUSE.SYS
   ```

   If you don't see this message, run SETUP again to modify your DOS start-up disk.

If you see the message Insufficient memory to run Word when you try to start Word, fewer than 360K of memory is available—not including the memory taken up by DOS. If your computer has only 256K or 320K of memory, you need to add more memory before you can run Word. If your computer has plenty of memory, you may have loaded some memory-resident programs, such as SideKick® or ProKey™, that are taking up too much memory space. Deactivate these programs, or reboot your computer, and try again.

Exploring the Word 5 Screen

The Word 5 screen contains two general areas, the *document window* (enclosed by the rectangular window border) and the *command area* (the four lines below the rectangle).

Note: If you like a "clean screen" look, you can hide the command menu and the window borders. (See "Hiding the Command Menu" in this chapter.) For more information on screen customization options, including choosing the colors you want, see Chapter 9, "Customizing the Screen and Using Windows."

The Document Window

When you start Word, the document window is *active*, which means that the alphanumeric keys you press will produce text in the document window. You can tell when the document window is active by looking at the *message line*, the next-to-last line on the screen. When the document window is active, the message line reads Edit document or press Esc to use menu (see fig. 1.1). When you see this message, Word is in its *edit mode*, and you can create or edit your document.

Fig. 1.1.

An active
document
window.

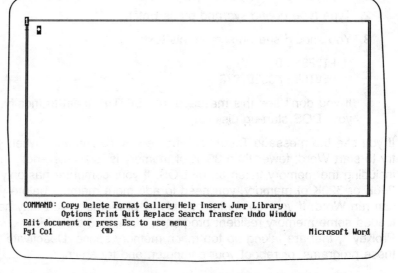

```
COMMAND: Copy Delete Format Gallery Help Insert Jump Library
         Options Print Quit Replace Search Transfer Undo Window
Edit document or press Esc to use menu
Pg1 Co1          {90}                              Microsoft Word
```

You can display up to eight windows at a time with Word 5. With more than one window on the screen, you can view more than one location in a document, or you can work with more than one document at a time. Word's windows, as figure 1.2 shows, are *tiled*, which means that opening a new window reduces the size of the existing one (or ones). But you can zoom any window to full size just by pressing Ctrl-F1. Windows are covered in detail in Chapter 9, "Customizing the Screen and Using Windows."

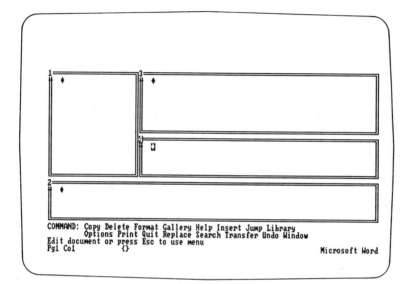

Fig. 1.2.

Word's tiled windows.

```
COMMAND: Copy Delete Format Gallery Help Insert Jump Library
         Options Print Quit Replace Search Transfer Undo Window
Edit document or press Esc to use menu
Pg1 Co1              {}                          Microsoft Word
```

You will find that windows are especially useful when you are working with two or more documents at a time or when you are moving text in a document (or between documents).

Every document window has the following basic features, which are indicated in figure 1.3:

❑ *Window number*. If only one window is displayed on the screen, it is called window 1 by default, and the number 1 appears in the window's upper left corner. If more than one window is displayed on the screen, you can tell which window is active by looking at the windows' numbers. The active window's number is highlighted. In figure 1.2, for instance, window 4 is active.

❑ *Position indicator*. A small horizontal line on the window's left border (hereinafter referred to as "left window border," "top window border," and so on), this indicator shows your relative position in a document. If the indicator is near the top of the border, you're at the beginning of the document. If the indicator is near the bottom of the border, you're near the end of the document.

Note: The indicator isn't totally accurate. It's only intended to give you a quick, relative idea of where you are in a document.

❏ *Cursor.* Sometimes called the *highlight* in Word's manuals, the cursor is the rectangular highlight on the screen that shows where text will appear when you type at the keyboard. When you begin with a blank document, the cursor is superimposed on the end mark. But after you've entered text in your document, the cursor and end mark separate. You can move the cursor around by using the arrows and other keys, but you can't move it past the end mark.

❏ *End mark.* This diamond-shaped mark displays at the end of the document. You can't use the arrow keys to go past the end mark (unless you have created footnotes or endnotes), so don't get frustrated if you are unable to move the cursor around on-screen when you first start Word. Just press the Enter key to create some "room" to move the cursor.

❏ *Document name.* After you save your document with the Transfer Save command, the name you gave your document appears on the right corner of the bottom window border.

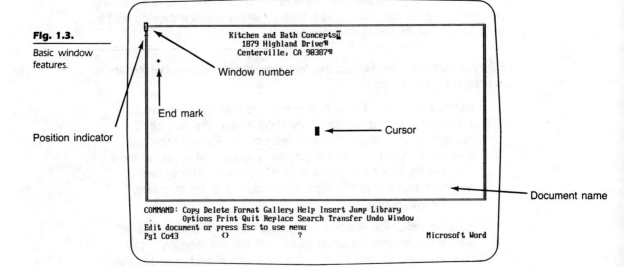

Fig. 1.3.

Basic window features.

Window number

End mark

Position indicator

Cursor

Document name

```
                     Kitchen and Bath Concepts¶
                        1879 Highland Drive¶
                        Centerville, CA 90387¶


COMMAND: Copy Delete Format Gallery Help Insert Jump Library
         Options Print Quit Replace Search Transfer Undo Window
Edit document or press Esc to use menu
Pg1 Co43          {}              ?                   Microsoft Word
```

The Document Window
for Mouse Users

If your system is equipped with a mouse, take note of these additional window features for mouse users:

❑ *Scroll bars*. The *left* and *bottom* window borders serve as scroll bars, which means that you can use them to scroll the screen. For more information on scrolling with the scroll bars and the mouse, see "Moving the Cursor and Scrolling" in this chapter.

❑ *Window split bars*. If you point to the *top* or *right* window borders and click the left mouse button, Word splits the current window. To cancel an unwanted window split, point to the border again and press *both* mouse buttons. (If your mouse has more than two buttons, refer to the instructions that came with it.) For more information on opening and closing windows with the mouse, see Chapter 9, "Customizing the Screen and Using Windows."

❑ *Selection bar*. Selection is an important operation in Word; you must select text by highlighting it before you can edit or format it. The vertical column next to the left window border is called the selection bar. If you click the mouse after placing the pointer in this column, you can quickly select lines, paragraphs, or even the whole document. For more information on selection and the selection bar, see Chapter 3, "Word 5 Editing Strategies."

❑ *Ruler switch*. The upper right corner of the window border is called the ruler switch. If you point to the switch and click the left button, a ruler appears on the top window border. Point to the same place and click both buttons simultaneously to turn off the ruler. For more information on using the ruler, see Chapter 5, "Word 5 Formatting Strategies: Page Formatting."

❑ *Zoom switch*. When you're using the mouse, the window number also serves as the zoom switch, which is useful when you're displaying more than one tiled window on the screen. When you click the left button on the zoom switch, that window zooms to full size. To shrink the window back to normal size, point to the window's number (the zoom switch) and click the *right* button. For more information on using the mouse to zoom and unzoom windows, see Chapter 9, "Customizing the Screen and Using Windows."

If you're not using the mouse, don't despair! Word provides good keyboard techniques for all the operations just mentioned. You will find a full discussion of these keyboard techniques in this chapter, as well as in Chapters 3, 5, and 9.

The Command Menu

The *command menu*, which is positioned below the document window, lists the commands you can use with Word. To activate the command menu, press the Esc key. After you do, the command menu becomes *active*, and Word is in the *command mode*: The program is ready to act on the commands you select. You can tell when the command menu is active because one of the command names is highlighted, and a brief description of the highlighted command appears on the message line (the next-to-last line on the screen). Figure 1.4 shows an example of an active Copy command. To activate the document window and return to the edit mode, press Esc again.

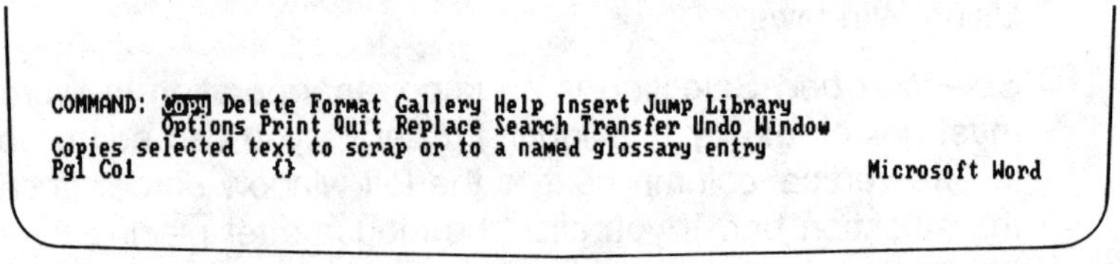

Fig. 1.4.

An active command menu.

```
COMMAND: Copy Delete Format Gallery Help Insert Jump Library
         Options Print Quit Replace Search Transfer Undo Window
Copies selected text to scrap or to a named glossary entry
Pg1 Co1          {}                                    Microsoft Word
```

Caution: Practice moving from the edit mode to the command mode and back to the edit mode until you're sure you recognize the difference. If you think you're in the edit mode when you're actually in the command mode, and you start typing text, Word interprets the characters you type as commands and tries to act on them. In most cases, however, this error will not have catastrophic results. You may see a command menu and the message Not a valid option on the message line. You must press Esc to cancel the command and return to the edit mode.

The Status Line

The status line, the last line on the screen, contains important information about Word and about the document on which you're working. Here's an overview of the contents of the status line, an example of which is shown in figure 1.5:

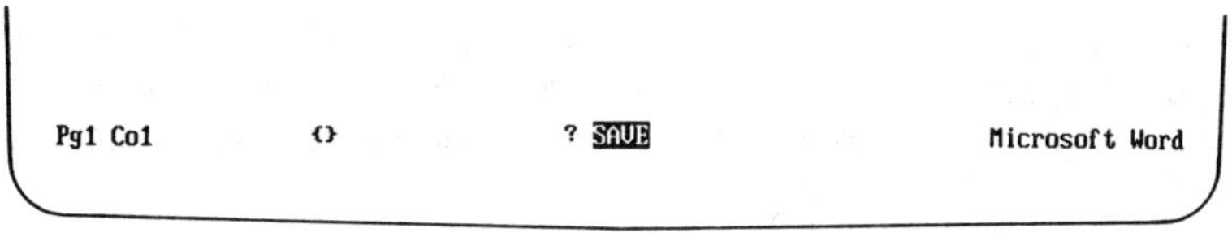

Fig. 1.5.

The status line.

```
Pg1 Co1          {}          ? SAVE                    Microsoft Word
```

❏ *Page and column indicators*. The page number indicator shows the number of the page within which the cursor is positioned. (Remember that the cursor shows you where text will appear if you start typing.) The column indicator shows the horizontal position of the cursor on the 80-column screen. In figure 1.5, the status line indicates that the cursor is on page 1, column 1.

❏ *Scrap*. Indicated by two curly braces, the scrap is a temporary storage place for the most recently deleted or copied text. If you see an ellipsis (. . .) within the braces, the text stored in the scrap is too lengthy to be displayed, so only the first and last characters are shown. As you'll quickly find when you begin editing documents, you can use the scrap as a convenient way to move text from one location to another in your document. For more information on using the scrap while editing, see Chapter 2, "Your First Word 5 Document —Quickly!"

❏ *SAVE indicator*. When the SAVE light comes on in the status line, save your documents, glossaries, and style sheets immediately by choosing the Transfer Save All command.

Caution: Be sure to save your work when the SAVE light comes on. If you have been writing all day, you may have to save all your work and use the Transfer Clear All command before the light disappears. For more information on the Transfer Clear All command, see Chapter 8, "Finding and Managing Documents."

❏ *Key status indicator*. This indicator is blank unless you have pressed one of the toggle keys listed in table 1.1. These keys are called toggle keys because you press the same key to turn an operating mode on or off. The F5 key, for instance, toggles between the overtype mode, in which the characters you enter rub out existing text, and the insert mode, in which the characters you enter push existing text right and down. After you press one of the toggle keys, a code (such as CL for Caps

Lock or OT for overtype) appears, warning you that Word is in a special operating mode. (Some keyboards also have little red or green lights that tell you when you have pressed Num Lock, Scroll Lock, or Caps Lock.)

Table 1.1
Key Status Indicator Codes

Code	Key or Command	Meaning
CL	Caps Lock	Letters entered as caps
CS	Shift-F6	Column-select mode on
EX	F6	Extend mode on
LD	Ctrl-F5	Line drawing mode on
MR	Format revision-Marks	Mark revisions mode on
NL	Num Lock	Numeric keypad enters numbers
OT	F5	Overtype mode on
RM	Shift-F3	Record macro mode on
SL	Scroll Lock	Arrow keys scroll the screen
ST	Ctrl-F3	Step mode on
ZM	Ctrl-F1	Active window is zoomed

Caution: The status line has room for as many as six different key status codes, but sometimes one code overwrites another (although both are still in effect). If you turn on both the overtype mode and the mark revisions mode, for instance, you don't see the OT code; only the MR code appears.

For now, don't worry about what all these modes do. Some of them are relevant only to advanced functions of Word 5.

Caution: If you're working with Word and the keyboard suddenly seems to behave oddly or the mouse won't work, check the key status indicator to see whether you have accidentally pressed one of these mode toggle keys. If so, just press the key again to cancel the mode.

If you are using a mouse with Word, a question mark, called a *help mark*, displays in the middle of the status line. If you point to this help mark and click either mouse button, Word displays information about the command you're using. See this chapter's section on "Getting Help" for more information.

Learning the Word 5 Keyboard

Like most programs, Word 5 makes use of the special keys on the IBM Personal Computer's keyboard, such as Ctrl, Ins, Del, Alt, Num Lock, and others. Just where these keys are located depends on which PC or compatible you're using. Figure 1.6 shows the keyboard layout used on early IBM Personal Computers and compatibles. Figure 1.7 shows the keyboard layout used with earlier Personal Computer AT and AT-compatible computers, and Figure 1.8 shows the latest layout for ATs.

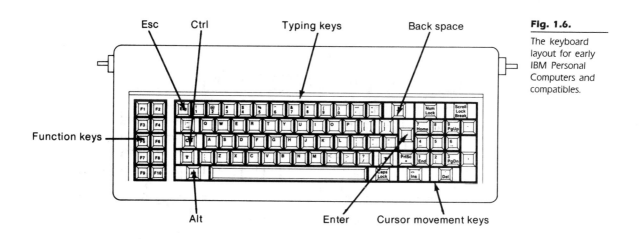

Fig. 1.6.

The keyboard layout for early IBM Personal Computers and compatibles.

Because every programmer is free to determine how most of these keys are used in a program, the keys' operations sometimes differ from program to program. You need to understand how the keys operate for the specific program you're using. Fortunately, Word's use of these keys is quite rational, so a brief overview of how the keys work in the edit mode will suffice.

Fig. 1.7.

The keyboard layout used with earlier Personal Computer ATs and compatibles.

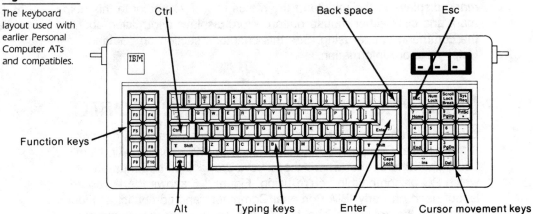

Ctrl

Back space

Esc

Function keys

Alt

Typing keys

Enter

Cursor movement keys

Fig. 1.8.

The latest keyboard design.

Esc

Function keys

Back space

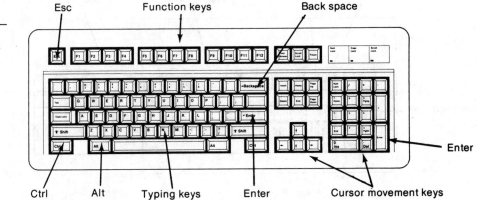

Enter

Ctrl

Alt

Typing keys

Enter

Cursor movement keys

In the edit mode, pressing the Enter key places a paragraph mark in your document. (You don't see the mark, however, unless you choose the Partial or All option in the **show non-printing symbols** field of the Options menu.)

Caution: You don't have to press Enter at the end of every line. In fact, you should insert a paragraph mark by pressing Enter only when you come to the end of a paragraph. Word, like all personal computer word processing programs, includes a feature called *word wrapping*, in which words "wrap" down to the next line if they would extend over the right margin.

Num Lock, *Scroll Lock*, and *Caps Lock* are irritants if you press them accidentally. Num Lock changes the numeric keypad so that the arrow and other cursor control keys enter numbers rather than move the cursor. If you're pressing the down-arrow key and getting the number 2 entered in your document, you must have inadvertently pressed Num Lock. Similarly, Scroll Lock changes the function of the arrow keys so that they scroll the document as well as move the cursor. The effect can be disconcerting if you press the key accidentally. And if everything you type appears in capital letters, you've probably pressed Caps Lock. Fortunately, Word tells you whether you've touched these keys; the codes NL, SL, or CL appear on the status line. To cancel one of these modes, just press the appropriate key again.

The *Del* key deletes the character on which the cursor is positioned and sends the character to the scrap. You can hold down the key to send into oblivion all the text to the right of the cursor (until you let go of the key).

The *Ins* key places the contents of the scrap in your document, precisely where the cursor is positioned. You also can hold down the Ins key to continue inserting the same scrap character(s).

The *Backspace* key deletes the character to the left of the cursor. Unlike the Del key, however, the Backspace key does *not* send the deleted text to the scrap. If you hold down the Backspace key, the cursor races back over the text you have typed, erasing it. (You can recover text deleted with this method if you use the Undo command immediately after the deletion occurs.)

Use the *space bar* only to enter a blank space between words or numbers. Don't use the space bar to move the cursor! To control cursor movement, use the arrow keys instead. Also, avoid using the space bar to align text in columns. Even if you succeed in lining the text on the screen, Word may not print it correctly.

The *Tab* key is useful for aligning text in columns on the screen. For more information on using tabs, see Chapter 11, "Creating Tables and Lists with Tabs, Autosort, and Math."

> **Caution:** Do not use the Tab key to indent paragraphs. A much better method is to set up a paragraph format that includes an automatic first-line indent. That way, you can eliminate or change the indent throughout your entire document with just one command. For more information on paragraph formatting, see Chapter 4, "Word 5 Formatting Strategies: Characters and Paragraphs."

To use *Ctrl* or *Alt*, you hold down the key while you press another key. (Throughout this book, a hyphenated key combination indicates that you should hold down the first key while you press the second. For example, Ctrl-F8 means that you hold down the Ctrl key and press F8; Alt-N means that you hold down the Alt key and press N.) These keys are used extensively for formatting and other commands. Many of these commands have menu equivalents, but if you're a good typist, you can enter a command more quickly by using the Ctrl- or Alt-key counterpart. Throughout *Using Microsoft Word 5*, you will learn many uses for these keys. Watch for the keyboard shortcut icons in the margins.

Word does not depend on *function keys* quite as much as WordPerfect® and other programs do, thanks to Word's excellent system of on-screen menus. (Fig. 1.9 shows the function key help screen for Word 5.) In some cases, however, no menu equivalents are available for function key commands (see table 1.2).

Fig. 1.9.

The function key summary provided by the Help Keyboard command.

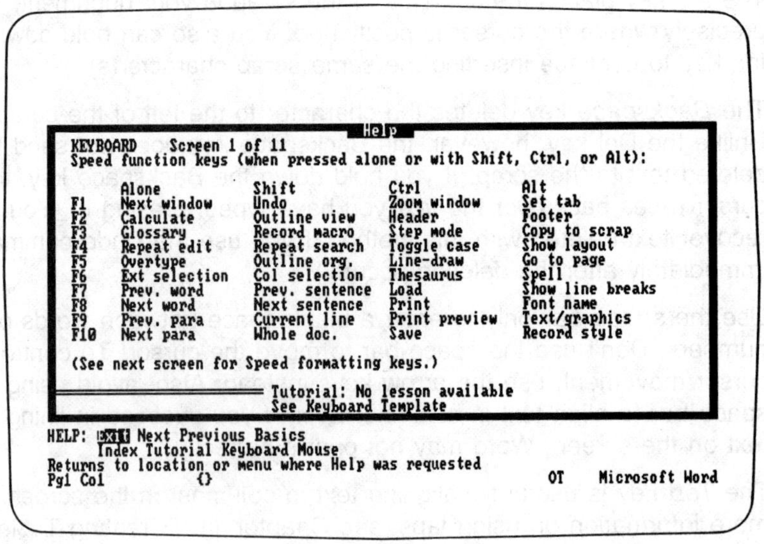

```
                                      Help
KEYBOARD     Screen 1 of 11
Speed function keys (when pressed alone or with Shift, Ctrl, or Alt):

          Alone          Shift           Ctrl            Alt
     F1   Next window    Undo            Zoom window     Set tab
     F2   Calculate      Outline view    Header          Footer
     F3   Glossary       Record macro    Step mode       Copy to scrap
     F4   Repeat edit    Repeat search   Toggle case     Show layout
     F5   Overtype       Outline org.    Line-draw       Go to page
     F6   Ext selection  Col selection   Thesaurus       Spell
     F7   Prev. word     Prev. sentence  Load            Show line breaks
     F8   Next word      Next sentence   Print           Font name
     F9   Prev. para     Current line    Print preview   Text/graphics
     F10  Next para      Whole doc.      Save            Record style

     (See next screen for Speed formatting keys.)

                           Tutorial: No lesson available
                           See Keyboard Template

HELP: EXIT Next Previous Basics
          Index Tutorial Keyboard Mouse
Returns to location or menu where Help was requested
Pg1 Col        {}                                    OT    Microsoft Word
```

Table 1.2
Function Key Commands Not Directly
Duplicated by Menu Commands

Key	Effect
F1	Move highlight to next window in numerical order
F2	Perform calculation on selected numbers
F3	Insert glossary with a name corresponding to the word typed on the screen
F4	Repeat last editing command
F5	Toggle overtype mode on and off
F6	Toggle extend mode on and off
Shift-F2	Toggle outline mode on and off
Shift-F3	Toggle record macro mode on and off
Shift-F5	Toggle outline organize mode on and off
Ctrl-F1	Zoom window to full size (if reduced) or reduce size (if zoomed)
Ctrl-F3	Toggle step mode on and off
Ctrl-F4	Toggle case
Ctrl-F5	Toggle line drawing mode on and off
Alt-F9	Switch between text and graphics modes
Alt-F10	Record style

If you misplace your function key template, or if you're using your copy of Word on another computer temporarily, choose **H**elp from the command menu and then choose **K**eyboard. The screen shown in figure 1.9 appears, listing the function key assignments.

Controlling the Display

You have already learned the difference between the edit mode and the command mode. If the video display adapter you're using has graphics capabilities, you need to learn another, equally important distinction: that between the *graphics mode* and the *text mode*. These modes control how Word displays your document on-screen (but they do not affect how the document is printed).

The Graphics Mode Versus the Text Mode

In the graphics mode, Word displays character emphasis (boldface, underlining, italic, superscript and subscript, small capitals, strikethrough formatting, and double underlining) the way it will appear when printed. If you're creating a document that uses both underlining and italic, seeing these formats on-screen the way they will print can be helpful. In the text mode, both formats are shown with underlining, and you can't distinguish them on-screen.

Another advantage of the graphics mode is that it shows the mouse pointer's shape changes, which let you know when the mouse is ready to carry out a certain kind of command. For example, when you move the pointer to the selection bar, the pointer points to the right rather than the left, which indicates that the mouse is ready to select. Table 1.3 lists the different pointer shapes in graphics mode.

Table 1.3
Mouse Shape Changes in Graphics Mode

Pointer Shape	Indicates
➤	Ready to click a new cursor location or select text
↕	Ready to scroll up or down (on left scroll bar)
↔	Ready to scroll right or left (on bottom scroll bar)
➤	Ready to select line, paragraph, or whole document (on selection bar)
▭	Ready to split window (on top or right window border)
▪▪▪	Ready to toggle ruler on or off (on ruler switch)
⇹	Ready to size window (on lower right window corner)

Despite these advantages, the graphics mode is slower than the text mode. On fast 80286 and 80386 systems, the graphics mode's performance is quite acceptable, but on 8088 machines it is sluggish. No matter which system you use, choose the text mode when speed matters more than display accuracy.

Choosing a Display Mode

With many video display adapters, you can choose among text and graphics display options as well as among two or more levels of graphics resolution. After you install Word with SETUP, you can see a list of your display options (and choose the one you want) with the Options command.

To choose a display mode, follow these steps:

1. Press Esc to enter the command mode.

2. Type *o* to select the **O**ptions command.

3. When the Options menu appears, use the arrow keys to highlight the **display mode** command field.

4. Press F1 to see a list of the display modes available with your video adapter. (For an example, see fig. 1.10).

5. Use the arrow keys to highlight the display mode you want.

6. Press Enter.

```
1   Text, 25 Lines, Monochrome
2   Text, 25 Lines, 16 colors
3   Graphics, 25 Lines, 2 colors




WINDOW OPTIONS for window number: 1        show hidden text:(Yes)No
         show ruler: Yes(No)     show non-printing symbols:(None)Partial All
        show layout: Yes(No)              show line breaks:(Yes)No
       show outline: Yes(No)               show style bar: Yes(No)

GENERAL OPTIONS mute:(Yes)No                summary sheet:(Yes)No
             measure:(In)Cm P10 P12 Pt       display mode: 1
            paginate:(Auto)Manual                  colors:
            autosave:                    autosave confirm: Yes(No)
           show menu:(Yes)No                show borders:(Yes)No
         date format:(MDY)DMY            decimal character:(,),
         time format:(12)24             default tab width: 0.5"
        line numbers: Yes(No)             count blank space: Yes(No)
        cursor speed: 3                   linedraw character: (|)
        speller path: A:\SPELL-AM.LEX
Enter mode number or press F1 to select from list
Pg1 Co1              {H}                            Microsoft Word
```

Fig. 1.10.

The Options menu and display mode options.

Press Alt-F9 to toggle between the last two video modes you chose in the **display mode** field of the Options menu. If the last two modes you chose were the high-resolution graphics mode (43 lines of text) and the standard graphics mode (24 lines of text), Alt-F9 toggles between these two options.

Moving the Cursor and Scrolling

Word 5 comes equipped with a variety of keys and mouse techniques for moving the cursor on the screen and scrolling up and down in your document. (If you've created lines longer than the 7.3-inch line lengths Word can display in a normal document window, you also can scroll left and right.)

Techniques for the Keyboard

The keys for cursor movement, which are listed in table 1.4, are simple, well organized, and convenient to use. Try all of them, especially the Home and End keys, which you will use often. Ctrl-PgUp and Ctrl-PgDn come in handy, too, for jumping immediately to the beginning or end of a document.

Note: If you hold down certain keys (those marked in the table with an asterisk), they repeat their action.

Table 1.4
Keys for Moving the Cursor

Key	Moves Cursor
Up arrow*	Up one line
Down arrow*	Down one line
Left arrow*	Left one column
Right arrow*	Right one column
Home	To beginning of line
End	To end of line
PgUp*	Up one screen
PgDn*	Down one screen

Table 1.4—Continued

Key	Moves Cursor
Ctrl-Home	To top of window
Ctrl-End	To bottom of window
Ctrl-right arrow*	To next word
Ctrl-left arrow*	To previous word
Ctrl-up arrow*	To previous paragraph
Ctrl-down arrow*	To next paragraph
Ctrl-PgUp	To beginning of document
Ctrl-PgDn	To end of document

*Key repeats action when held down

As you will quickly learn when you explore the effects of these keys, holding down the up- or down-arrow keys causes the screen to scroll when you reach the top or bottom borders. But it doesn't scroll *until* you touch the borders. If you want to have more control over scrolling, press the Scroll Lock key and try the up- and down-arrow keys again. (Note that the code SL appears in the status line.) After you press Scroll Lock, the functions of the arrow keys change, as shown in table 1.5. Instead of just moving the cursor, the arrow keys also scroll the screen, even before the cursor reaches the window border. To exit the Scroll Lock mode and restore the arrow keys' original functions, just press Scroll Lock again so that the SL code disappears from the status line.

Table 1.5
Scrolling the Screen (with Scroll Lock On)

To scroll	Press
Up one line	Up arrow
Down one line	Down arrow
Left (1/3 screen)	Left arrow
Right (1/3 screen)	Right arrow

Caution: If you haven't created a line longer than Word's screen, the left and right arrows won't work when Word is in the Scroll Lock mode (with the SL code displayed on the key status indicator). To get the left and right arrow keys to work again, press Scroll Lock to toggle off the Scroll Lock mode.

Techniques for the Mouse

One of the best reasons to use the mouse is the ease with which you can reposition the cursor on the screen. With the mouse, moving the cursor is as simple as pointing to the place you want to make a change and clicking the left button. In most cases, you would need many strokes of the arrow keys to accomplish the same end.

You can also use the mouse to scroll the screen. To scroll down, do the following:

1. Position the pointer on the left scroll bar (the left window border).

2. When the pointer changes shape (becomes a two-headed arrow pointing up and down in graphics mode, and a large rectangle in text mode), click the *left* mouse button.

To scroll up, follow these instructions:

1. Position the pointer on the left scroll bar.

2. When the pointer changes shape, click the *right* mouse button.

You can control how much of the screen scrolls by positioning the pointer higher or lower on the scroll bar. The lower you position the pointer, the more the screen scrolls.

If you have created lines longer than the document window, you can also scroll left and right. Position the pointer on the bottom scroll bar, and click the left button to scroll left, or the right button to scroll right.

Caution: Scrolling with the mouse differs from keyboard scrolling with PgUp or PgDn in one important way. When you scroll with PgUp, PgDn, or other keys, the cursor tags along. When you scroll with the mouse, however, the cursor stays put. For this reason, you may be in for a surprise if you scroll to a new section of your document and start typing. Suddenly, the screen moves back to where you started scrolling, and the text you've typed appears there. What has happened is that Word has returned to the place you left the cursor. Remember, the cursor's function is to show you where the text you type will appear.

To avoid this problem, after scrolling with the mouse, click the left mouse button on the place you want your text to appear. The cursor moves to the place you clicked.

Using a mouse technique called "thumbing," you can quickly scroll to a relative position in your document, such as one-third or one-half of the way through the file. Follow these two simple steps:

1. Place the pointer on the left scroll bar so that the pointer's position corresponds to the portion of the document you want to see. For instance, if you want to scroll one-third of the way down a document, place the pointer one-third of the way down the left scroll bar.

2. Click *both* mouse buttons simultaneously. The screen immediately scrolls to the position you've chosen, and the position indicator moves down the scroll bar to that position.

Note: This technique is not very precise. If your document is paginated, you may want to use the Jump Page command, which is described in Chapter 3, "Word 5 Editing Strategies," to go to a specific page.

Using Word's Menu Commands

The command menu at the bottom of the Word screen is your door to a world of word processing power. In this menu, you will find commands to format and print your text, check spelling and sort lists, and perform dozens of other word processing operations. See table 1.6 for a brief overview of these commands, but don't worry if you don't understand just yet what some of them do.

Table 1.6
An Overview of Word's Menu Commands

Command Name	Task
Copy	Copy selected text to the scrap or a glossary
Delete	Delete selected text to the scrap or a glossary
Format	Format characters, paragraphs, and page styles; add footnotes, annotations, and bookmarks; search and replace styles throughout document
Gallery	Create and edit style sheets
Help	Obtain on-line help
Insert	Insert text from the scrap or a glossary
Jump	Jump to a page, a footnote, an annotation, or a bookmark
Library	Sort, retrieve documents, hyphenate, link to spreadsheets, use DOS, use the Thesaurus, use Spell
Options	Set window and general operating options
Print	Print document to file or printer; repaginate document and preview before printing
Quit	Quit Word and return to DOS
Replace	Replace text throughout document
Search	Search for specified text
Transfer	All file operations: load, save, clear, merge, delete, and rename documents and glossaries
Undo	Restore file to its state before the last command or editing change
Window	Split, close, or move window

Some commands, like Quit, have only one level. When you choose these commands, you set them in motion. In other cases, however, a submenu appears when you choose a command. The submenu lists more named options. Figure 1.11 shows an example of such a submenu: the Format menu.

```
FORMAT: Character Paragraph Tab Border Footnote Division Running-head Stylesheet
        sEarch repLace revision-Marks pOsition Annotation bookmarK
Sets character format (bold, italic, hidden, etc.) and fonts
Pg1 Col           {}                                      SL        Microsoft Word
```

Fig. 1.11.

The submenu of command options for the Format command.

When you reach the final level of most commands, you see a menu with several command fields, such as those shown in figure 1.12 for the Format Character command. Currently selected options are enclosed in parentheses. Some of the fields have named options, such as Yes or No. Other fields require you to type information yourself. For example, in the **font size** field in figure 1.12, you must type the appropriate number.

```
FORMAT CHARACTER bold: Yes  @        italic: Yes(No)       underline: Yes(No)
        strikethrough: Yes(No)       uppercase: Yes(No)    small caps: Yes(No)
        double underline: Yes(No)    position:(Normal)Superscript Subscript
        font name: Courier           font size: 12         font color: Black
        hidden: Yes(No)
Select option
Pg1 Col           {}                                      SL        Microsoft Word
```

Fig. 1.12.

The command fields for the Format Character command.

If a command field requires you to type information, check the message line to see whether you can press F1 to see a list of options. In figure 1.13, for example, the message Enter font name or press F1 to select from list appears when you highlight the **font name** field of the Format Character command. And when you press F1, a list of your available options appears, as shown in figure 1.14. (The list of available fonts will vary depending on the printer you have installed.)

```
FORMAT CHARACTER bold: Yes(No)       italic: Yes(No)       underline: Yes(No)
        strikethrough: Yes(No)       uppercase: Yes(No)    small caps: Yes(No)
        double underline: Yes(No)    position:(Normal)Superscript Subscript
        font name: Courier           font size: 12         font color: Black
        hidden: Yes(No)
Enter font name or press F1 to select from list
Pg1 Col           {}                                                Microsoft Word
```

Fig. 1.13.

Highlighting the **font name** field.

Selecting from a list of available items is almost always better than typing the information yourself. If you select from a list, you get a better idea of just which options are available, and that helps you to learn the program. What's more, you don't have to memorize long lists of option names.

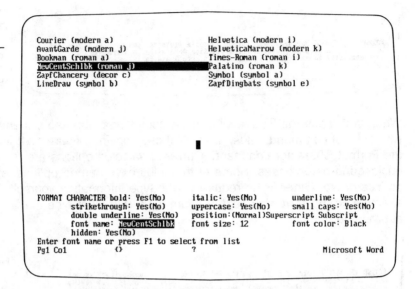

Fig. 1.14.

The menu of
font name
options that is
displayed after
you press F1.

Note that for most commands, *choosing* a command is not the same thing as *executing* a command—or "carrying it out" (Microsoft's phrase). When you choose a command, you have an opportunity to select options in command fields. But you still can cancel the command by pressing Esc or by clicking both mouse buttons. When you carry out a command, you tell Word that you're serious about the options you've chosen and that you want the program to act on them. To carry out a command, press Enter or click the left button on the command name. The next section describes the different ways you can choose a command.

Options for Choosing Commands

You can choose commands in several ways. You can use a variety of cursor-movement keys to navigate through command menus, submenus, and command fields. An even easier way, however, is to choose a command by typing the capitalized letter. And if you have a mouse, you can choose and carry out many commands without even touching the keyboard.

To choose commands with the keyboard, follow these steps:

1. Press Esc to enter the command mode.

2. Use the space bar, the Tab key, or the right-arrow key to move the highlight to the right in the command menu; use

the Backspace or left-arrow key to move left. Use the down- or up-arrow to move the highlight directly to the next line down or up in the command menu.

3. When you have highlighted the command you want, press Enter.

4. If a submenu appears, use the techniques given in step 2 to highlight the command you want.

5. When the menu of command fields appears, use the arrow keys to select the field you want to modify. Alternatively, use the Tab key to move right and down in the command menu, and use Shift-Tab to move left and up.

6. If the command field you want to modify contains named options, such as Yes or No, use the space bar or Backspace key to highlight the option you want. If you must supply the information yourself, check the message line to see whether you can press F1 to see a list of available options. If so, press F1. Choose an option from the list by highlighting it with the arrow keys and pressing Enter.

7. Press Enter (or click the command name) to carry out the command. To cancel the command, press Esc.

To choose commands by typing the command's capitalized letter, follow these steps:

1. Press Esc to enter the command mode.

2. Type the capitalized letter of the command. If you're choosing the **F**ormat command, for instance, type *f* (the case doesn't matter; you can use either an upper- or a lowercase letter).

3. If a submenu appears, type the capitalized letter of the option you want. To select the **C**haracter option in the Format menu, for instance, type *c*.

4. If a menu containing command fields appears, as is the case with most commands, you must use the space bar, arrow keys, or Backspace key to select the command field you want.

5. If the command field contains a list of options, and the options begin with capital letters (such as Yes or No), you can choose the option by typing the option's first letter. To choose the **Y**es option in a command field, for instance, type *y*.

6. Press Tab to move the cursor through the other fields, if you need to set them. After you make all your choices, press Enter (or click the command name) to carry out the command. To cancel the command, press Esc.

Learn to use the first-letter approach to choosing commands. You will quickly learn to press Esc (to activate the command menu) and type *ts*, for instance, for the Transfer Save command, or *fp* for the Format Paragraph command. And the command choices you memorize in this way will figure prominently in the macros you're sure to write as your Word mastery increases. The capital-letter approach is the best way to include commands in macros. (See Chapter 21, "Creating and Using Word 5 Macros," for more information.) To help you learn to choose commands in this way, the capital letters of Word 5 commands are boldfaced throughout this text whenever you're instructed to choose the command.

Note, however, that this first-letter technique does *not* work for choosing command fields—although it *does* work for named, capitalized options within command fields. In general, if the first letter of a command or option name is capitalized, you can choose the command or name by typing that letter; but if there is not a capitalized letter, you can't choose the command by typing a letter.

To choose commands with the mouse, follow these steps:

1. Point to the command you want to choose, and click the left mouse button.

2. If a submenu appears, point to the option you want, and click the left mouse button.

3. When the menu of command fields appears, point to a command field and use the left button to click the option you want. If you must type a response, click the field and type your chosen option (or press F1 and click the option you want from the list that appears). Select additional options in the same way.

4. When you are finished choosing options, click the command name or press Enter to carry out the command. To cancel the command, press Esc or click *both* buttons at the same time.

If you click the *right* button on a command name or submenu choice, Word chooses the command *and* carries it out at the same time. This feature is useful when you have finished making several choices in a command menu by clicking the left button, and you have come to the last choice. If you point to this choice and click the right button, Word saves you the trouble of having to carry out the command in a separate operation.

Hiding the Command Menu

Many people find the command menu distracting. Fortunately, you can hide it, giving you an additional three lines of working space in the bargain. And, unless you're using the mouse, you pay almost no cost for doing so; you can press Esc to bring the command menu back to the screen. The only real disadvantage to hiding the menu is that you cannot use the mouse to enter the command mode and choose a command simultaneously by clicking a command name. You have to press Esc to enter the command mode first.

To hide the command menu, do the following:

1. Choose the **O**ptions command and highlight the **show menu** command field.

2. Choose the **N**o option and carry out the command.

3. Carry out the command by pressing Enter or clicking the command name.

Using the Undo Command

As you learn Word, you will find yourself giving commands or performing editing operations and then wishing you hadn't. But remember that Word gives you a remarkable parachute: the Undo command. Undo can't fix everything, however. Table 1.7 lists what it *can* undo. Keep this list in mind as you're learning Word.

Caution: If you do give a command or perform an editing operation whose effects you regret, remember that Undo works only if you use it immediately after the error. After you use a command, don't type any new text, perform any insertions or deletions, or use any additional commands until you have checked the command's effects and you're satisfied that they are okay.

Table 1.7
What the Undo Command Undoes

Last editing operation	Effect of pressing Undo
Copied text to the scrap	Previous scrap contents restored
Inserted text from the scrap	Insertion canceled
Copied text with the mouse	Copied text disappears
Moved text with the mouse	Move canceled; text reappears in original position with highlighting
Deleted text to the scrap	Deletion canceled; text reappears in original position with highlighting
Deleted text with the Backspace key	Deletion canceled; text restored

Last command used	Effect of pressing Undo
Copy	Previous contents of the scrap restored
Format	Formatting canceled
Format Replace	Operation canceled; all substitutions restored to original
Gallery	No effect (Choose Exit to return to your document.)
Help	No effect (Choose Exit to return to your document.)
Insert	Insertion canceled
Jump	No effect

Table 1.7—Continued

Last command used	Effect of pressing Undo
Library Autosort	Sort canceled; text returned to order before command was given
Library Hyphenate	Hyphenation canceled; all hyphens that command inserted are removed
Library Index	Index that command created is removed
Library Number	Numbering canceled; numbers removed
Library Run	No effect (Give a DOS command and press a key to return to Word.)
Library Spell	No effect (Choose **Q**uit to return to Word.)
Library Table	Table that command created is removed
Library Thesaurus	Word substitution canceled; original restored
Options	No effect (To cancel choices in the Options menu, use the command again and restore the original settings.)
Print	No effect (Press Esc to stop printing.)
Quit	No effect (If you see a message, press Esc to return to Word.)
Replace	Word substitutions removed and originals restored throughout document
Search	No effect (Press Esc to cancel search while still in progress.)

Table 1.7—Continued

Last command used	Effect of pressing Undo
Transfer Load	No effect
Transfer Merge	No effect
Undo	Undoes effect of last Undo command; restores changes

A nice feature of Undo is that you can undo the command's own effects. Suppose that you make an editing change, such as adding a sentence to a paragraph. You aren't sure that you like the result, so you use Undo. Then, seeing the paragraph without the sentence, you realize that the paragraph was better when you left the sentence in it. Choose Undo again, and the sentence reappears.

Getting Help

Word is equipped with an excellent on-line help utility, which provides information about commands or program functions at a keystroke. You can obtain Quick Help, which provides an informative screenful of information about the command or feature you were using when you gave the command. If you want, you can obtain Tutorial Help, which calls up the appropriate lesson in the Learning Word computer-based training program. You also can access a list of help topics.

Alt-H

Quick Help

To ask for Quick Help about a command, follow these steps:

1. Highlight the command name or command field.

2. Press Alt-H.

To use the mouse to ask for Quick Help about a command, do the following:

1. Highlight the command name or command field.

2. Point to the help mark (?) on the status line.

3. Click the left mouse button.

To see a list of help topics, follow these steps:

1. Choose the **H**elp command from the command menu.

2. When the Help menu appears, choose the Index option.

3. When the help topic index appears (see fig. 1.15), use the arrow keys to highlight the topic you want to study.

4. Press Enter.

```
Autosave            Hyphens             Ruler
Backup              Indent              Running heads
Block               Index               Save
Bold                Italics             Screen borders
Bookmarks           Jump                Search
Bulleted list       Justify             Select text
Calculate           Keyboard            Show layout
Center              Leader character    Side by side
Colors              Line break          Small caps
Columns             Line drawing        Sort
Commands            Line spacing        Speed keys
Copy                Load document       Spell
Cross referencing   Macros              Spreadsheet link
Delete              Mailing labels      Strikethrough
Division break      Margins             Style sheets
Doc retrieval       Move text           Sub/Superscript
DOS, OS/2 and back  Mouse               Summary sheets
Double Space        Networks            Table of Contents
File formats        Numbering           Tables

HELP INDEX: File formats

Select Help topic; press PgDn for more topics
Pg1 Co1            {}                        OT    Microsoft Word
```

Fig. 1.15.

The help topic index.

To return to your document after viewing the help topic index, choose the **E**xit command from the Help menu, and press Enter.

Tutorial Help

If you want computer-based training lessons on a subject, you can ask for Tutorial Help, which uses the Learning Word computer-based tutorial. You can take these lessons right in the middle of an editing session with Word.

To get Tutorial Help on a command or command field, follow these steps:

1. Highlight the command or field you do not understand.

2. Press Alt-H to display the Help menu and the Quick Help screen about the command or field.

3. Choose the **T**utorial option from the Help menu.

4. Choose the **L**esson option on the Help Tutorial submenu.

To choose a tutorial from an index of topics covered, do the following:

1. Choose the **H**elp command or click the help mark.

2. When the Help menu appears, choose the **T**utorial option.

3. When the Help Tutorial submenu appears, choose the **I**ndex option.

4. Use the arrow keys or the mouse to highlight the lesson you want, and press Enter.

Ctrl-Q

To quit Tutorial Help at any time, press Ctrl-Q. To quit the Help menu, choose **E**xit.

Saving Your Work

When you create a document with Word 5, the program temporarily stores the document in your computer's internal memory and in several temporary disk files. No permanent record of the document is made until you deliberately save the document to disk by using the Transfer Save command.

Ctrl-F10

Using the Transfer Save Command

To make a permanent record of your document, follow these steps:

1. Press Esc to enter the command mode.

2. Choose the **T**ransfer **S**ave command or use the Ctrl-F10 keyboard shortcut.

3. When the **filename** field appears, as shown in figure 1.16, type a name for your document. The name must conform to DOS rules about valid characters. You can use the letters A through Z, the numbers 0 through 9, and the following characters:

   $ & % ` ( ) - @ ^ { } ~ ' ! _

   If you omit the period and extension, Word automatically uses its default extension (.DOC).

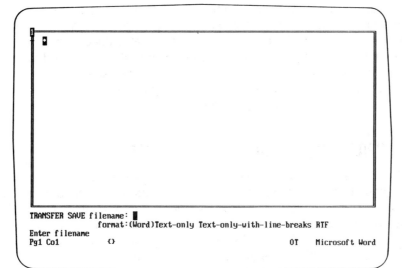

Fig. 1.16.

The Transfer Save menu.

```
TRANSFER SAVE filename: █
                format:(Word)Text-only Text-only-with-line-breaks RTF
Enter filename
Pg1 Co1          {}                              OT    Microsoft Word
```

4. Be sure that the **Word** option is selected (surrounded with parentheses) in the **format** field. If it isn't, highlight that option before carrying out the command.

5. Press Enter.

6. After Word saves your document, a document summary sheet appears. Always type a long version of the document's name in the **title** field. Then think of two or three words that describe your document's content; type them in the **keywords** field. If more than one person will use your computer, type your name in the **author** field. As you will learn in Chapter 8, "Finding and Managing Documents," completing the document summary sheet greatly facilitates document-retrieval tasks. Press Enter to close the document summary sheet.

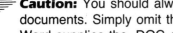 **Caution:** You should always use Word's default extension (.DOC) for documents. Simply omit the period and extension when you save files; Word supplies the .DOC extension automatically. Word expects its documents to be named with this extension. If you use some other extension to name your documents, you will find that retrieval operations from disk are more complicated. For more information, see Chapter 8, "Finding and Managing Documents."

Note: Unless you specifically tell it otherwise, Word always saves documents to the current drive or directory—that is, the drive or directory from which you started Word. You can save a document to a drive or directory other than the current one if you prefer. You need to specify the full path name, however, as well as the file name, when you use the Transfer Save command. For more information, see Chapter 8, "Finding and Managing Documents."

Automatically Storing Changes

New to Word 5 is the autosave feature, which you access in the Options menu. This new feature automatically stores the changes you make to documents and, in the event of a power loss or computer failure, allows you to reconstruct work that you haven't saved with the Transfer Save command. With this new feature, using Word for critical professional writing applications is much less risky than it used to be. Autosave works more or less imperceptibly; the only drawback to using it is that it does consume some additional disk space. Unless you're using a dual floppy system or you're otherwise short on disk space, you will want to use autosave all the time.

To turn on the autosave feature, follow these steps:

1. Choose the **O**ptions command and move the highlight to the **autosave** field (see fig. 1.17).

2. Type the number of minutes you want to elapse between backup operations. To back up your work every 10 minutes, for instance, type *10*.

3. Carry out the command by pressing Enter or clicking the command name.

To restore your work after a power failure, simply do the following:

1. Restart your computer after the power comes back on.

2. Start Word. A message on-screen informs you that your work was not saved and gives you the option of restoring all unsaved files, including style sheets and glossaries. Press Y to restore your last work.

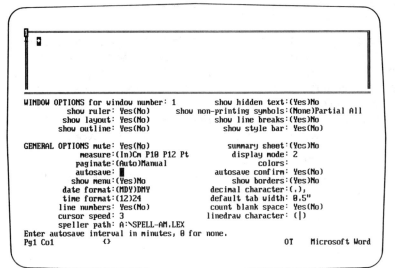

Fig. 1.17.

The **autosave** field in the Options menu.

```
WINDOW OPTIONS for window number: 1          show hidden text:(Yes)No
          show ruler: Yes(No)      show non-printing symbols:(None)Partial All
         show layout: Yes(No)            show line breaks:(Yes)No
        show outline: Yes(No)            show style bar: Yes(No)

GENERAL OPTIONS mute: Yes(No)             summary sheet:(Yes)No
            measure:(In)Cm P10 P12 Pt     display mode: 2
           paginate:(Auto)Manual              colors:
           autosave: █                  autosave confirm: Yes(No)
          show menu:(Yes)No               show borders:(Yes)No
        date format:(MDY)DMY            decimal character:(.),
        time format:(12)24             default tab width: 0.5"
       line numbers: Yes(No)           count blank space: Yes(No)
       cursor speed: 3                 linedraw character: (|)
       speller path: A:\SPELL-AM.LEX
Enter autosave interval in minutes, 0 for none.
Pg1 Co1        {}                               OT   Microsoft Word
```

Caution: Using the autosave feature is not the same as using the Transfer Save command. Autosave is merely a backup procedure to be used in case of a computer crash or power failure. Even if you're using autosave, you must still save your work to disk by using the Transfer Save command.

Quitting Word

If you haven't saved your work by choosing the Transfer Save command, Word does not let you quit the program without confirming that the work should indeed be discarded.

To quit Word at the end of an editing session, do the following:

1. Choose the **Q**uit command from the command menu.

2. If you see the message Enter Y to save changes to document, N to lose changes, or Esc to cancel, press Y if you want to save your document. Otherwise, press N.

Caution: Do not quit Word simply by turning the power off in the midst of an editing session. The Quit command does far more than merely return you to DOS. Quit also erases many temporary files and closes the document on which you're working.

Chapter Summary

This chapter prepared you to begin using Microsoft Word 5 by showing you how to use the Learning Word program to familiarize yourself with Word and how to start the Word program itself. In this chapter, you also explored the screen and the keyboard, the differences between the text and graphics modes, and how to move the cursor and scroll the screen. You learned also how to choose commands, use the Undo command, get help, save your documents, and exit from Word.

Now that you're familiar with these Word fundamentals, you're ready to begin using Word. Chapter 2 steps in where this chapter leaves off and shows you how to create "Your First Word 5 Document—Quickly!"

2

Your First Word 5 Document—Quickly!

Word is well known as one of the most powerful word processing programs available for any computer, but the program is quite easy to use at an elementary level. You can start producing letters, memos, and brief reports immediately. In this chapter, you learn how to use Word in a straightforward, simple way. Specifically, you create, format, edit, save, and print a simple document (a business letter).

If you're just getting started with word processing, this chapter helps by explaining and illustrating fundamental word processing concepts as well as the basics of using Word 5. As you will see, word processing enables you to keep revising your work until it meets the highest professional standards. You will understand why almost everyone who has tried word processing cannot imagine going back to a typewriter!

Even if you already have some familiarity with Word, however, this chapter may be well worth skimming. The material is elementary, but it presents an approach to Word that has been developed by experts through long experience with the program. Take note, particularly, of the Power User Tips and Caution icons. Another reason for skimming this chapter is that the rest of the chapters in Part I develop and extend the topics covered here. All these chapters show how to go beyond the fundamentals and take full advantage of Word 5's remarkable features.

In this chapter, you learn how to do the following:

❏ Create a new Word 5 document and enter text, correcting errors as you type

❏ Center and boldface text—and, along the way, learn important concepts about how Word handles text formatting

❏ Insert the current date automatically, using one of Word's built-in glossaries

❏ Join and split paragraphs the way Word experts do

❏ Select and delete text

❏ Undo a deletion by using the Undo command

❏ Insert new text into existing text

❏ Move text from one location to another with the keyboard or the mouse

❏ Set up a special tab format for typing a complimentary close

❏ Preview your letter's appearance on the screen to check the balance on the page

❏ Print your document

Please remember: This chapter draws on the Word 5 knowledge introduced in Chapter 1, "Preparing To Use Word 5." In particular, you should know how to start Word, understand the basic features of the Word screen, know how to move between the edit mode and the command mode, know some of the commonly used keys for cursor movement, understand how to navigate through Word's command menus, and know how to save and quit.

This chapter assumes, too, that you've chosen your favorite way of giving commands (using the keyboard, typing the command's capitalized letter, or using the mouse). From this point on, instructions that mention commands use this format:

Choose the **No** option from the **show menu** field of the Options menu.

If you need some help getting around in command menus, review the Chapter 1 section on "Choosing Commands."

Creating and Formatting the Letter

Writing business letters is a big responsibility. Every time you send a first-class letter, you put yourself and your organization on the line.

You have the opportunity to create either a favorable or a negative impression of your company. For this reason, preparing letters with a fine word processing program like Word 5 is a good idea. Using a word processor enables you to experiment with the wording until you get it exactly right.

This entire chapter is a single tutorial, one that walks you through a "real world" writing experience. You start with a poorly written letter and alter it until it meets the professional standards of today's business environment. Here's the situation: Suppose that you're the director of a small training firm which specializes in training corporate employees in security techniques. You frequently use videos to illustrate potential security problems. Last week, you spent a day training some employees at Atlantic Electronic Enterprises, Inc. Everything went fine, except that the video projection device's bulb blew during the final moments of the presentation. You had a backup, though, and were soon back in action. A week later, you receive a letter from Mr. Nelson T. Jones, your contact at the firm, thanking you for the presentation but complaining—rather unfairly and gruffly—about the equipment breakdown. The ball's in your court now; you must answer the letter.

If your computer doesn't have a clock-calendar board, be sure to set the date correctly with DOS when you start your system. To set the date when you start your system, type the date in mm-dd-yy format (such as 02-28-89) when the Enter today's date prompt appears. If you don't see this prompt, type *date* at the system prompt.

Start Word with a new, unnamed document. If you've been working with Word already and have a document on the screen, choose the **T**ransfer **C**lear **A**ll command. (If you haven't saved your work, Word asks whether you want to do so.) Check to make sure that no codes (such as OT, CL, or RM) are visible on the key status indicator (the space just to the left of Microsoft Word on the status line). If you see a code, check table 1.1 to find out which toggle key to press in order to turn off the code.

Typing and Centering the Return Address

Begin this tutorial by typing the return address.

1. Choose the **C**entered option in the **alignment** field of the **F**ormat **P**aragraph menu (see fig. 2.1) and then execute the command. Alternatively, use the Alt-C keyboard shortcut. The cursor jumps to the middle of the screen.

Alt-C,

Fig. 2.1.

Centering text
with the Format
Paragraph
command.

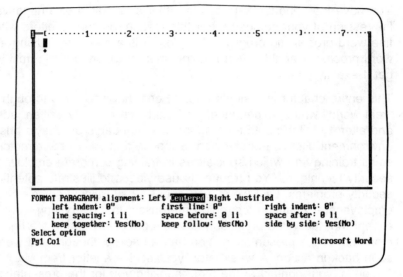

```
[·········1·········2·········3·········4·········5·········]·········7·····]




FORMAT PARAGRAPH alignment: Left Centered Right Justified
     left indent: 0"          first line: 0"        right indent: 0"
    line spacing: 1 li       space before: 0 li      space after: 0 li
   keep together: Yes(No)     keep follow: Yes(No)    side by side: Yes(No)
Select option
Pg1 Co1              {}                                    Microsoft Word
```

2. Now type the return address as follows, pressing Enter at the end of each line. If you make a mistake, use the Backspace key to rub out the error.

    Albemarle Valley Associates
    Business Security Training and Development
    13987 Oakfair Parkway
    Suite 128
    Charlottesville, VA 22987
    (804) 111-9000

    When you press Enter, Word copies the centered format to the next line automatically. In fact, the format remains in effect until you deliberately cancel it.

3. When you finish typing the telephone number, press Enter.

4. Choose the **F**ormat **P**aragraph command again, but this time choose the **L**eft option in the **alignment** field. Then execute the command. Alternatively, use the Alt-P keyboard shortcut. The cursor jumps back to the left margin.

Your document should look like figure 2.2. Welcome to what-you-see-is-what-you-get word processing!

Alt-P

The normal paragraph keyboard shortcut (Alt-P) is especially useful. Use it whenever you want to cancel a special paragraph format, such as centered text or double-line spacing, and return to Word's default text entry format, which prints your text single-spaced and flush left.

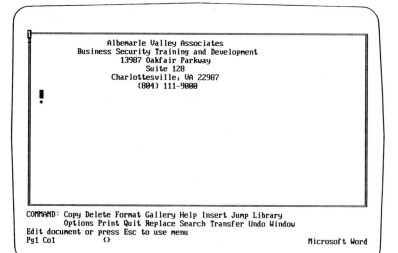

Fig. 2.2.

Letter with centered return address.

```
Albemarle Valley Associates
Business Security Training and Development
13987 Oakfair Parkway
Suite 128
Charlottesville, VA 22987
(804) 111-9000
```

```
COMMAND: Copy Delete Format Gallery Help Insert Jump Library
         Options Print Quit Replace Search Transfer Undo Window
Edit document or press Esc to use menu
Pg1 Co1          {}                                  Microsoft Word
```

Selecting and Boldfacing Your Firm's Name

Now boldface your firm's name (Albemarle Valley Associates). To attach character emphasis, such as boldface, to text you have already typed, you need to select the text so that it is highlighted on the screen. Selecting the text is your way of telling Word which text you want affected by a formatting command. To boldface your firm's name, using the keyboard, follow these steps:

Alt-B

1. Use the arrow keys or the mouse to place the cursor on the first character of the firm's name. (If you're not sure how to reposition the cursor, see "Moving the Cursor and Scrolling" in Chapter 1.)

2. Press the F6 (Extend) key.

Note that the code EX appears in the key status indicator, as shown in figure 2.3. This code informs you that Word is in the extend mode.

3. Press the End key. The highlight extends immediately to the end of the line.

4. Choose the **Y**es option in the **bold** field of the Format Character menu (see fig. 2.4) and then execute the command. Alternatively, use the Alt-B keyboard shortcut.

Fig. 2.3.

The EX code, indicating that Word is in the extend mode.

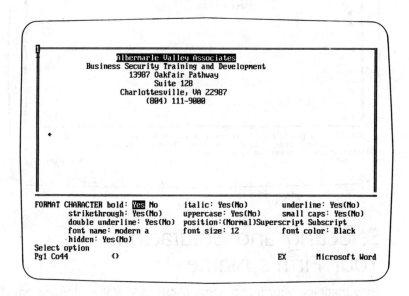

```
Pg1 Co44          {}                              EX      Microsoft Word
```

Fig. 2.4.

Boldfacing text with the Format Character command.

```
                        Albernarle Valley Associates
                  Business Security Training and Development
                          13987 Oakfair Pathway
                               Suite 128
                         Charlottesville, VA 22987
                            (804) 111-9000




        ·



FORMAT CHARACTER bold: Yes No       italic: Yes(No)      underline: Yes(No)
         strikethrough: Yes(No)     uppercase: Yes(No)   small caps: Yes(No)
         double underline: Yes(No)  position:(Normal)Superscript Subscript
         font name: modern a        font size: 12         font color: Black
         hidden: Yes(No)
Select option
Pg1 Co44          {}                              EX      Microsoft Word
```

5. Press the down-arrow key to cancel the highlighting. With most monitors, the firm's name now appears in bold.

Note that Word automatically cancels the extend mode after you format a selection. If you extend a selection but do not use the Format command, press F6 again to toggle off the extend mode.

Mouse users can use a technique called "clicking and dragging" to extend a selection. Substitute the following two steps for steps 2 and 3 in the preceding exercise:

2. Point to the first character you want to select. Then press the right button and hold it down.

3. As you are holding down the right button, move the mouse to the right until you have selected the firm's name.

Distinguishing between Paragraph and Character Formatting

Basic to Word is a distinction between paragraph formatting and character formatting. Paragraph formats, which affect all the text in a paragraph, include the following:

❑ The alignment of text (whether it's positioned flush left, centered, flush right, or justified on both margins)

❑ Indentation from the right or left margins and on the paragraph's first line

❑ Line spacing, such as single- or double-spacing

❑ Blank lines before and after the paragraph

Word defines a *paragraph* as all the text you type until you press Enter. Note that this definition is not semantic; it has nothing to do with the paragraphs with which you are familiar, which are units of meaning. On the contrary, Word defines paragraphs only in a mechanical way. A Word paragraph can be just one line (such as the company's name in the letter you're writing), a heading, or an ordinary text paragraph. After you choose a special paragraph format and start typing, Word continues to use that format until you cancel it by pressing Alt-P.

Character formats include emphasis (such as boldface, italic, and underlining); position (subscript, superscript, or normal); and font (type style, such as Pica, Elite, or Helvetica). Character formats can affect any unit of text, from one character to an entire document. After you choose a special character format and start typing, Word continues to use that format until you cancel it by pressing Alt-space bar.

You need to notice one more distinction. You can format characters (with emphases such as boldfacing) and paragraphs (with formats such as centering) in the following two ways:

❑ *As you type.* With this technique, you "program" the cursor to "lay down" a format as you enter the text. You used this method when you typed your letter's return address. The Alt-key formatting commands (Alt-P and Alt-space bar) program the cursor to lay down Word's *default* formats (single-spaced, flush-left paragraphs and characters without special emphases).

❑ *Later.* With this technique, you type your text first, as you did with the firm's name in the letter you're typing. Later, you select or highlight the text and give a formatting command. When you format this way, you needn't mark the end of the format with Alt-P or Alt-space bar.

Both types of formatting, formatting-as-you-type and formatting later, are explored in Chapters 4 and 5. For now, let's proceed with the letter.

Automatically Inserting the Date

You can type the date manually, if you prefer, but Word can do it for you. Just follow these steps:

1. Use the down-arrow key to move the cursor to the end-of-file mark. Then press Enter two or three times to leave some blank space under the return address.

2. Choose the Insert command and, when the Insert from: prompt appears, press F1.

3. When the menu appears, as shown in figure 2.5, use the arrow keys to select the **date** option; then execute the command by pressing Enter. Word enters the current date automatically.

Fig. 2.5.

Automatically inserting the current date.

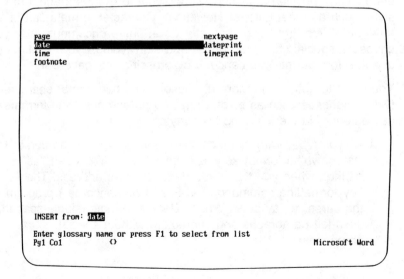

You have just used one of Word's built-in glossaries, which are discussed thoroughly in Chapter 12, "Using Glossaries and Bookmarks." A *glossary* is a storage place for holding a certain type of information, which you can insert into your document as you please.

As you can see from this example, the menu technique requires so many keystrokes that you might as well type the date yourself. The keyboard shortcut, however, is much faster; this shortcut illustrates why learning at least some of the shortcut techniques can be worth your while. The following two steps show you how to insert a built-in glossary, using the keyboard shortcut:

F3

1. Type the glossary's name, *date*.

2. Press F3. The glossary name disappears, and in its place, the current date appears.

Typing the Text of the Letter

Now you need to type the correspondent's address, the salutation, and the body of the letter, as shown in figure 2.6. You will improve this business letter later.

Joining and Splitting Paragraphs

As you look at the body of this letter, you remember that business letters should be positive and emphasize the reader's point of view. You therefore look critically at the business letter you've just typed. Something is wrong, but you're not sure what it is, so you experiment. First, you decide to join the first two paragraphs.

Joining Paragraphs

To join paragraphs, follow these steps:

1. Choose the **Partial** option in the **show non-printing symbols** field of the **O**ptions menu (see fig. 2.7). When the screen reappears, as shown in figure 2.8, you can see that Word has displayed paragraph marks at every spot where you pressed Enter.

2. Use the F6 (Extend) key or the click-and-drag technique to select both of the paragraph marks that divide the first and second paragraphs. To extend the selection to the second

paragraph mark, use the down-arrow key (the F6 technique) or drag down (the mouse technique).

3. After selecting both marks, press Del. Word then joins the paragraphs, as shown in figure 2.9.

Fig. 2.6.

A first draft of a business letter.

```
                    Albernarle Valley Associates
               Business Security Training and Development
                        13987 Oakfair Pathway
                             Suite 128
                       Charlottesville, VA 22987
                          (804) 111-9000


         January 29, 1989

         Nelson T. Jones
         Engineering Development
         Atlantic Electronic Enterprises, Inc.
         5878 Sycamore Drive
         Beltway, VA 22787

         Dear Mr. Jones:

         Thank you for your letter of January 22.  I'm disappointed
         you weren't happy with the equipment failure that occurred
         during our recent training session.

         I'm sure you understand, however, that machines do sometimes
         fail!  Really, an engineer ought to know that!  We had a
         substitute machine and got it up and running immediately.

         We have replaced the unreliable projection display system
         that failed during our final presentation.  Now that the new
         wide-screen direct display systems are available, we--and
         our customers--won't have to rely on those inefficient and
         unreliable projection systems.



         ◆

COMMAND: Copy Delete Format Gallery Help Insert Jump Library
         Options Print Quit Replace Search Transfer Undo Window
Microsoft Word Version 5.0 release 17
Pg1 Co1          {¶}                                  Microsoft Word
```

Some users find on-screen paragraph marks distracting. But as you can see, rejoining paragraphs is easy when the paragraph marks are displayed. If they're invisible, joining and splitting paragraphs is like groping in the dark. For editing purposes, you need to be able to see precisely where you have pressed Enter.

 Caution: If you're editing without displaying paragraph marks, you can easily delete a mark by accident. And if you do, the second paragraph "collapses" into the first one. See the next section, "Splitting Paragraphs," to learn how to restore the second paragraph.

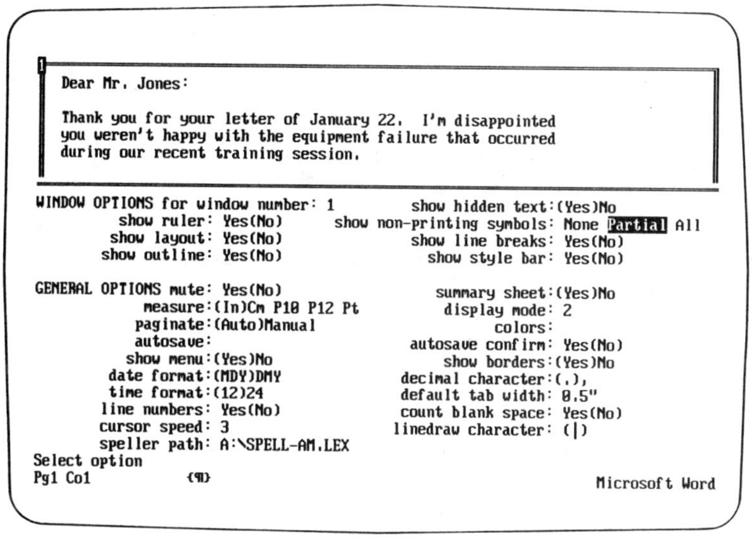

Fig. 2.7.

Using the Options menu to display paragraph marks.

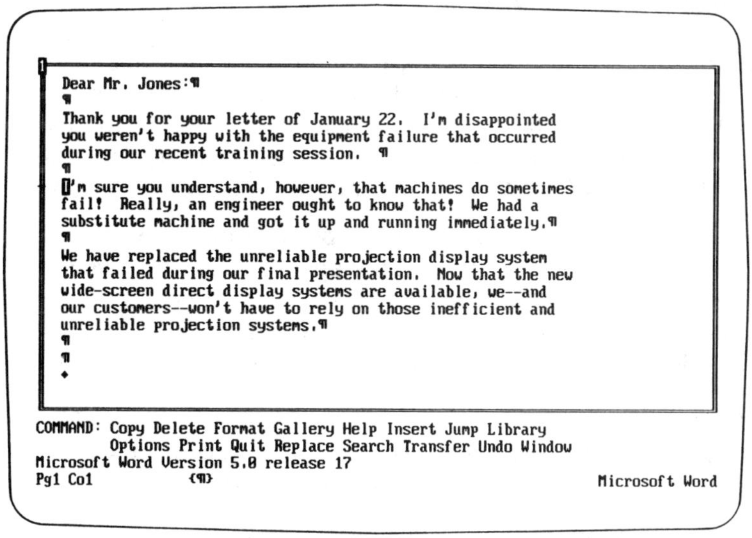

```
Dear Mr. Jones:

Thank you for your letter of January 22.  I'm disappointed
you weren't happy with the equipment failure that occurred
during our recent training session.



WINDOW OPTIONS for window number: 1         show hidden text:(Yes)No
           show ruler: Yes(No)     show non-printing symbols: None Partial All
          show layout: Yes(No)           show line breaks: Yes(No)
         show outline: Yes(No)             show style bar: Yes(No)

GENERAL OPTIONS mute: Yes(No)                summary sheet:(Yes)No
            measure:(In)Cm P10 P12 Pt        display mode: 2
           paginate:(Auto)Manual                  colors:
           autosave:                     autosave confirm: Yes(No)
          show menu:(Yes)No               show borders:(Yes)No
        date format:(MDY)DMY            decimal character:(.),
        time format:(12)24             default tab width: 0.5"
        line numbers: Yes(No)            count blank space: Yes(No)
        cursor speed: 3                 linedraw character: (|)
        speller path: A:\SPELL-AM.LEX
Select option
Pg1 Co1           {¶}                              Microsoft Word
```

Fig. 2.8.

Displaying paragraph marks to see where you have pressed Enter.

```
Dear Mr. Jones:¶
¶
Thank you for your letter of January 22.  I'm disappointed
you weren't happy with the equipment failure that occurred
during our recent training session.  ¶
¶
I'm sure you understand, however, that machines do sometimes
fail!  Really, an engineer ought to know that!  We had a
substitute machine and got it up and running immediately.¶
¶
We have replaced the unreliable projection display system
that failed during our final presentation.  Now that the new
wide-screen direct display systems are available, we--and
our customers--won't have to rely on those inefficient and
unreliable projection systems.¶
¶
¶
◆

COMMAND: Copy Delete Format Gallery Help Insert Jump Library
         Options Print Quit Replace Search Transfer Undo Window
Microsoft Word Version 5.0 release 17
Pg1 Co1           {¶}                              Microsoft Word
```

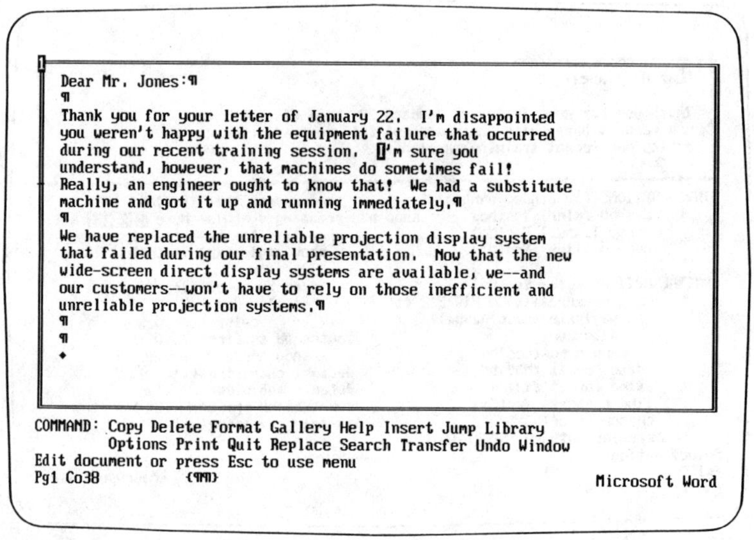

Fig. 2.9.

After joining the first and second paragraphs.

```
┌─                                                              ─┐
│▌                                                              │
│  Dear Mr. Jones:¶                                             │
│  ¶                                                            │
│  Thank you for your letter of January 22.  I'm disappointed  │
│  you weren't happy with the equipment failure that occurred  │
│  during our recent training session.  ▯'m sure you           │
│  understand, however, that machines do sometimes fail!       │
│  Really, an engineer ought to know that!  We had a substitute│
│  machine and got it up and running immediately.¶             │
│  ¶                                                            │
│  We have replaced the unreliable projection display system   │
│  that failed during our final presentation.  Now that the new│
│  wide-screen direct display systems are available, we--and   │
│  our customers--won't have to rely on those inefficient and  │
│  unreliable projection systems.¶                             │
│  ¶                                                            │
│  ¶                                                            │
│  ◆                                                            │
│                                                              │
│                                                              │
│ COMMAND: Copy Delete Format Gallery Help Insert Jump Library  │
│          Options Print Quit Replace Search Transfer Undo Window│
│ Edit document or press Esc to use menu                        │
│ Pg1 Co38           {¶M}                        Microsoft Word │
└─                                                              ─┘
```

Splitting Paragraphs

You will have many occasions to split paragraphs. For example, a real paragraph—not the mechanical one defined by Word—should be unified; it should express and develop a single idea. If you have more than one idea in a paragraph, you should split the paragraph into two. To practice the technique for splitting a paragraph, follow these steps:

1. Use the mouse or the arrow keys to position the cursor on the character at which you want the split to occur. Because you're just experimenting, position the cursor at the beginning of any sentence in one of the letter's paragraphs. (You will rejoin the split paragraphs in a moment.)

2. Press Enter.

As you can see, Word breaks the paragraph into two. Press Enter again to leave a blank line between the two paragraphs, if you prefer.

To rejoin the paragraphs you split, simply select the new paragraph marks Word has inserted, and use the **D**elete command (or press the Del key).

Deleting and Undeleting a Paragraph

As you inspect your letter after joining the two paragraphs, you decide that the entire first paragraph must go. It's too negative, and it violates the first principle of professional business communication: focus on the customer, not your own feelings and preoccupations. To delete the paragraph, using the keyboard, follow these steps:

1. Place the cursor anywhere in the first paragraph.

2. Press F10 to select the whole paragraph (see fig. 2.10).

3. Press Del. The paragraph is cut to the scrap, as shown in figure 2.11.

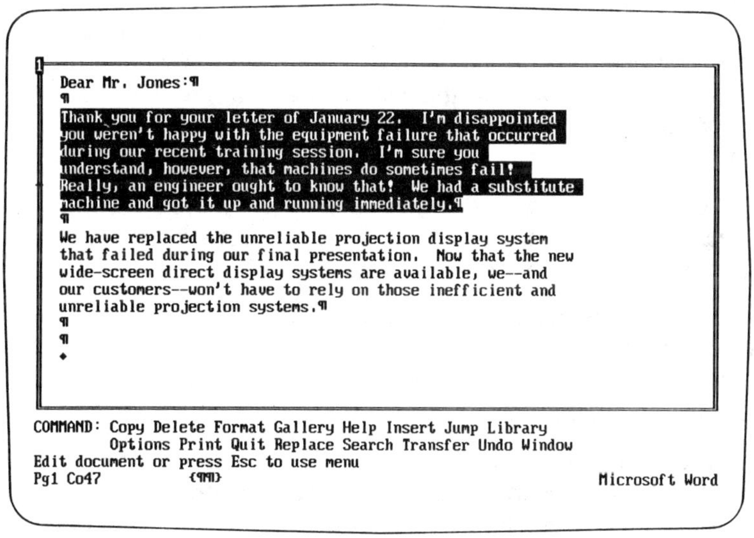

```
Dear Mr. Jones:¶
¶
Thank you for your letter of January 22.  I'm disappointed
you weren't happy with the equipment failure that occurred
during our recent training session.  I'm sure you
understand, however, that machines do sometimes fail!
Really, an engineer ought to know that!  We had a substitute
machine and got it up and running immediately.¶
¶
We have replaced the unreliable projection display system
that failed during our final presentation.  Now that the new
wide-screen direct display systems are available, we--and
our customers--won't have to rely on those inefficient and
unreliable projection systems.¶
¶
¶
◆



COMMAND: Copy Delete Format Gallery Help Insert Jump Library
         Options Print Quit Replace Search Transfer Undo Window
Edit document or press Esc to use menu
Pg1 Co47          {¶¶}                        Microsoft Word
```

Fig. 2.10.

Selecting a paragraph with F10.

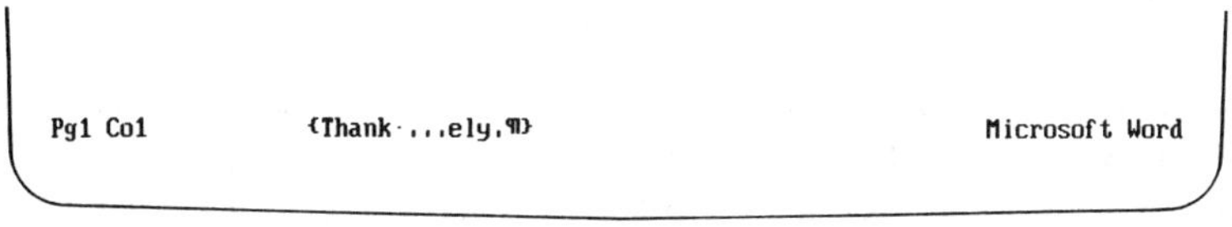

```
Pg1 Co1          {Thank···ely.¶}              Microsoft Word
```

Fig. 2.11.

Cutting the paragraph to the scrap.

Note that the scrap shows only the first and last five characters of the paragraph, including the paragraph mark.

To delete a paragraph with the mouse, do the following:

1. Place the pointer in the selection bar, which is the first vertical column on the screen, located just to the right of the left scroll bar. You will know the pointer is in the right position when its shape changes. If you're in the graphics mode, the pointer changes to a right-facing arrow. If you're in the text mode, the pointer changes to a small rectangle.

2. Move the pointer up or down the selection bar until the pointer is beside the paragraph you want to delete.

3. Click the right mouse button to select the paragraph.

4. Press Del to cut the paragraph to the scrap.

Before you do anything else, try using the **U**ndo command to restore the deletion—and use the command again to delete the paragraph once more. You can use Undo in this way to "test" the effect of an editing change, cycling back and forth between the change and the original text.

One of the nicest things about editing with Word is that you can always reconsider a deletion, even if you have cut huge amounts of text. You can restore a deletion in two ways:

Ins

❑ As mentioned previously, the Undo command puts your text back the way it was before the deletion. Undo restores the deletion to the exact spot from which it was cut. Use the Undo command to cancel a deletion.

❑ The Insert command (as well as the Ins key) restores the text you have cut but reinserts it at the cursor's location. Use the Insert command (or the Ins key) to copy or move text from one location to another in your document.

Caution: The topics of copying and moving text are introduced elsewhere in this chapter. For now, however, note this one important caution about the scrap: *The scrap holds only one deletion at a time.* The next time you cut something, the new cut text wipes out the scrap's contents. Therefore, if you have just cut a huge amount of text, and you're not sure whether you should have done so, think twice before you cut more text to the scrap and thus make retrieving all that text impossible.

Inserting Additional Text

While looking over the remaining text of the letter, you realize that you goofed when you deleted the whole first paragraph—nothing is wrong with the sentence "Thank you for your letter of January 22." You could bring the whole paragraph back from the scrap, but retyping the sentence is almost as easy. Follow these instructions to insert the new sentence at the beginning of the letter:

1. Check the status line. If the key indicator says OT, press F5 to cancel the overtype mode.

2. Use the arrow keys or the mouse to put the cursor on the second paragraph mark below the salutation.

3. Type *Thank you for your letter of January 22.* To continue with your new effort to emphasize the positive, also type the additional text shown in figure 2.12 (*Mr. Jones, it was a pleasure*...). Press Enter when you come to the end of the paragraph.

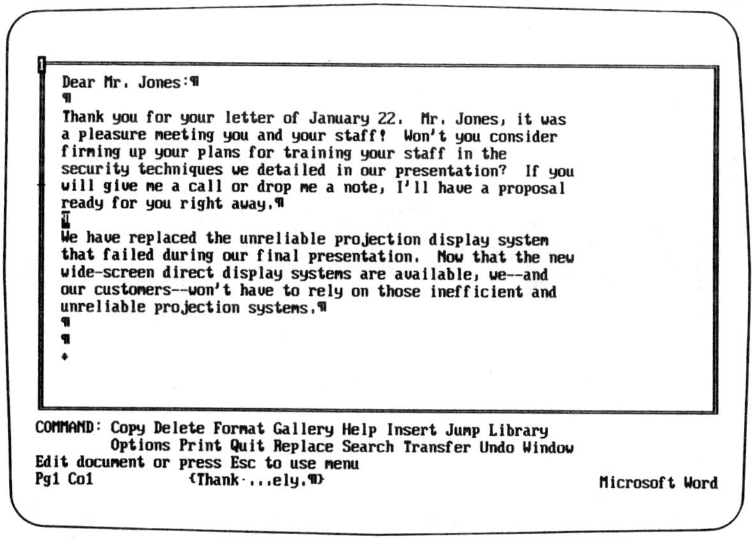

```
Dear Mr. Jones:¶
¶
Thank you for your letter of January 22. Mr. Jones, it was
a pleasure meeting you and your staff! Won't you consider
firming up your plans for training your staff in the
security techniques we detailed in our presentation? If you
will give me a call or drop me a note, I'll have a proposal
ready for you right away.¶
¶
We have replaced the unreliable projection display system
that failed during our final presentation. Now that the new
wide-screen direct display systems are available, we--and
our customers--won't have to rely on those inefficient and
unreliable projection systems.¶
¶
¶
↓



COMMAND: Copy Delete Format Gallery Help Insert Jump Library
         Options Print Quit Replace Search Transfer Undo Window
Edit document or press Esc to use menu
Pg1 Co1          {Thank·...ely.¶}              Microsoft Word
```

Fig. 2.12.

Inserting text.

Note that existing text moves right and down automatically. This feature is called *automatic reformatting* and—like word wrapping—is one of the reasons computers make writing a pleasure.

Moving Text

This letter is looking better, but as you read over what you have inserted, you realize that some of this material belongs at the end of the letter, not the beginning. You therefore decide to do a block move.

A *block move*, as the name suggests, involves moving a block of text from one part of a document to another. Doing block moves with Word is exceptionally easy. You must first select the text you want to move. (You can select any amount of text, from a single character to dozens of pages.) Then you cut the text to the scrap by using the Delete command (or the Del key), move the cursor to the new location, and use the Insert command (or the Ins key) to paste the text from the scrap into the new location. (Mouse users take note: You can use a special technique that bypasses the scrap entirely. See "Moving Text with the Mouse" for more information.)

The following steps show you how to move the text in the letter:

1. Use the F6 (Extend) key or the click-and-drag technique to select the text, as shown in figure 2.13. Don't select the paragraph mark at the end of the first paragraph. If you do, you lose the blank line that separates the two paragraphs.

Fig. 2.13.

Selecting the text to be moved.

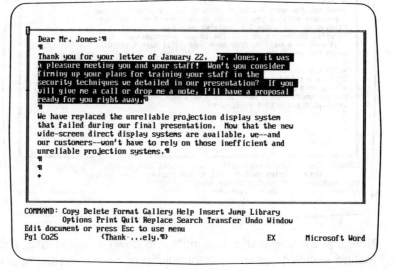

```
        Dear Mr. Jones:¶
        ¶
        Thank you for your letter of January 22. Mr. Jones, it was
        a pleasure meeting you and your staff! Won't you consider
        firming up your plans for training your staff in the
        security techniques we detailed in our presentation?  If you
        will give me a call or drop me a note, I'll have a proposal
        ready for you right away.¶
        ¶
        We have replaced the unreliable projection display system
        that failed during our final presentation.  Now that the new
        wide-screen direct display systems are available, we--and
        our customers--won't have to rely on those inefficient and
        unreliable projection systems.¶
        ¶
        ¶
        ♦


COMMAND: Copy Delete Format Gallery Help Insert Jump Library
         Options Print Quit Replace Search Transfer Undo Window
Edit document or press Esc to use menu
Pg1 Co25           {Thank·...ely.¶}                EX       Microsoft Word
```

Del

2. Choose the **D**elete command. When the Delete menu appears, you can see that Word has proposed a response, which is highlighted, in the **delete to** field (see fig. 2.14). This proposed response is none other than the scrap. (As you will learn in Chapter 12, "Using Glossaries and Bookmarks," you also can delete to glossaries, which are essentially *named* scraps.) Press Enter to cut the selected text to the scrap. As an alternative to using the Delete command, just press Del.

```
DELETE to: {}

Enter glossary name or press F1 to select from list
Pg1 Co25          {Thank·,,.ely,¶}                EX     Microsoft Word
```

Fig. 2.14.

Using the Delete command.

3. Move the cursor to the end of the document.

4. Choose the **I**nsert command. When the Insert menu appears, the **insert from** command field's proposed response is the scrap (see fig. 2.15). Press Enter to accept that response. As an alternative to using the Insert command, just press the Ins key.

Ins

```
INSERT from: {}

Enter glossary name or press F1 to select from list
Pg1 Co1           {Mr.·Jo...·away.}                      Microsoft Word
```

Fig. 2.15.

Using the Insert command.

Become accustomed to using the Del and Ins keyboard shortcuts for moving text. They're much faster than the Delete and Insert commands, which have their greatest uses when you are cutting text to glossaries and retrieving text from glossaries. For more information on glossaries, see Chapter 12.

The letter should now look like figure 2.16. Welcome to computer-assisted writing.

Mouse users can use an even easier and speedier technique to move text. To move text with a mouse, follow these steps:

1. Use the click-and-drag technique to select the text you want to move.

2. Point to the place you want to move the text.

3. Hold down the Ctrl key and click the left button.

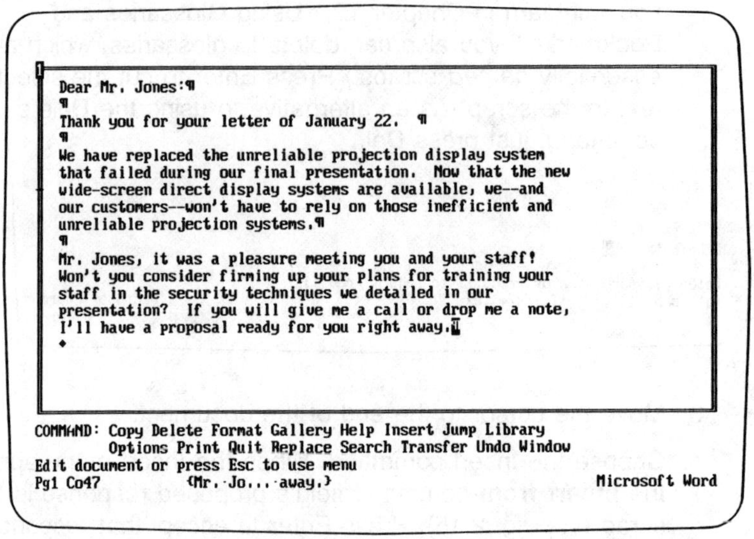

Fig. 2.16.

Text in its new location after a block move.

```
┌┐
│▌ Dear Mr. Jones:¶
│ ¶
│ Thank you for your letter of January 22.  ¶
│ ¶
│ We have replaced the unreliable projection display system
│ that failed during our final presentation.  Now that the new
│ wide-screen direct display systems are available, we--and
│ our customers--won't have to rely on those inefficient and
│ unreliable projection systems.¶
│ ¶
│ Mr. Jones, it was a pleasure meeting you and your staff!
│ Won't you consider firming up your plans for training your
│ staff in the security techniques we detailed in our
│ presentation?  If you will give me a call or drop me a note,
│ I'll have a proposal ready for you right away.▓
│ ◆
└
COMMAND: Copy Delete Format Gallery Help Insert Jump Library
         Options Print Quit Replace Search Transfer Undo Window
Edit document or press Esc to use menu
Pg1 Co47          {Mr. Jo...away.}                  Microsoft Word
```

Setting Tabs and Using the Newline Command

Now you need to add the complimentary closing. You can indent the closing manually if you prefer, but setting up a tab format is easier and more convenient. If you change your mind about the tab settings, you can easily set up a new format. Follow these steps to set up your tab format and to type the closing:

1. Use the arrow keys or the mouse to select the last paragraph mark in your document. Press Enter to insert a blank line after the last paragraph.

2. Choose the **F**ormat **T**ab **S**et command. When the **position** field appears, type *3.5* and press Enter.

3. Choose the **O**ptions command and select **Y**es in the **show ruler** command field. Press Enter, and Word displays a ruler along the top window border, showing the tab stop you set.

4. Press Tab. The cursor jumps to the new tab stop.

5. Type *Sincerely,* but don't press Enter. Instead, use the Newline command (Shift-Enter). Press Shift-Enter four times.

6. Press Tab, type *Diane B. Smith, Director* and press Shift-Enter again.

7. Press Tab again, and type *Corporate Training.* Figure 2.17 shows the completed closing.

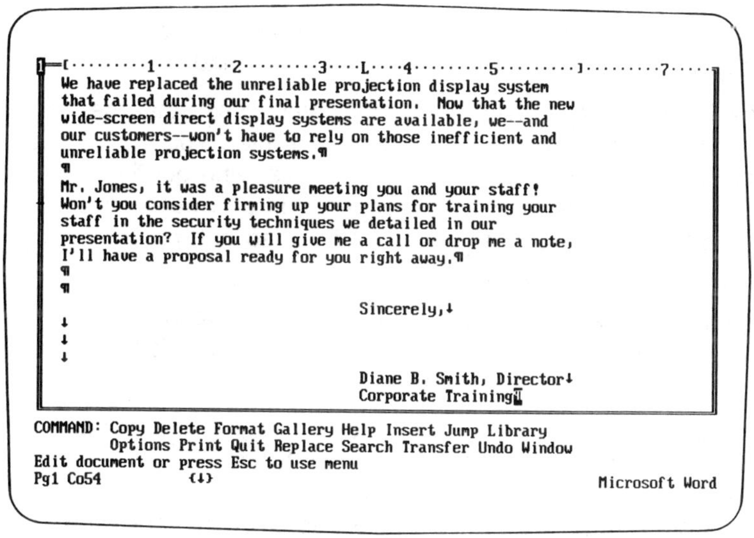

Fig. 2.17.

Complimentary closing created with the Newline command (Shift-Enter).

What's all this business about Shift-Enter? Here's the point: In Word, tab stops are a paragraph format. The tab stops you choose when you use the Format Tab Set command attach only to the paragraph that is selected (the one in which the cursor is positioned) when you use the command. The Format Tab Set command thus affects only one paragraph at a time. The Newline command (Shift-Enter) starts a new line without starting a new paragraph. Therefore, if you use Shift-Enter rather than Enter to enter several lines of text, you can change the tab stops for all those lines with just one Format Tab Set command. Use the Newline command whenever you want to control a line break but don't want to begin a new paragraph.

Follow these instructions to change the tab stop so that you can see in practice what all this information means:

1. Position the cursor anywhere within the complimentary closing.

2. Choose the **Format Tab Set** command. When the command menu appears, press F1.

3. Now press the up- or down-arrow key to select the tab stop you set (3.5 inches).

4. Press Ctrl-left arrow to move the tab stop left, or Ctrl-right arrow to move the tab stop right. Experiment with the position until you're happy with it.

5. When you have decided where you want the closing to be positioned, press Enter to carry out the command.

Users of earlier versions of Word will be delighted to see that the text moves around as you move the tab mark on the ruler. You can adjust the text until it's just the way you want it before carrying out the command and making the change "permanent." In previous versions, you didn't see the change until after you had carried out the command.

Mouse users, as usual, can take advantage of special, easy techniques for setting and moving tabs. These techniques are discussed in Chapter 11, "Creating Tables and Lists with Tabs, Autosort, and Math."

As you may have already discovered, Word comes with preset tabs every 0.5 inch. (You can change this setting by typing a new measurement in the **default tab width** field of the Options menu.) When you set custom tabs with the Format Tab Set command, you delete the preset tabs, but only for the paragraph(s) selected when you use the command. Additionally, Word deletes only the preset tabs to the left of the custom tabs you set.

Previewing Your Letter before Printing

Now is a good time to explore a new Word 5 feature, Print preView. This command shows you how your document will appear on the printed page. For business letters, Print preView is especially valuable because you can see how well the text is balanced on the page. Good business-letter practice suggests that the body of a letter should be positioned so that it's slightly above the place it would be if it were exactly centered. If the letter is too far up, however, it can look as if it is jammed against the return address. If the letter is too far down, it can appear "heavy" and unattractive.

To preview your letter before printing, do the following:

1. Choose the **P**rint pre**V**iew option. Alternatively, use the Ctrl-F9 keyboard shortcut.

2. When the preview screen appears, as shown in figure 2.18, note how the text is laid out relative to the entire page.

Ctrl-F9

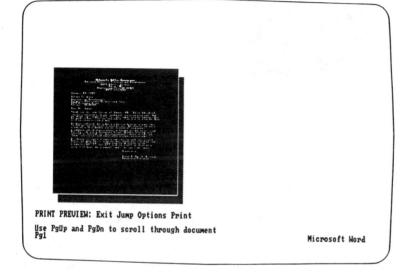

Fig. 2.18.

Using Print preView.

3. To leave Print preView, choose **E**xit.

As you can see, the text is too high—it's crowded against the return address. To cure the problem, follow these steps:

1. Use the arrow keys or mouse to move the cursor to the paragraph mark just below the return address, and press Enter three or four times.

2. Press Ctrl-PgDn to move to the bottom of the file, and make sure that you haven't entered so many lines that Word has started a new page. If you did, a row of dots appears across the screen, showing you where the page break will occur. To remove the page break and make sure that all the text prints on one page, use Ctrl-PgUp and delete two or three of the paragraph marks you entered.

Choose **P**rint pre**V**iew again (see fig. 2.19) to make sure that your letter is balanced.

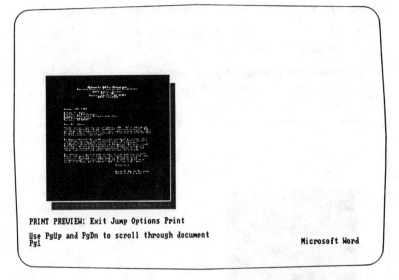

Fig. 2.19.

Previewing the
letter after
moving down
the body.

Printing Your Letter

Now you need to print the letter. By this time, you should have
followed the instructions in the appendix to get your printer working,
including choosing a printer description file and installing it with the
Print Options command. If you haven't taken these steps already, save
your work and consult the appendix.

Ctrl-F8

To print your document, simply follow these steps:

1. Make sure that your printer is turned on and selected (ready
   to receive instructions), and that the cable is securely
   connected between your computer and the printer.

2. Choose the **P**rint **P**rinter command. Alternatively, use the
   Ctrl-F8 keyboard shortcut.

Caution: Because you can use so many different printers with an
IBM-format personal computer, this book cannot go into all the
problems that can occur when you try to get your printer working. If
you're having trouble, ask the dealer who sold you the printer for
help. Or ask someone who's experienced in IBM-format computing to
help you. As you will discover, such people are usually willing to help
because they know only too well what new users have to go through
to conquer these problems.

When you're finished printing your letter, save your work to disk by choosing the **T**ransfer **S**ave command (or use the Ctrl-F10 shortcut).

Chapter Summary

In this chapter, you learned the basics of how to write, format, edit, and print a simple business letter. The next three chapters explore editing and formatting in detail, showing you many more command options and techniques. You will find complete lists of Word's text editing and formatting commands and their keyboard shortcuts. For now, however, congratulations on finishing this tutorial! You have learned a great deal about Word, and you have had an opportunity to explore this wonderful program's personality.

3

Word 5 Editing Strategies

One of the joys of word processing is the ease with which you can revise your work once you have created it. You needn't send anything out the door until your text looks and reads as if it were created by a professional.

You have already learned much of what you need to know in order to edit your text with Word. In Chapter 2, you learned how to revise a letter until it was exactly right. This chapter expands your knowledge of Word writing and editing techniques. In this chapter, you learn how to do the following:

❑ Retrieve files you have created and saved to disk

❑ Enter foreign-language and technical characters

❑ Prevent Word from separating two words that belong together

❑ Use the full range of options for selecting, deleting, and inserting text

❑ Use the overtype mode for quick editing

❑ Copy and transpose text

❑ Search your document for text you specify, or automatically replace one text string with another throughout your document

❑ Move around in a large document without paging through it manually

You don't need to memorize everything in this chapter in order to learn Word effectively. Word gives you many options for accomplishing basic editing tasks, so you can choose the methods that suit you best. For this reason, you will be wise if you try all the techniques in this chapter, striving all the while to develop a "short list" of the techniques you prefer.

Experienced computer users often learn a new program by using some "old-fashioned" technology: a blank 5-by-8-inch card. After you try the many options Word gives you for such operations as moving and selecting text, list on a card the commands and techniques you like best. Then you can use the card as a quick reference guide. Writing down your favorite methods helps you remember them, and you can keep your highly focused guide right by your computer to refresh your memory when necessary.

Work through this chapter with your computer and a "guinea pig" file at hand, one that's at least two or three pages long. If you haven't already created and saved a two- or three-page document, create and save one now. But because you're experimenting, don't work with anything valuable.

Computers Are Great, But . . .

Any medium for writing is bound to have some liabilities, and terrific as it is, computerized word processing is no exception. Writing teachers often find that students who write with word processing programs don't rewrite bad passages but instead merely add new words and sentences to try to clarify them. The result? A "bloated" manuscript that's stilted, lengthy, and tedious to read. You can avoid this problem by remembering a simple rule: If a passage seems unclear or poorly written, don't try to fix it by adding new text to it. Place the cursor above it, rewrite it, compare the two versions, and delete the poorer one.

Computer-assisted writing causes another problem: a computer doesn't show you much of your document on the screen. With Word, you see only about one-third of a page. Keeping your document's overall structure in mind as you write and edit is therefore difficult. (For this reason, the editors of many university presses say that they're not surprised when a word-processed manuscript is poorly organized.) A good cure for this problem is to use a printed copy of your document as a guide for revision. An even better solution is to use Word's wonderful outlining feature, which shows your document's overall structure at a keystroke. This feature, unique to Word, is one of the most innovative and useful features ever devised for professional writing applications. (For more information on outlining, see Chapter 10.)

To hide the command menu and thus see more of your document, choose the **N**o option in the **show menu** command field of the **O**ptions menu. If you want to display the menu again, press Esc.

Retrieving Files

You can start Word and load an existing document at the same time. Or if you're already working in Word, you can use the Transfer Load command to retrieve a document from disk.

Starting Word and Loading a Document

Before you can practice editing with Word 5, you must load a file. To start Word and load a document, do the following:

1. Start your computer and go to the DOS prompt. Log on to the drive or directory that contains your document (for more information, see the Appendix).

2. Type *word filename*, where "filename" is the name of your document. If you have used Word's default extension (.DOC), you can omit the period and the extension.

If you see the message Enter Y to create file, Word cannot find the document you named. Press Esc, and refer to "If Word Can't Find Your Document" in this chapter for information on how to proceed.

Retrieving Documents after Starting Word

After you start Word, use the Transfer Load command to move documents from disk to Word's memory. The Transfer Load menu is shown in figure 3.1.

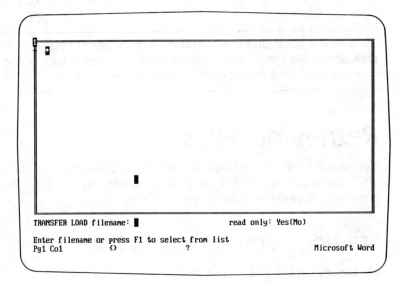

```
TRANSFER LOAD filename: █                    read only: Yes(No)

Enter filename or press F1 to select from list
Pg1 Co1            {}              ?                    Microsoft Word
```

To avoid errors and frustration, you need to know the following two facts about the way Transfer Load works.

❏ If you type the file name without a period or extension, Word assumes that you have used the default document extension (.DOC), and looks for a file with that extension. If you saved the document with some other extension, you must type the extension. Otherwise, Word will not find the document.

❏ Unless you specify additional path information, Word assumes that the document is in the current drive or directory. If the document is in some other drive or directory, you can type the path information in the filename command field of the Transfer Load menu.

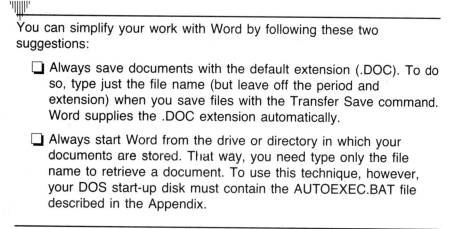

You can simplify your work with Word by following these two suggestions:

❏ Always save documents with the default extension (.DOC). To do so, type just the file name (but leave off the period and extension) when you save files with the Transfer Save command. Word supplies the .DOC extension automatically.

❏ Always start Word from the drive or directory in which your documents are stored. That way, you need type only the file name to retrieve a document. To use this technique, however, your DOS start-up disk must contain the AUTOEXEC.BAT file described in the Appendix.

Retrieving Documents from the Current Drive or Directory

If you want to edit a document you created earlier, you must retrieve it. To retrieve a document that's in the current drive or directory, follow these steps:

1. Choose the **T**ransfer **L**oad command (or use the Ctrl-F7 keyboard shortcut).

Ctrl-F7

2. In the **filename** field, type the document's file name (and the period and extension, if you used an extension other than .DOC). To retrieve the file REPORT.DOC, for instance, type *report* in the **filename** field, as shown in figure 3.2.

3. Carry out the command by pressing Enter or clicking the command name.

Note: Word ignores lower- and uppercase letters when saving and retrieving files, so the case of your file name doesn't matter.

If you see the message Enter Y to save changes to document, N to lose changes, or Esc to cancel, you have created some text but haven't saved it. Press Y to save the text or N to abandon it.

Viewing a List of Drives, Directories, and Files

You can view a list of the currently available drives, directories, and .DOC files by following these steps:

1. Choose the **T**ransfer **L**oad command.

2. When the command menu appears, the **filename** option is highlighted. Press F1.

3. A list of the currently available drives and directories appears (see fig. 3.3). Some documents may be present, too, but the drives and directories are enclosed in brackets.

Fig. 3.2.

Retrieving a file with the default extension (.DOC).

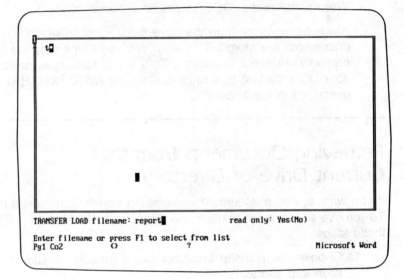

```
 t

                       TRANSFER LOAD filename: report           read only: Yes(No)

                       Enter filename or press F1 to select from list
                       Pg1 Co2              {}              ?                    Microsoft Word
```

Fig. 3.3.

The list of drives and directories displayed after you press F1.

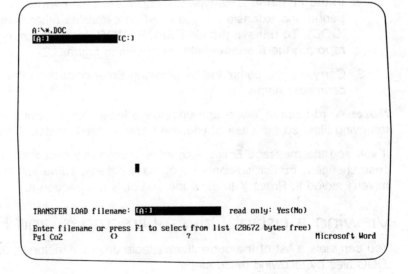

```
A:\*.DOC
[A:]                          [C:]




                       TRANSFER LOAD filename: [A:]              read only: Yes(No)

                       Enter filename or press F1 to select from list (28672 bytes free)
                       Pg1 Co2              {}              ?                    Microsoft Word
```

4. Highlight the name of the drive, directory, or document you want, and press Enter. If you choose a document, Word loads the document. If you choose a drive or directory, however, Word displays another list. This list shows the files available in the chosen drive or directory (see fig. 3.4). Select the file you want, or if a directory is available, continue searching directories for files.

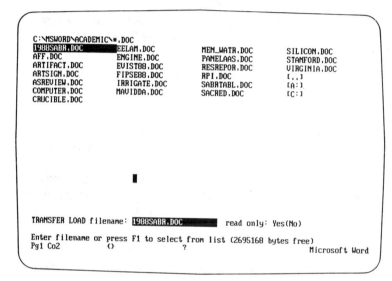

Fig. 3.4.

The list of files in a drive or directory you have selected.

In previous versions of Word, pressing F1 displayed only the .DOC files in the current drive or directory. And if you couldn't remember the names of other directories in which documents were stored, you were out of luck. You had to use the Library Run command (see Chapter 8, "Finding and Managing Documents") and then the DOS DIR command.

If Word Cannot Find Your Document

If you try to load a document while starting Word and see the message Enter Y to create file, or if you type your document's name in the **filename** field only to see the message File does not exist. Enter Y to create or Esc to cancel, don't panic. Getting one of these messages doesn't necessarily mean that your document has disappeared into the void! The message may mean simply that one of the following situations is involved:

❏ *The file isn't in the current drive or directory.* Press Esc and use the **T**ransfer **L**oad command again. Press F1 to see a list of available drives and directories, and continue as explained in "Viewing a List of Drives, Directories, and Files."

❏ *You saved the file with an extension other than .DOC.* Press Esc, and use the **T**ransfer **L**oad command again. This time, type the file name and the extension.

❏ *The document is on some other disk.* Make sure that you have placed the right disk in your computer. Press Esc, change the disk, and use the **T**ransfer **L**oad command again.

If you think that you erased your document by accident, do not save anything to the disk from which you erased your file until you consider your options.

As you will learn in Chapter 8, "Finding and Managing Documents," Word automatically creates a backup file (with the .BAK extension) every time you save a file with Transfer Save. The .BAK file contains the next-to-last version of your file. If you save your work frequently, this file contains most of your work. You can load a .BAK file by using Transfer Load; just remember to type the .BAK extension.

If you haven't saved any additional work to the disk, you can use an "unerase" utility program to restore the file. Such programs are available in commercial or shareware versions. For more information, contact your software dealer.

Examining Other Document-Retrieval Options

As you will learn in Chapter 8, "Finding and Managing Documents," Word has even more document-retrieval options, including these:

❏ You can use the Transfer Load command and F1 to find and list documents with extensions other than .DOC.

❏ Word comes equipped with a sophisticated and powerful document search-and-retrieval system for hard disk users. You can use this system to search a huge hard disk for all the files by a certain author, all the files created after a certain date, or just the one document that contains certain text. This system is available with the Library Document-retrieval command.

❑ You can use the Transfer Options command to change the current drive or directory during an editing session.

❑ With the Transfer Merge command, you can load one document into another so that the two are merged into one.

See Chapter 8 for more information on these options.

Creating a New Blank Document

As you have already learned, when you start Word by typing *word* at the DOS prompt, the program starts and loads a new blank document. To load a new blank document after you have been working with another one in the same editing session, however, you need to use the Transfer Clear command.

To clear the screen and load a new blank document, do the following:

1. Choose the **T**ransfer **C**lear **W**indow command.

2. If you see the message Enter Y to save changes to document, N to lose changes, or Esc to cancel, decide whether you want to save the current document or abandon it. To save it, press Y; to abandon it, press N.

More about Creating Text with Word

In Chapters 1 and 2, you learned the basics of creating a new document with Word. This section presents additional information about creating text with Word; you may find some of this material helpful to you for specific writing purposes.

Using Foreign and Special Characters

The IBM Personal Computer was designed for an international marketplace as well as for scientific and engineering applications. The computer therefore comes equipped with many foreign-language characters and technical symbols. To use one of these special characters, follow these steps:

1. Look up the character's three-number code in figure 3.5.

2. Hold down the Alt key and type the three-number code on the numeric keypad.

Fig. 3.5.

Alt-key codes for
foreign and
special characters.

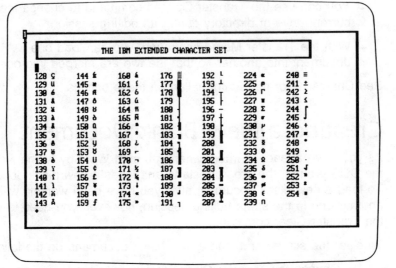

 Caution: Just the fact that your printer is said to be "IBM compatible"
doesn't mean that it can print the foreign-language and technical
characters, even though your computer can display them on-screen.
Consult your printer's manual to make sure that it can print "extended"
or "higher-order" characters. If you're looking for a printer and planning
to use these characters in your work, insist that the salesperson
demonstrate the printer's capability to print the extended character set.

Using Nonbreaking Spaces

Occasionally, you may want to prevent Word from separating two
words (such as a first and last name) or breaking a mathematical
formula when the program prints your document. (The line breaks you
see on the screen aren't necessarily the ones Word uses when you
print.) To prevent Word from separating two words, connect them with
a nonbreaking space.

To enter a nonbreaking space, simply do the following:

1. Type the first word.

2. Press Ctrl-space bar.

3. Type the second word.

Rather than create a line break between the words linked by a nonbreaking space, Word will move both words to the next line if necessary.

By choosing the **A**ll option in the **show non-printing symbols** field of the **O**ptions command (see fig. 3.6), you can see where you have entered nonbreaking spaces. After you choose the All option, Word displays a small, nonprinting dot at every point at which you pressed the space bar. Word leaves a blank space, however, where you pressed Ctrl-space bar.

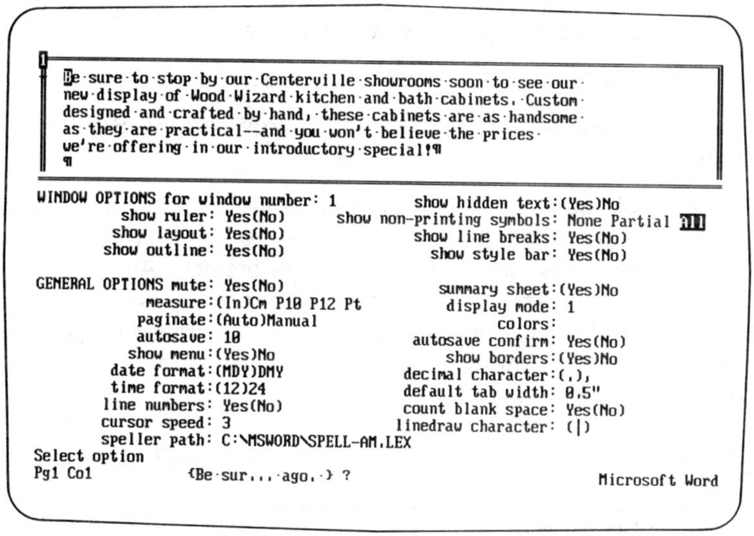

Fig. 3.6.

Displaying nonbreaking spaces.

Using Nonbreaking Hyphens

If you are typing two words or numbers separated by a hyphen, as in "E. E. Evans-Pritchard," you may want to prevent Word from placing a line break at the hyphen. Rather than type an ordinary hyphen, use a nonbreaking hyphen. Follow these steps:

1. Type the first word.

2. Press Ctrl-Shift-hyphen (hold down the Ctrl and the Shift keys and press the hyphen key).

3. Type the second word.

Word will not create a line break between the words linked by a nonbreaking hyphen; instead, the program will move both words down to the next line.

Manually Starting a New Page

Word is preset with the Auto option chosen in the **paginate** field of the Options menu. And with this option selected, the program paginates your document automatically. These automatic page breaks—each a row of dots and spaces across the screen—appear as you type. If you insert or delete text above one of the breaks, Word automatically repositions the break. Any time you want, however, you can insert a page break manually. A manual page break forces Word to start a new page at the place you give the manual page break command.

To force Word to start a new page, follow this procedure:

1. Place the cursor where you want Word to start a new page.

2. Press Ctrl-Shift-Enter (hold down the Ctrl key and the Shift key and press Enter).

A manual page break looks like a row of dots without spaces. It differs from an automatic page break, in which the dots are separated by spaces. (Fig. 3.7 compares the two types of page breaks.) Another way to tell the difference between automatic and manual page breaks is that you can't select or position the cursor on an automatic page break, but you *can* select a manual page break. You can thus delete it if you decide that you don't need it.

Fig. 3.7.

Automatic and manual page breaks.

```
┌─────────────────────────────────────────────────────────────┐
│in·our·introductory·special!¶                                 │
│¶                                                             │
│About·Wood·Wizard·Cabinets.··In·February,·1947,·John·and·     │
│Marsha·Williams·couldn't·find·the·cabinets·they·wanted·for·   │
│their·kitchen·remodeling·plans,·and·so·they·decided·to·build· │
│them·in·their·basement·shop.··Avid·woodworking·hobbyists,·    │
│John·and·Marsha·created·a·kitchen·that·their·friends·and·     │
│neighbors·admired--so·much·so,·in·fact,·that·they·found·      │
│ . . . . . . . . . . . . . . . . . . . . . . . . . . . . . . │
│themselves·swamped·in·orders!··Realizing·that·many·people·    │
│wanted·their·hand-crafted·cabinets,·John·and·Marsha·founded·· │
│Wood·Wizard·Kitchen·and·Bath·Cabinets,·Inc,·the·next·year.¶  │
│¶                                                             │
│.............................................................│
│Although·Wood·Wizard·Kitchen·and·Bath·Cabinets·has·just·      │
│celebrated·its·40th·birthday·and·sells·over·a·million·        │
│dollars'·worth·of·cabinets·annually,·every·kitchen·and·bath·  │
│cabinet·we·make·is·a·hand-crafted·product,·just·like·the·     │
│ones·that·John·and·Marsha·made·decades·ago.·¶                │
│                                                             │
│COMMAND: Copy Delete Format Gallery Help Insert Jump Library  │
│         Options Print Quit Replace Search Transfer Undo Window│
│Edit document or press Esc to use menu                        │
│Pg1 Co1          {Be·sur...ago.·} ?          Microsoft Word   │
└─────────────────────────────────────────────────────────────┘
```

To remove a manual page break, follow these steps:

1. Place the cursor on the page break so that the whole row of dots is highlighted.

2. Press Del.

When you delete a manual page break to the scrap, Word stores the break there as it would any other deleted text or symbol. You can use the Insert command or the Ins key to insert the break elsewhere.

 Caution: Use manual page breaks sparingly, particularly if you plan to subject your document to moderate or heavy editing. As you delete and insert text above the forced page break, the manual break may become unnecessary. As a general rule, you should insert manual page breaks only when you have finished editing your document and are ready to print. And preview all your page breaks, automatic and manual, by using the Print Repaginate command. For more information on Print Repaginate, see Chapter 7, "Printing Your Work."

Don't use manual page breaks to keep headings from appearing by themselves at the bottom of a page. A far better method is to format headings by choosing the **Yes** option in the **keep follow** field of the **Format Paragraph** command. For more information on ways to format headings, see the section titled "Controlling Page Breaks" in Chapter 5, "Word 5 Formatting Strategies: Page Formatting."

Selecting Text for Editing or Formatting

As you learned in Chapter 2, you frequently need to select text so that it is highlighted on the screen. Selection is necessary for editing operations; you must select the text you want to delete, copy, or move. Selection is also necessary for formatting operations when you are formatting after entering the text (the "formatting later" approach). You must select the text you want to format so that Word knows which text you want affected.

Word gives you many keyboard and mouse options for selecting text. You can select words, sentences, paragraphs, and even the whole document. In most cases, these units of text correspond to the way they are used in everyday language. But you need to realize that Word defines units of text in a mechanical way. Take a moment to look at table 3.1, which explains the rules Word follows to distinguish between such units as "words" and "characters."

Table 3.1
How Word Defines Units of Text

Text unit	Includes
Character	Anything you can type at the keyboard, as well as the paragraph and newline marks Word inserts in your document
Word	Any group of characters that is set off by spaces, tabs, hyphens, or punctuation (could even be a group of characters like *MXPTX11995*); includes trailing spaces but not punctuation
Line	All the characters on a single line
Sentence	Any group of characters that is surrounded by sentence-ending punctuation (periods, question marks, exclamation marks) or by a paragraph or newline mark (could even be a jumbled group of characters such as *Mrpph alkjd 331.*); includes trailing punctuation and spaces
Paragraph	Any group of characters that ends with a paragraph mark (could even be a one-word heading); includes the trailing paragraph mark
Column	A vertical line of characters on the screen (If you use the screen borders, you can display 75 columns of text on the screen; if you hide the borders by using the Options command, you can display 77.)
Document	All the characters in a document except footnotes, running heads, and page numbers

Pay special attention to what is included with each unit in Word's definitions. For example, when you select a word and delete it, Word also deletes the space that follows the word. When you select a sentence and delete it, Word deletes the punctuation and spaces that immediately follow it. When you select a paragraph and delete it, Word also deletes the paragraph mark, eliminating the blank line that would have remained on the screen after the paragraph was deleted.

(Note in table 3.1 that Word can select columns, or vertical rectangles of text on the screen. This technique is extremely handy for rearranging columns of data in tables but seldom used for other purposes. For this reason, selecting columns is discussed in Chapter 11, "Creating Tables and Lists with Tabs, Autosort, and Math.")

Whether you are using the keyboard or the mouse, you can select fixed or variable amounts of text. Selecting a *fixed* amount of text means that you select one of the text units that Word knows how to identify, such as a word, a sentence, a line, or a paragraph (see table 3.1). When you select a *variable* unit of text, as you did in Chapter 2, by using F6 or the click-and-drag technique, you select just the amount of text you want—such as part of a word, part of a sentence, or part of a paragraph. You also can use this technique to expand the highlight to include additional text after you select a fixed amount.

As you can see in table 3.1, Word defines a word to include trailing spaces, a sentence to include trailing punctuation and spaces, and a paragraph to include the trailing paragraph mark. When you're deleting or moving text, then, always use commands that select these fixed units. That way, you don't have any extraneous spaces, punctuation, or lines left after you perform the editing operation.

Selecting Fixed Units of Text with the Keyboard

Word uses function keys F7 through F10 for text-selection functions. Try some of the keyboard text-selection techniques listed in table 3.2 to see which ones you find most convenient. To cancel a selection, just press any key that moves the cursor.

Table 3.2
Selecting Fixed Units of Text with the Keyboard

To select	Press this key
Character right	Right-arrow key
Character left	Left-arrow key
First character on line	Home
Last character on line	End
Character up	Up-arrow key
Character down	Down-arrow key
Preceding word	F7
Next word	F8
Preceding sentence	Shift-F7
Next sentence	Shift-F8
Preceding paragraph	F9
Next paragraph	F10
Current line	Shift-F9
Whole document	Shift-F10

Note:. The functions of these keys repeat when you hold down the keys. For example, if you press and hold down the F10 key, Word selects the next paragraph and then continues selecting subsequent paragraphs, one after another. If the selection moves too fast, enter a lower number in the **cursor speed** field of the **O**ptions menu.

Selecting Fixed Units of Text with the Mouse

Mouse users also can select fixed units of text. Try some of the techniques listed in table 3.3; you're sure to find several of them useful.

Table 3.3
Selecting Fixed Units of Text with the Mouse

To select	Point to	Click
Character	Character	Left button
Word	Word	Right button
Sentence	Sentence	Both buttons
Line	Selection bar	Left button
Paragraph	Selection bar	Right button
Document	Selection bar	Both buttons

When you're selecting a paragraph for formatting (not editing), you needn't highlight the whole paragraph. Just position the cursor anywhere within the paragraph and use the **F**ormat **P**aragraph command. For more information on paragraph formatting, see Chapter 4, "Word 5 Formatting Strategies: Characters and Paragraphs."

Selecting Variable Amounts of Text with the Keyboard

In Chapter 2, you learned how to use the F6 (Extend) key to select variable amounts of text. Here's a quick review of how to extend the selection with the F6 (Extend) key:

1. Place the cursor where you want the highlight to begin.

2. Press F6. The code EX appears in the key status indicator.

3. Press any cursor-movement key to expand the highlight.

4. When you are finished expanding the highlight, choose the command you want to use (such as **D**elete or **F**ormat).

Most commands cancel the extend mode. To cancel it manually, just press F6 again.

You also can select variable amounts of text by using the Shift key. Follow these steps to select variable amounts of text:

1. Hold down the Shift key and press any key that moves the cursor. As long as you hold down the Shift key, the highlight is "anchored" at the cursor's original location, and you can expand the highlight as needed.

2. When you have finished expanding the highlight, release the Shift key.

The highlight remains on the screen. To cancel the highlight, just touch one of the cursor-movement keys.

The only real difference between the F6 and Shift-key techniques is that you must continue to hold down the Shift key as you're expanding the highlight. When you press F6, however, you begin a mode that stays in effect until you press F6 again.

Selecting Variable Amounts of Text with the Mouse

In Chapter 2, you learned how to use the click-and-drag technique to expand the highlight. To refresh your memory, you use the following technique:

1. Position the cursor at the beginning of the text you want to select.

2. Hold down the left or right button and drag to expand the highlight. If you hold down the left button, you can stop the selection within a word. If you hold down the right button, the selection expands word-by-word, preventing you from stopping the selection within a word.

You can easily select variable amounts of text this way. If you drag to the top or bottom window borders, Word scrolls the screen and continues to expand the highlight.

You can use the mouse with the F6 (Extend) key if you prefer. To extend the selection with the mouse and the F6 key, use the following procedure:

1. Click the left button on the first character you want selected.

2. Press F6. The code EX appears in the key status indicator.

3. Click the last character you want selected.

Most commands turn off the extend mode. To turn it off manually, press F6 again.

Deleting Text

To delete text, you need to select it first, using one of the keyboard or mouse techniques. Then choose the **D**elete command (or press the Del key) to delete the selection to the scrap and close up the space left by the deletion. You can restore the deletion by choosing the **U**ndo command, the Insert command, or the Ins key.

Note: When you restore a deletion by choosing Undo, Word always puts the deleted text back where you deleted it. If you choose the Insert command or press the Ins key, however, Word inserts the deleted text at the cursor's location. If you have moved the cursor away from the deletion's location, you must move it back before choosing Insert or pressing the Ins key to restore the deletion.

As you have already learned, you can delete text also by pressing the Backspace key. This key deletes the character to the left but does not affect the scrap. You cannot retrieve from the scrap the text you rub out with the Backspace key. You can, however, restore all the text, or much of it, by choosing the **U**ndo command.

Caution: If you have stored some text in the scrap and want to use the text again, be careful not to wipe it out by performing a second deletion. This accident often occurs in block moves. For example, suppose that you delete a paragraph to the scrap, thinking you will insert the text elsewhere. While scrolling to the new location, however, you notice a word that's not necessary. You select it and delete it. When you get to the new location, you find that the paragraph you wanted to move is gone! The scrap now contains the single word you deleted on the way to your new location.

If you accidentally wipe out text that you intended to use again, here's a trick you can use to recover the scrap's contents:

1. Without giving any additional commands or entering any additional text, choose the **U**ndo command.

2. Word restores the second deletion to your document, and the scrap's original contents reappear in the scrap.

Shift-Del

Word offers a shortcut you can use to delete text without affecting the scrap's contents: Shift-Del. You can use this command on a single character, a selected unit of text, or an extended selection. Use Shift-Del whenever you want to delete text from your document but preserve the scrap's contents. To recover a deletion you made with Shift-Del, use the **U**ndo command immediately.

To prevent accidents when you are moving valuable text from one location to another, delete the text to glossaries rather than the scrap. For more information on glossaries, see Chapter 12, "Using Glossaries and Bookmarks."

Inserting Text from the Scrap

Shift-Ins

As you learned in Chapter 2, the Insert command (and its keyboard counterpart, Ins) inserts the scrap's contents at the cursor's location.

Here's a helpful variation on text insertion. The keyboard shortcut Shift-Ins replaces the highlighted selection with the contents of the scrap in one operation. In other words, this shortcut deletes the currently selected text and inserts the scrap at the selection's location. Shift-Ins saves you the trouble of deleting the text before inserting it.

Suppose that you decide to move a paragraph to a new location, replacing a paragraph that's already there. Follow these steps to save keystrokes by using Shift-Ins:

1. Delete the paragraph you want to move.

2. Select the paragraph you want to replace.

3. Press Shift-Ins.

To cancel the effects of this command, choose **U**ndo.

Using the Overtype Mode

Most word processing programs have two text-creation modes, an insert mode and an overtype mode. In the insert mode, which is Word's default mode, the text you type pushes existing text right and down. In the overtype mode, which you can use by pressing F5, the text you type erases existing text. Some people are happy to write in the insert mode at all times, but you may want to experiment with the overtype mode. It can be useful when you're doing extensive rewriting. Writing experts know that wiping out a bad paragraph and rewriting it from scratch is usually better than just adding clarifying words here and there.

Note that the Backspace key does not work the same way in the overtype mode as it does in the insert mode. In overtype mode, backspacing doesn't delete characters to the left, and you can't go past the place where you started typing.

 Caution: If you toggle on the overtype mode by mistake, you might think Word is behaving oddly or about to crash because the Backspace key doesn't work. Whenever you think something's wrong with Word, check the key status indicator: you may have accidentally toggled on a mode. For more information, see "The Status Line" in Chapter 1.

Moving and Copying Text

As you learned in Chapter 2, moving text with Word is easy, whether you're using the keyboard or the mouse. Using variants of the same techniques, you also can copy text from one location in your document to another.

When you're moving or copying text from one part of a document to another, or from one document to a second document, try using two windows. You can display both locations (the source and destination) at the same time, so you more easily can keep track of what you're doing. And because you don't have to scroll or load a second document while the text you cut or copied is in the scrap, you have less chance of using a command that wipes out that text.

Moving Text: A Review

Keyboard and mouse techniques for performing block moves have already been discussed in Chapter 2, but here's a quick review.

To perform a block move, use the following method:

1. Select the text you want to move.

2. Choose the **D**elete command or press the Del key.

3. Move the cursor to the text's new location.

4. Choose the **I**nsert command or press Ins.

To perform a block move with the mouse, follow these steps:

1. Select the text you want to move.

2. Move the pointer to the text's new location.

3. Hold down the Ctrl key and click the left button.

Copying Text

You can use the keyboard or the mouse to copy text you previously typed. You also can use the F4 (Repeat) key to repeat text you just typed.

Alt-F3

Copying Text You Previously Typed

To copy text with the keyboard, do the following:

1. Select the text you want to copy.

2. Choose the **C**opy command and press Enter to copy the text to the scrap. Alternatively, use the Alt-F3 keyboard shortcut.

3. Move the cursor to the spot where you want to copy the text.

4. Choose the **I**nsert command or press Ins.

To copy text with the mouse, follow these steps:

1. Select the text you want to copy.

2. Move the pointer to the spot where you want to copy the text.

3. Hold down the Shift key and click the left button.

Repeating the Last Text You Typed

The F4 (Repeat) key has its own special memory. F4 stores all the keys you have pressed since the last time you moved the cursor to enter new text or issued a command. You can use F4 to copy text throughout your document. When you press F4, Word enters at the cursor's location whatever is stored in F4's memory.

To copy text with the F4 key, use the following procedure:

1. Press Esc twice to clear F4's memory.

2. Type the text you want to copy.

3. Move the cursor to a new location and press F4. The text you typed appears at the new location.

4. To repeat the text again, move the cursor to another new location and press F4. Continue to move the cursor to new locations and press F4 to repeat the text throughout your document.

Do not press Enter, type more text, or give a command along the way because doing so clears F4's memory.

If you are working with the Yes option chosen in the **show menu** field of the Options menu, clicking either button on COMMAND has the same effect as pressing F4.

Transposing Text with the Mouse

Mouse users can transpose (switch the positions of) characters, words, or sentences. The technique is a variation of the block move procedure discussed earlier in this chapter. Follow these steps to transpose text:

1. Select the second unit of text you want to transpose, using the text-selection techniques introduced in this chapter. (To transpose characters, select the second character. To transpose words, select the second word; and to transpose sentences, select the second sentence.)

2. Point to the first unit of text (character, word, or sentence) and hold down the Ctrl key.

3. To transpose characters, click the left button. To transpose words, click the right button. To transpose sentences, click both buttons.

Searching for Text

Once you have created a document that's several pages long, searching the document on-screen for a certain passage is tedious—and tiresome for the eyes. And why bother, when Word can do it for you? Using the Search command, you can specify *search text*—a series of characters—that you want Word to find. Word then goes through your document at high speed, trying to find an *exact* match for the search text in your document. Whenever you think, "I know I discussed such-and-such somewhere, but where?" use the Search command. Put that expensive computer to work!

Doing a Simple Search

To search for text in your document, follow these steps:

1. If you want to search your entire document, press Ctrl-PgUp to position the cursor on the first character of the document. Word searches from the cursor position to the end of the document (if you're searching down) or to the beginning (if you're searching up). Word is preset to search down, toward the end of the document.

2. Choose the **S**earch command.

3. When the **S**earch menu appears (see fig. 3.8), type in the **text** command field the text you want to find. You can type up to 250 characters of text, spaces included.

   To speed the search, keep the search string short, but not so short that Word will find unwanted matches. For example, if you want to search for the word *all-inclusive*, type the whole word. If you use just the first few letters, *all*, Word will find *alley*, *alligator*, and *all-important*.

4. In the **direction** field, choose **D**own (the default) to search from the cursor's position to the end of the document, or choose **U**p to search toward the document's beginning.

5. Carry out the command.

```
 ┌──────────────────────────────────────────────────────────┐
 │ ▯e·sure·to·stop·by·our·Centerville·showrooms·soon·to·see·our· │
 │ new·display·of·Wood·Wizard·kitchen·and·bath·cabinets.·Custom │
 │ designed·and·crafted·by·hand,·these·cabinets·are·as·handsome· │
 │ as·they·are·practical--and·you·won't·believe·the·prices·    │
 │ we're·offering·in·our·introductory·special!¶                │
 │ ¶                                                            │
 │ About·Wood·Wizard·Cabinets.··In·February,·1947,·John·and·    │
 │ Marsha·Williams·couldn't·find·the·cabinets·they·wanted·for· │
 │ their·kitchen·remodeling·plans,··and·so·they·decided·to·build· │
 │ them·in·their·basement·shop.··Avid·woodworking·hobbyists,·  ▮ │
 │ John·and·Marsha·created·a·kitchen·that·their·friends·and·    │
 │ neighbors·admired--so·much·so,·in·fact,·that·they·found·     │
 │ themselves·swamped·in·orders!··Realizing·that·many·people·  │
 │ wanted·their·hand-crafted·cabinets,·John·and·Marsha·founded·· │
 │ Wood·Wizard·Kitchen·and·Bath·Cabinets,·Inc.·the·next·year.¶ │
 │ ¶                                                            │
 │ Although·Wood·Wizard·Kitchen·and·Bath·Cabinets·has·just·     │
 │ celebrated·its·40th·birthday·and·sells·over·a·million·       │
 │ dollars'·worth·of·cabinets·annually,·every·kitchen·and·bath· │
 ├──────────────────────────────────────────────────────────┤
 │ SEARCH text: Wood Wizard Kitchen and Bath Cabinets▮        │
 │        direction: Up(Down) case: Yes(No) whole word: Yes(No) │
 │ Enter text                                                   │
 │ Pg1 Co1          {Be·sur...ago.·} ?            Microsoft Word │
 └──────────────────────────────────────────────────────────┘
```

Fig. 3.8.

The Search menu.

If Word finds a match for the text string you entered, the program scrolls the screen to the first match down (or up) and highlights it.

If Word can't find the text string, you see the message `Search text not found`. Choose the **S**earch command again and double-check your spelling and menu choices. As you will see, Word displays the last search text you used in the **text** command field. Check that text to make sure that it contains *exactly* what you are looking for. Remember, so far as Word is concerned, *cat* is as different from *chat* as *feline* is from *conversation*. Computers may be fast, but they are literal to the extreme.

Repeating the Search

If Word finds a match for your search text, and you want to look for additional places in your document that contain the text, choose the **S**earch command again. The search text you just used is visible in the **text** command field, so simply carry out the command to repeat the search. Or you can use the Shift-F4 keyboard shortcut to repeat the search without using the Search command at all. This key combination repeats the last Search command you gave in the current editing session, using all the command field settings you chose. (You can't use Shift-F4 unless you have used the Search command at least once in the current editing session.)

Shift-F4

Customizing the Search

You can tailor your search, using the **case** and **whole word** fields of the Search menu. For instance, you can customize a search so that Word matches *HIMALAYAS* but not *Himalayas*. This search, a *case-sensitive* search, tries to match the exact case pattern (lower- and uppercase) of the text you enter. You also can customize a search so that Word matches *cat* but not *catatonic*, *catastrophe*, or *Magnificat in C Major*. This search, a *whole-word* search, matches the search string only if the "match" is surrounded by spaces or punctuation.

To search for an exact match of the search text's case pattern, the steps to take are the following:

1. Enter the search text in the **text** field of the Search menu.

2. Choose the **Y**es option in the **case** field.

3. Carry out the command.

To do a whole-word search, use this procedure:

1. Enter the search text in the **text** field of the Search menu.

2. Choose the **Y**es option in the **whole word** command field.

3. Carry out the command.

Replacing Text

Like the Search command, the Replace command finds text that matches the search text you specify. This command works in exactly the same way the Search command does; you can search for up to 250 characters, you can search for precise case configurations, and you can do a whole-word search. But the Replace command has one crucial difference: it deletes the text that matches the search string and replaces that text with other text you specify.

Here's how to do a simple replace operation:

1. Press Ctrl-PgUp to move to the beginning of the document. (Like the Search command, Replace searches from the cursor's position to the bottom or top of the document. To replace text throughout your document, therefore, you need to place the cursor on the first character.)

2. Choose the **R**eplace command.

3. In the **text** command field, type the text you want to remove.

4. In the **with text** command field, type the text you want Word to substitute for the search text.

5. Carry out the command.

When Word finds a match, you see the message `Enter Y to replace, N to ignore, or type Esc to cancel`. If you press Y or N, Word either replaces or ignores the text, and then continues searching for the next match. To cancel the replace operation, press Esc.

As with the Search command, you can use the Yes options in the **case** and **whole word** fields of the Replace command. If you would rather not confirm each replacement as it occurs, choose the **No** option in the **confirm** command field. But be wary! Word may make changes you don't like.

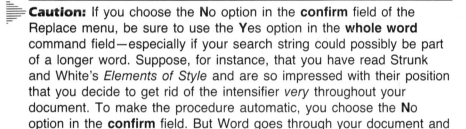

Caution: If you choose the **No** option in the **confirm** field of the Replace menu, be sure to use the **Yes** option in the **whole word** command field—especially if your search string could possibly be part of a longer word. Suppose, for instance, that you have read Strunk and White's *Elements of Style* and are so impressed with their position that you decide to get rid of the intensifier *very* throughout your document. To make the procedure automatic, you choose the **No** option in the **confirm** field. But Word goes through your document and changes *everything* to *ething*.

Moving Around in a Lengthy Document

With Word Version 5, pagination is automatic—that is, Word automatically decides where page breaks should occur and enters page-break marks on the screen. And the page-number indicator on the status line shows you at any given time where the cursor is positioned in your document. (Before Version 5, the page-number indicator read `Pg1` until you printed or repaginated your document—even if you had typed dozens of pages of text.)

Because Word now paginates automatically and actively as you write and edit, the Jump Page command is useful for navigating in any document longer than four or five pages. The PgUp and PgDn keys

Word
5

don't move you from page to page but from screen to screen, so the actual amount of text traversed may amount to considerably less than a full page. For this reason, scrolling with the Jump Page command is faster and easier.

Alt-F5

To jump to a specific page, do the following:

1. Choose the **J**ump **P**age command. Alternatively, use the Alt-F5 keyboard shortcut.

2. When the **number** field appears, type the page to which you want to jump (see fig. 3.9). Word's proposed response to this field is the page in which the cursor is currently positioned. To erase that default setting, just type the page number you want.

3. Carry out the command.

Fig. 3.9.

The Jump Page command.

```
│ Be·sure·to·stop·by·our·Centerville·showrooms·soon·to·see·our·
  new·display·of·Wood·Wizard·kitchen·and·bath·cabinets.·Custom·
  designed·and·crafted·by·hand,·these·cabinets·are·as·handsome·
  as·they·are·practical--and·you·won't·believe·the·prices·
  we're·offering·in·our·introductory·special!¶
  ¶
  About·Wood·Wizard·Cabinets.··In·February,·1947,·John·and·
  Marsha·Williams·couldn't·find·the·cabinets·they·wanted·for·
  their·kitchen·remodeling·plans,·and·so·they·decided·to·build·       ▮
  them·in·their·basement·shop.··Avid·woodworking·hobbyists,·
  John·and·Marsha·created·a·kitchen·that·their·friends·and·
  neighbors·admired--so·much·so,·in·fact,·that·they·found·
  themselves·swamped·in·orders!··Realizing·that·many·people·
  wanted·their·hand-crafted·cabinets,·John·and·Marsha·founded··
  Wood·Wizard·Kitchen·and·Bath·Cabinets,·Inc.·the·next·year.¶
  ¶
  Although·Wood·Wizard·Kitchen·and·Bath·Cabinets·has·just·
  celebrated·its·40th·birthday·and·sells·over·a·million·
  dollars'·worth·of·cabinets·annually,·every·kitchen·and·bath·

JUMP PAGE number: 4▮

Enter page number
Pg1 Co1              {Be·sur...ago.}·?                    Microsoft Word
```

If you see the message pagination is required, you either have not entered more than one page of text, or you have set the **paginate** field of the Options menu to Manual. Add some more text, or modify the Options setting.

If you plan to create lengthy documents with headings and subheadings, you can use Word's outline mode to move quickly from one section of your document to another. For more information, see Chapter 10, "Organizing Your Document with Outlining."

Chapter Summary

This chapter rounds out your knowledge of Word editing techniques. You learned how to accomplish many fundamental editing tasks, such as retrieving files; using nonbreaking spaces and hyphens; selecting, deleting, inserting, copying, and transposing text; searching for and replacing text; and moving around in a lengthy document.

To complete your editing skills, however, be sure to read Chapter 9, "Customizing the Screen and Using Windows," Chapter 10, "Organizing Your Document with Outlining," and Chapter 12, "Using Glossaries and Bookmarks." Multiple-window, outlining, and glossary techniques aid your revision efforts in ways that are unimaginable without computer experience—and without Word. Imagine working with five or six documents at a time, each in its own window, and being able to zoom each window to full size—or shrink it—at a keystroke. Imagine, too, restructuring your document's overall organization with just a few keystrokes in the outline organize mode! These techniques, and more, are discussed in Part II.

4

Word 5 Formatting Strategies: Characters and Paragraphs

Word is one of the best programs on the IBM-format market for formatting your text—that is, enhancing and arranging it so that it prints the way you want. You can see many character formats (such as boldface and underlining) and nearly all paragraph formats (such as indentation and line spacing) right on-screen as you write.

In Chapter 2, you learned the basics of formatting with Word, including centering text, attaching boldface character emphasis, joining and splitting paragraphs, and adding custom tab stops. You learned the difference between character and paragraph formatting, and you learned that you can format in two ways: as you type and after you type. Chapter 3 added to this knowledge by showing you more ways to select fixed and variable units of text, a step that's necessary to format characters after you type.

This chapter broadens your knowledge of character and paragraph formatting with Word 5. You will learn how to do the following:

❑ Use Word's default character and paragraph formatting settings, the ones the program applies if you issue no formatting commands

❑ Use the many measurement options available with this precision program

❑ Use character emphasis (such as boldface or italic), employ your printer's special fonts and font sizes, and add hidden comments to your document

❑ Control paragraph alignment (including right margin justification), paragraph indentation, and line spacing

❑ Determine the format currently assigned to any character or paragraph

❑ Copy character and paragraph formats quickly and easily from one part of your document to another

❑ Search for character and paragraph formats so that you can quickly locate a given format in your document

❑ Replace character and paragraph formats so that Word automatically substitutes one format (such as boldface) for another (such as underlining) throughout your document

Before reading this chapter and trying out the new formatting techniques with your computer, be sure that you have installed your printer as described in the appendix. Be sure, too, to use the Print Options command to name your printer. These steps are necessary so that Word can tell which fonts and font sizes your printer can handle.

In addition, before you begin, choose the **O**ptions command and select the **P**artial option in the **show non-printing symbols** field. This choice displays paragraph marks. You need to see paragraph marks on-screen if you want to avoid formatting errors. Once you choose this option, Word saves your preference and displays paragraph marks even when you start the program in a new editing session. (For more information on which options Word saves from session to session, see the appendix.)

The following character and paragraph formats are covered elsewhere in this book:

❑ To format a paragraph so that Word does not break pages within or after the paragraph, see Chapter 5, "Word 5 Formatting Strategies: Page Formatting."

❑ To set new default character styles for page numbers, line numbers, and footnote reference marks, and to set new default paragraph styles for footnotes, running heads, and headings, see Chapter 20, "Using Style Sheets."

❑ To create lines and boxes with the Format Border command, see Chapter 17, "Creating Forms and Illustrations."

❏ To create side-by-side paragraphs with the Format Paragraph command, see Chapter 19, "Creating Multiple-Column Text and Newsletters."

Examining Word's Default Formats

Every word processing program comes with certain default formatting settings. These settings are the ones the program uses unless you give commands to the contrary. Word's default character and paragraph formats are listed in table 4.1. (For a list of the default page style formats, see table 5.1 in the next chapter.) As you will learn when you create or print a document that has more than one page, the default formats ensure that your document prints with well-proportioned margins, page breaks, and—thanks to wordwrap—an attractively aligned right margin.

Table 4.1
Word's Default Character and Paragraph Formats

Format	Setting
Emphasis	None
Font	Printer's standard (such as Pica or Courier)
Line height	12 point (6 lines to an inch)
Measurement	Inches
Paragraphs	Single-spaced, flush-left alignment
Tabs	Every 0.5 inch
Type size	12 point height, 10 to an inch (10 pitch)

As explained in Chapter 4, you can alter any of these formats in a document. After you change a format, Word saves your changes with the document so that they're available the next time you edit. Every time you create a new blank document, however, all the default formats listed in table 4.1 are in effect.

You can create new default formatting settings in a number of ways. You can change the default tab stops by entering a new measurement in the **default tab width** field of the Options menu. As you learn in

Chapter 5, you can set new default margins by using the Format Division Margins command. But the best way to set new defaults is to create a custom style sheet and make it the new default for the program. If you want Word to come on-screen at the start of every editing session with precisely the font, font size, margins, and other choices you want, be sure to read Chapter 21, "Using Style Sheets." Choosing your own defaults is the best of many good reasons for using style sheets regularly.

Knowing Your Measurement Options

As indicated in table 4.1, by default Word measures horizontally in inches (including fractions of an inch). For the most part, the program measures vertically in 12-point lines (6 to an inch). You can see these measurements in the command fields of the Format Paragraph menu and other command menus. And when you type numbers in these fields to change default formats, Word assumes that you are using these measurements. In figure 4.1, for instance, the **left indent**, **first line**, and **right indent** command fields display the measurements in inches ("), while the **line spacing**, **space before**, and **space after** fields show the measurements in lines (li).

Fig. 4.1.

Default measurement formats (inches and lines).

```
FORMAT PARAGRAPH alignment: Left Centered Right Justified
     left indent: 0"              first line: 0"           right indent: 0"
     line spacing: 1 li           space before: 0 li       space after: 0 li
     keep together: Yes(No)       keep follow: Yes(No)     side by side: Yes(No)
Select option
Pg1 Co1              {}                    ?                      Microsoft Word
```

Word responds to measurements entered not only in inches and lines but also in printer's points, metric units, and fixed-font character positions.

Changing the Default Measurement Format

If you are accustomed to metric measurements, prefer to think in terms of spaces for indents, or want to use printer's points for precision formatting, you probably want to change the default measurement format. Follow these steps:

1. Choose the **O**ptions command.

2. Choose one of the options in the **measure** command field, as shown in figure 4.2. (Table 4.2 describes the measurement codes.)

3. Carry out the command.

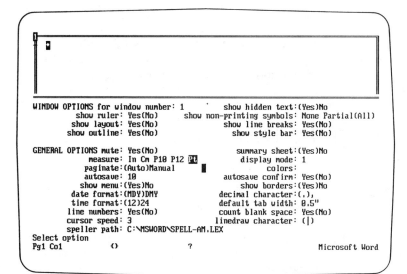

Fig. 4.2.

Changing the default measurement format.

WINDOW OPTIONS for window number: 1   show hidden text:(Yes)No
        show ruler: Yes(No)   show non-printing symbols: None Partial(All)
        show layout: Yes(No)   show line breaks: Yes(No)
        show outline: Yes(No)   show style bar: Yes(No)

GENERAL OPTIONS mute: Yes(No)   summary sheet:(Yes)No
            measure: In Cm P10 P12 █▌   display mode: 1
            paginate:(Auto)Manual   █   colors:
            autosave: 10   autosave confirm: Yes(No)
            show menu:(Yes)No   show borders:(Yes)No
            date format:(MDY)DMY   decimal character:(.),
            time format:(12)24   default tab width: 0.5"
            line numbers: Yes(No)   count blank space: Yes(No)
            cursor speed: 3   linedraw character: (|)
            speller path: C:\MSWORD\SPELL-AM.LEX
Select option
Pg1 Co1   {}   ?   Microsoft Word

Table 4.2
Measurement Codes and Format Options

Code	Format
In or "	inches (default)
Cm	centimeters
P10	character positions in Pica fixed-width font (10 characters per inch)
P12	character positions in Elite fixed-width font (12 characters per inch)
Pt	printer's points (72 per inch)

After you change the **measure** field, Word displays all measurements in the format you selected. If you chose printer's points, for instance, both vertical and horizontal formats are measured in points (see fig. 4.3).

Fig. 4.3.

New default measurement format (printer's points).

```
FORMAT PARAGRAPH alignment: Left Centered Right Justified
         left indent: 0 pt        first line: 0 pt        right indent: 0 pt
         line spacing: 12 pt      space before: 0 pt      space after: 0 pt
         keep together: Yes(No)   keep follow: Yes(No)    side by side: Yes(No)
Select option
Pg1 Co1                  {}                   ?                    Microsoft Word
```

Once you have changed the default, Word saves it so that it's available the next time you use the program. To change back to the original settings, just choose the **In** option in the **measure** field of the Options menu.

Overriding the Default Measurement Format

Whether you're using Word's default measurement format or a new one you have chosen from the Options menu, you can override the default for a specific measurement by typing a number and one of the measurement codes from table 4.2. To specify a line height in printer's points rather than lines, for instance, you can type *14 pt* in any field that accepts line measurements.

Caution: If you omit the measurement code, Word uses the default measurement format. Thus if you're using the default settings (lines and inches), and you type *14* in the **line spacing** field, Word leaves 14 lines blank between each printed line! To enter a line spacing of 14 points, you must type *14 pt*.

Formatting Characters

When you format characters, you attach character emphasis (such as boldface or italic), change the character's position (normal, superscript, or subscript), or assign the character's type style (font and font size). You also can hide text so that it doesn't appear on the screen or on the printout (unless you want it to).

Using Character Emphasis and Controlling Position

Character emphases such as boldface, italic, and underlining add drama and meaning to your document—provided, of course, that you don't overuse them. Word gives you a full storehouse of emphasis options, including strikethrough text (useful for showing clauses that have been struck out of legal contracts) and small caps (text that prints in small-sized capital letters). You also can format text so that it's positioned above the line (superscript) or below it (subscript).

Caution: Your printer may not be able to print all these character emphases and positions. Before formatting a document with them, create a test document and use all the formats so that you can see which ones print and which ones don't. Consult your printer's manual for more information on the printer's capabilities.

What You See on the Screen

As you can see in figure 4.4, Word can display all the emphasis and position options on-screen, provided that (1) your computer can display graphics, and (2) you're using Word in graphics mode. With most monitors, much of the formatting becomes invisible (or indistinguishable from other emphases) in text mode (see fig. 4.5).

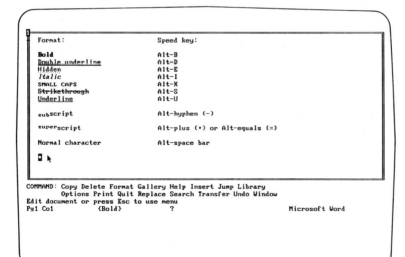

Fig. 4.4.

Screen display of character emphasis and position in graphics mode.

Fig. 4.5.

Screen display of character emphasis and position in text mode.

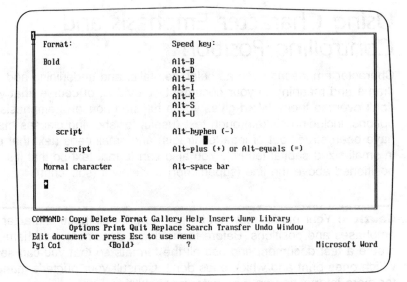

```
Format:                    Speed key:

Bold                       Alt-B
                           Alt-D
                           Alt-E
                           Alt-I
                           Alt-K
                           Alt-S
                           Alt-U

    script                 Alt-hyphen (-)

      script               Alt-plus (+) or Alt-equals (=)

Normal character           Alt-space bar



COMMAND: Copy Delete Format Gallery Help Insert Jump Library
         Options Print Quit Replace Search Transfer Undo Window
Edit document or press Esc to use menu
Pg1 Co1              {Bold}           ?                 Microsoft Word
```

If you have a color monitor, you can assign the colors you like to each character emphasis and position so that the character formats are visible even in text mode. For more information, see Chapter 9, "Customizing the Screen and Using Windows."

Using Keyboard Shortcuts for Formatting Characters

Normally, using keyboard shortcuts is best when you're entering just one character emphasis at a time. Keyboard shortcuts are much faster and require fewer keystrokes than when you use the Format Character menu. Table 4.3 lists the keyboard shortcuts for character emphasis formatting. You can use these shortcuts to format as you type, or you can format later (but be sure to select the text first).

Table 4.3
Keyboard Shortcuts for Character Emphases

Emphasis	Shortcut
Bold	Alt-B
Double underline	Alt-D
Hidden	Alt-E
Italic	Alt-I
Small caps	Alt-K

Table 4.3—Continued

Emphasis	Shortcut
Strikethrough	Alt-S
Subscript	Alt- − (minus)
Superscript	Alt- + (plus) or Alt- = (equal sign)
Underline	Alt-U
Cancel formats	Alt-space bar

To format character emphasis as you type, using the keyboard shortcuts, follow these steps:

1. Position the cursor where you want the text to appear.

2. Use the keyboard shortcut, such as Alt-B or Alt-U.

3. Type the text.

4. When you are finished typing the text you want to emphasize, press Alt-space bar.

Caution: If you are using a font other than the default one, do not use Alt-space bar to cancel character emphasis. Alt-space bar cancels all character formatting, including fonts and font sizes, and applies the default formats. To cancel just the emphasis but leave the font unchanged, select the text and use the Format Character command. Choose the **N**o option in the format's command field and carry out the command.

To format character emphasis after you type, do the following:

1. Select the text you want to format.

2. Use the keyboard shortcut, such as Alt-B or Alt-U.

Caution: If you are formatting a single character that you already typed, you must use the keyboard shortcut twice.

See Chapter 14, "The Legal and Scholarly Word," for information on ways to enter superscripted footnote reference marks automatically.

Using Two or More Character Emphases

You can apply two or more character emphases to a selection. For example, you can format a heading with both underlining and boldface. Just select the text and, while it is highlighted, use two or more keyboard shortcuts. In such cases, it might be easier to use the Format Character command in the following manner:

1. Choose the **F**ormat **C**haracter command.

2. Choose the **Y**es option in the fields of all the formats you want.

3. Carry out the command by pressing Enter or clicking the command area.

Removing Character Emphasis

To remove character emphasis from text you have already formatted, follow these steps:

1. Select all the text that contains the format you want to remove.

2. Press Alt-space bar.

If you are using fonts other than your printer's default font, cancel the emphasis by choosing the **F**ormat **C**haracter command and selecting the **N**o option in the appropriate field.

Solving Problems with Unwanted Character Emphasis

Many new Word users find that boldface, underlining, and other character emphases pop up where they aren't needed. To understand why, you need to realize that the paragraph mark is a character like any other in that it can receive character formatting. And when you press Enter, Word creates a new paragraph mark with the same formatting. Later, if you position the cursor on this new paragraph mark and start typing, your text will have the paragraph mark's formatting—which is the same as the text you have been typing.

This concept is easier to grasp if you take the following quick tutorial. Be sure to try it; it reveals a peculiarity of Word that most users learn only through frustrating experience.

1. In a new blank Word document, choose the **O**ptions command and make sure that the **show hidden text** field is set to the **P**artial option.

2. Press Enter twice and press the up-arrow key so that the cursor is positioned on a paragraph mark. Type a word.

3. Use a variable text selection technique to select the word and the paragraph mark. Try using the F6 key or, if you have a mouse, the click-and-drag technique.

4. Press Alt-B to boldface the selection. Note that the paragraph mark appears in boldface, too!

5. Place the cursor on the paragraph mark and press Enter several times. All the new paragraph marks display in boldface.

6. Place the cursor on any of the new paragraph marks and start typing. The text appears in boldface.

Now you know another reason why displaying paragraph marks as you work is so important. If you don't, you could format a paragraph mark without realizing it and get unwanted character formatting.

To cancel character formatting in a paragraph mark, follow these steps:

1. Position the cursor on the mark.

2. Press Alt-space bar twice.

The following mini-tutorial illustrates one other way you can wind up with emphasis—underlining, to be specific—where you don't want it:

1. In a new blank Word document, type a word and underline it, using any of the available techniques.

2. Place the cursor on the word's first character and press Tab twice.

Note that the blank spaces created by the tab strokes are underlined!

To avoid unwanted underlining when tabbing, press Alt-space bar on the first character of text you have already formatted before you press Tab.

Using Your Printer's Fonts

Today's printers, even the cheapest ones, are capable of printing more than one font and font size. Word gives you a high degree of control over these fonts. You can use several fonts and font sizes in one document—indeed, you can even mix fonts and font sizes in one line.

To format your text with a variety of fonts and font sizes, use the techniques you have already learned for formatting as you type or formatting later. You must use the Format Character command, however, because no keyboard shortcuts are available for font and font-size formatting.

Viewing a List of Available Fonts

When you name a printer using the Print Options command (see the appendix), Word reads information from one of the printer description files stored on the Printers Disks. This printer description file includes a list of the fonts and font sizes available with your printer. If you have named a printer, you can press F1 to see a list of which fonts and font sizes are available.

With Word, fonts and font sizes are just like any other character format. To format characters with a distinctive font, you use the Format Character command's **font** and **font size** fields. You can format as you type or format later, just as you would with character emphasis. You can change fonts and font sizes as often as you want within a document.

Alt-F8

To choose fonts and font sizes from a list, follow this procedure:

1. Choose the **F**ormat **C**haracter command and position the cursor in the **font name** field. Alternatively, use the Alt-F8 keyboard shortcut.

2. Press F1 to see the list of fonts available with your printer. Figure 4.6 shows an example.

3. Highlight the font you want, but don't carry out the command yet. Word places the font name you have chosen in the **font name** command field.

4. Press Tab to move the highlight to the **font size** command field.

5. Press F1 to see a list of the font sizes available for the font you have chosen. Figure 4.7 shows an example.

6. Choose a font size and carry out the command.

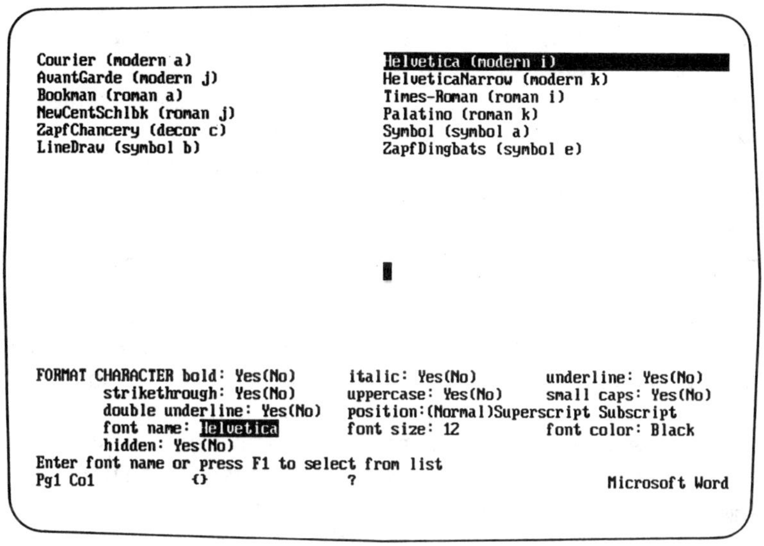

```
Courier (modern a)              Helvetica (modern i)
AvantGarde (modern j)           HelveticaNarrow (modern k)
Bookman (roman a)               Times-Roman (roman i)
NewCentSchlbk (roman j)         Palatino (roman k)
ZapfChancery (decor c)          Symbol (symbol a)
LineDraw (symbol b)             ZapfDingbats (symbol e)




                                    ▌




FORMAT CHARACTER bold: Yes(No)      italic: Yes(No)        underline: Yes(No)
          strikethrough: Yes(No)    uppercase: Yes(No)     small caps: Yes(No)
          double underline: Yes(No) position:(Normal)Superscript Subscript
          font name: Helvetica      font size: 12          font color: Black
          hidden: Yes(No)
Enter font name or press F1 to select from list
Pg1 Co1              {}                 ?                  Microsoft Word
```

Fig. 4.6.

Choosing a font
from a list.

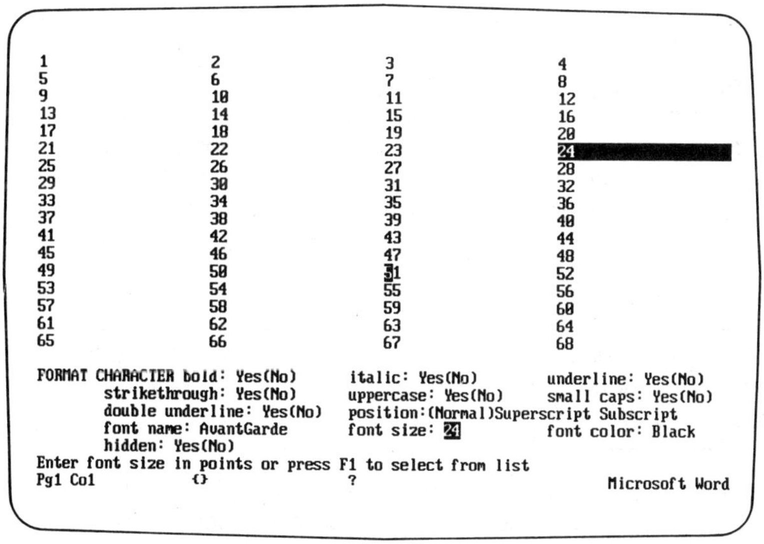

```
1            2            3            4
5            6            7            8
9            10           11           12
13           14           15           16
17           18           19           20
21           22           23           24
25           26           27           28
29           30           31           32
33           34           35           36
37           38           39           40
41           42           43           44
45           46           47           48
49           50           51           52
53           54           55           56
57           58           59           60
61           62           63           64
65           66           67           68

FORMAT CHARACTER bold: Yes(No)      italic: Yes(No)        underline: Yes(No)
          strikethrough: Yes(No)    uppercase: Yes(No)     small caps: Yes(No)
          double underline: Yes(No) position:(Normal)Superscript Subscript
          font name: AvantGarde     font size: 24          font color: Black
          hidden: Yes(No)
Enter font size in points or press F1 to select from list
Pg1 Co1              {}                 ?                  Microsoft Word
```

Fig. 4.7.

Choosing a font
size from a list.

Caution: If you're using a laser printer, Word's list may include several fonts and font sizes that your printer cannot print without a special cartridge. Be sure to read your printer's manual carefully so that you understand which fonts and sizes are actually available.

One major advantage of using style sheets is that you can create several of them, each with its own standard or default font. This capability will be of especially great interest to owners of laser printers with multiple-font capabilities. You can create a style sheet called REPORT, for instance, that prints in Times Roman, and another style sheet called LETTER that prints in Helvetica. For more information on style sheets, see Chapter 20.

Caution: With Word, character size and line height are independent. If you choose an extremely large (14- or 18-point) or a tiny (6- to 8-point) font, you may want to change Word's line spacing setting, too. Otherwise, the lines of text may be jammed up against one another (with large fonts) or widely separated (with small fonts). To adjust line spacing, see "Controlling Line Spacing" in this chapter.

Using More Than One Font and Font Size in a Document

Although you can use more than one font or font size in a document, Word does not display your font and font size choices on-screen. All on-screen text is displayed in fixed-width "typewriter" font. For this reason, the text alignment and line breaks you see on-screen may not be those that appear when your document is printed. In figure 4.8, for example, the text entered in an 8-point font looks exactly like the text entered in a 14-point font.

If you have a color monitor, you can use the **O**ptions command to assign distinctive colors to font sizes. See Chapter 9, "Customizing the Screen and Using Windows," for more information.

By choosing the **Y**es option in the **show line breaks** field of the Options menu (see fig. 4.9), however, you can see where Word will break lines when you print. Note that lines printed with small-sized fonts run off the screen. The text won't look that way when printed; with a small font, many more characters can fit on a line.

```
This text is written in 8-point Times Roman.  With a font
size this small, many characters will fit on one line.

This text is written in 14-point Times Roman.  With a font
this large, few characters will fit on one line.█




                          █




COMMAND: Copy Delete Format Gallery Help Insert Jump Library
         Options Print Quit Replace Search Transfer Undo Window
Edit document or press Esc to use menu
Pg1 Co49          {}              ?                Microsoft Word
```

Fig. 4.8.

Text of different font sizes displayed with fixed-width screen font.

```
This text is written in 8-point Times Roman.  With a font size this small, m
This text is written in 14-point Times Roman.  With a font this large, few
characters will fit on one line.█

WINDOW OPTIONS for window number: 1        show hidden text:(Yes)No
          show ruler: Yes(No)       show non-printing symbols:(None)Partial All
         show layout: Yes(No)               show line breaks: Yes No
        show outline: Yes(No)              show style bar: Yes(No)
                                                          █
GENERAL OPTIONS mute: Yes(No)             summary sheet:(Yes)No
            measure:(In)Cm P10 P12 Pt       display mode: 1
            paginate:(Auto)Manual                colors:
            autosave: 10            autosave confirm: Yes(No)
           show menu:(Yes)No               show borders:(Yes)No
         date format:(MDY)DMY        decimal character:(.),
         time format:(12)24          default tab width: 0.5"
        line numbers: Yes(No)         count blank space: Yes(No)
        cursor speed: 3             linedraw character: (|)
        speller path: C:\MSWORD\SPELL-AM.LEX
Select option
Pg1 Co32          {}              ?                Microsoft Word
```

Fig. 4.9.

Choosing the Yes option in the **show line breaks** field of the Options menu.

Alt-F7

Do you really need to see where Word will break lines? In most cases, probably not. Line breaks are critical only when you're typing tables or any other tabular information that must be clearly arranged. (For more information, see Chapter 11, "Creating Tables and Lists with Tabs, Autosort, and Math.") You can toggle the display of line breaks on and off by using the Alt-F7 keyboard shortcut. Toggle on the actual line breaks only when you need to see them.

Many of today's printers can print proportionally spaced text, in which wide letters such as *m* receive more space than their narrower counterparts. The result is a printout that looks as if it had been professionally typeset. The trouble with proportional spacing, however, is that because Word always displays all text in a fixed-width, monospace font, even if the program will later print the same text with proportional spacing, you cannot be sure that the printout will resemble what you see on-screen. Even if you use the Options menu to display line breaks, you see only where Word will break lines. You can't see how each of those lines will be spaced.

 Caution: Do not try to align columns of proportionally spaced text with the space bar, because the text will not print the way it looks on-screen. Instead, use Tab, or set paragraph indents by using the Format Paragraph command.

Changing the Font for the Whole Document

You may find that you prefer to print in a font other than your printer's default. The default font for most laser printers, for instance, is the fixed-width "typewriter" font, Courier. If you have purchased a cartridge to print in a more handsome font, such as Helvetica or Times Roman, you may want to print all or most of your documents in this alternate font.

The easiest way to make sure that your documents automatically print in the font you want is to create a new default style sheet. With a style sheet, you can define a standard character style so that, even when you press Alt-space bar, Word always considers that font to be the standard font. If you have a laser printer and you frequently use fonts such as Helvetica or Times Roman, you should explore style sheets as soon as possible. (For more information on style sheets, see Chapter 20.)

 Caution: Without using style sheets, you still can format your whole document so that it prints with a nondefault font, but the process is tricky and tedious. You have to go through the procedure for every document you create, and your printout will often contain text printed in the default format here and there. Every time you unthinkingly press

Alt-space bar (to cancel some other aspect of character formatting, such as character emphasis), Word returns to the default Pica font for your printer. If you have a laser printer, you thus get Courier fonts in a document you thought you formatted only with Helvetica or Times Roman.

To format your entire document so that it prints in a font or font size other than the default font, follow these steps:

1. Do not choose a font name or size until you have completely finished editing your document. Until then, just type with the default font.

2. Press Shift-F10 to select the whole document.

3. Choose the **F**ormat **C**haracter command and type a font name or size in the **font name** or **font size** field (or choose from a list by pressing F1).

4. Carry out the command and print your document.

The reason you should make changing the font the last step before printing is that every time you press Alt-space bar, as cautioned previously, Word restores all the default formats—including font names and sizes. Because you can't see fonts on-screen, you can't tell when you have accidentally wiped out a font assignment.

Changing Case

New to Word 5 is a command, Ctrl-F4, that controls lower- and uppercase formatting. You can still format characters in uppercase by choosing the Yes option in the **uppercase** field of the Format Character command, but as always, this format is lost if you save your document in any format other than Word's. (You may save your document without formatting, for instance, so that you can upload it through electronic mail links, or swap it with colleagues who use other word processing programs.) You don't have that problem with Ctrl-F4 case formatting. When you choose case (lower or upper) with Ctrl-F4, the text remains as it appears on-screen, even if you save your file without formatting.

To use Ctrl-F4, select the text you want to affect. Then press Ctrl-F4 once, and the text appears in all lowercase letters. If you press Ctrl-F4 again, the text appears in all uppercase letters. If you press Ctrl-F4 a third time, the text appears with each word capitalized (see fig. 4.10).

Fig. 4.10.

Controlling case
with Ctrl-F4.

```
 Original text.  The aircraft did not just perform well; in
 fact, it seemed to float and sail through the air with
 incredible poise and balance, responding precisely and
 instantly to every touch at the controls.

 All lower case.  the aircraft did not just perform well; in
 fact, it seemed to float and sail through the air with
 incredible poise and balance, responding precisely and
 instantly to every touch at the controls.

 All upper case.  THE AIRCRAFT DID NOT JUST PERFORM WELL; IN
 FACT, IT SEEMED TO FLOAT AND SAIL THROUGH THE AIR WITH
 INCREDIBLE POISE AND BALANCE, RESPONDING PRECISELY AND
 INSTANTLY TO EVERY TOUCH AT THE CONTROLS.

 Every word capitalized:  The Aircraft Did Not Just Perform
 Well; In Fact, It Seemed To Float And Sail Through The Air
 With Incredible Poise And Balance, Responding Precisely And
 Instantly To Every Touch At The Controls.

COMMAND: Copy Delete Format Gallery Help Insert Jump Library
         Options Print Quit Replace Search Transfer Undo Window
Edit document or press Esc to use menu
Pg1 Co42            {T}              ?                    Microsoft Word
```

Using Hidden Text

Hidden text has many uses in Word 5, as you will learn in several of the chapters in Part II. You can use hidden text, for instance, to mark words for later inclusion in an index or table of contents. You can also use hidden text to insert nonprinting comments in a document—and you can hide all such comments with a single keystroke. Because you will have many occasions to use hidden text, learning how to create, display, hide, and print hidden text passages is well worth your while.

Creating Hidden Text

Alt-E

To create hidden text, you format it as if it were a character format. You can create hidden text as you type, or hide it later.

To create hidden text as you type, follow these steps:

1. Choose the **Yes** option in the **show hidden text** field of the **O**ptions menu. Also choose the **P**artial option in the **show non-printing symbols** field of the same command menu.

2. Choose the **Yes** option in the **hidden** command field of the **F**ormat **C**haracter menu. Alternatively, use the Alt-E keyboard shortcut.

3. Type the text you want to hide. As you type, it appears with a special dotted underline, the hallmark of hidden text when displayed on-screen (see fig. 4.11).

4. When you come to the end of the text, press Ctrl-space bar to cancel hidden text formatting.

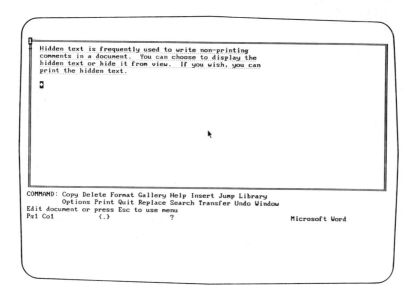

Fig. 4.11.

Text formatted as hidden.

To format hidden text after you type, do the following:

1. Choose the **Y**es option in the **show hidden text** field of the **O**ptions menu. Also choose the **P**artial option in the **show non-printing symbols** field of the same command menu.

2. Select the text you want to hide. Be sure to include trailing spaces. If the text is a word, line, or sentence, use one of the fixed-unit selection techniques discussed in Chapter 3.

3. Choose the **Y**es option in the **hidden** command field of the **F**ormat **C**haracter menu. Alternatively, use the Alt-E keyboard shortcut.

Hiding the Text on the Screen

To hide the text on the screen, follow these two steps:

1. Choose the **O**ptions command.

2. Select the **No** option in the **show hidden text** field, and carry out the command.

If you choose the All or Partial option in the **show non-printing symbols** field of the **O**ptions menu, Word displays a double-headed arrow at every spot at which you have hidden text (see fig. 4.12). The symbol does not show, however, if you choose the None option in the **show non-printing symbols** field.

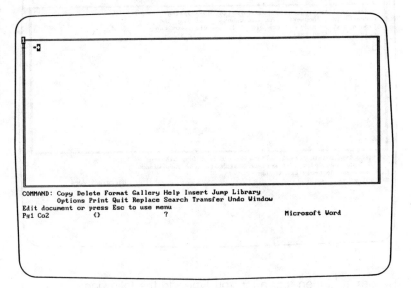

Fig. 4.12.

The arrow symbol showing the location of hidden text.

Printing Hidden Text

To print hidden text (whether or not it is displayed on-screen), follow these steps:

1. Choose the **P**rint **O**ptions command.

2. Select the **Yes** option in the **hidden text** command field.

3. Carry out the command and print your document.

Normally, you should leave this option set to No. As you will learn in Part II, you handle some operations—such as indexing and linking to spreadsheets—by embedding commands in your document and formatting them as hidden text. You don't want these commands to print.

Formatting Paragraphs

When you choose a paragraph format, Word assigns the format to the paragraph or paragraphs you have selected. (A paragraph, remember, is simply the text between two paragraph marks.) You can't change a paragraph format within a paragraph; all paragraph formats apply to the entire paragraph or to the multiple paragraphs you have selected.

Paragraph formats include paragraph alignment, indentation, and line spacing (see fig. 4.13). All these formats appear on-screen, so you can easily visualize how your text will be arranged on the page. Whenever you start a new paragraph, you can change these formats. You easily can create a document that includes both double-spacing and single-spacing, for instance.

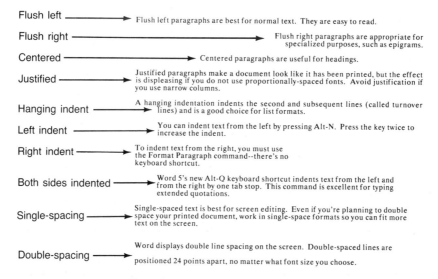

Fig. 4.13.

Word's paragraph formats.

The Format Paragraph command is your key to paragraph formats. You can enter many of them, however, with keyboard shortcuts. The available shortcuts are listed in table 4.4.

Table 4.4
Keyboard Shortcuts for Paragraph Formatting

Format	Shortcut
Automatic first-line indent	Alt-F
Blank line before paragraph	Alt-O (letter, not zero)
Centered alignment	Alt-C
Decrease left indent	Alt-M
Double line spacing	Alt-2
Hanging indent	Alt-T
Increase left indent	Alt-N
Indent left and right	Alt-Q
Justified alignment	Alt-J
Flush-left alignment	Alt-L or Alt-P
Flush-right alignment	Alt-R
Cancel formats	Alt-P

Caution: Paragraph formats do not include left and right margins. With Word, left and right margins—and line length, which is determined by margin settings—are page formats, not paragraph formats. A page format runs through an entire document or a section of a document. For more information on margins and line length, see Chapter 5, "Word 5 Formatting Strategies: Page Formatting."

If you like to format as you type, begin your document by setting up a standard paragraph format. For example, choose justification, an automatic first-line indent, double line spacing, and one blank line before each paragraph. Then type the first paragraph. When you press Enter, Word automatically copies all these formats to the next paragraph.

Controlling Paragraph Alignment

You can use the following four types of paragraph alignment:

Flush left (default)	The left margin is aligned, but the right margin is ragged.
Flush right	The right margin is aligned, but the left margin is ragged.
Centered	Text is centered between the left and right margins.
Justified	Both margins are aligned.

Caution: If your printer does not have a proportionally spaced font, Word justifies your text by inserting spaces between words. Sometimes this technique produces unsightly gaps in your text. Most documents look better with flush-left formatting, which is easier to read.

**Alt-J,
Alt-R,
Alt-C**

To change paragraph alignment as you type, use this procedure:

1. Choose the **Format Paragraph** command and select an option in the **alignment** field (see fig. 4.14). Alternatively, press Alt-R for flush-right, Alt-C for centered, or Alt-J for justified alignment.

```
FORMAT PARAGRAPH alignment: Left Centered Right Justified
     left indent: 0"          first line: 0"          right indent: 0"
     line spacing: 1 li       space before: 0 li      space after: 0 li
     keep together: Yes(No)   keep follow: Yes(No)    side by side: Yes(No)
Select option
Pg1 Co1              {}                  ?                       Microsoft Word
```

Fig. 4.14.

Choosing text alignment.

2. Type the text. Every time you press Enter, Word repeats the alignment format automatically, so you don't need to give the command again.

3. To return to the default paragraph format (flush left, single-spaced), press Alt-P.

To format paragraph alignment after you type, do the following:

1. Place the cursor in the paragraph you want to format. Alternatively, select several paragraphs, using one of the variable text selection techniques discussed in Chapter 3. To select the whole document, press Shift-F10.

2. Choose the **F**ormat **P**aragraph command and select an option in the **alignment** field. Alternatively, press Alt-R for flush-right, Alt-C for centered, or Alt-J for justified alignment.

Controlling Paragraph Indentation

Word provides many options for indenting paragraphs from the margins. You can use keyboard shortcuts to indent text by amounts conforming to the default tab width setting. For more flexibility, you can control paragraph indentation with the Format Paragraph menu.

Do not use these indentation techniques to set new margins. To change Word's default margin settings, see Chapter 5, "Word 5 Formatting Strategies: Page Formatting."

You can control the amount of indentation entered by Alt-F (automatic first-line indent), Alt-N (increase left indent), Alt-M (decrease left indent), Alt-T (hanging indent), and Alt-Q (indent left and right). When you use these commands, Word always indents by one default tab width. To change this width, enter a new measurement in the **default tab width** field of the **O**ptions menu.

Using an Automatic First-Line Indent

You need not use the Tab key to indent the first line of every paragraph—and, in fact, you shouldn't. If you set up a paragraph format that includes an automatic first-line indentation, Word enters the indent for you automatically.

Alt-F

To set up the program so that Word automatically indents the first line of a paragraph as you type, follow these steps:

1. Choose the **F**ormat **P**aragraph command and type in the **first line** field the amount of indentation you want (see fig. 4.15). Alternatively, use the Alt-F keyboard shortcut.

```
FORMAT PARAGRAPH alignment:(Left)Centered Right Justified
     left indent: 0"          first line: 0.5█      right indent: 0"
     line spacing: 1 li       space before: 0 li    space after: 0 li
     keep together: Yes(No)   keep follow: Yes(No)  side by side: Yes(No)
Enter measurement
Pg1 Co1              {}                  ?                     Microsoft Word
```

Fig. 4.15.

Using automatic first-line indentation.

2. Type your text. Every time you press Enter, Word repeats the alignment format automatically, so you don't need to give the command again.

3. To return to the default paragraph format (flush left, single-spaced), press Alt-P.

To indent the first line of a paragraph after you type the paragraph, do the following:

1. Place the cursor in the paragraph you want to format. Alternatively, select several paragraphs, using one of the variable text selection techniques discussed in Chapter 3. To select the whole document, press Shift-F10.

2. Choose the **Format Paragraph** command and type in the **first line** field the amount of indentation you want. Alternatively, use the Alt-F keyboard shortcut.

Indenting Text from the Margins

You can indent an entire paragraph from the left margin, the right margin, or both. But don't simply press Enter and use tabs or spaces; if you do, you'll have to realign all the text by hand if you insert or delete text later. Use the Format Paragraph command instead.

To indent text as you type, follow these steps:

**Alt-N,
Alt-Q**

1. Choose the **Format Paragraph** command and type measurements in the **left indent** and the **right indent** command fields. Alternatively, use Alt-N to indent the left margin, or Alt-Q to indent both the left and the right margins. (Word offers no keyboard shortcut for indenting only the right margin.)

2. Type the text. Every time you press Enter, Word repeats the alignment format automatically; you don't need to give the command again.

3. To return to the default paragraph format (flush left, single-spaced), press Alt-P.

To indent a paragraph after you type, use the following method:

1. Place the cursor in the paragraph you want to format. Alternatively, select several paragraphs, using one of the variable text selection techniques discussed in Chapter 3. To select the whole document, press Shift-F10.

2. Choose the **F**ormat **P**aragraph command and type measurements in the **left indent** and the **right indent** command fields. Alternatively, press Alt-N to indent the left margin, or Alt-Q to indent both the left and the right margins.

Caution: Indenting both the left and right margins isn't the same as changing the margins. To change the margins in your document, use the Format Division Margins command. For more information, see Chapter 5, "Word 5 Formatting Strategies: Page Formatting."

Alt-M

Creating Stepped Paragraphs

The Alt-N keyboard shortcut indents the left margin of a paragraph by the default tab width. If you press Alt-N twice, you indent the paragraph by two tab widths. If you press the key combination three times, you indent three tab widths, and so on. If you have indented a paragraph with Alt-N, you can "unindent" it by pressing Alt-M. Alt-M reduces the left indent by one tab width. You can use Alt-N and Alt-M to create *stepped paragraphs*, as shown in figure 4.16.

Alt-T

Creating Hanging Indents

Hanging indents, in which the first line extends left of the paragraph's left indent, are frequently used in list formats (such as bibliographies). The easiest way to create a hanging indent is to use the Alt-T keyboard shortcut. This key combination formats the first line flush to the left margin and indents subsequent lines, called *turnover lines*, by one default tab width.

You can create hanging indents with other measurements by using the Format Paragraph command. The trick is to place a negative number in the **first line** command field, by following these steps:

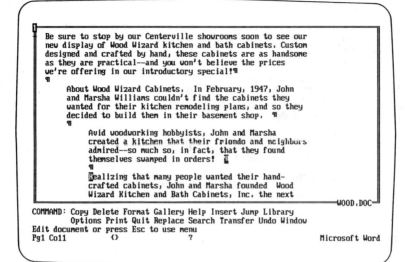

Fig. 4.16.

Stepped paragraphs created with Alt-N.

1. Choose the **F**ormat **P**aragraph command and type in the **left indent** command field the indentation you want for the turnover lines. For example, if you want the turnover lines indented 1 inch, type *1* in this field.

2. Select the **first line** command field and, using a negative number, indicate how far to the left of the turnover lines you want the first line to be positioned. To position the first line 0.5 inch to the left of the turnover lines, for instance, type *−0.5 in* in this field.

3. Carry out the command.

Figure 4.17 shows a document with hanging indents

Creating Bulleted or Numbered Lists

Once you learn how to create a hanging indent, formatting a bulleted or numbered list (see fig. 4.18) is easy. On the first line of every hanging-indent paragraph, enter a number, a hyphen, or a bullet (try Alt-248 or Alt-254). Then press Tab. The tab stop should line up with the turnover lines.

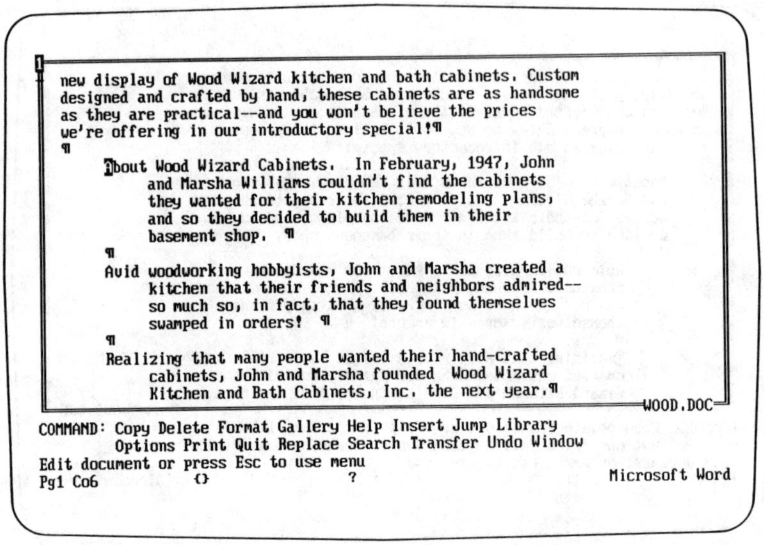

Fig. 4.17.

Formatting a
hanging indent.

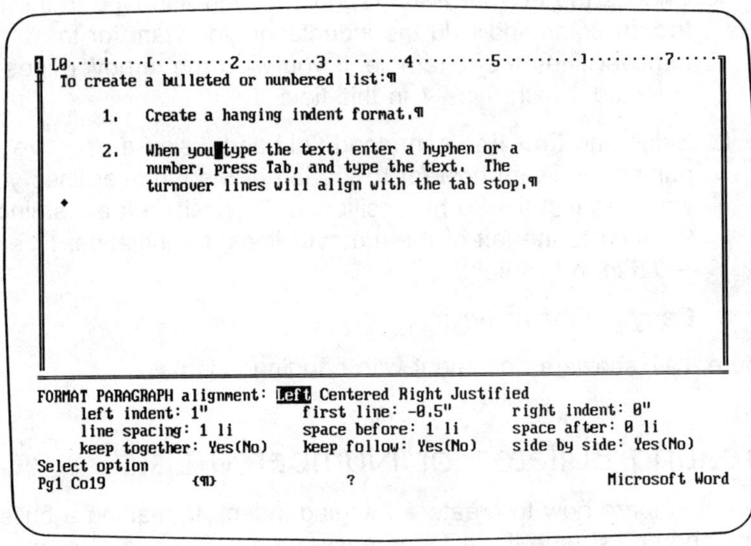

```
    new display of Wood Wizard kitchen and bath cabinets. Custom
    designed and crafted by hand, these cabinets are as handsome
    as they are practical--and you won't believe the prices
    we're offering in our introductory special!¶
    ¶
        About Wood Wizard Cabinets.  In February, 1947, John
            and Marsha Williams couldn't find the cabinets
            they wanted for their kitchen remodeling plans,
            and so they decided to build them in their
            basement shop.  ¶
        ¶
        Avid woodworking hobbyists, John and Marsha created a
            kitchen that their friends and neighbors admired--
            so much so, in fact, that they found themselves
            swamped in orders!  ¶
        ¶
        Realizing that many people wanted their hand-crafted
            cabinets, John and Marsha founded  Wood Wizard
            Kitchen and Bath Cabinets, Inc. the next year.¶
                                                        WOOD.DOC
    COMMAND: Copy Delete Format Gallery Help Insert Jump Library
                Options Print Quit Replace Search Transfer Undo Window
    Edit document or press Esc to use menu
    Pg1 Co6              {}               ?            Microsoft Word
```

Fig. 4.18.

A numbered list.

```
L0····1···[········2·········3·········4·········5·········]·········7·····
    To create a bulleted or numbered list:¶

        1.    Create a hanging indent format.¶

        2.    When you type the text, enter a hyphen or a
            number, press Tab, and type the text.  The
            turnover lines will align with the tab stop.¶
    ◆



    FORMAT PARAGRAPH alignment: Left Centered Right Justified
        left indent: 1"            first line: -0.5"      right indent: 0"
        line spacing: 1 li         space before: 1 li     space after: 0 li
        keep together: Yes(No)     keep follow: Yes(No)   side by side: Yes(No)
    Select option
    Pg1 Co19             {¶}              ?            Microsoft Word
```

Understanding the Ruler

You may have noticed that when you use the Format Paragraph
command, a ruler appears on the top window border. You can turn the
ruler on so that it appears at all times; just choose the **Y**es option in
the **show ruler** field of the **O**ptions menu.

The ruler doesn't measure the page as it prints; the ruler measures lines of text from the left margin. By default, Word is set up with a 6-inch line length, which is produced by its 1.25-inch left and right margins. To change these margins (and alter the default line length), use the Format Division Margins command. For more information, see Chapter 5.

 Caution: You don't need to indent paragraphs to create a left margin, because a 1.25-inch left margin is already included in Word's default margin settings. If you indent all your text 1 inch on the screen, you will get a 2.25-inch left margin on your printout.

As you can see in figure 4.18, the ruler contains symbols that help you understand the formatting settings for the selected paragraph (the one in which the cursor is positioned). Here are what these symbols mean:

¦	First-line indent (or hanging indent's first line)
[	Left indent from margin
]	Right indent from margin

You should know one more important point about the ruler. It always shows the indents of the currently selected paragraph. As you move the cursor from one paragraph to another that has different indents, you see the ruler change.

The ruler shows the custom tab stops you have chosen for a paragraph, too. For more information, see Chapter 11, "Creating Tables and Lists with Tabs, Autosort, and Math."

Indenting Text with the Mouse

New to Word 5 is a simplified technique for indenting text with the mouse. Previously, you had to choose the Format Paragraph command before using this technique. Now you can perform it any time the ruler is displayed.

To indent text with the mouse, do the following:

1. Place the cursor in the paragraph you want to format, or select several paragraphs by using one of the variable text selection methods. To select the whole document, press Shift-F10. If the ruler doesn't appear, click the ruler switch in the upper right corner of the window.

2. Point to the symbol of the indent you want to change.

3. Hold down the Alt key and the right mouse button, and drag the symbol to its new location.

Note: The first-line indent symbol (¦) is often superimposed on the left-indent symbol ([) so that you can't see the left-indent symbol. When the two are superimposed, the first one to move is always the left indent. To set an automatic first-line indentation, then, begin by moving the left-indent symbol off the first-line indent symbol. Then move the first-line indent symbol to the location you want. Finally, move the left-indent symbol back to its original location.

Controlling Line Spacing

Word's line spacing is exceptionally versatile and easy to use. You can double-space your entire document, if you prefer, or you can mix single- and double-spaced text. You also can create paragraph formats that automatically include blank lines before and after each paragraph, saving you the trouble of pressing Enter to create a blank line.

Double-Spacing Your Document

If you want to print your document double-spaced, you can attach the format as you type, or format later. In either case, you see the double line spacing right on-screen. Formatting later may be preferable if you plan to edit your document heavily; with single-spacing, you can see more lines of text in the document window.

Alt-2

To double-space your text as you type, follow these steps:

1. Choose the **Format Paragraph** command and type the line spacing you want (2 *li*) in the **line spacing** command field. Alternatively, use the Alt-2 keyboard shortcut.

2. Type the text. Every time you press Enter, or every time Word wraps to a new line, Word repeats the double-spacing format automatically, so you don't need to give the command again.

3. To return to the default paragraph format (flush left, single-spaced), press Alt-P.

To double-space your text after you type, do the following:

1. Place the cursor in the paragraph you want to double-space. Alternatively, select several paragraphs, using one of the

variable text selection techniques discussed in Chapter 3. To select the whole document, press Shift-F10.

2. Choose the **Format P**aragraph command and type the line spacing you want (*2 li*) in the **line spacing** command field. Alternatively, use the Alt-2 keyboard shortcut.

Adding Blank Lines before and after a Paragraph

The **space before** and **space after** fields of the Format Paragraph command are useful for specifying blank lines. If you are single-spacing your document, for instance, you may want to establish a paragraph format that automatically enters a blank line before a paragraph when you press Enter.

Caution: Do not get into the habit of creating blank lines in your document by pressing Enter. Although you can do so in many cases without harmful results, you will find later that this method forecloses some advanced options for you, such as automatic list sorting and the prevention of widowed headings. If you want blank lines between paragraphs, always create them by setting up a paragraph format that includes blank lines in the **space before** or **space after** field.

To enter a blank line before each paragraph as you type, follow these steps:

Alt-O

1. Choose the **Format P**aragraph command and type *1 li* in the **space before** command field. Alternatively, use the Alt-O keyboard shortcut.

2. Type the text. Every time you press Enter, Word repeats the alignment format automatically, so you don't need to give the command again.

3. To return to the default paragraph format (flush left, single-spaced), press Alt-P.

To enter blank lines after you type, use the following method:

1. Place the cursor in the paragraph you want to format. Alternatively, select several paragraphs, using one of the variable text selection techniques discussed in Chapter 3. To select the whole document, press Shift-F10.

2. Choose the **F**ormat **P**aragraph command and type *1 li* in the **space before** command field. Alternatively, use the Alt-O keyboard shortcut.

Controlling Line Spacing with Large or Small Fonts

With Word, line spacing and font size are independent. In other words, if you choose a 14-point font with the Format Character command, Word still uses the default single line spacing. Because an inch contains 72 points (6 lines), each line is 12 points in height. For this reason, the lines will look as if they are jammed together too closely. Similarly, if you use a tiny font (6 or 8 points), Word still uses 12-point lines, and the lines will look double- or triple-spaced, even if you intended single line spacing.

When you use a large or small font, therefore, you should adjust the **line spacing** field accordingly. You may have to experiment to get the spacing right, but begin by typing the font's size in the **line spacing** field. If you're using a 14-point font, for instance, select all the text you have formatted with that font, choose the **F**ormat **P**aragraph command, and type *14 pt* in the **line spacing** field.

Being Careful with Paragraph Marks

Think of a paragraph's ending paragraph mark as the place where Word "stores" the paragraph formats you chose for that paragraph. When you delete the paragraph mark, therefore, the paragraph loses all the formatting you gave it.

This fact comes into play in two situations—one intentional, and one accidental. If you're joining two paragraphs, as you learned to do in Chapter 2, you delete the first paragraph's paragraph mark; that's the only way you can join the two paragraphs. But if you're editing without displaying the paragraph marks, you might delete a mark accidentally.

In both cases, the result is the same: the two paragraphs join, and the first paragraph takes the formatting of the second. Why? Remember that a paragraph gets its formatting from the information stored in the paragraph mark at the end of the paragraph. Therefore, in the joined paragraph, the paragraph mark that determines the format is the only mark left: the one at the end of what used to be the second paragraph.

If the two paragraphs are formatted exactly the same way, joining them has no adverse consequences. If they're formatted differently, however, joining them can give you an unwanted surprise. Just use the **Format P**aragraph command again (or use a keyboard shortcut) to restore the formatting you want.

Caution: After you format your document, be sure to save it with the **W**ord option chosen in the **format** field of the **T**ransfer **S**ave command. This option is the default setting. If you accidentally choose another, Word asks you to press Y to confirm the loss of formatting when you save. If you see this message when you use **T**ransfer **S**ave, press Esc to cancel the command. Use **T**ransfer **S**ave again, and make sure that the **W**ord option is selected. For more information on your options when saving, see Chapter 8, "Finding and Managing Documents."

Checking the Current Formats

One of Word's best features is its capability to display most formats on-screen. Even so, you can't see some formats (such as fonts and font sizes), and judging measurements precisely on the screen is difficult ("Is that paragraph indented 0.5 inch or 0.75 inch?"). You can use the Format Character and Format Paragraph menus, however, to check the formats you have applied to a particular character or paragraph. Check the formats whenever you're in doubt about which formats or measurements you have applied to your text.

Checking the Current Character Formats

To check the formats you have applied to a character, simply do the following:

1. Select a single character whose format you want to check.

2. Choose the **Format C**haracter command and inspect the settings in the command menu.

The currently selected options are shown in parentheses, except for the field that contains the highlight (the highlight is positioned on the currently selected option in that field). In figure 4.19, for example, the command menu shows that underlining has been chosen for the selected character.

Fig. 4.19.

Checking the current character format.

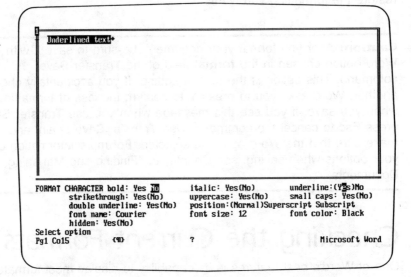

Checking the Current Paragraph Formats

To check the formats you have applied to a paragraph, follow these instructions:

1. Place the cursor anywhere in the paragraph whose formats you want to check.

2. Choose the **F**ormat **P**aragraph command and inspect the settings in the command menu.

In figure 4.20, for instance, the command menu shows that full justification and a 1-inch left indent have been chosen for the selected paragraph.

```
▌L8····!····[········2········3········4········5········]········7·····▐

        This paragraph is typed with a  hanging  indentation.
        The first l▌ne "hangs" over the subsequent  lines,
        which are called turnover lines.  The paragraph is
        also formatted  with  blank  lines  and  justified
        alignment.▌
    ◆



▌
▌
▌
▌
▌
─────────────────────────────────────────────────────
FORMAT PARAGRAPH alignment: Left Centered Right █Justified█
     left indent: 1"        first line: -8.5"     right indent: 8"
     line spacing: 1 li      space before: 1 li    space after: 0 li
     keep together: Yes(No)  keep follow: Yes(No)  side by side: Yes(No)
Select option
Pg1 Co21            {or·}              ?                  Microsoft Word
```

Fig. 4.20.

Checking the
current paragraph
format.

 Caution: If you select more than one character or paragraph, and if
some of the text within the selection is formatted differently, the Format
menu options are displayed blank, and you can't check the formatting.
(As you will learn later in this chapter, this feature allows you to add
new formats to text without canceling or altering existing ones.) To
ensure that you don't see a blank menu when checking formats, select
just one character or paragraph at a time.

Copying Character and Paragraph Formats

Whether you format as you type or format later, you will find that
knowing how to copy formats from one selection to another can be a
convenient tool. Copying saves you the trouble of giving the formatting
command all over again. This section explains how you can copy
character and paragraph formats with the mouse, and provides an
undocumented—but nifty—technique for copying paragraph formats
with the keyboard.

Copying Character Formats

To copy a character format with the mouse, do the following:

1. Select the characters to be formatted.

2. Point to a character that already has the format you want.

3. Hold down the Alt key and click the left button.

If the format you want to copy isn't on-screen, split the screen into two windows and scroll one window so that both the selection and the format are displayed. For more information on windows, see Chapter 9, "Customizing the Screen and Using Windows."

Copying Paragraph Formats

You can copy paragraph formats with the keyboard or the mouse. The keyboard method, by the way, isn't in Word's documentation, but many users figure out how to do it anyway. The technique becomes obvious once you understand that Word stores paragraph formatting information in paragraph marks.

To copy a paragraph format with the keyboard, follow these steps:

1. Display the paragraph marks by choosing the **P**artial or **A**ll option in the **show non-printing symbols** field of the **O**ptions menu.

2. Select the paragraph mark you want to copy.

3. Use the **C**opy command or Del command or key and press Enter to copy the mark to the scrap.

4. Position the cursor where you want the mark to appear. If the text you want to format already exists, position the cursor on the text's paragraph mark.

5. Use the **I**nsert command or press Ins. The inserted mark pushes the cursor down to the next line.

6. Press the left- or up-arrow key to move the cursor back to the mark you just inserted, and start typing.

To copy a paragraph format with the mouse, follow these steps:

1. Place the cursor in the paragraph whose format you want to copy.

2. Move the pointer to the selection bar next to the paragraph you want to format.

3. Hold down the Alt key and click the right button.

Searching for Character and Paragraph Formats

After formatting a lengthy document, you may want to find a place where you used a specific character or paragraph format. You can search for a format with the Format sEarch command.

To search for a character format or formats, use the following procedure:

1. To search your entire document, press Ctrl-PgUp to position the cursor at the beginning.

2. Choose the **F**ormat s**E**arch **C**haracter command.

3. When the command menu appears (see fig. 4.21), choose the **D**own option in the **direction** field.

```
FORMAT SEARCH CHARACTER direction: Up Down
          bold: Yes No          italic: Yes No          underline: Yes No
          strikethrough: Yes No   uppercase: Yes No        small caps: Yes No
          double underline: Yes No position: Normal Superscript Subscript
          font name:              font size:              font color:
          hidden: Yes No
Select option
Pg1 Co1            {or·}            ?                       Microsoft Word
```

Fig. 4.21.

The Format sEarch Character menu.

4. Select the format or formats for which you want to search. To find Helvetica text with bold formatting, for instance, highlight **Y**es in the **bold** field and type *Helvetica* in the **font name** field.

5. Carry out the command.

Word tries to match the format or formats you selected. If you chose more than one format, Word finds a match only if it contains all the formats you selected.

To search for a paragraph format or formats, use the following method:

1. To search your entire document, press Ctrl-PgUp to position the cursor at the beginning.

2. Choose the **F**ormat s**E**arch **P**aragraph command.

3. When the command menu appears (see fig. 4.22), choose the **D**own option in the **direction** field.

Fig. 4.22.

The Format sEarch Paragraph menu.

```
FORMAT SEARCH PARAGRAPH direction: Up Down
          alignment: Left Centered Right Justified
          left indent:            first line:         right indent:
          line spacing:           space before:       space after:
          keep together: Yes No   keep follow: Yes No  side by side: Yes No
Press capital letter of the menu item you want
Pg1 Co1              {or·}              ?                    Microsoft Word
```

4. Select the format or formats for which you want to search.

5. Carry out the command.

Replacing Character and Paragraph Formats

Here's a terrific productivity feature. Suppose that you have just finished formatting a lengthy manuscript, and you used italic type extensively. Now you find out that the style guidelines you're working with don't permit italic; you must use underlining instead. Without the Format repLace command, you would have to scroll through your document and manually reformat every instance of italic. But this command can do the whole job automatically.

To replace a format automatically throughout a document, do the following:

1. Press Ctrl-PgUp to move the cursor to the beginning of the document.

2. Choose the **F**ormat rep**L**ace **C**haracter or the **F**ormat rep**L**ace **P**aragraph command.

3. When the command menu appears (see fig. 4.23), choose the format you want removed from your document. Choose **N**o in the **confirm** field if you want Word to perform all the

substitutions without confirmation. Choose **Y**es if you want to check each substitution.

Performing this search-and-replace operation on formats is much less risky than it is on text. Generally, you can use the **N**o option without risk of unwanted changes—but be sure you want to change every instance of the format before you choose this option.

```
FORMAT REPLACE PARAGRAPH confirm: Yes No
      alignment: Left Centered Right Justified
      left indent:          first line:           right indent:
      line spacing:         space before:         space after:
      keep together: Yes No keep follow: Yes No   side by side: Yes No
Select option
Pg1 Col            {or·}              ?                   Microsoft Word
```

Fig. 4.23.

The Format repLace Paragraph menu.

4. When the **replace with** menu appears (see fig. 4.24), choose the format you want word to insert in your document.

```
REPLACE WITH PARAGRAPH FORMAT alignment: Left Centered Right Justified
      left indent:          first line:           right indent:
      line spacing:         space before:         space after:
      keep together: Yes No keep follow: Yes No   side by side: Yes No
Select option
Pg1 Col            {or·}              ?                   Microsoft Word
```

Fig. 4.24.

The Replace With Paragraph Format menu.

5. Carry out the command by pressing Enter or clicking the command name. If you chose the **Y**es option in the **confirm** field, press **Y** to confirm the substitution, **N** to ignore this instance of the format, or Esc to stop searching and return to the search's beginning point.

Why You Should Learn Style Sheet Formatting

You may be surprised to learn this fact, but you're already using a style sheet: Word's default style sheet, NORMAL.STY. A style sheet defines the formats you enter with keyboard shortcuts, such as Alt-T or Alt-I.

As you have probably already learned, the keyboard shortcut formats defined in NORMAL.STY are appropriate for many uses, but you probably want to change at least some of them. You may, for instance, want to have a key combination that would, in one keystroke, create a paragraph with all these formats:

❑ Automatic 0.5-inch first-line indent

❑ Double line spacing

❑ Justified right margin

❑ 10-point Helvetica font

You can do exactly that with a style sheet. After creating a style sheet and defining a keyboard shortcut with these formats, you can enter all of them in just one stroke of that key. Obviously, your efforts in learning style sheet formatting will be handsomely repaid!

Before reading Chapter 20 ("Using Style Sheets"), however, you should read the next chapter on page formatting. After you complete the next chapter, you will have all the knowledge you need in order to tackle style sheet formatting.

Chapter Summary

Word's default formats include an 8 1/2-by-11-inch page size, top and bottom margins of 1 inch, left and right margins of 1.25 inches, tabs every 0.5 inch, single line spacing, flush-left alignment, and (with most printers) a "plain vanilla" Pica type style and size. Even if you do no formatting at all, your text will still print on separate pages with neat margins (but without page numbers). If you format your document, Word saves your formatting instructions with the document, so they're available the next time you load the document.

This chapter introduced you to character and paragraph formatting. You learned how to use different units of measurement; control character emphasis and position; use your printer's fonts; use hidden text; control paragraph alignment, indentation, and line spacing; copy character and paragraph formats; and search for and replace character and paragraph formats. The next chapter explores Word 5 formatting even further by introducing you to page formatting.

5

Word 5 Formatting Strategies: Page Formatting

As you have already learned, Word distinguishes between character formatting and paragraph formatting, the subjects of the preceding chapter. Character formats affect emphasis, position, font style, and font size, in units of text ranging from one character to an entire document. Paragraph formats affect alignment, indentation, and line spacing for one or more paragraphs.

This chapter focuses on the third level of formatting, page formatting. With Word, page formats include margins, page size, page numbers, and running heads. (Running heads are short versions of a document's title that print at the top or bottom of every page.) You can set page formats for your entire document, or if you prefer, you can break your document into two or more divisions, each with its own distinctive page formats.

With Word, you can create a single but complex document, such as a business report, that has distinct divisions (chapters and appendixes), each with its own running heads, margins, page-number styles, and page-number sequence. Most of the time, however, you will create documents with just one page format running throughout the document, so this chapter is primarily about document-wide page formatting.

151

In this chapter, you learn how to do the following:

❏ Work with Word's default page style formats, the ones the program uses unless you give your own page format commands

❏ Use the Format Division command to format page formats

❏ Change Word's default page size and margins, and set new defaults for every document you create

❏ Add running heads to your document, using the new, easy Word 5 formatting features

❏ Add page numbers to your document and get them to print precisely the way you want

❏ Control page breaks so that you never see a heading left alone at the bottom of a page

❏ Break up your document into two or more divisions, each with its own distinctive pattern of page styles

Some page formats, such as footnotes and multiple-column formatting, are discussed elsewhere in this book. For information on footnotes, see Chapter 14, "The Legal and Scholarly Word"; for multiple-column formatting, see Chapter 19, "Creating Multiple-Column Text and Newsletters." Line numbers, used most frequently in legal documents, are also discussed in Chapter 14. In addition, see Chapter 18, "Integrating Text and Graphics," for a discussion of page design with figures and illustrations.

Getting To Know Word's Default Page Styles

Word's default settings for page styles define the way your document will print unless you give commands to the contrary. Table 5.1 lists these default settings.

Table 5.1
Word's Default Page Styles

Style	Default setting
Margin: bottom	1.0″
Margin: left	1.25″
Margin: right	1.25″
Margin: top	1.0″
Page length	11″
Page number position	0.5″ from top of page, 7.25″ from left
Page number style	Arabic (1, 2, 3, and so on)
Page numbering	Start at 1
Page numbers	No (off)
Page width	8.5″
Running head position	0.5″ from top or bottom of page

If you're used to some other word processing program, some of these settings may seem peculiar to you. For instance, Word doesn't print page numbers automatically (you must deliberately turn on page numbering for each document you create, using the Format Division Page-numbers command). Remember, though, that some of the documents you create will be one-page letters, and you don't want a page number on a single-page letter. As you will learn in this chapter, turning on page numbers for longer documents like reports and proposals is easy.

Altering any of these defaults is easy, and—as you learn in this chapter's section on "Setting Page Size and Margins"—you can save new default margins, a new page width, and a new page length. The key to changing these defaults, and to most other aspects of page style formatting, is the Format Division command.

Using the Format Division Command

Word has a number of oddly named commands, such as Transfer (why not "File"?) and Gallery (why not "Style-sheet"?), but the Format

Division command is the one most likely to baffle users. It ought to be called something like "Format Page-style." To be sure, you can use Format Division to format sections or divisions of your document, but you're formatting page styles when you do. If you think of the command as the "Format Page-style" command, you may get less confused about how to use it. In most cases, you use the command to determine a page style for your whole document. Unless you deliberately break your document into two or more divisions, the choices you make in the Format Division menu affect your entire document.

Working with the Command's Options

When you choose the Format Division command, you see a submenu that lists several options (see fig. 5.1). Here's a summary of what you can do with each option:

Margins	Set margins, page size, and running head location; set gutters and mirror margins for two-sided printing of your document; save settings as the new defaults
Page-numbers	Turn on automatic page numbering, specify page number position, specify starting number, and set page number style (such as Arabic or Roman numerals)
Layout	Choose location for footnotes (on the same page or at the end of the document), set up multiple columns, and control page breaks when a new division is started
line-Numbers	Add line numbers that print in the margin of legal documents

About the Division Mark

After you make a choice in one of the Format Division command's menus, Word inserts a *division mark* in your document (see fig. 5.2). This mark, a double row of dots across the screen, appears at the end of your document, just above the end-of-file mark. You see the division mark no matter which option you choose in the **show non-printing symbols** field of the Options menu.

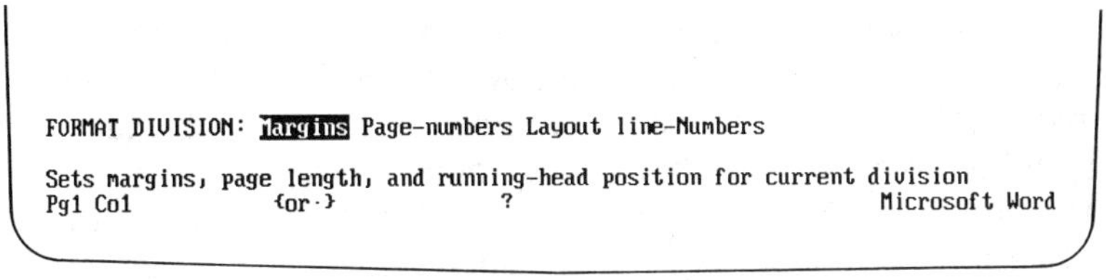

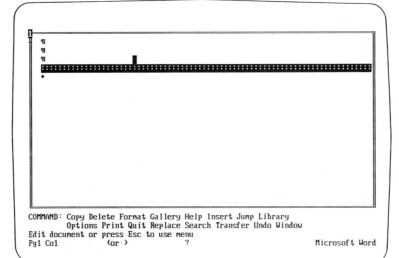

Fig. 5.1.

The Format Division menu.

Fig. 5.2.

A division mark at the end of a document.

Caution: The division mark is like a paragraph mark: it "stores" the formats you choose. If you delete the mark, you lose the page style formats you have chosen. If you accidentally delete the division mark while editing at the end of your document, choose the **U**ndo command.

After the division mark appears, be sure to type above it, not below it. Only the text above the division mark will have the page style formats you chose.

Setting Page Size and Margins

If you're using Word outside the North American context, you may want to change the page size to suit local standards. And you may want to change Word's default left and right margins, which produce a line length of only 60 characters with standard Pica (10-pitch) fonts. Line lengths of 65 characters are the norm for most documents.

With previous versions of Word, you had only one way to change these default settings: create and use a new default style sheet. But here's some good news: With Word 5, you can save a new default page size and margins just by choosing an option in the Format Division Margins menu (see fig. 5.3). This new feature is just one of the many little touches that make Word 5 such a pleasure to use.

Fig. 5.3.

The Format Division Margins menu.

```
FORMAT DIVISION MARGINS
      top: [1"]                bottom: 1"
      left: 1"                  right: 1"
      page length: 11"         width: 8.5"      gutter margin: 0"
      running-head position from top: 0.5"      from bottom: 0.5"
      mirror margins: Yes(No)                   use as default: Yes(No)
Enter measurement
Pg1 Col              {or·}            ?                      Microsoft Word
```

Setting Page Size

Word can print on nearly any size of standard paper. If you're using a paper size other than 8.5 by 11 inches, just enter new measurements in the **page length** and **width** fields of the Format Division Margins menu (see fig. 5.3).

In previous versions of Word, if you used a laser printer, you frequently had to use a 10.5-inch setting in the **page length** field to get your printer to work properly with Word. In Word 5, the adjustment is included in Word's printer drivers. Another thoughtful touch!

Setting Margins

The word *margins* refers to the white space at the top, bottom, left, and right of the printed page. By default, Word prints margins of 1 inch at the top and bottom, and 1.25 inches on the left and right.

Caution: You need to distinguish margins from the paragraph indents you can create with the Format Paragraph command. A left or right paragraph indent *adds* to the existing margin. For example, if you choose a left indent of 1 inch in the Format Paragraph menu, Word prints 2.25 inches of blank space in the left margin of that paragraph.

Setting new margins for your document is easy. Just enter new measurements in the **top**, **bottom**, **left**, and **right** fields of the Format Division Margins menu (see fig. 5.3).

Using Negative Paragraph Indents as "Outdents"

Those of you who have used typewriters are probably familiar with the margin release key, which permits you to type beyond the right margin if the need arises. In some word processing programs, this function is called *outdenting*—making text go beyond the margin temporarily. You can outdent with Word by placing a negative number in the **right indent** field of the Format Paragraph menu. This technique is useful when you are typing a table, for instance, that doesn't quite fit in the margins you have set. You cannot outdent the left margin, however.

To outdent text temporarily, use the following procedure:

1. Set the margins for the whole document, using the **Format Division Margins** command.

2. When you want to type text that goes beyond the left or right margin, press Enter to start a new paragraph.

3. Choose the **Format Paragraph** command.

4. To outdent text from the right margin, type a negative number in the **right indent** command field (see fig. 5.4).

5. Carry out the command.

```
FORMAT PARAGRAPH alignment: Left Centered Right Justified
        left indent: 0"         first line: 0"        right indent: -1"
        line spacing: 1 li      space before: 0 li    space after: 0 li
        keep together: Yes(No)  keep follow: Yes(No)  side by side: Yes(No)
Select option
Pg1 Co1              {or·}              ?                Microsoft Word
```

Fig. 5.4.

"Outdenting" the right margin.

If the ruler is visible, you can see the right-margin symbol (]) jump past the margin measurement you have specified. When you're finished typing the text you want outdented, press Enter to start a new paragraph. Then choose the **Format Paragraph** command again and type *0"* in the **right indent** command field.

Using Mirror Margins

New to Word 5 is a *mirror margins* feature, which reverses the left and right margin settings on even-numbered pages. This option is useful when you are creating a document that will be duplicated on both sides of the page and bound.

If you set a 1.5-inch left margin and a 1-inch right margin and choose **Ye**s in the **mirror margins** field of the Format Division Margins menu (see fig. 5.3), Word prints these margins on odd-numbered pages. On even pages, however, Word prints a 1-inch left margin and a 1.5-inch right margin. Then when you duplicate both sides of the pages and bind them so that odd-numbered pages are on the right and even-numbered pages are on the left, the 1.5-inch margin is always on the side to be bound, thus allowing ample room for the binding.

Adding Gutters

The term *gutter* refers to extra white space that is added to the left side of odd-numbered pages, and to the right side of even-numbered pages, to facilitate binding. Like mirror margins, gutters are useful when you plan to duplicate documents on both sides of the page. In fact, gutters do exactly the same thing that mirror margins do. Word gives you two ways to accomplish the same thing.

To add a gutter, type a measurement in the **gutter margin** field of the Format Division Margins menu (see fig. 5.3). If you type *0.5* in this field, for instance, Word adds half an inch to the left margin of odd-numbered pages, and the same space to the right margin of even-numbered pages.

Setting New Default Margins

To save as defaults any of the settings in the Format Division Margins menu, follow these steps:

1. Choose the **F**ormat **D**ivision **M**argins command.

2. Choose the page size, margins, running head position, mirror margins, or gutter width that you want to apply to every document you create. (For information on running heads, see "Creating Running Heads" in this chapter.)

3. Choose the **Y**es option in the **use as default** field.

One advantage (among many) of creating style sheets is that you can create several of them, each with its own default margins. You can create a style sheet called REPORT, for instance, which has mirror margins appropriate for a business report that will be duplicated on both sides of the page. You can create a second style sheet called LETTER, which has margins appropriate for a business letter. For more information on style sheets, see Chapter 20.

Creating Running Heads

Running heads are short versions of a document's title, that are printed within the top or bottom margin of each page. (Sometimes running heads include the author's name or other information.) Running heads positioned at the top of the page are called *headers*, and those at the bottom are called *footers*.

Word's capabilities for running heads are unusually flexible. For example, you can do the following:

❏ Create headers and footers that print just on odd pages, just on even pages, or on both

❏ Include running heads on page 1, if you prefer

❏ Use running heads that have more than one line of text (Word automatically expands the margins to make room)

❏ Change running head text within your document

❏ Include automatic page numbers in running heads

And with Version 5, experienced Word users will find that formatting running heads is much easier than with earlier versions. Running head margins are now flush with the left and right margins set in the Format Division Margins command.

This section discusses all aspects of creating and formatting running heads, except one: creating running heads that print page numbers. For information on page numbers in running heads, see this chapter's section on "Adding Page Numbers."

Adding Headers or Footers to Your Document

**Ctrl-F2,
Alt-F2**

To add a running head to your document, follow these steps:

1. Type the running head text at the beginning of your document and press Enter. Figure 5.5 shows a sample running head.

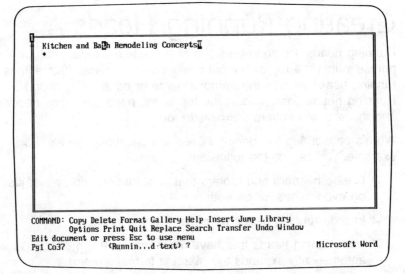

Fig. 5.5.

Typing the running head text.

```
Kitchen and Bath Remodeling Concepts




















COMMAND: Copy Delete Format Gallery Help Insert Jump Library
         Options Print Quit Replace Search Transfer Undo Window
Edit document or press Esc to use menu
Pg1 Co37        {Runnin...d text} ?              Microsoft Word
```

2. Press the up arrow to position the cursor in the paragraph you have just created.

3. Choose the **F**ormat **R**unning-head command.

4. When the Format Running-head menu appears (see fig. 5.6), choose the **T**op option in the **position** field to create a header, or choose the **B**ottom option in the same field to create a footer. Then carry out the command. Alternatively, use the Ctrl-F2 keyboard shortcut to create a header, or Alt-F2 to create a footer.

After you carry out the Format Running-head command, a caret (ˆ) appears in the selection bar next to the running head text (see fig. 5.7). The caret tells you that the paragraph will print as running head text, not as normal text.

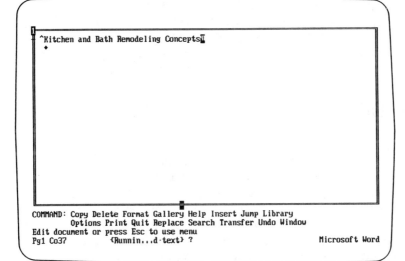

```
FORMAT RUNNING-HEAD position: Top Bottom None
        odd pages:(Yes)No  even pages:(Yes)No  first page: Yes(No)
        alignment:(Left-margin)Edge-of-paper
Select option
Pg1 Co37          {Runnin...d text} ?              Microsoft Word
```

Fig. 5.6.

Using the Format Running-head command.

```
^Kitchen and Bath Remodeling Concepts
 ◆









COMMAND: Copy Delete Format Gallery Help Insert Jump Library
         Options Print Quit Replace Search Transfer Undo Window
Edit document or press Esc to use menu
Pg1 Co37          {Runnin...d text} ?              Microsoft Word
```

Fig. 5.7.

The caret symbol (^) that marks running head text.

Note: With the Format Running-head menu, you can add character emphasis and other formats to your running head, including lines, boxes, and shading with the Format Border command.

Headers and footers look clean and professional with lines running across the page. To insert a line below a header, choose the **Yes** option in the **below** field of the **F**ormat **B**order command, and also choose the **L**ines option in the **type** field. To insert a line above a footer, choose the **L**ines option in the same command menu, but choose the **Y**es option in the **above** field. (For more information on the Format Border command, see Chapter 17, "Creating Forms and Illustrations.")

Choosing Options for Headers and Footers

By default, Word prints running heads on both odd and even pages but not on the first page. Headers are printed 0.5 inch from the top of the page, and footers are printed 0.5 inch from the bottom. The default horizontal placement for running heads has changed with Word 5. Previously, running-head paragraphs were printed flush with the left side of the page unless you deliberately indented them. With Word 5, running head paragraphs are flush with the margins indicated in the Format Division menu. You can alter these default settings to create more interesting and complex running heads for your documents.

Using Different Running Heads for Odd and Even Pages

If you're planning to duplicate your document on both sides of the page, consider creating different running heads for the odd (right) and even (left) pages. The following tutorial shows you how to create an attractive pattern of headers for such a document. On the odd-numbered pages, the header text appears flush to the right margin. On the even-numbered pages, the header text appears flush to the left margin. Follow these steps to create headers for this type of document:

Alt-R

1. Type the header text you want to display on the odd-numbered (right) pages. Press Alt-R to format the text flush to the right margin, and then press Enter (see fig. 5.8).

Alt-P

2. Type the header text you want to display on the even-numbered (left) pages. Press Alt-P to format the text flush to the left margin, and then press Enter (see fig. 5.9).

3. Place the cursor on the first header, and choose the **Top** option in the **position** field. Then choose the **Yes** option in the **odd pages** field of the Format Running-head menu, but choose the **No** option in the **even pages** field (see fig. 5.10). Carry out the command.

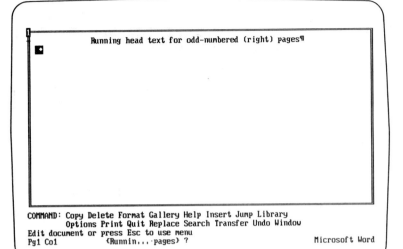

Fig. 5.8.

Header text for
odd-numbered
pages.

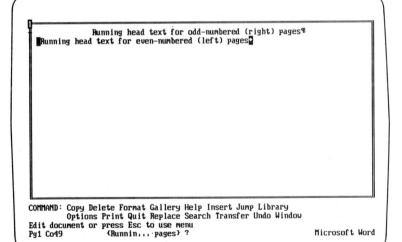

Fig. 5.9.

Header text for
even-numbered
pages.

4. Place the cursor on the second header, the one for even
   pages, and choose the Format Running-head command
   again. Choose the Top option in the **position** field. Then
   select the Yes option in the **even pages** field, but choose
   the No option in the **odd pages** field (see fig. 5.11). Carry
   out the command.

Fig. 5.10.

Formatting the header for odd-numbered pages.

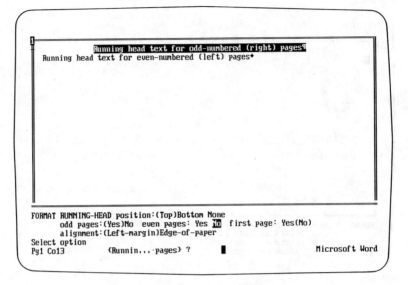

Fig. 5.11.

Formatting the header for even-numbered pages.

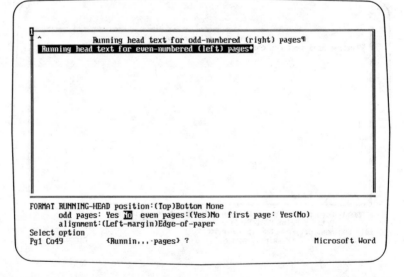

You can improve the appearance of these running heads even further by adding lines with the Format Border command, as suggested in the preceding power user tip.

Once you have entered several pages of text, you can preview your running heads with the Print preView command.

Understanding Running Head Codes

If you create more than one kind of running head, as suggested in the preceding tutorial, you may want to display running head codes. These codes tell you how you have formatted the running heads. To turn on the running head codes, follow these steps:

1. Choose the **O**ptions command.

2. When the command menu appears, as shown in figure 5.12, choose the **Y**es option in the **show style bar** field.

3. Carry out the command.

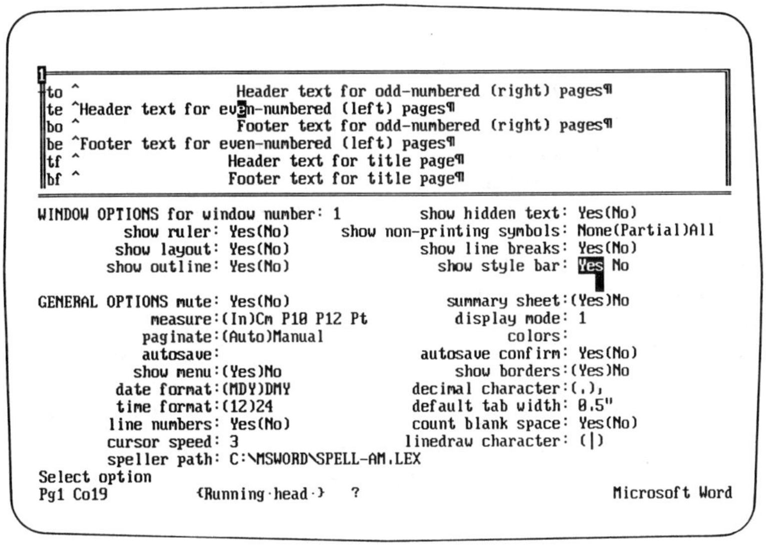

Fig. 5.12.

The Options menu.

As shown along the left side of figure 5.12, the style bar then displays the running head codes. See table 5.2 for a list of these codes and their meanings.

Table 5.2
Running Head Codes in the Style Bar

Code	Meaning
t	Top (header), odd and even pages
tf	Top (header), first page only
te	Top (header), even pages only
to	Top (header), odd pages only

Table 5.2—Continued

Code	Meaning
b	Bottom (footer), odd and even pages
bf	Bottom (footer), first page only
be	Bottom (footer), even pages only
bo	Bottom (footer), odd pages only

Changing the Running Head's Vertical Position

As mentioned previously, Word by default prints header text 0.5 inch from the top of the page and footer text 0.5 inch from the bottom. You can change this vertical position of the running head text by typing new measurements in the **running-head position from top** and **from bottom** command fields of the Format Division Margins command.

When should you change the vertical position? If you're happy with Word's default top and bottom margins of 1 inch, you have no reason to—your running heads will print right in the middle of the top and bottom margins. If you reduce or expand the top or bottom margin, however, you should change the **running-head position from top** or **from bottom** setting to reposition the running head text in the middle of the margin. If you're using a 1.25-inch top margin, for instance, type *0.625"* in the **running-head position from top** field of the Format Division Margins menu.

Positioning Running Heads beyond the Left or Right Margin

Earlier versions of Word were preset to format running heads flush to the left side of the page, not flush with the left margin. This setting allowed you easily to extend the running head a little beyond the left margin for even-numbered pages, an arrangement that some document designers prefer. Forgetting to indent the running head paragraph from the left and right edges of the page, however, was also easy to do. Because earlier versions of Word didn't have Print preView, you could print your whole document before noticing that the running heads were misaligned.

By default, Version 5's running heads are aligned flush with the left margin, and every running head text's paragraph has the same right margin as the rest of the document. For this reason, you can align running heads flush right with Alt-R, and the text lines up neatly with the text's right margin.

If you want to extend the running heads a little beyond the margins, however, you have to do some fancy formatting. You can extend them by following these instructions:

1. Create the running head text and format it as usual with the **Format Running**-head command. Choose the **Edge-of-paper** option before carrying out the command (see fig. 5.13). Notice that the indent markers on the ruler now show an 8.5-inch line length (if you're using paper that is 8.5 inches wide).

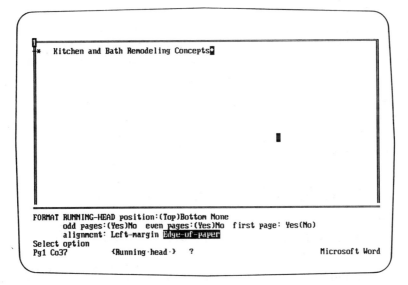

Fig. 5.13.

Positioning the running heads flush to the left and right sides of the page.

2. Choose the **Format Paragraph** command.

3. Enter the margins you want for running heads in the **left indent** and **right indent** fields of the Format Paragraph menu, as shown in figure 5.14. If you are using Word's default margins (1.25 inches right and left), for example, type *0.75* in both fields. Then carry out the command.

4. Preview the results with **Print preView**.

Fig. 5.14.

Indenting the running heads 3/4 inch from the left and right sides of the page.

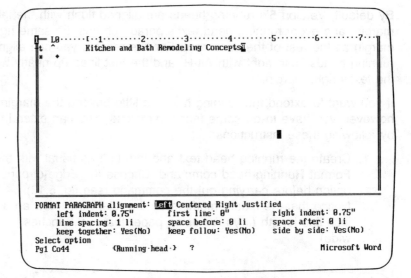

```
     L0·····[··1········2········3········4·······5········6········7···]
t  ^           Kitchen and Bath Remodeling Concepts
*  ◆


                                                      ▮



   FORMAT PARAGRAPH alignment: Left Centered Right Justified
        left indent: 0.75"        first line: 0"        right indent: 0.75"
        line spacing: 1 li        space before: 0 li    space after: 0 li
        keep together: Yes(No)    keep follow: Yes(No)  side by side: Yes(No)
   Select option
   Pg1 Co44           {Running·head·}   ?                   Microsoft Word
```

If you formatted the running-head text flush left, the running head extends slightly beyond the text's left margin. If you formatted the text flush right, it extends just beyond the text's right margin.

Note: You don't see the text formatted this way on the screen unless you choose the **Yes** option in the **show layout** field of the Options menu. For more information on this option, see Chapter 9, "Customizing the Screen and Using Windows."

Deleting a Running Head

If you want to remove a running head from your document, simply position the cursor on the running head, press F10 to select it, and press Del.

You can delete the running head formatting while saving the text (a new Word 5 feature) by using this simple procedure:

1. Position the cursor on the running head you want to change back to normal text.

2. Choose the **None** option in the **position** field of the Format Running-head menu.

Changing Running Head Text in a Document

Sometimes you may want to change the text of a running head in your document. For example, suppose that you want one version of a header to appear on pages 2 through 10, and another version to appear on pages 11 through 20. To do so, simply insert the new text before a page break; the new running head will appear on the next page. To start the new running head on page 11, for example, insert the new text at the bottom of page 10. Be sure to format the new text as running head text, using the Format Running-head command.

Adding Page Numbers

Unlike most word processing programs, Word doesn't automatically print page numbers on your documents. You must deliberately turn on page numbering. You can add page numbers in two ways: (1) by choosing the Yes option in the Format Division Page-numbers command, or (2) by adding a page number slug to a running head.

Of the two methods, the second is by far the best. If you add page numbers by using a running head, you can do the following:

❏ Suppress the printing of page numbers on page 1 of your document

❏ Format the page number characters the way you want— without using a style sheet

❏ Add text, such as "Page" or surrounding hyphens

Using the Format Division Page-numbers Command

To add page numbers with this method, follow these steps:

1. Choose the **F**ormat **D**ivision **P**age-numbers command.

2. When the command menu appears (see fig. 5.15), choose the **Y**es option.

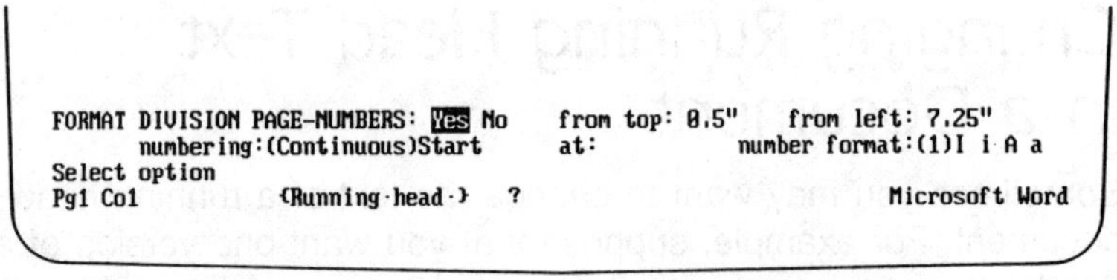

Fig. 5.15.

Choosing automatic page numbers.

```
FORMAT DIVISION PAGE-NUMBERS: Yes No     from top: 0.5"    from left: 7.25"
          numbering:(Continuous)Start    at:               number format:(1)I i A a
Select option
Pg1 Co1          {Running·head·}    ?                        Microsoft Word
```

3. By default, the **Yes** option in this command prints page numbers 0.5 inch from the top of the page and 7.25 inches from the left (in the upper right corner of each page, in other words). To change the position, type new measurements in the **from top** and **from left** fields. To print page numbers centered at the bottom of the page, for instance, type *10.5"* in the **from top** field and *4.25"* in the **from left** field.

4. Carry out the command.

Note: The measurements you place in the **from top** and **from left** fields of the Format Division Page-numbers command do not affect the placement of page numbers in running heads.

After you select the Yes option in this command, Word prints page numbers—including page 1—in your printer's default font. You can't suppress the printing of page numbers on page 1 if you add page numbers this way. Worse, you can't format the page number characters unless you create a style sheet. For these reasons, you may want to add page numbers with running heads rather than with the Format Division Page-numbers command.

Adding Page Numbers to Running Heads

The best way to add page numbers to your document is to create a running head that includes a *page number slug*, a symbol that tells Word to print the current page number at precisely the spot at which you have placed the slug.

To insert a page number slug, use this procedure:

1. Press Ctrl-up arrow to move the cursor to the beginning of your document.

2. Press Enter to create a blank line at the top of your document, and press the up-arrow key to select the blank line.

3. Choose the Insert command. When the **from** prompt appears, press F1. When the list appears, as shown in figure 5.16, choose **page** and press Enter.

You also can use a keyboard shortcut to insert the page number slug. Type *page* and press F3.

F3

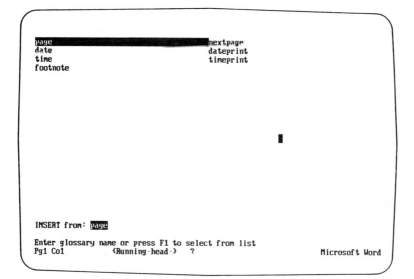

Fig. 5.16.

Inserting a page number slug.

```
page                          nextpage
date                          dateprint
time                          timeprint
footnote




                                  █



INSERT from: page
Enter glossary name or press F1 to select from list
Pg1 Co1          {Running·head·}   ?                 Microsoft Word
```

The word *page* then appears in parentheses in your document, as shown in figure 5.17. The parentheses tell you that the word is not an ordinary one but a page number slug.

4. To format the page numbers, select the slug and choose the **Format Character** command. Choose the emphasis, font name, and font size you want.

5. Add text or surrounding hyphens if you prefer. Press Alt-C to center the page numbers, or Alt-R to format them flush right.

6. This step is important: don't forget to format the text as running head text, using the **Format Running-head** command.

Fig. 5.17.

Formatting the page number slug as running head text.

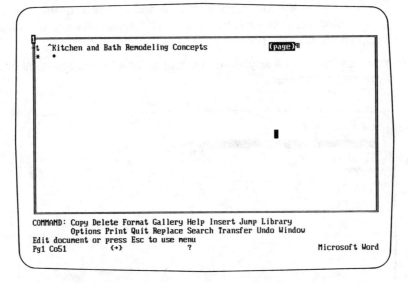

```
t  ^Kitchen and Bath Remodeling Concepts              (page)¶
*    ◆




                              ▮




COMMAND: Copy Delete Format Gallery Help Insert Jump Library
          Options Print Quit Replace Search Transfer Undo Window
Edit document or press Esc to use menu
Pg1 Co51          {+}                ?              Microsoft Word
```

You can insert other slugs by pressing F1 after choosing the command. **Date** inserts the system date, and **time** inserts the system time. **Dateprint** and **timeprint** insert the system date and time at the time you print the document. If you work collaboratively and revise your documents frequently, you may want to insert the dateprint and timeprint slugs in your drafts' running heads so that you know precisely when a draft was printed and circulated.

Caution: If you add page numbers with running heads, be sure to choose the **N**o option in the **F**ormat **D**ivision **P**age-numbers command. If you choose the **Y**es option, you could get page numbers in two different places on your printout. If you discover double page numbers in your document, use the **F**ormat **D**ivision **P**age-numbers command and choose **N**o.

Starting with Different Page Numbers

Whether you add page numbers with the Format Division Page-numbers command or with running heads, you can start the page numbering with a number other than 1. You may want to do so, for example, when you have divided a document into separate files to facilitate handling and backup. Suppose that after printing your

Chapter 1, you find that the first page of Chapter 2 should be page 21. To start the numbering of Chapter 2 at page 21, open the file that contains Chapter 2 and choose the **Format Division Page-numbers** command. Choose the **Start** option in the **numbering** field, and type *21* in the **at** field.

Controlling Page Breaks

In Chapter 3, you learned how to insert manual page breaks by pressing Shift-Ctrl-Enter. You were cautioned, though, that you should probably avoid manual page breaks, particularly if you will edit your document and thus possibly insert or delete text above the manual page break. In this section, you learn how to format headings, tables, and other material so that Word never inserts a page break where you do not want one.

Preventing Orphaned Headings

Perhaps the most unsightly outcome of automatic page formatting is the *orphaned heading*, a heading that appears all alone at the bottom of a page, separated from its accompanying text by a page break automatically inserted by the program. You can prevent orphaned headings by always formatting headings as follows:

1. Type the heading on a line, and press Enter to make it a paragraph (in Word's definition of the term).

2. Press the up-arrow key to select the heading.

3. Choose the **Format Paragraph** command.

4. To leave a blank line under the heading, type *1 li* in the **space after** field.

5. Choose the **Yes** option in the **keep follow** field.

6. Carry out the command.

The **keep follow** field tells Word that it should always keep this paragraph (the heading) on the same page as the paragraph that follows it. Once you have chosen this option, Word will never insert a page break immediately after this paragraph.

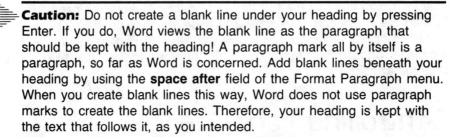

Caution: Do not create a blank line under your heading by pressing Enter. If you do, Word views the blank line as the paragraph that should be kept with the heading! A paragraph mark all by itself is a paragraph, so far as Word is concerned. Add blank lines beneath your heading by using the **space after** field of the Format Paragraph menu. When you create blank lines this way, Word does not use paragraph marks to create the blank lines. Therefore, your heading is kept with the text that follows it, as you intended.

You can use style sheets to set up an Alt-key formatting command for headings. If you do, be sure to format the keyboard shortcut so that it keeps the heading with the following paragraph and enters blank space after the heading. For information on style sheets, see Chapter 20.

Keeping an Entire Paragraph on a Page

If you choose the Yes option in the **keep together** field of the Format Paragraph command, Word does not put a page break within the paragraph. Instead, if a page break is needed, the program moves the whole paragraph to the next page and starts printing the paragraph at the top of that page.

This option is useful for creating tables. When you type a table, use the Newline command (Shift-Enter) rather than Enter to begin each new line. (The whole table is thus one paragraph.) Then choose the **Format Paragraph** command and the **Yes** option in the **keep together** field. Word will not divide the table onto two pages. For more information on tables, see Chapter 11, "Creating Tables and Lists with Tabs, Autosort, and Math."

Using Two or More Divisions in a Document

So far, this chapter has covered page styles as if they applied to an entire document. And normally they do. If you prefer, however, you can insert a division break in your document by pressing Ctrl-Enter. After using this command, Word places a division mark (a double row of dots across the screen) at the cursor's location. The division mark created by Ctrl-Enter looks just like the division mark Word places at the end of your document when you choose options in the Format Division menus.

After you insert a division mark, your document has two parts: Division 1 and Division 2. The status line changes to show the current division number, such as D1 or D2, in addition to the page and column numbers. You can create as many division marks in your document as you need.

You don't need to break your document into divisions unless you want to change some aspect of page style formatting within a portion of your document. Just as paragraph formats apply to a unit of text (the paragraph), so too do page style formats apply to a unit: the division. Normally, your document contains only one division, so page styles apply to the whole document. But if you split the document, you can use one set of page styles for Division 1 and another set for Division 2.

One reason you may want to change divisions is to change margins. For example, after inserting a division mark, you can format Division 1 with 1-inch margins all around, but Division 2 can have a 1.5-inch left margin. You may find other reasons to insert division marks. With Word 5, for instance, you can blend single-column and multiple-column text on a page. You separate the two formats by inserting a division mark.

When you create a division break, Word does the following:

- ❏ Collects all the endnotes for a division (when you print) and places them at the end of the division

- ❏ Restarts the footnote and endnote numbering sequence (After the division break, the first footnote you insert is numbered 1, even if the first division has many footnotes.)

- ❏ Cancels all running heads (If you want the second division to have running heads, you must insert new running head entries after the division break.)

- ❏ Creates a page break (You can suppress the page break, or force Word to break the page so that the new division starts on a new column or an odd-numbered or even-numbered page.)

All these features enable you to create a single document with separate chapters. If you divide the chapters with division breaks, you can have all the endnotes for each chapter printed at the chapter's end. You can format each division so that Word must start the new chapter on an odd-numbered page. And each division can have its own running heads, with short versions of the chapter's title as appropriate.

Is creating a complex, multidivision document in this way a good idea? It could be, depending on what kind of document you're writing, how long the document is, and what kind of system you're using.

If you're creating a report, a proposal, or documentation that will be reproduced directly from Word's printouts, consider creating one large document that contains all the chapters in separate divisions. This way, you can use Word's powerful indexing and table-of-contents generation functions (see Chapter 13, "Creating Indexes and Tables of Contents").

A document of about 100 to 150 printed pages can be created in a single file without taxing the resources of your computer, provided you have a hard disk. If your document will be substantially longer, however, think twice about placing it in just one Word file. The longer the file, the slower Word becomes when performing operations like searching and scrolling.

If you have a basic system (an 8088 chip with 512K or 640K of main memory), Word will perform sluggishly with a lengthy document, and you may run out of memory when you attempt such operations as sorting and searching. If you plan to create lengthy, multidivision documents frequently, consider upgrading your system by adding an expanded memory board that conforms to the Lotus-Intel-Microsoft specifications (Version 3.2 or later). Consider, too, using a system with the 80286 or 80386 processing chips.

Previewing Page Formatting

Print preView, a feature new to Word in Version 5, displays your document's pages one or two at a time, showing you aspects of page style formatting that you don't normally see. These aspects include several page style formats discussed in this chapter, such as margins, running heads, and page numbers.

Note: To use Print preView, you must install your printer by using the Print Options command. For more information, see the appendix.

To preview your document, do the following:

1. Choose the **P**rint pre**V**iew option. Alternatively, use the Ctrl-F9 shortcut. Word displays the page on which the cursor is positioned. If the cursor is on page 19 of your document, you see page 19 in the preview mode.

2. Press PgDn or PgUp to scroll through your document. Use the **J**ump option to jump to a specific page.

3. To leave the preview mode, choose the **E**xit command in the **P**rint pre**V**iew menu.

If you're not happy with the formatting you have seen, use the **F**ormat **D**ivision or **F**ormat **R**unning-head command and make corrections as necessary.

Chapter Summary

In this chapter, you took another step toward understanding the full capabilities of Word's formatting features. You learned how the Format Division command controls most aspects of page style formatting, including setting margins and page size, as well as setting new defaults for these formats. You also learned how to use this powerful command to turn on page numbering and specify page-number or running-head locations.

You also learned a few tricks of the trade, such as how to "outdent" text from the right margin, use mirror margins, add a gutter, prevent widowed headings, keep all the lines of a paragraph together on a page, divide your document into two divisions, and preview your page style formatting.

The next chapter helps you perfect your documents with Word's Thesaurus and with Spell, the spell-checking program. For more information on formatting documents, be sure to read Chapter 20, "Using Style Sheets."

6

Using the Thesaurus, Checking Spelling, and Controlling Hyphenation

One of Word's best features is its 220,000-word thesaurus. Seamlessly integrated with Word, Thesaurus opens the pages of a massive synonym dictionary at a keystroke. Simply place the cursor after a word that doesn't seem quite right, call up the Thesaurus, choose the synonym you want from the list, and Word makes the substitution automatically. As you quickly discover, the synonym lists are extensive and fascinating; it is no exaggeration to say that these lists, created by Microlytics, Inc. specifically for Thesaurus, are a distinguished scholarly achievement. Word uses the same computer-based thesaurus that motivated the normally cautious William F. Buckley, Jr., to declare that it had "changed his life." With Thesaurus, all the richness of the English language awaits you, just a keystroke away.

Until Version 5, the quality of Word's Thesaurus was not matched by Spell, which earned an unenviable reputation as one of the slowest and clumsiest spell checkers around. But all that is rectified in Word 5. Spell is now fully integrated with Word; your document no longer disappears when you use Spell, and the program runs lickety-split. Improvements in Spell, moreover, enable the program to catch errors other than spelling, such as nonstandard capitalization and repeated words (for example, "the the"). Spell is now up to the standards set by the rest of Microsoft Word.

Word 5 also includes an automatic hyphenation utility, which inserts optional hyphens in your document automatically. Optional hyphens appear only when needed to adjust line breaks. Although this utility isn't 100-percent accurate, it almost always breaks words in ways conforming to the strictures of style handbooks. If you plan to use multiple columns, right-margin justification, or proportional spacing, you may find it helpful to use automatic hyphenation to avoid unsightly gaps between words.

This chapter covers these utilities in detail. In this chapter, you learn how to do the following:

❑ Use Thesaurus to find the right word—or explore the many shades of meaning for a word

❑ Check your document's spelling and add correctly spelled words to the dictionary

❑ Modify the way Spell works to suit your writing practices and needs

❑ Create and use your own user and document dictionaries

❑ Hyphenate your document automatically

Finding the Right Word: Thesaurus

A wonderful aid for creative writers, Thesaurus enriches your writing by supplying synonyms for words that you highlight in your document. Because Thesaurus is organized by 15,000 root words, it's rare (uncommon, extraordinary, exceptional) to use Thesaurus and find no synonyms for the word you highlight. When you see a synonym list, you will be impressed by the range and depth; after all, 220,000 words are stored in this thesaurus, most of them cross-referenced in dozens or even hundreds of ways. Remember, though, that familiar words are almost always clearer, and more meaningful, than exotic ones.

Thesaurus is also useful for more practical purposes. When you're writing a business letter, for instance, being as clear as you can is important—often, being clear means finding the simplest word. If you write "Please send the parcel in an expeditious fashion," think twice: that sentence doesn't motivate action, it puts people to sleep! A little work with Thesaurus persuades you to say, "Please send the parcel quickly."

Use Thesaurus, too, to make sure that you grasp the full meaning of a word—particularly its connotations. Suppose, for instance, that you write a letter with the following sentence: "Thank you for your trenchant criticism of our presentation. We need to hear from our customers to improve our services!" *Trenchant*, as you quickly discover with Thesaurus, isn't the right word: its synonyms include *caustic*, *cutting*, *vulgar*, and *obscene*. Obviously, "trenchant" isn't the best word to describe friendly constructive criticism; or more to the point, even if the criticism *was* caustic, your job in a business letter of this sort is to redefine the situation so that the unfriendly criticism is interpreted as friendly and constructive. It's better to say, "Thank you for your helpful criticism."

There's still no substitute for a dictionary, but a good thesaurus—like Word's—can deepen your grasp of a word's meaning in ways that no dictionary can. If you use an unfamiliar word whose meaning and range of connotations aren't completely clear to you, use Thesaurus to make sure that you're not alluding to connotations you don't want.

Looking Up Synonyms

If you use Word on a system with two floppy drives, you must insert the Thesaurus disk when prompted to do so. If you use a hard drive, be sure to install Thesaurus in the directory that contains Word. For more information on installing Word, see the Appendix.

To look up a word in Thesaurus, do the following:

Ctrl-F6

1. Press F8 or click the right mouse button to highlight the word you want to look up (see fig. 6.1).

2. Choose the **L**ibrary th**E**saurus command. Alternatively, use the Ctrl-F6 keyboard shortcut.

If Thesaurus doesn't list synonyms for the word you chose, the program checks to see whether the word is listed in another form. If you highlight *officiously*, for instance, and call up Thesaurus, you see synonyms for *officious*.

If Thesaurus cannot find the word or any of its roots, you see the message, The word was not found. Please choose another word to look up. A list of 30 words closest in spelling to the word you highlighted then appears. Use the arrow keys to highlight another word in the list, or press Esc.

3. When the Thesaurus window appears (see fig. 6.2), use the arrow keys to highlight the word you want from the list.

4. Press Enter to insert the word you have highlighted into your document. (Mouse users: point to the synonym you want and click the right button.) Word makes the substitution automatically. Alternatively, press Esc to leave Thesaurus without making a change.

Fig. 6.1.

Highlighting the word to look up in Thesaurus.

```
2 L[········1·········2·········3·········4·········5·········]·········7····
  ¶
  Arthur J. Stone¶
  Stone Construction Co.¶
  14787 Southwest Highway¶
  Central City, VA 22887¶
  ¶
  Dear Mr. Stone:¶
  ¶
  Thanks for your letter of January 14, and particularly,
  thanks for your trenchant criticism of our presentation to
  your employees two weeks ago.  We need to hear from our
  customers if we hope to improve our services!  ◆




                                              ┌─LETTER.DOC─┐
  Pg1 Co26          {1}            ?              2M       Microsoft Word
```

Fig. 6.2.

Synonyms for the highlighted word.

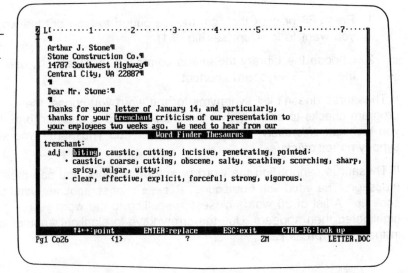

```
2 L[········1·········2·········3·········4·········5·········]·········7····
  ¶
  Arthur J. Stone¶
  Stone Construction Co.¶
  14787 Southwest Highway¶
  Central City, VA 22887¶
  ¶
  Dear Mr. Stone:¶
  ¶
  Thanks for your letter of January 14, and particularly,
  thanks for your trenchant criticism of our presentation to
  your employees two weeks ago.  We need to hear from our
  ├────────────────────── Word Finder Thesaurus ──────────────────────┤
  trenchant:
  adj • biting, caustic, cutting, incisive, penetrating, pointed;
       • caustic, coarse, cutting, obscene, salty, scathing, scorching, sharp,
         spicy, vulgar, witty;
       • clear, effective, explicit, forceful, strong, vigorous.




  ├─────── ↑↓←→:point ────── ENTER:replace ───── ESC:exit ────── CTRL-F6:look up ───────┤
  Pg1 Co26          {1}            ?              2M            LETTER.DOC
```

If you have just typed a word and want to look up its synonyms, don't bother selecting it. Just press Ctrl-F6. In such situations, Word always looks up the first word to the left of the cursor, ignoring punctuation and spaces.

Looking Up Synonyms of Synonyms

When the Thesaurus window is open, you can look up synonyms of any of the words displayed. You also can type a word and see synonyms of it. **Warning:** This feature is addictive. When you use it, you set off on a voyage through the interconnections of the English language—and, to the extent you have internalized these interconnections by learning English, you journey through your own mind's pathways.

To see synonyms of words in a Thesaurus list, do the following:

1. Open Thesaurus by highlighting a word and pressing Ctrl-F6.

2. Highlight a word in the synonym list.

3. Press Ctrl-F6 again. (Mouse users: click the words `Ctrl-F6:look up` on the Thesaurus window's bottom border.)

4. When the new synonym list appears, choose a synonym. Press Enter (or click the right button) to insert the word in your document. Alternatively, press Ctrl-F6 to see more synonyms.

You can continue viewing synonyms of synonyms indefinitely. To see the preceding list of synonyms, press Ctrl-PgUp or click the words `Ctrl-PgUp:last word` on the bottom border of the window.

To type in the Thesaurus window a word for which you want to see synonyms, do the following:

1. With the Thesaurus window open, type the first letter of the word you want to look up.

2. When the Look Up window appears (see fig. 6.3), type the rest of the word (see fig. 6.4).

3. Press Enter. Thesaurus displays a synonym list for the word you typed.

Fig. 6.3.

The Thesaurus
Look Up window.

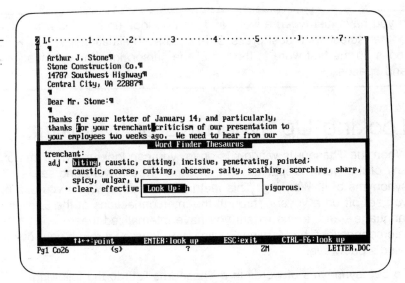

Fig. 6.4.

Typing a word to
look up in
Thesaurus.

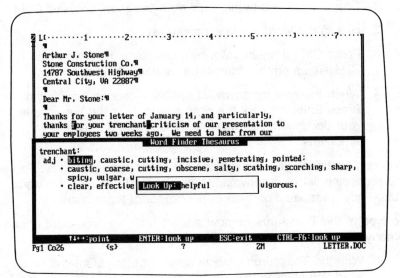

Checking Spelling: Spell

New to Version 5 of Word is a much-improved Spell, formerly the bane
of Word users for its sluggish performance and inflexibility. In those
days, Spell was little more than an awkward add-on program; when
you used Spell, Word saved your document, cleared the screen

(panicking novice users, who exclaimed, "Whoa! Where's my work?"), spent inordinate amounts of time loading this and loading that, and then—seemingly hours later—presented you with an enormous list of unknown words. Horrendous. Many Word users found themselves buying add-on, memory-resident spell checkers to overcome this deficiency—others gave up and bought WordPerfect. (Fans of the business scene, note: here's a key chapter in the tale entitled, "How to cripple an otherwise superior product and lose market leadership.")

The new Spell splits the screen, leaving your document in view, and immediately begins checking from the cursor location to the end of the document. (You can check the whole document, if you want, by pressing Ctrl-PgUp before using Spell, or you can check just selected text.) When Spell finds a word it cannot match in its dictionaries, the program tries to find the correct spelling. Spell then displays a list of all the words closest to the misspelled word. If the correct spelling is in the list, correcting the word is as simple as choosing the correct spelling from the list displayed. If Spell cannot find any words close to the misspelled word, or if none of the words Spell finds to replace the misspelled word is correct, you can type the correct spelling on the Correct line. Spell makes corrections as you go, which means that you can exit at any time without losing your changes. All this is good news indeed for Word veterans!

If you use Word on a system with two floppy drives, you must insert the Spell disk when prompted to do so.

If you use Word on a system with a hard drive, you should ordinarily install Spell in the same directory as the one in which Word is installed. If you place Spell elsewhere, type the directory path name and file name in the **speller path** field of the Options command menu. For more information, see the Appendix.

Checking Spelling

To check the spelling of a document by using the keyboard, do the following:

Alt-F6

1. Position the cursor where you want to begin spell checking or select the text you want checked.

To check the entire document, press Ctrl-PgUp to position the cursor at the beginning of the file. To check a selection, highlight the text you want to check. You can select a single word, if you want.

2. Choose the **L**ibrary **S**pell command. Alternatively, use the Alt-F6 keyboard shortcut.

   Spell begins checking the document or the selection immediately. Users of previous versions of Word will be delighted to learn that it's no longer necessary to choose the Proof command after the Spell menu appears.

   When Spell finds a word it cannot match with the correctly spelled words in its dictionary, the message Not found appears, and Spell tries to locate the correct spelling automatically. If Spell finds a list of potentially correct spellings, it displays them (see fig. 6.5).

3. To correct the misspelled word, highlight the correctly spelled word in the generated list and press Enter. If Spell cannot find the word's correct spelling, choose the **C**orrect command and type the correct spelling in the **Correct** command field. To leave the word as it is, just choose the Ignore command.

If you want Spell to make the correction for this error automatically in future spell-checking sessions, choose the **Y**es option in the **remember correction** field. The next time you run Spell, the program will automatically make the correction you just made if the same error is found. Choose this option to fix errors you tend to make repeatedly, like leaving out an *r* in *occurred.*

If you type a correction, Spell tries to check the correction you type against its dictionaries. If it cannot find a match, this message appears: Word not in dictionary. Enter Y to confirm, N to retype, or Esc to cancel. (Don't let this message concern you; it appears frequently when you correct proper nouns or jargon.) If you're sure that you have spelled the word correctly, press Y.

4. If you make a mistake or want to type the correction over again, choose **U**ndo from the **S**pell command menu immediately after making the change.

5. When Spell comes to the end of the document, this message appears: Enter Y to continue checking spelling from the top of the document, N to exit, or Esc to cancel. Press Y if you want Spell to check the rest of the document.

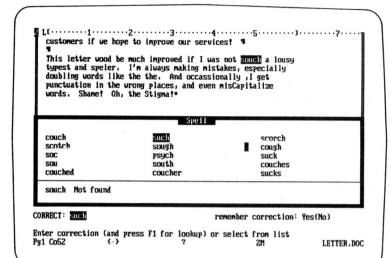

Fig. 6.5.

A list of possible corrections generated by Spell.

![Caution icon] **Caution:** Like all computer spell checkers, Spell doesn't actually check spelling. It tries to match the words in your document with its "dictionaries," which are merely lists of correctly spelled words. This means that the following are true:

❑ Spell questions some words even though you spell them correctly; examples include proper nouns (names of people and places), possessives of familiar words (cat's, organizations'), and jargon (processual, hyperdynamic).

❑ Spell fails to detect an error if the error is a correctly spelled word (for example, the letter in figure 6.5 contains *wood*, a correctly spelled word, instead of *would*).

To check spelling using the mouse, do the following:

1. Position the cursor where you want to begin spell checking or select the text you want checked.

   To check the entire document, press Ctrl-PgUp to position the cursor at the beginning of the file. To check a selection, highlight the text you want to check. You can select a single word, if you want.

2. Click the **Library S**pell command. Alternatively, use the Alt-F6 keyboard shortcut.

Spell begins checking the document or the selection immediately. Users of previous versions of Word will be delighted to learn that it's no longer necessary to choose the **P**roof command after the Spell menu appears.

When Spell finds a word it cannot match with the correctly spelled words in its dictionary, the message Not found appears and Spell tries to locate the correct spelling automatically. If Spell finds a list of potentially correct spellings, it displays them (see fig. 6.5).

3. To correct the misspelled word, point to the correctly spelled word in the generated list and click the right button. If Spell cannot find the word's correct spelling, click the **C**orrect command and type the correct spelling in the **Correct** command field. To leave the word as it is, just click the **I**gnore command.

   If you want Spell to make this correction automatically for the rest of the document or the selection, click the **Y**es option in the **remember correction** field. Click this option, for instance, if you discover that you consistently misspelled a place name or person's name and want to make the correction through your document.

   If you type a correction, Spell tries to check the correction you type against its dictionaries. If it cannot find a match, this message appears: Word not in dictionary. Enter Y to confirm, N to retype, or Esc to cancel. (Don't let this message concern you; it appears frequently when you correct proper nouns or jargon.) If you're sure that you have spelled the word correctly, press Y.

4. If you make a mistake or want to type the correction over again, click **U**ndo from the **S**pell command menu immediately after making the change.

5. If you started Spell anywhere besides the beginning of your document, you see this message when Spell reaches the end of the document: Enter Y to continue checking spelling from the top of the document, N to exit, or Esc to cancel. Press Y if you want your whole document checked.

Editing Your Document While Checking Spelling

Sometimes you cannot fix a spelling mistake by retyping just one word; the whole phrase is wrong. In figure 6.5, for example, the improperly capitalized word, *misCapitalize*, isn't just improperly capitalized; it is also a neologism and ought to be banished from the letter. Doing so, however, isn't possible by just typing a new word. The whole sentence must be rewritten so that the final phrase reads "and even capitalize words improperly." Fixing an error like this one is easy with Word 5's much-improved Spell. Just choose the Exit command to leave Spell, and then edit your document (the program saves the changes you already made). Then choose Spell again; spell-checking resumes from the cursor's location.

Correcting Errors Other than Spelling Errors

A spiffy new feature of Spell in Version 5 is its ability to catch several types of errors other than spelling errors, including some kinds of improper punctuation (see fig. 6.6) and improper capitalization (see fig. 6.7). If Spell detects errors of these types in your document, just choose Correct, and Spell makes the changes automatically.

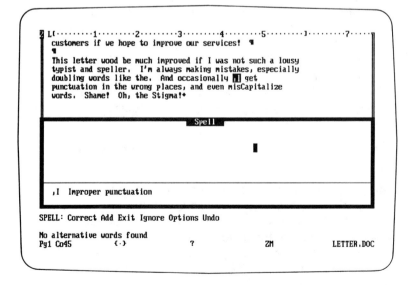

Fig. 6.6.

Spell detects improper punctuation in a document.

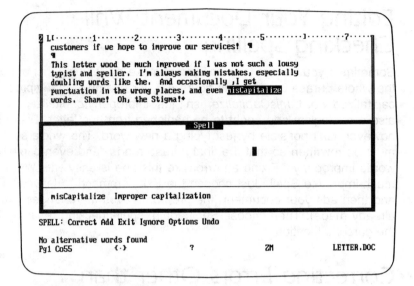

Fig. 6.7.

Spell detects improper capitalization in a document.

Adding Unknown Words to the Dictionary

Spell's dictionary contains more than 120,000 words. Among these words are many common place names (including Charlottesville, Washington, and Virginia, but not Crozet or Uppsala), and common personal names (such as Smith, Jones, Sue, Tom, and Ed, but not Suzanne or Javier). In addition, Spell's dictionary—although copious—doesn't contain technical terms related to professional or scientific specialties. If you write business letters using many proper nouns, or scientific or professional reports or articles using many technical terms, you may want to add correctly spelled words to one of Word's three dictionaries. After you add these words, Spell won't flag them as potential errors, and the program checks spelling much more quickly.

When you add words, you can add them to any of the following three different dictionaries:

❏ Standard dictionary. Spell always uses the words in this dictionary when it checks your spelling. Add words to this dictionary if they're likely to appear in many or most of the documents you create. Examples include your name, your street, your city (if it's not already in Spell's dictionary), and names of coworkers.

Note: The Standard dictionary isn't the same as Spell's own dictionary, contained in a special, nondocument file (SPELL-AM.LEX). The words you add to the standard dictionary go into a file called UPDAT-AM.CMP. This file is an ordinary document file. If you accidentally add an incorrectly spelled word to the standard dictionary, therefore, you can undo the damage by simply editing UPDAT-AM.CMP.

❑ Document dictionary. This dictionary is stored with the document whose spelling you're checking. Spell consults this dictionary only when you recheck this particular document. Choose this dictionary to store correctly spelled words you're not likely to use in any other document.

❑ User dictionary. In addition to checking SPELL-AM.CMP and the standard dictionary (UPDAT-AM.CMP), Spell also checks the user dictionary. By default, this dictionary file name is SPECIALS.CMP. Adding words to the default user dictionary isn't much different from adding words to the standard dictionary, because Spell checks the default user dictionary every time you use the program. You can, however, create a new user dictionary and give it a distinctive name. If you do, Spell does not use the new user dictionary unless you specifically tell it to do so by naming the dictionary in the Options menu of the Library Spell command. Use a distinctively named user dictionary to store words that you use for certain documents (but not for others). If more than one person uses Word on your system, create user dictionaries for each user.

Caution: There's no limit to the number of words you can add to these dictionaries. Because they're stored in ordinary document formats, however, lengthy word lists slow Spell down. (Spell's own dictionary, SPELL-AM.LEX, is stored in a special file format for super-fast retrieval.)

Adding Words to the Dictionaries

To add correctly spelled words to the standard or document dictionaries, do the following:

1. When Spell reports that a correctly spelled word isn't in its dictionary, choose the **A**dd command.

2. When the Add menu appears, choose **S**tandard to add the word to the standard dictionary, or **D**ocument to add the word to the document dictionary.

To create a user dictionary and add words to it, do the following:

1. Start Spell by selecting the **L**ibrary **S**pell command. When the Spell menu appears, choose the **O**ptions command in the **S**pell menu.

2. When the command menu appears, type a new user dictionary name in the **user dictionary** field.

3. Carry out the command by pressing Enter or clicking the command name. Press Y to confirm creating the new user dictionary.

4. To add words to the user dictionary you've just created, continue checking your spelling. When Spell flags a word you want to add, use the **A**dd command and choose the **U**ser option.

The new user dictionary's name must have the extension CMP. Be sure to choose a name that describes the dictionary's contents. If the dictionary contains legal terms, use a file name like LEGAL.CMP. If the dictionary contains Karen's additions, name it KAREN.CMP.

Word saves as the new default the choices you make in the **user dictionary** field, so Spell uses the specified dictionary the next time you check spelling. To switch user dictionaries, start Spell and choose the Spell Options command again. Type the name of the dictionary you want to use in the **user dictionary** field.

To speed Spell's operation, choose **M**anual in the **alternatives** field of the **S**pell **O**ptions menu. Word does not look up the correct spelling until you use the Correct command.

Other Spell Options

You can choose other options in the Spell Options menu to control the way Spell works. If you check a document likely to contain nonstandard punctuation, such as a program file, choose the **No** option in the **check punctuation** field. If your document contains nonstandard capitalization, such as acronyms or command names, choose the **Yes** option in the **ignore all caps** field.

Hyphenating Your Document: Hyphenate

If you plan to create multiple-column text (see Chapter 19), you find that narrow columns produce unsightly effects—especially if you justify the right margins (see fig. 6.8). The only way to correct this problem is to hyphenate your document. The job could be tedious if you had to do it manually. But Word's Library Hyphenate command can do the job for you automatically. If you want, you can confirm each hyphen's placement before Word makes the insertion.

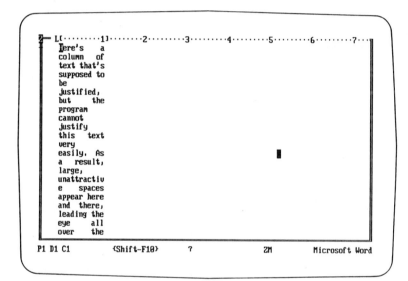

Fig. 6.8.

The effect of no hyphenation on a multiple-column document.

To hyphenate your document without confirming the insertion of hyphens, do the following:

1. Select the text you want to hyphenate.

   To hyphenate the whole document, press Ctrl-Pgup to move the cursor to the top of the document.

2. Choose the **L**ibrary **H**yphenate command. When the Library Hyphenate command appears (see fig. 6.9), carry out the command by pressing Enter or clicking the command name.

Word inserts optional hyphens automatically at every possible location. By no means will all words be hyphenated; Word's hyphenation dictionary contains only an abbreviated dictionary. The optional hyphens will affect line breaks only if using them would even out lines.

If you choose **No** in the **confirm** field, watch out for two-letter prefixes (such as "de-" or "re-") at the ends of lines. Unfortunately, Word will hyphenate this way.

Fig. 6.9.

The Library Hyphenate command for automatic insertion.

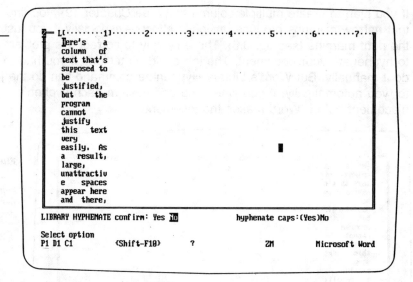

To remove all the hyphens Word has inserted automatically, choose the **U**ndo command immediately after using the **L**ibrary **H**yphenate command. If you add text or choose another command, Undo won't remove the hyphen.

If you set very narrow margins for your document, you may have to manually insert additional optional hyphens to improve the margins. To insert optional hyphens manually, position the cursor at an appropriate point in the word and press Ctrl-hyphen.

To confirm or modify each hyphen's placement, do the following:

1. Select the text you want to hyphenate.

   To hyphenate the whole document, press Ctrl-Pgup to move the cursor to the top of the document.

2. Choose the **L**ibrary **H**yphenate command. When the Library Hyphenate command appears (see fig. 6.10), choose the **Y**es option in the **confirm** field.

3. Carry out the command by pressing Enter or clicking the command name.

Before Word inserts hyphens, the program displays the message `Enter Y to insert hyphen`, `N to skip word`, `or use direction keys to reposition` (again see fig. 6.10). To reposition the hyphen, press the up- or down-arrow keys to move to the preceding or next positions in the word that Word has identified as a potential breaking point. To reposition the break manually, use the left or right arrow keys.

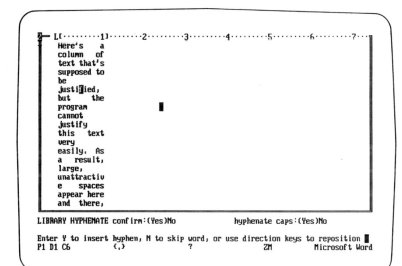

Fig. 6.10.

The Library Hyphenate command for confirmed insertion.

Chapter Summary

In Word 5, the excellence of Thesaurus is finally matched by Spell, for years the forgotten stepchild of Word's world. Use Thesaurus at every opportunity; it's useful for practical applications as well as creative writing. Use it to make sure that you grasp all the connotations of words with which you're not completely familiar. Spell checking is, of course, a necessity for business and professional writing, and you will be pleased to find how easy this much-improved version is to use. Be sure to do a final, manual proofreading before sending the document to your boss, a funding agency, or an important customer! If you create documents with narrow columns, Word's Hyphenate utility can help make the column margins more professional looking.

7

Printing Your Work

Word 5's printing features are flexible and easy to use. In most cases, printing your work is as simple as choosing options in the Print Options command menu and then using the Print Printer command. Word prints the document displayed on the screen. If you prefer, you can preview your document's formatting and page breaks before printing.

This chapter assumes that you have installed your printer, using the SETUP program (see the Appendix, "Word and Your Computer"), and that your printer is connected to your computer and working properly. In this chapter, you learn to do the following:

❏ Preview document formatting and page breaks

❏ Choose printing options, such as graphics resolution, number of copies, and draft printing

❏ Print your document with the Print Printer command

❏ Use other printing strategies, such as printing directly and printing to a file

❏ Get the most out of your laser printer

❏ Solve common printer problems

About the Print Command

Word's Print command brings up a submenu (see fig. 7.1) with nine options. Following is a brief overview of these options.

Option	Description
Printer	Starts printing the document in the active window, using the choices made in the Options command menu
Direct	Sends keystrokes directly to the printer
File	Prints document to a file
Glossary	Prints the contents of the active glossary file
Merge	Prints multiple copies of a document, using information drawn from a list, such as a mailing list
Options	Displays a menu from which you can choose several printing options, such as multiple copies or graphics resolution
Queue	Starts a mode in which you can continue to type and edit while printing goes on in the background
Repaginate	Previews and adjusts page breaks
preView	Previews formatting

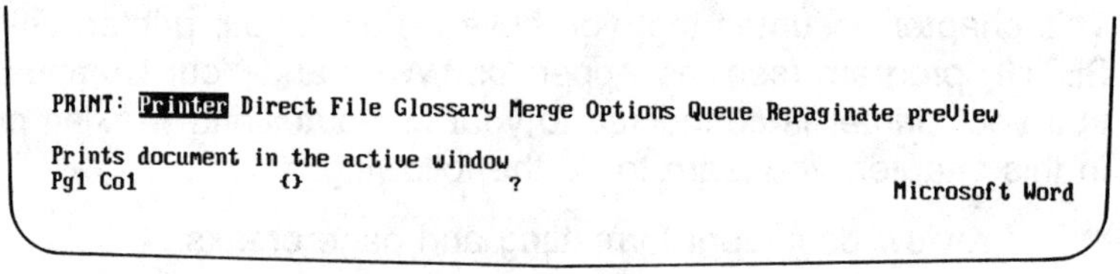

Fig. 7.1.

The Print command submenu.

```
PRINT: Printer Direct File Glossary Merge Options Queue Repaginate preView

Prints document in the active window
Pg1 Co1              {}              ?                    Microsoft Word
```

Getting Ready To Print: Previewing Formatting and Page Breaks

You do not have to preview your document's formatting and page breaks before printing but you can save money if you do—particularly if you own a laser printer. Toner cartridges are expensive! Why print a 35-page document, only to find that you haven't used the Format Running-head command on your running head text, or that a bad page break is on page 3? The next sections explain how you can preview the formatting and page breaks of your document before you print it.

Previewing Formatting

New to Word 5 is the Print preView command, already introduced in Chapters 4 and 5. Use Print preView to check document formats before you print. You can see margins, running heads, page numbers, character formatting, and paragraph formatting with this command. If you find a problem, note the page number on which it occurs, choose Exit to return to your document, and use Jump Page to scroll directly to the page with the problem.

A Print preView Checklist

As you preview your document in Print preView, use this checklist to make sure that everything is as you formatted it:

❑ Do the running heads appear in the top or bottom margin? If not, you probably forgot to use the Format Running-head command to format headers or footers.

❑ Are there no page numbers, even though you wanted them? If not, return to your document and choose the **Yes** option in the Format Division Page-numbers command menu. If you entered page numbers in a running head, remember that you must insert the page number slug from the glossary by using the Insert command. You cannot just type *(page)* as ordinary text. (See Chapter 4 for more information about including page numbers in running heads.)

❑ Do paragraphs appear appropriately spaced? If you're printing a single-spaced document, you may find that the document looks more attractive if a blank line appears between paragraphs. To insert a blank line, return to your document, select all the text paragraphs, and press Alt-O.

❑ If you're printing a letter, does it look balanced on the page? A letter should be positioned vertically on the page so that the text's center point is slightly above the center of the page. If the text is too high, return to your document, position the cursor under the letterhead, and press Enter several times. Make the margins wider (1.5 inch left and right) if the letter is brief; make the margins narrower (1.0 inch) if the letter is lengthy.

❏ Did you use character emphasis consistently? Have you switched from italic to underlining? To make your emphasis consistent, return to your document, and choose the **Format** rep**L**ace **C**haracter or **F**ormat rep**L**ace **P**aragraph command to make global changes.

❏ If you use a nonstandard font or font size, are there sections of your document where Word has inserted the normal font or font size against your wishes? Remember that pressing Alt-space bar cancels all special character formatting, including fonts and font sizes. If you write a document with the Helvetica 10 font, and then press Alt-space bar, Word returns to Courier 12. (You cannot see font changes in Print preView, unfortunately, but you can see font size changes.) Return to your document, select the inappropriately formatted text, and use the **F**ormat **C**haracter command to change the font.

❏ Does a heading appear at the bottom of a page? If so, return to your document, select the heading, and choose the **Yes** option in the **keep follow** field of the Format Paragraph command. (Make sure that the blank lines under the heading are entered with measurements in the **space after** field of the Format Paragraph command, not with Enter keystrokes.)

You can preview page breaks with Print preView, but the recommended way is to do so with the Print Repaginate command. Print Repaginate not only previews the page breaks but provides tools to adjust their placement.

If you don't see any problems with your document, you can print directly from the Print preView menu by choosing the Print option in the Print preView menu. Word uses the options currently chosen in the Print Options command menu (for more information on Print Options, see the section entitled "Choosing Printing Options" later in this chapter).

If you have a full-page monitor (a monitor that displays a full 66 lines of text), choose the **1**-page option in the **display** field of the **P**rint preView **O**ptions command. If you format your document with different running heads on odd and even pages, choose the **F**acing-pages option in the same command menu so that you can check placement and balance of these elements.

Previewing and Adjusting Page Breaks

Sure signs of hasty word processing are found in bad page breaks: headings positioned by themselves at the bottoms of pages, tables broken over two pages, chapters starting halfway down an even-numbered page. Experienced writers know that it pays to preview page breaks before printing, and Word makes that process easy. If you choose the **Y**es option in the **confirm page breaks** field of the Print Repaginate command, Word takes you through your document one page at a time, giving you the opportunity to adjust the page breaks if you want. Print Repaginate also displays line breaks the way they look when the document is printed.

Because Word 5 can display page breaks actively on the screen, you aren't required to use the Print Repaginate command to see where Word places page breaks—you can simply scroll through your document to preview the page breaks. (If you don't see the automatic page breaks on your screen as you write and edit, choose the **A**uto option in the **paginate** field of the Options command menu.) However, using Print Repaginate is faster and easier than searching for page breaks manually. This command hunts down all the page breaks for you automatically, so save your eyes!

To preview page breaks with **P**rint **R**epaginate, do the following:

1. Choose the **Y**es option in the **confirm page breaks** field of the Print Repaginate command menu (see fig. 7.2). Word scrolls to the document's first page break and displays the message, Enter Y to confirm page break or use direction keys to reposition.

2. Press Y to accept the page break, or press the up-arrow key to reposition the break at a better location and press Y. You can only move a page break *up* from its proposed position.

3. Continue previewing page breaks until you reach the end of the document.

If you entered any manual page breaks using Ctrl-Shift-Enter, Word highlights the break and displays the message, Enter Y to confirm or R to remove. In most cases, remove the manual page break unless you see a good reason to retain it.

 Caution: If you press Esc to cancel the Print Repaginate command before reaching the end of your document, Word discards all the breaks you reposition.

Fig. 7.2.

Confirming page
breaks with the
Print Repaginate
command.

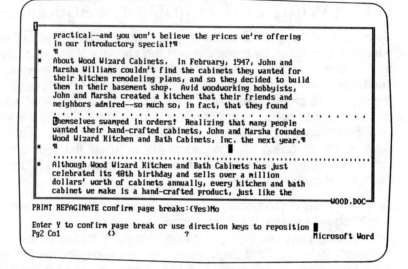

After you use Print Repaginate, Word returns to the Print command's
submenu. To print your document, choose **P**rinter from the submenu.

Choosing Printing Options

Use the Print Options command menu (shown in fig. 7.3) to choose
special printing options: multiple copies, manual or continuous paper
feed, ranges of pages, draft copies, double-sided printing, graphics
resolution, and background printing. Each of these options is explained
in the following sections.

The Print Options command also is used to identify your printer and
route the printing signal from your computer to your printer. For more
information on these functions, see the Appendix.

Printing Multiple Copies of
a Document

To print multiple copies of a document, do the following:

1. Choose the **P**rint **O**ptions command.

2. Type the number of copies you want in the **copies** command
   field. The default for this option is 1.

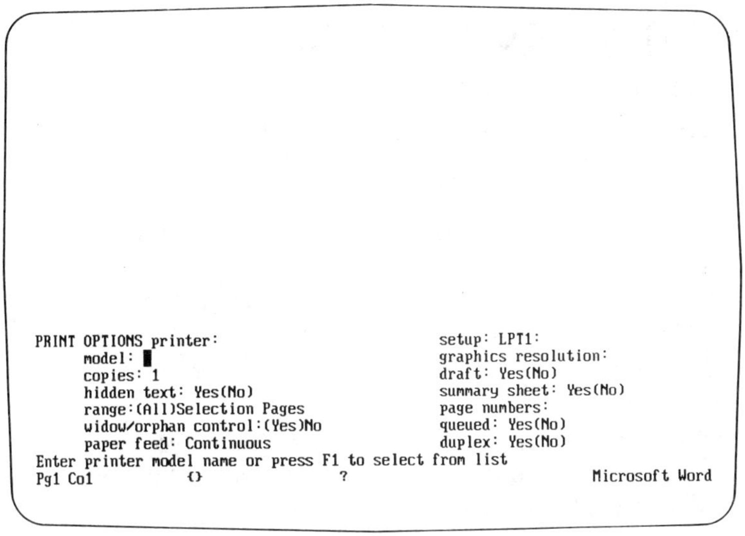

Fig 7.3.

The Print Options command menu.

```
PRINT OPTIONS printer:                   setup: LPT1:
       model: ▉                          graphics resolution:
       copies: 1                         draft: Yes(No)
       hidden text: Yes(No)              summary sheet: Yes(No)
       range:(All)Selection Pages        page numbers:
       widow/orphan control:(Yes)No      queued: Yes(No)
       paper feed: Continuous            duplex: Yes(No)
Enter printer model name or press F1 to select from list
Pg1 Col          {}              ?                    Microsoft Word
```

3. Carry out the command by pressing Enter or clicking the command name.

Caution: Word does not save the choice you make in the **copies** field when you quit Word. The selection remains in effect as long as you are in the editing session. If you print a second document in the same session but want only one copy of it, be sure to use the Print Options command again and reset the default value.

Choosing Manual or Continuous Paper Feed

If your printer has a sheet feeder or can use tractor-fed continuous paper, type *continuous* in the **paper feed** field of the Print Options menu. To insert sheets manually before Word prints a page, type *manual*. If you choose the manual option, Word pauses to give you time to insert the sheet before printing the page.

Note: Some printers have additional feed options, such as multiple paper bins or a special envelope feeder. Word controls these features if your printer has them. To see a list of the options available for your printer, select the **paper feed** field and press F1. Choose the **paper feed** option you want and press Enter.

Printing a Range of Pages

To print a range of pages, do the following:

1. Choose the **P**rint **O**ptions command.

2. Choose the **P**ages option in the **range** field.

3. Type the page numbers you want to print in the **page numbers** field.

You can print individual pages by separating each page number with a comma (for example, *8,15,27*). You can type a range of pages using a hyphen (*8-27*) or colon (*8:27*). You can also type a range and individual pages (for example, *8-27,32,68*).

If you divided your document into two or more divisions, you must specify the page number and the division number, giving the page number first (for example, *8D2-27D2,32D3,68D4*).

4. Carry out the command by pressing Enter or clicking the command name.

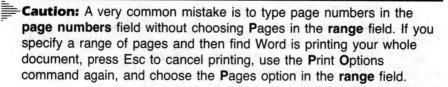

Caution: A very common mistake is to type page numbers in the **page numbers** field without choosing **P**ages in the **range** field. If you specify a range of pages and then find Word is printing your whole document, press Esc to cancel printing, use the **P**rint **O**ptions command again, and choose the **P**ages option in the **range** field.

Printing a Draft

Choose the **Y**es option in the **draft** field of the **P**rint **O**ptions command to print a draft of your document without graphics or justification. Printing speed is enhanced when you select this option.

Choosing Graphics Resolution

Laser printers can print at several different levels of *graphics resolution*, a term referring to the density of the printing. Graphics resolution is measured in dots per inch (dpi). If your printer can print graphics at different resolutions, you can choose the resolution you want. The Hewlett-Packard LaserJet, for instance, can print at resolutions of 75 dpi, 150 dpi, and 300 dpi. Chose the lower resolutions for fast draft printing; choose the highest for the final draft.

Note: Some printers require additional memory to print graphics at 300 dpi.

To change the graphics resolution, do the following:

1. Choose the **P**rint **O**ptions command.

   Make sure that you have selected a printer in the **printer** command field.

2. Select the **graphics resolution** field and press F1.

3. Choose the desired resolution from the list Word displays and press Enter.

Controlling Widows and Orphans

By default, Word suppresses widows (a *widow*, in typesetting parlance, is the last line of a paragraph when it appears alone at the top of the page) and *orphans* (the first line of a paragraph when it appears by itself at the end of a page).

Professional document designers consider widows and orphans to be flaws, but you may want to turn Word's widow and orphan control off in some cases. When you're creating a multiple-column newsletter, for instance, you probably want both columns to have exactly the same number of lines; otherwise, the columns will look uneven at the tops and bottoms. To turn off widow/orphan control, select **No** in the **widow/orphan control** field on the Print Options command menu.

Using Background Printing

You can edit or write while printing with Word when you choose **Y**es in the **queued** field of the Print Options command menu. After you choose this option, Word acts differently when you choose the **P**rint **P**rinter command. Instead of tying up your screen while your document prints, Word formats the document and then returns the screen to your control while the program sends signals to the printer. Once queued printing has started, you can use the **P**rint **Q**ueue command to pause or restart printing. For more information on the Print Queue command, see "More about Queued Printing," later in this chapter.

Caution: Most users find queued printing unsatisfactory; it slows your computer to a crawl. If your time constraints are such that you really must write as you print, consider buying a printer buffer, a memory device placed between your computer and printer. A printer buffer takes the signal from your computer, stores it, and sends it on to your printer. As far as your computer is concerned, the buffer is a super-fast printer, so your computer sends the print signals at the highest possible rate.

Creating a Document to be Printed on Another System

This chapter assumes that you have installed your printer and named it in the **printer** and **model** fields of the Print Options command menu. Nothing stops you, however, from naming a different printer in these fields—even if that printer isn't directly connected to your computer. To name a printer that isn't directly connected to your computer, go to the DOS prompt:

1. Insert the Word Utilities Disk #1 into the disk drive and type *SETUP.*

2. Choose the **P** option to install the additional printer you want to use.

After you run SETUP, you will find in Word's directory two printer description files: the file for the printer you chose when you first ran SETUP and the file for the printer you just added. From now on, you can choose between these two printers by using the Print Options command.

You may want to name a different printer in this field if you're working at home but want to print your document at work on the boss's fancy laser printer. Once you specify the name and model of the printer in the Print Options command menu, save your document to a floppy disk. Then take the floppy disk to the computer connected to the fancy printer, start Word on that system, and print your document.

Word saves the choices you make in the **printer** and **name** fields when you choose Quit. The next time you use your system, be sure that you change the settings in these fields to be appropriate for your printer.

Other Print Options

You can choose additional options in the Print Options menu. These options are described briefly in the following list:

❏ Choose **Yes** in the **hidden text** field to print hidden text, whether or not the text is visible on the screen. For more information about hidden text, see Chapter 4, "Word 5 Formatting Strategies: Character and Paragraphs."

❏ Choose **Ye**s in the **summary sheet** field to print your document's summary sheet. You fill out the summary sheet when you save a new document with Word. This sheet is printed on a separate page at the end of the document.

❏ Choose **S**election in the **range** field to print the text selected on the screen.

❏ If your printer is capable of printing on both sides of the page, choose **Ye**s in the **duplex** field to choose double-sided printing.

Saving Your Choices in the Print Options Menu

Table 7.1 shows which options in the Print Options command menu are saved—and which ones aren't—when you quit Word. The options Word saves are in effect the next time you use the program. The options Word doesn't save remain in effect through the Word session, even if you clear the screen and load a new document.

Table 7.1
How Word Stores Your Print Options Choices

Option	Description of Option
Options not saved when you quit Word	
copies	Chooses multiple copies
graphics resolution	Chooses resolution of graphics
page numbers	Prints range of pages
queued	Prints while editing
range	Prints range or selection
summary sheet	Prints summary sheet
Options saved when you quit Word	
draft	Omits graphics and justification
duplex	Prints on both sides of page
hidden text	Prints hidden text

Table 7.1—Continued

Option	Description of Option
model	Specifies printer model
paper feed	Specifies manual or continuous feed
printer	Specifies printer brand
setup	Specifies printer port (serial or parallel)
widow/orphan control	Toggles control on/off

Ctrl-F8

Printing Your Document

Printing your document with Word is simple. Once you choose the options you want with the **P**rint **O**ptions command, use the **P**rint **P**rinter command to start printing. Alternatively, use the Ctrl-F8 shortcut.

You can use more complicated printing strategies, if you want. You can interrupt queued printing so that you regain your computer's full speed. You can chain documents together with the INCLUDE command so that the documents have continuous pagination. You can print directly from the keyboard, and you can print to a file.

Each of these approaches to printing is described in the following sections.

More about Queued Printing

If you choose **Y**es in the **queued** field of the Print Options command menu, your document prints in the background, allowing you to write and edit as the printer works. You will find, however, that your computer slows down considerably. For this reason, you may want to use the **P**rint **Q**ueue command to interrupt background printing so that you can use your computer at full speed for a time. You can continue the printing later.

To interrupt queued printing, use the **P**rint **Q**ueue command and select **P**ause. To resume printing, use the **P**rint **Q**ueue command again, but this time choose the **C**ontinue option. To restart the printing from page 1, choose **P**rint **Q**ueue **R**estart. To stop queued printing, choose **P**rint **Q**ueue **S**top.

Caution: You cannot use the Print Queue command to begin printing a document in the background. To start queued printing, choose **Yes** in the **queued** field of the Print Options command menu. Then choose the **Print Printer** command.

You can use queued printing to print several files at once. The best way to print multiple files is to use the **Library Document-retrieval Print** command. For more information, see Chapter 8, "Finding and Managing Documents."

Chaining Documents for Continuous Printing and Pagination

If your system is slow or has limited disk space, you still can create a lengthy document with continuous pagination. Instead of creating one large document, break the document into separate sections or chapters and put each in a separate file. When you are ready to print the entire document, chain the files together by using the INCLUDE command.

To chain documents using the INCLUDE command, do the following:

1. Use the **Transfer Load** command to load the file containing the first section of your document.

2. Choose the **Yes** option in the **Format Division Page-numbers** command.

If you want to add page numbers with running heads, you must insert running heads with a page number slug into every file chained with the INCLUDE command. For more information on running heads, see Chapter 5, "Word 5 Formatting Strategies: Page Formatting."

3. Press Ctrl-PgDn to move the cursor to the end of the file.

4. Hold the Ctrl key and press the left bracket key ([) to enter a left chevron («).

5. Type the word *include*, press the space bar, and type the file name of the second section of your document.

6. Hold the Ctrl key and press the right bracket key (]) to enter a right chevron (»).

If the second section is named CHAP2.DOC, for example, the following should be the last line of the file:

«INCLUDE CHAP2.DOC»

7. Press Enter to start a new line.

8. Repeat steps 4 through 7 for each additional file you want to include in the printing and pagination process.

    When you're finished, you have a list of INCLUDE statements.

9. Use the **P**rint **M**erge command to start printing.

If you use the **P**rint **P**rinter command, Word does not chain the documents named.

If you use the default setting (**page**) in the **F**ormat **D**ivision **L**ayout command's **division break** field, Word starts a new page at the beginning of every new file.

Printing to a File

You can print your document to a file by using the Print File feature, if you want. The major reason for doing so with previous versions of Word was to create a plain ASCII file—a file containing nothing but standard ASCII characters and an Enter keystroke (paragraph mark) at the end of every line. New to Word 5, however, is a **T**ext-only-with-line-breaks option in the **format** field of the Transfer Save command menu. This option makes it much easier to save files to pure ASCII format. For more information on ASCII files, see Chapter 8, "Finding and Managing Documents."

Printing Directly

Choose the **P**rint **D**irect command to send keystrokes directly to the printer. The keystrokes you press after you select this command do not appear on your screen; they are printed on the printer. When you're finished typing to the printer, press Esc to exit the **P**rint **D**irect mode. You may find it difficult to control direct printing; with some experimentation you may find a use for this mode.

If you want to interrupt your work to type a quick memo or note to somebody and print it, it may be better to use the **S**election option in the **range** field of the Print Options command menu. Choose this option, type the memo, select the memo so that all of it is highlighted, and choose **P**rint **P**rinter. Word prints only the selection highlighted. When the printing is finished, press Del to erase the highlighted memo and continue working.

Other Ways To Print

You can start printing a document in **P**rint pre**V**iew, as already mentioned, and also by using the **P**rint option in the Library Document-retrieval command menu. For more information on Library Document-retrieval, see Chapter 8, "Finding and Managing Files."

Troubleshooting Common Printing Problems

This section assumes that you can make your computer print by using DOS (or with other programs). If your computer doesn't print with DOS, reread your printer manual or get help from the store from which you bought the printer. If you're new to personal computers, you will almost surely need help if you bought a serial printer! The focus of this section, however, is with printer problems involving Word.

If You See the Message "Enter a Printer Name in Print Options"

If you see the message Enter a Printer Name in Print Options when you try to print, chances are you haven't properly installed your printer. You may have run SETUP, for example, without selecting the option that copies the printer description file to your Word directory. If so, run SETUP again. See the Appendix for instructions.

If You See the Message "Printer Is Not Ready"

Moments after displaying the Printer Is Not Ready message, Word erases it and replaces it with Enter Y to continue or Esc to cancel. If you are away from the computer when it is printing (or supposed to be printing) and return to find this message on the screen, you have a printing problem. Word was trying to send the print signal to your printer, but the printer didn't respond.

To correct the printer-not-ready condition, check the following:

❏ Is your printer plugged in and turned on?

❏ Is your printer "selected," or ready to receive output from the computer?

❏ Is the cable connected tightly to both the computer and the printer?

❏ Have you specified the correct port in the **setup** field of the Print Options menu?

❏ Is the printer out of paper?

If you still cannot get your printer to work, recheck your installation procedure. See the Appendix for details.

If Word Formats Your Document But Doesn't Print It

If Word formats your document but doesn't print anything when you select the Print Printer command, you probably told Word to print a selection or a range of pages not included or highlighted in the document. Use the **P**rint **O**ptions command and select the **A**ll option in the **range** field, specify page numbers contained in your document, or highlight something before you specify **S**election in the **range** field.

If the Formatting Is Wrong or You See Garbage Characters

If Word prints your entire document with incorrect formatting or odd characters, make sure that you have named the correct printer in the **printer** and **model** fields of the Print Options menu. If most formats are correct, check the commands you used to format the text that isn't printing properly. See Chapters 4 and 5 for more information on formatting commands.

Chapter Summary

To make sure that your document has been formatted and paginated properly before printing, use the Print preView and Print Repaginate commands. Check running heads, page numbers, paragraph spacing, page balancing, character emphasis, font sizes, and headings in Print preView. Even if you're by using Word's automatic (active) page breaks, it's a good idea to preview page breaks using the **Yes** option in the **confirm page breaks** field of the Print Repaginate menu. Get to know the Print Options command menu: it's your key to printing flexibility with Word.

This chapter ends the discussion of the fundamentals of Word 5. In the next part of this book, "Word 5's Features and Applications," you learn how to use many of the features that have helped seal Word's reputation as one of the top programs on the market. Don't be afraid to read this section if you're a newcomer to personal computing! Anyone can learn how to use Word's file management, windowing, and outlining features; you will find that these features are indispensable after you have tried them.

II

Word 5's Features and Applications

Includes

Finding and Managing Documents

Customizing the Screen and Using Windows

Organizing Your Document with Outlining

Creating Tables and Lists with Tabs, Autosort, and Math

Using Glossaries and Bookmarks

Creating Indexes and Tables of Contents

The Legal and Scholarly Word

Enhancing Group Productivity: Using Annotations and
Redlining

Creating Form Letters

8

Finding and Managing Documents

A good word processing program makes it easy to create and save documents—so easy, in fact, that you will be amazed at how fast you can fill up a 40-megabyte hard disk with dozens or even hundreds of document files. What began as a pleasure—the ease of using a high-quality word processing system—turns into a nightmare. Someone has to cope with organizing the files, with their cryptic names (11XMRPH.DOC) and unidentifiable origins. The problem is compounded when more than one person uses a machine. No sooner do you erase an apparently useless file than someone comes charging angrily into the office, saying "You've just wiped out the only copy of a $50,000 contract!" If this happens to you, incidentally, the retort of choice is, "Our procedures call for disk and print-based backup at the end of every session." But it's far better to avoid the whole problem by using Word intelligently.

A professional word processing program doesn't help you just create documents; it also helps you find and manage the documents you create. With the new Version 5 additions to Library Document-retrieval, Word's document management command, Word moves to the top of its class. When you know the file name and location of a document, the easiest and fastest way to load a document is with the Transfer Load command. If you're not sure where a document is or what its file name is, Library Document-retrieval gives you powerful tools to search the contents of an entire hard disk to track down an elusive file. Here's a brief overview of what you can do with this splendid command:

217

❑ You can search for documents using any of the fields in the document summary sheet, such as **title**, **author**, **date of creation**, **date of revision**, **version number**, or **keywords**. Using this technique, you can track down the first version of the document entitled "Letter to J.P. Jones" written on November 19th.

❑ You can retrieve all the documents that meet specific criteria. You can ask, in effect, "Show me all the documents on the whole disk that were written by JONES in 1989," and the list appears in seconds.

❑ You can search for documents containing specific text anywhere in the files themselves! You can ask, in effect, "Show me any document mentioning that blasted McAndrews contract!" and the list appears on the screen.

New Version 5 Document-retrieval features make it a cinch to organize your hard disk, back up your documents on floppies, and delete unwanted files. You can mark documents simply by highlighting them and pressing Enter or the space bar; and then you can copy, delete, or print all the marked documents in a batch operation. This feature makes it unnecessary to spend money on a hard-disk management program and greatly increases Word's value.

In this chapter, you find a comprehensive approach to file and disk management, covering the following:

❑ Loading documents with the Transfer Load command, including the use of path statements and wild cards

❑ Using the Transfer Save command, including filling out summary sheets and saving documents in ASCII format

❑ Searching for documents with Library Document-retrieval

❑ Using Library Document-retrieval's wonderful disk management capabilities to the fullest extent

❑ Gaining access to DOS while working with Word

An introduction to the Transfer Save command is presented in Chapter 2, "Your First Word 5 Document—Quickly!" For an introduction to the Transfer Load command, see Chapter 3, "Word 5 Editing Strategies."

Note: This chapter presupposes a basic working knowledge of hard disk organization with DOS. You should know what directories are and how to create, change, and delete directories.

About the Transfer Command

Like many other commands, the Transfer command displays a submenu (shown in fig. 8.1) with several options. Table 8.1 gives a quick overview of the options on this submenu and their functions.

Table 8.1
Transfer Command Options

Option	Description
Load	Transfers a document from disk to Word's memory and displays it in the document window
Save	Transfers a document from Word's memory to disk
Clear	Removes documents from Word's memory. If you see the SAVE warning on the status line, use this command to make the warning disappear.
Delete	Removes documents from disks. You can't use Transfer Delete on any document opened during the current editing session.
Merge	Loads the file you name into the one displayed in the document window. Use this command to combine two files. Word inserts the named file at the cursor location.
Options	Changes the default drive or directory. By default, this command's **setup** field shows the default directory, that is, the directory from which you started Word. New to Version 5 is a **save between sessions** field. You can create a permanent default directory by choosing the **Y**es option in this field. This directory will be the default no matter which directory you are in when you start Word.
Rename	Changes the file name of the document currently in the document window. This command changes the DOS file name, just as if you used the DOS Rename command.
Glossary	Loads or merges a glossary from disk. For more information on glossaries, see Chapter 12, "Using Glossaries and Bookmarks."

Table 8.1—Continued

Option	Description
Allsave	Saves all the changes made to documents, glossaries, and style sheets. If you use windows to load and display more than one document, Word saves all of them.

Fig. 8.1.

The Transfer command submenu.

```
TRANSFER: Load Save Clear Delete Merge Options Rename Glossary Allsave

Loads named document
Pg1 Co1          {}              ?              Microsoft Word
```

More About the Transfer Load Command

In Chapter 3, you learned to use the Transfer Load command to load documents previously created and saved. You learned that the best way to start Word is from the directory or disk that contains your documents so that you need not provide path information when you type the file name in the **filename** field.

In this section, you learn to load a document that is not in the default drive or directory by including path statements with the file name. You also learn to create (and save, if you want) a new default drive or directory during an editing session. Last, you learn to find a file whose file name you cannot quite remember by using wild cards and the F1 key.

Using Path Statements

A path statement tells DOS how to find a file. Path information can be included any time you type a file name. To indicate a disk drive, type the drive's letter followed by a colon (for example, C: or A:). To indicate a directory, type a backslash followed by the directory's name (for example, \DOCS or \LETTERS. To add a file name to the path statement, type a backslash before the file name. Here's a path statement that tells DOS, "The file called REPORT88.DOC is in the DOCS directory on drive C":

C:\DOCS\REPORT88.DOC

You can use path statements with the Transfer Load command to load a file not on the default disk or directory. To accomplish this, do the following:

1. Choose the Transfer Load command.

2. Type the full path name, including the drive name if the file is on a disk drive other than the default drive (see fig. 8.2).

   Type *A:\BACKUP\REPORT88.BAK*, for instance, to load the file called REPORT88.BAK in the \BACKUP directory of the disk in drive A.

3. Carry out the command by pressing Enter or clicking the command name.

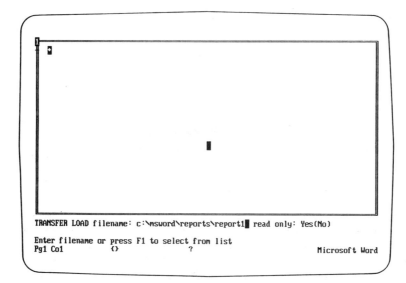

TRANSFER LOAD filename: c:\msword\reports\report1█ read only: Yes(No)

Enter filename or press F1 to select from list
Pg1 Co1   {}   ?   Microsoft Word

Fig. 8.2.

Using a path name to save a document to a drive or directory other than the default.

Viewing a List of Directory Names

A very nice feature of Word 5 is that you don't have to remember the names of all your directories. You can use the Transfer Load command to display all the directories and subdirectories you have created.

To see a list of valid directory names, do the following:

1. Choose the **T**ransfer **L**oad command and press F1.

2. When the list of drive letters or directories appears (refer to fig. 8.3), highlight the drive or directory you want and press F1 again to display the list of files or subdirectories in that directory.

If you want to see the names of subdirectories within a directory, highlight the directory's name and press F1 again.

When the list of files appears, highlight the desired file name and press Enter to load the file. Press Esc to cancel the command.

Fig. 8.3.

List of documents, drives, and directories.

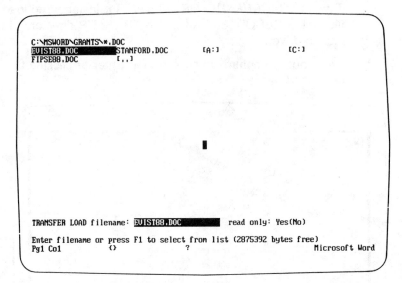

Typing path names is tedious, and what's worse, mistakes are easy to make. To save time and trouble, avoid situations where you have to type path information. Start Word from a document directory. After starting the program, use the **T**ransfer **O**ptions command, described later in this chapter, to change the default drive or directory. Make full use of the Library Document-retrieval command's capability to display a list of documents in every directory, allowing you to load a document in just two keystrokes or clicks.

Using Wild Cards and F1 with Transfer Load

You can use the two DOS wild cards with Transfer Load to control the list of files that appears when you press F1. The valid DOS wild cards, together with illustrations of their use, appear in table 8.2.

Table 8.2
Using DOS Wild Cards with Word

Wild card	Function
?	Matches any single character or number. For instance, REPORT8?.DOC matches REPORT87.DOC, REPORT88.DOC, and REPORT89.DOC.
*	Matches any single or multiple characters. For instance, REPORT88.* matches REPORT88.DOC, REPORT88.BAK, and REPORT88.TXT.
*.DOC	Matches any file name with the DOC extension
*.BAK	Matches any backup file that Word automatically creates when you use the Transfer Save command.
.	Matches any file name

Wild cards come in handy in many situations. Following are two of these instances:

❏ To display a list of all the backup documents Word has created in a drive or directory other than the default, type the path name and *.BAK* (for example, A:\DOCS*.BAK) and press F1.

❏ To see a list of *all* the files, not just Word documents, on a drive or directory, type the path name and *.* (for example, C:\ARCHIVE*.*).

To load any Word document displayed by using a wild-card character and the F1 key, just highlight the file name and press Enter.

If You Get an Error Message with Transfer Load

If you see the message Enter Y to save changes in document, N to lose changes, or Esc to cancel, you are trying to load a new document without having saved the changes made to the current document. Press Y if you want to save the changes made to the current document or N to abandon them.

If you see the message, File does not exist. Enter Y to create or Esc to cancel, Word cannot find the file you named. Press Esc to cancel the Transfer Load command. Before panicking, consider this list of possible errors:

❑ You typed the file name or directory name incorrectly. Use the Transfer Load command and try again.

❑ The file you want isn't in the directory or disk you named. Use the Transfer Load command and try again.

❑ You left out a directory name. If the file is in a subdirectory (a directory within a directory), you must name the entire path (for instance, C:\DOCS\REPORTS\REPORT88.DOC).

❑ You didn't use Word's default extension DOC when you saved the file. To load a file with some other extension, type the extension (for example, REPORT88.BAK). If you saved the file without any extension at all, type the file name followed by a period (for example, REPORT88.).

If you still cannot find the file, search for it by using the Transfer Load command and wild cards, as described in "Using Wild Cards and F1" earlier in this chapter. Better, use the Library Document-retrieval command to search for the missing document.

Using the Transfer Options Command

If you followed the advice in Chapter 2 and started Word from the directory containing your documents, you don't have to worry about adding path information to file names when using the Transfer Load command. In the middle of an editing session, however, you may decide to use documents in another directory. As explained in the preceding section, you can load such documents by including path information with the file name. If you plan to work with several documents in that directory, you can save yourself the trouble of typing the path name over and over. Use the **T**ransfer **O**ptions command to define a new default drive or directory.

To change the default drive or directory during an editing session, do the following:

1. Choose the **T**ransfer **O**ptions command.

2. Type the new drive or directory in the **setup** command field, shown in figure 8.4. To see a list of valid drive and directory names, press F1. Choose the desired drive or directory from this list.

3. Carry out the command by pressing Enter or clicking the command name.

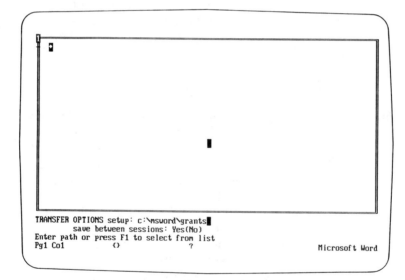

```
TRANSFER OPTIONS setup: c:\nsword\grants█
              save between sessions: Yes(No)
Enter path or press F1 to select from list
Pg1 Co1            {}               ?                Microsoft Word
```

Fig. 8.4.

The Transfer Options command.

If you see the message, Not a valid drive or directory, you have typed a drive or directory name that doesn't exist. You may have misspelled the name. Try the command again, and before you type anything in the **setup** field press F1 to see a list of valid drive and directory names.

New with Version 5 is a handy addition to the Transfer Options command: you can save the default drive or directory choice made in the **T**ransfer **O**ptions command **setup** field. Just choose the **Y**es option in the **save between sessions** field to save your directory choice for the next Word session.

Unless you keep all your documents in one directory, however, leave this field set to **No**. That way, the **setup** field automatically contains the name of the directory from which you started Word. If you start Word from the directory \MSWORD\REPORTS, for instance, the **setup** field automatically contains that directory name. This feature has advantages for style sheet users, as Chapter 20 explains.

More about the Transfer Save Command

As you already learned in Chapter 2, you should fill out the summary sheet that appears when you use Transfer Save if you want to make the most of the Library Document-retrieval command. In this section, you learn more about what the various fields of the command mean. You also learn how to save your file to a drive or directory other than the default, how to save documents in pure ASCII format, and how to cope with a full disk and other problems when saving files.

Filling Out Summary Sheets

The first time you save a document with Transfer Save, Word displays a blank summary sheet. Following are some tips for filling it out.

Field	Length	Description
Title	40	Use this field to type a short version of the document's title, with the most significant words first. (Word displays only the first two or three words of the title when you view lists with Library Document-retrieval.) If your document is entitled, "Report to the Directors on the Advisability of Investing in OK Products, Inc.," type *OK Products Report to Directors* in the **title** field. Note: The document title in the summary sheet has nothing to do with the document's DOS file name. By typing a title in the summary sheet, you do not change the DOS file name.
Author	40	You don't need to fill out this field unless your computer is used by more than one person. If it is, be sure to fill out this field

Field	Length	Description
		for every document that you (and all other users) create. Be consistent: always use one spelling and one form of your name. Don't type *Dr. Margaret Smith* for one document and *Peggy* for the next.
Version Number	10	If you want to keep track of the versions of a document you save, type a number (or any identifying text up to 10 characters in length) in this field. Note: Word does not update version numbers automatically.
Operator	40	Use this field only if you're typing someone else's document. Type your name in this field.
Creation Date	8	Word fills in this field automatically. If you forgot to set the system time and date, however, Word fills in these fields with the beginning of time (so far as MS-DOS is concerned): early in the morning of January 1, 1980. You can edit these fields to set the correct date and time.
Revision Date	8	Word fills in and updates this field automatically.
Keywords	80	Use this field to enter a few short, descriptive words that identify your document's contents. Use descriptors, or key words that classify your document (such as *letter*, *contract*, *report*, *memo*) as well as identifiers, or key words that identify its specific content (such as *Jones*, *Acme Manufacturing*, or *National Science Foundation*).
Comments	220	Use this field to add any text that might help you identify the contents of a document (for example, *Contains the text of a proposal to the National Science Foundation for a study of professional ethics in artificial intelligence*).

If you don't want to fill out the summary sheet, just press Enter when it appears. But think twice before doing so! Months from now, will you be able to tell what's in a file just by looking at that cryptic, 8-character DOS file name?

If you didn't fill out a summary sheet when you saved a document, you can update it at any time by using the **L**ibrary **D**ocument-retrieval **U**pdate command. For more information on this command, see "Finding Documents with Library Document-retrieval," later in this chapter.

Saving to a Nondefault Drive or Directory

To save your document to a drive or directory other than the default, choose one of these two techniques:

❏ Type the full path name of the desired drive or directory where you want to store this file in the **filename** field when you use the **T**ransfer **S**ave command.

❏ Choose the **T**ransfer **O**ptions command and type the drive or directory name you want to use. Then use the **T**ransfer **S**ave command and type the file name.

If you see the message, Not a valid drive or directory, Word cannot find a drive or directory with the name you typed. To see a list of valid drives and directories, use the **T**ransfer **L**oad command and press F1. When you have identified the correct name of the drive or directory, press Esc to cancel the **T**ransfer **L**oad command and use the **T**ransfer **S**ave command again, specifying the correct drive and directory.

About the .BAK Files Word Creates

As you have already learned, Word creates an automatic backup file (with the extension .BAK) when you resave your document. (No backup file is created the first time you save.) This backup file, however, does not contain the current version of your document, the one saved in the .DOC file. Rather, the backup file contains the previous version of the file.

The .BAK file Word creates is very useful, then, if you want to throw out the changes made since the last time you saved a document. The .BAK file isn't a true backup file. To back up the current version of your document, you must do so deliberately.

An easy way to back up your documents is to use the Library Document-retrieval Copy command. For more information about this command, see "Managing Documents with Library Document-retrieval," later in this chapter.

Saving Documents in ASCII-File Format

Here's a welcome Word 5 feature for anyone who must save documents in pure ASCII-file format. A pure ASCII file has no formatting or printer commands, and each line ends with a carriage return (displayed as a paragraph mark with Word). If you want to upload your file through electronic mail links, you may need to save it as an ASCII file.

Before Version 5, saving files in ASCII format with Word was an extremely tedious process. Now it's easy. Just choose the **T**ext-only-with-line-breaks option in the **format** field of the **T**ransfer **S**ave command menu. If you have used any formatting commands, you will see the message Enter Y to confirm loss of formatting. Press Y to abandon the formats you have entered. If you want to keep a copy of the file that retains these formats, however, press Esc to cancel the command and use **T**ransfer **S**ave again. Save the file by using the **W**ord option in the **format** field. Then use **T**ransfer **S**ave again to save the file to a new file name, and choose the **T**ext-only-with-line-breaks option. Press Y to confirm loss of formatting.

Using Transfer Allsave

If you work with more than one document at a time, or if you create new glossaries or style sheets, you can save all your changes at once by using the Transfer Allsave command, a new feature of Word 5.

If You Get an Error Message with Transfer Save

If you see the message, Document Disk Full, you're probably working with a dual floppy system. To save your work, take out the disk in drive B and insert a blank, formatted disk. (If you don't have any disks formatted, see "Using DOS in Word: The Library Run Command" later in this chapter for instructions on using the Library Run command to run DOS programs within Word. Format the disk, and return to Word.) Then use the **T**ransfer **S**ave command again. You may have to switch disks in and out several times.

For tips on using a dual floppy system with Word, see the Appendix. If you have filled up your hard disk, save your work to a floppy disk.

Finding and Loading Documents with Library Document-Retrieval

If you're reasonably sure that you know the name of a document, what's in it, and where it's located, use the Transfer Load command to find and load the file. If you have any doubt about a document's name, contents, or location, or if you want to see a list of all the files conforming to specific criteria, use the Library Document-retrieval command. Using this command, you can display a list of all the documents in every directory on an entire hard disk, or you can narrow the list by telling Word to retrieve only those documents conforming to criteria you specify, such as title, author, or creation date. Word examines the document summary sheets of the documents you have created and lists the documents that match the stated criteria. With this command, in other words, you never have to browse through the contents of a huge hard disk manually. Let Word do it for you!

Library Document-retrieval is terrific, but it's important to understand what Word does—and doesn't—do when you use the command. First, the command is a disk retrieval command like Transfer Load, so that Word displays only the files you have saved to disk. Second, Library Document-retrieval displays only the files you have saved with the default extension, .DOC. (You can display files with different extensions by typing an asterisk, a period, and the extension in the **path** field of the Query command menu. To see a list of files with the extension .BAK, for instance, you type

    *.BAK

in the Query command's **path** field. See the next section for more information on using the Query command.

Note: The Library Document-retrieval command is most useful for hard disk users. If you use a two-floppy system, however, you may find this command useful for backing up your work. Refer to "Managing Files with Library Document-retrieval" in this chapter for more information.

Getting into Library Document-retrieval—and back out again—is easy. Just choose the Library Document-retrieval command. Your document disappears, but don't worry—when you leave Library Document-retrieval, Word takes you back to the cursor's location in your document. To leave Library Document-retrieval, press Esc to activate the Library Document-Retrieval command menu and choose the Exit option.

Changing the Default Path in the Query Command Field

In Version 4 of Microsoft Word, Word saved what you typed in the **path** field of the Library Document-Retrieval Query command menu. In Version 5, however, this field contains the current setting in the **setup** field of the Transfer Options command, and Word doesn't save the **path** field's setting when you quit the program.

When you use the Library Document-retrieval command in Version 5, therefore, Word searches for .DOC files in the directory named in the **setting** field of the Transfer Option command menu. If you want to search for documents in another directory, you must change the directory named in the Query command's **path** field.

To change the setting in the **path** field of the Library Document-retrieval Query command, do the following:

1. Choose the **Library D**ocument-retrieval command.

2. When the command submenu appears as shown in figure 8.5, choose the **Q**uery option. The Query option displays the command menu shown in figure 8.6.

3. In the **path** field of the Query command, type the path names of the directory or directories that may contain the documents for which you are searching. You can type more than one directory if you separate the path names by commas (see fig. 8.7).

4. Carry out the command by pressing Enter or clicking the command name.

Fig. 8.5.

The Library
Document-
retrieval submenu.

```
DOCUMENT-RETRIEVAL: Query Exit Load Print Update View Copy Delete

Press Spacebar to mark-unmark file, Ctrl+Spacebar to mark all, or Esc for menu
                            ?                                Microsoft Word
```

Fig. 8.6.

The Library
Document-
retrieval Query
command menu.

```
QUERY path: C:\MSWORD\GRANTS
     author:
     operator:
     keywords:
     creation date:                    revision date:
     document text:
     case: Yes(No)                     marked files only: Yes(No)
Enter search directories separated by commas or press F1 to select from list
                            ?                                Microsoft Word
```

Fig. 8.7.

Separating path
names with
commas.

```
QUERY path: C:\MSWORD\GRANTS,C:\MSWORD\REPORTS,C:\MSWORD\LETTERS
     author:
     operator:
     keywords:
     creation date:                    revision date:
     document text:
     case: Yes(No)                     marked files only: Yes(No)
Enter search directories separated by commas or press F1 to select from list
                            ?                                Microsoft Word
```

Unless there are hundreds of documents on your disk, put the names
of all the directories in which you store Word documents into the **path**
field of the Library Document-Retrieval Query command menu. After
you change the **path** field this way, Library Document-retrieval may
display more documents than one screen can show. But you can use
PgUp and PgDn to scroll the list, and as you learn in the following
section, you can narrow the list as you please.

Narrowing the Search

If you enter all the directories in which you store Word documents into
the **path** field in the Library Document-Retrieval Query command
menu, Word finds and displays all the .DOC files in every directory you
named. To narrow the scope of the search and reduce the number of
documents displayed in the window, you can type additional
information in the Query command's other fields. For example, to view
only those documents created by Peggy Smith, type *Peggy Smith* in
the **author** field and carry out the command. Word then searches the

summary sheets of all the documents in the specified directories. If it finds a match or matches, Word displays a list of the file or files in the window.

To narrow the scope of a search, do the following:

1. Choose the **Li**brary **D**ocument-retrieval command. A list of documents appears in the window.

2. Press Esc to enter the Library Document-retrieval command mode. The **Q**uery option is highlighted.

3. Press Enter. The Query submenu appears.

4. Highlight one or more of the fields and type the search criterion or criteria you want. To search for all the documents Peggy Smith created, for instance, type *Peggy Smith* in the **author** command field.

5. Carry out the command.

Note: When you fill out fields in the Query command menu, you tell Word to display a list of only those files that contain all the criteria you specify. For instance, if you type *Peggy Smith* in the **author** field and *1/19/89* in the **creation date** field, Word tries to find documents containing Peggy Smith in the **author** field of the summary sheet *and* 1/19/89 in the **date** field. The more fields you fill out, the more specific the search is, and the more you reduce the number of documents displayed after you carry out the command.

Caution: To add dates to the **creation date** or **revision date** fields of the Query command menu, you must use precisely the date format specified in the **date format** field of the Options command menu. The default format is mm/dd/yy.

If You See an Error Message

If Word cannot match the criteria you specify to the information contained in document summary sheets, you see the message, No matching files found. This message doesn't mean the document you want has been erased. The search may have gone awry for any of the following reasons:

❏ You haven't listed all the document directories by typing path names in the **path** command field. Be sure to include all the directories that contain documents, separating path names by commas.

❏ The text you type isn't exactly the same as the text you entered into the documents' summary sheets. If you typed *Margaret* in the **author** field of summary sheets, but search for all the documents by *Peggy*, Word won't retrieve the documents. Be consistent when you fill out summary sheets.

❏ You used too many criteria and narrowed the search too much. Suppose that you typed *Peggy* in the **author** field, *1/19/89* in the **creation date** field, and *Acme, Inc.* in the **keywords** field. But it happens that Peg didn't create any documents about Acme, Inc. that day. Try broadening the search by eliminating one or more of the criteria.

Focusing the Search Using Logical Operators

In any field of the Library Document-retrieval Query command menu, you can use logical operators to focus your search for documents more precisely. A *logical operator* is a symbol that specifies the relationship between two search terms. (The symbols are listed in table 8.3.) For example, the & symbol (or a space) stands for the AND operator. If you link two terms using the AND operator, Library Document-retrieval lists only those documents containing both linked terms in the document's summary sheet. If you type *Acme, Inc. & contract* in the Query command **keywords** field, Word lists only those documents (if any) containing both these terms in the summary sheet's **keywords** field.

If you have any experience with a database management program, you're already familiar with logical operators and their effects on a search. Table 8.3 is a brief overview of logical operators and their effects.

Table 8.3
Logical Operators and Their Effects on a Search

Operator	Description
AND	Use this operator to narrow a search. Both criteria must be satisfied before Word lists the document. You can search, for example, for all documents with both Acme, Inc. and contract in the **keywords** field (type *Acme, Inc. & contract* in the **keywords** field).
OR	Use this operator to broaden a search. Word lists any document whose summary sheet contains either of the linked terms. You can search, for example, for all the documents created by Peggy or Linda (type *Peggy, Linda* in the **author** field).
NOT	Use this operator to exclude documents containing the second term in their summary sheets. You can search, for example, for all the documents containing the word "contract" in the **keywords** field of their summary sheets, but not the ones that also contain the words "Acme" (type *contract~Acme* in the **keywords** field).
LESS THAN GREATER THAN	These operators are very useful for searches involving the **creation date** or **revision date** fields. You can search, for example, for all documents created after 11/19/88 (type *>11/19/88* in the **creation date** field).

Note: These operators link terms within a field of the Query command menu. When you fill out two or more different fields, you have effectively linked the criteria with the AND operator. Word does not list the documents unless their summary sheets match all the specified terms.

Table 8.4 lists logical operators for use with the Library Document-retrieval command.

Table 8.4
Logical Operators for Use with Library Document-retrieval

Character	Operator
, (comma)	OR operator (retrieves documents satisfying either criterion)
& (ampersand) or space	AND operator (retrieves only those documents satisfying both criteria)
~ (tilde)	NOT operator (retrieves all the documents satisfying the first criterion but not the ones that also satisfy the second)
< (less than)	LESS THAN (dates only)
> (greater than)	GREATER THAN (dates only)

Instead of spending money on a text retrieval program, use logical operators and the **document text** field in the Query command menu. To search for a document or documents containing the words *technology* or *artifact*, for instance, type *technology,artifact* in the Query command **document text** field. Word searches the full text of all the documents included in the **path** field's list of directory names. The search naturally takes some time, more (a few minutes) or less (a few seconds) depending on how many documents you have created and saved. Also, doing a search on a floppy disk-based system is much slower than doing the same search on a hard disk-based system.

Viewing the Document List

When you retrieve documents with the Library Document-retrieval command, Word displays them in the default format, the **S**hort format. In this format, Word lists only the path names and file names for each file (see fig. 8.8).

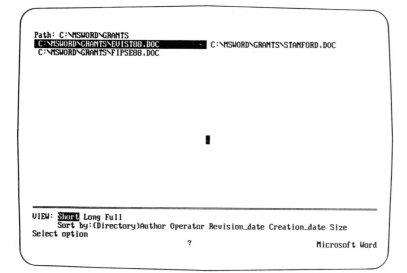

Fig. 8.8.

The Short display option in the Library Document-retrieval View menu.

You can alter the display format using the View command in the Library Document-Retrieval command menu. If you choose the **L**ong option, Word displays the documents' author and title as well as the path name and file name (see fig. 8.9). If you choose the **F**ull option, Word displays the summary sheet of the highlighted file (see fig. 8.10).

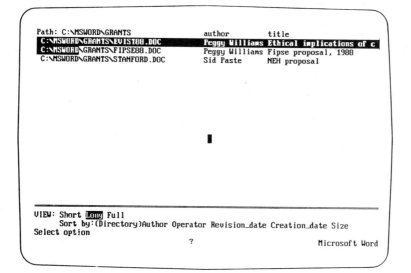

Fig. 8.9.

The Long display option in the Library Document-retrieval View menu.

Fig. 8.10.

The Full display option in the Library Document-retrieval View menu.

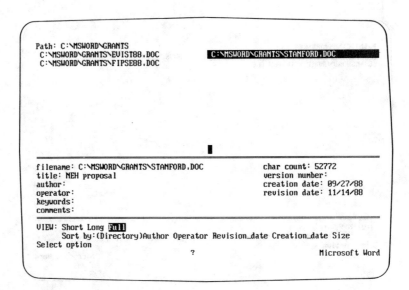

```
Path: C:\MSWORD\GRANTS
      C:\MSWORD\GRANTS\EVIST88.DOC          C:\MSWORD\GRANTS\STANFORD.DOC
      C:\MSWORD\GRANTS\FIPSE88.DOC




                                       ▌




filename: C:\MSWORD\GRANTS\STANFORD.DOC          char count: 52772
title: NEH proposal                              version number:
author:                                          creation date: 09/27/88
operator:                                        revision date: 11/14/88
keywords:
comments:

VIEW: Short Long █Full█
      Sort by:(Directory)Author Operator Revision_date Creation_date Size
Select option
                                   ?                        Microsoft Word
```

To change the view of the summary of the retrieved documents, do the following:

1. After displaying a list of documents with **L**ibrary **D**ocument-retrieval, press Esc to enter the Library Document-Retrieval command menu.

2. Choose the **V**iew command.

3. When the submenu appears, choose the **F**ull or **L**ong option.

4. Carry out the command.

Sorting the Document List

The Library Document-Retrieval View command menu lists several options you can choose for sorting documents: by directory (the default), by author, by operator, by revision or creation date, or by size (in characters).

To choose a sort option, do the following:

1. Choose the **L**ibrary **D**ocument-retrieval command. When the document list appears, press Esc to enter the Library Document-retrieval command mode.

2. Choose the **V**iew option. Choose the **L**ong option. If you use the **S**hort option, Word sorts the document list as you specify, but it won't list the document characteristics (such as author's name or file size) by which it has sorted them.

3. Choose a sort option in the **sort by** field.

4. Carry out the command.

Word displays headings on the screen and sorts the document list as specified (see fig. 8.11).

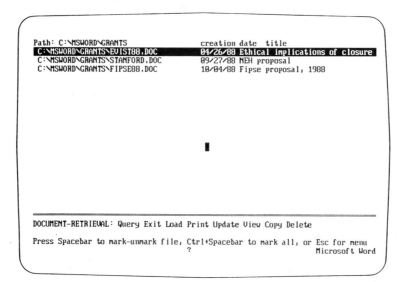

Fig. 8.11.

Document list sorted by creation date.

Updating Summary Sheets

If you haven't filled out your document summary sheets properly, or if you want to update one, use the Library Document-retrieval Update command.

To update the summary sheet for any document, do the following:

1. Choose the **L**ibrary **D**ocument-retrieval command. When the document list appears, highlight the name of the document whose summary sheet you want to update.

2. Choose the **U**pdate command.

3. When the summary screen appears, make the additions or changes you want.

4. Press Enter to carry out the command.

5. Select **E**xit to leave Library Document-retrieval.

Loading Documents

When you have identified the document you want to load, using the Library Document-retrieval command, follow these steps to load it so you can edit it or print it:

1. Highlight the document's name in the list displayed by Word.

2. Choose the **L**oad command.

3. Carry out the command by pressing Enter or clicking the command name.

Word loads the document, just as if you had used the Transfer Load command.

Managing Documents with Library Document-Retrieval

With the addition of two new commands (Copy and Delete) to the Library Document-Retrieval command menu, Word 5 has become a first-rate document management tool. You can use the Library Document-retrieval command to back up your work, move one or several files from one directory to another, delete unwanted documents, and even print several files at a time. The following sections explain each of these features.

Backing Up Your Work

To back up your work at the end of a session, do the following:

1. Choose the **Li**brary **D**ocument-retrieval command.

2. When the list of files appears, use the arrow keys or mouse to highlight the first file you want to back up.

3. Choose the **C**opy command on the Library Document-Retrieval command menu. When the Library Document-Retrieval Copy command menu appears, type the name of the destination drive or directory in the **marked files to drive/directory** field.

4. Carry out the command.

You can back up several files at once in a batch operation by marking them before using the Library Document-retrieval Copy command. To mark a file, highlight it and press space bar or Enter. When a file is marked, an asterisk appears in the style bar to the left of the file name. To unmark a marked file, just press space bar or Enter again. To mark all the displayed files, press Ctrl-space bar. To unmark all of them, press Shift-Ctrl-space bar.

To back up several files in a batch operation, do the following:

1. Choose the **L**ibrary **D**ocument-retrieval command.

2. When the list of files appears, mark the files you want to copy by highlighting them and pressing space bar or Enter.

3. When you have finished marking all the files you want to back up, choose the **C**opy command on the Library Document-Retrieval command menu.

4. When the Library Document-Retrieval Copy command menu appears, type the name of the destination drive or directory in the **marked files to drive/directory** field.

5. Carry out the command.

If you back up to a floppy disk and Word runs out of room on the disk, the copy operation ceases, and the files Word did not completely copy are left marked. Switch disks and choose the Copy option again to continue the operation.

Moving Documents

A welcome feature of Word 5's new Library Document-retrieval Copy command is the **delete files after copy** field. If you choose **Y**es in this field, Word deletes the original files and retains only the backups.

You can easily clutter up your hard disk with hundreds of files of letters. Rather than deleting them, move them to one or more floppy disks using the Library Document-retrieval Copy command. Choose **Y**es in the **delete files after copy** field to remove them from your hard disk after the backup operation is complete.

Deleting Documents

After using the Library Document-retrieval command to display a list of documents, you can delete one or several documents by marking them and using the **L**ibrary **D**ocument-retrieval **D**elete command. Mark all the files you want to delete by highlighting them and pressing the space bar. Then choose the **D**elete command in the Library Document-Retrieval command menu. Press Y to confirm each deletion.

Printing with Library Document-Retrieval

Here's an easy way to print several files in one unattended operation so that you can put your computer to work during one of those long meetings.

1. Choose the **L**ibrary **D**ocument-retrieval command. When the list of files appears, mark the files you want to print by highlighting them and pressing the space bar.

2. When you finish marking the files you want to print, choose **P**rint from the Library Document-Retrieval command menu.

3. When the Print submenu appears, choose **D**ocument to print just the documents selected, **S**ummary to print just the summary sheets of the selected documents, or **B**oth to print both.

4. Carry out the command.

Using DOS in Word: The Library Run Command

Any time you work with Word, you can leave Word temporarily, return to DOS, use DOS commands or other programs, and return to Word. The key to using DOS in Word is the Library Run command. Suppose, for example, that you're ready to print a document and you find that you did not use the program that downloads fonts to your printer. Without Library Run, you have to save your document, quit Word, use the downloading program, start Word, and load your document again. Obviously, Library Run can come in very handy.

To use Library Run, do the following:

1. Save your work with **T**ransfer **S**ave (or **T**ransfer **A**llsave, if you have more than one document open or if you use a glossary or style sheet) and choose the **L**ibrary **R**un command.

   Always save your work before using Library Run! Word is nearly crash-proof, but other programs you run from DOS may not be!

2. When the Library Run command menu appears, type the DOS command you want to use. To check a disk, for instance, type *A:CHKDSK* and press Enter.

   If you use a dual-floppy system, Word prompts you to insert a disk if necessary. To run CHKDSK, for instance, you must insert your DOS disk into drive A. When you have inserted the appropriate disk, press Y.

3. When the program you have started from DOS is finished, you see the message, Press a key to resume Word. After pressing a key, Word (and your document) returns to the screen.

 Caution: Don't use Library Run to delete or move files. The DOS file deletion and moving commands do not contain safeguards against deleting files Word needs during an editing session. Use the Library Document-retrieval command to delete files instead.

Chapter Summary

If you're reasonably sure that you know the name and location of a file you're trying to retrieve, use the Transfer Load command. Don't forget that this command has capabilities to load documents not on the default drive or directory. Use wild cards and F1, too, with the Transfer Load command, especially if you cannot find the desired file. If you're working with dozens or hundreds of files on a hard disk, make acquaintance with the Library Document-retrieval command. Even if you don't think that you will use the command right now, fill out the document summary sheets! Some day, you may be very glad you did.

To make the best use of Library Document-retrieval, update the Query command's **path** field with the names of all the directories in which you store Word documents. After all, when you fish with a net, you want to cast your net as wide as possible! When you specify all the directories, a long list of documents appears when you use the command. But when you do a search by typing information in the Query menu's fields, Word searches all the document directories to find just the files you specify, and a very abbreviated list appears on the screen. You can search for all the documents written by a certain author, for instance, on a certain date or range of dates. You can even search the full text of every Word document on your whole disk to find the one file, the maddeningly missing one, that contains precisely the text you specify. You don't need an expensive disk-searching program with Word—you already have one!

Make regular use of Library Document-retrieval to back up your work and clean up Word directories. Designed for use with Word documents, Library Document-retrieval performs these functions safely and effectively. If you need DOS while working with Word, use the Library Run command. Keep this command in mind if you run out of space on a disk and don't have any formatted disks at hand! You can use Library Run to format a disk without losing your document.

9

Customizing the Screen and Using Windows

Once you have mastered the basics of a word processing program, it's time to make the program look and behave on the screen precisely the way you want. Word makes the screen customization process easy. By choosing options from Word 5's new Options command menu, you can choose virtually any screen configuration you like, including WordPerfect's much-ballyhooed "clean screen."

Word also provides tools for splitting the screen so that multiple windows are displayed. Using this technique, you can display two or more sections of the same document at the same time, greatly facilitating copying and moving operations. You can also display two or more different documents at a time, and it's just as easy to copy or move text among them. Using Word's wonderful window zoom mode, you can open up to eight different documents at a time and move among them at a keystroke!

This chapter covers screen customization and windows in detail. In this chapter you learn

❑ How to create new default settings for Word's many display options so that they are available every time you start Word

❑ How to hide the command menu so that 22 lines of text are visible on the screen—and, if you want, how to hide the window borders to produce a "clean screen" effect

245

❑ How to use the show layout mode, a new feature of Word 5 that lets you edit while displaying special document formats such as running heads and multiple-column text

❑ How users of color monitors can customize their screens to display font sizes and other character emphases in distinctive colors

❑ How to open, size, zoom, and close windows, and how to use multiple windows for high-speed text editing

About the Options Command

The Options command fields shown in figure 9.1 provide many ways to customize Word's screen and operating characteristics—and you're already acquainted with these fields. You know how to display hidden text, turn on the ruler, display nonprinting symbols, select measurements, and change the default tab width. This section covers more Options menu choices, especially those that affect the screen display.

Fig. 9.1.

The Options command menu.

```
WINDOW OPTIONS for window number: █      show hidden text:(Yes)No
            show ruler: Yes(No)   show non-printing symbols: None(Partial)All
          show layout: Yes(No)          show line breaks: Yes(No)
         show outline: Yes(No)           show style bar: Yes(No)

GENERAL OPTIONS mute: Yes(No)        █      summary sheet:(Yes)No
              measure:(In)Cm P10 P12 Pt    display mode: 1
             paginate:(Auto)Manual              colors:
             autosave:                  autosave confirm: Yes(No)
           show menu:(Yes)No              show borders:(Yes)No
          date format:(MDY)DMY         decimal character:(.),
          time format:(12)24           default tab width: 0.5"
         line numbers: Yes(No)          count blank space: Yes(No)
         cursor speed: 3               linedraw character: (|)
          speller path: C:\MSWORD\SPELL-AM.LEX
Enter number
Pg1 Co1              {}              ?                    Microsoft Word
```

If you have used previous versions of Word, you notice right away that Version 5 displays a much larger Options command menu. It includes window options formerly hidden in the Window command submenu. If you're a Word veteran, you will appreciate the convenience of having all these options together in one place.

Whether you're new to Word or not, it is important to understand that the menu is divided into two distinct parts:

Window Options. This part of the menu contains options for the window with the number shown in the **for window number** field. If only one window is open on the screen, this field displays the number 1. Choices made in this part of the menu affect only one window. If you open additional windows, you can make different choices for them.

General Options. This part of the menu contains options for all windows. When you make a choice in this part of the menu, the choice affects all documents you display, edit, and print.

The differences in these parts of the menu come into play only when more than one window is open on the screen.

If you choose window options with 1 displayed in the **for window number** field, Word saves your choices as the default settings for window 1, the window that comes on the screen when you start Word. To choose default settings, therefore, make sure that the **for window number** field contains 1.

Caution: When you make choices in the Options command menu, Word saves these choices to disk in a file called MW.INI. This file is automatically stored on the Word program disk or in the directory in which you placed Word. Every time you start Word, the program consults this file to see which options are selected and treats them as default settings. If you delete this file, however, your choices are lost, and Word reverts to its original default settings. If this happens, use the Options command and choose your options a second time.

Customizing the Screen

Word's default display screen mode includes the command menu, a single window with borders, and a plain top border (without a ruler). You can change all these features, and can produce even the much-vaunted "clean screen" if you choose. With Word 5, users of color systems can assign distinctive colors to a variety of screen elements, including font sizes, character emphases, menus, and borders. Word saves all the changes you make, so they become the new default. You see them on the screen the next time you start Word.

The following sections explain how you can customize the screen.

Hiding the Command Menu

By default, Word displays 19 lines of text (see fig. 9.2). You can increase the display to 22 lines by hiding the command menu. To do so, choose **N**o in the **show menu** field of the Options command menu (refer to fig. 9.1). Three additional lines of text are then visible, as shown in figure 9.3. To use the command menu, just press Esc, and it pops back on the screen.

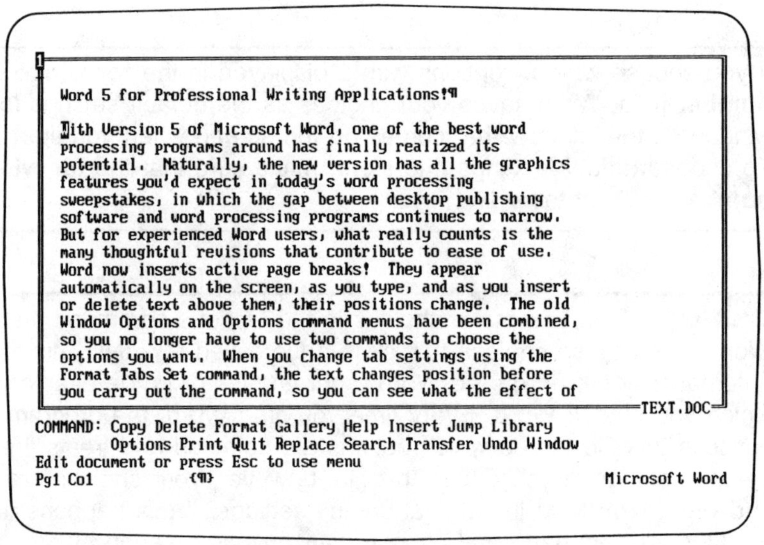

Fig. 9.2.

Default screen with 19 lines of text.

```
┌──────────────────────────────────────────────────────────────┐
│█                                                              │
│  Word 5 for Professional Writing Applications!¶               │
│                                                               │
│  █ith Version 5 of Microsoft Word, one of the best word       │
│  processing programs around has finally realized its          │
│  potential. Naturally, the new version has all the graphics   │
│  features you'd expect in today's word processing             │
│  sweepstakes, in which the gap between desktop publishing      │
│  software and word processing programs continues to narrow.   │
│  But for experienced Word users, what really counts is the    │
│  many thoughtful revisions that contribute to ease of use.    │
│  Word now inserts active page breaks! They appear             │
│  automatically on the screen, as you type, and as you insert  │
│  or delete text above them, their positions change. The old   │
│  Window Options and Options command menus have been combined, │
│  so you no longer have to use two commands to choose the      │
│  options you want. When you change tab settings using the     │
│  Format Tabs Set command, the text changes position before    │
│  you carry out the command, so you can see what the effect of │
│                                                      ─TEXT.DOC─│
│ COMMAND: Copy Delete Format Gallery Help Insert Jump Library  │
│          Options Print Quit Replace Search Transfer Undo Window│
│ Edit document or press Esc to use menu                        │
│ Pg1 Co1            {¶}                          Microsoft Word │
└──────────────────────────────────────────────────────────────┘
```

Why isn't the command menu hidden by default? After all, it comes back on the screen when you press Esc (which you have to do anyway to access the command mode in the keyboard version of Word), and you can see significantly more of your document—16 percent more, to be precise. The answer lies in Microsoft's plan to emulate Macintosh-style word processing. If you use the mouse, the visible command menu lets you choose commands by pointing and clicking. If you hide the menu, you have to press Esc before using commands.

```
Word 5 for Professional Writing Applications¶
¶
With Version 5 of Microsoft Word, one of the best word
processing programs around has finally realized its
potential.  Naturally, the new version has all the graphics
features you'd expect in today's word processing
sweepstakes, in which the gap between desktop publishing
software and word processing software continues to narrow.
But for experienced Word users, what really counts is the
many thoughtful revisions that contribute to ease of use.
Word now inserts active page breaks!  They appear
automatically as you type, and as you insert or delete text
around them, their positions change.  The old Window Options
and Options command menus have been combined, so you no
longer have to use two commands to choose the options you
want.  When you change tab settings using the Format Tabs
Set command, the text changes position before you carry out
the command, so you can see what the effect of your change
will be.  Bravo, Microsoft!¶
        A new command, Format pOsition, provides the tools you
need to "anchor" graphics at absolute positions on the page.
Once "anchored" in this way, the text you insert will

Pg1 Co57        {¶}            ?                    Microsoft Word
```

Fig. 9.3.

The command menu hidden, showing 22 lines of text.

Hide the command menu for day-to-day use of Word. You can see more of your document, and you make the menu reappear by pressing Esc. Even if you use the mouse, the benefit of a larger display window probably outweighs the penalty of pressing Esc before using commands.

Removing Window Borders

One of WordPerfect's claims on the marketplace is its "clean screen," which shows nothing but your document and a status line. Not to be outdone, Microsoft has included an option in Word to hide window borders, producing a "clean screen" (see fig. 9.4). To hide the borders, choose **N**o in the **show borders** field of the Options command menu. You see 24 lines of text on the screen.

Caution: Hiding the window borders disables the mouse scrolling capabilities discussed in Chapter 3. If you like to use the mouse to scroll, don't hide the borders.

Fig. 9.4.

The "clean screen," showing 24 lines of text.

```
 -  Word 5 for Professional Writing Applications¶
    ¶
    With Version 5 of Microsoft Word, one of the best word
    processing programs around has finally realized its
    potential.  Naturally, the new version has all the graphics
    features you'd expect in today's word processing
    sweepstakes, in which the gap between desktop publishing
    software and word processing software continues to narrow.
    But for experienced Word users, what really counts is the
    many thoughtful revisions that contribute to ease of use.
    Word now inserts active page breaks!  They appear
    automatically as you type, and as you insert or delete text
    around them, their positions change.  The old Window Options
    and Options command menus have been combined, so you no
    longer have to use two commands to choose the options you
    want.  When you change tab settings using the Format Tabs
    Set command, the text changes position before you carry out
    the command, so you can see what the effect of your change
    will be.  Bravo, Microsoft!¶
        A new command, Format pOsition, provides the tools you
    need to "anchor" graphics at absolute positions on the page.
    Once "anchored" in this way, the text you insert will
    "float" around the graphic automatically--even if you're
    using the Insert mode.◆
 Pg1 Co49              {¶}              ?              Microsoft Word
```

Alt-F4

Displaying the Document Layout

New to Version 5 is the **show layout** field of the Options command menu. If you choose the **Yes** option in this field, Word displays running heads, side-by-side paragraphs, and multiple-column text right on the screen—and you can edit the text while displaying it this way.

As you quickly learn if you use this option, however, Word slows down considerably—so much so, in fact, that you may prefer to edit in the normal mode and switch to the show layout mode only if you want to see whether you have correctly created a complex format (such as running heads or multiple columns). The **show layout** toggle key, Alt-F4, is useful in this scenario. Use Alt-F4 to switch with a keystroke between the Yes and No options on the **show layout** field.

Using Color

New to Version 5 is a far more versatile color customization option than was previously available. You can display virtually every feature of the screen, including font sizes, character emphases, borders, and menus, in precisely the colors you want. The reasons for doing so go beyond the artistic. In Word's text mode, which is considerably faster than graphics mode, you cannot tell the differences among many character emphases, such as italic and underlining. For most purposes, the speed improvement is worth the loss of display accuracy. If you have a color monitor, however, you can assign distinctive colors to character emphases, so that you can tell the differences among them even in text mode. What's more, you can assign distinctive colors to font sizes—the only way you can see font size assignments on the screen. If you work with multiple font sizes, this fact is reason enough to equip your system with a color video card and monitor. The better your color system, the more color choices you have. You can truly paint the screen as you want with EGA and VGA systems.

To customize screen colors, do the following:

1. Choose the **O**ptions command, select the **colors** field, and press F1.

2. When the Colors menu appears (see fig. 9.5), use the arrow key or the mouse to select the display feature you want to customize.

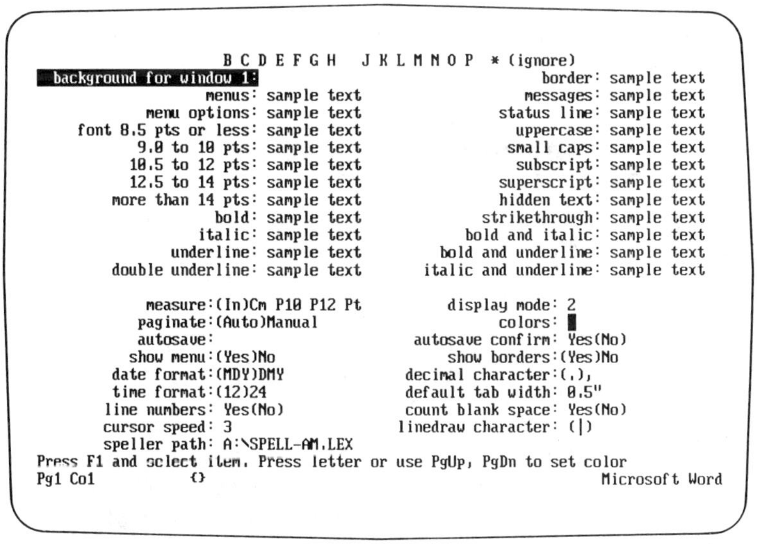

Fig. 9.5.

Choosing display colors with the Options command.

3. To apply one of the colors displayed on the top line to the selected display feature, press the letter of the color. Alternatively, press PgUp or PgDn to go through the gamut of color options.

As you peruse the colors for the selected display feature, the words *sample text* for the feature take on the currently selected color to provide a visual perception of what you are selecting.

4. After you choose a color for the selected display feature, use the arrow keys or the mouse to select another display feature.

5. Repeat steps 2 through 4 until you finish customizing all the display features you want to change.

6. Carry out the command by pressing Enter or clicking the command name.

Word saves the choices you make so that they are available the next time you use the program.

Note: If you have a CGA (Color Graphics Adapter) video card and monitor, you can choose colors only in text mode. With EGA and VGA monitors, you can choose colors in all modes.

Other Options

Table 9.1 is a brief overview of Options command choices not covered elsewhere in this book.

Table 9.1
Other Options Menu Choices

Option	Default	Description
show outline	No	Choose **Yes** to display the document text in outline mode, just as if you pressed Shift-F2. For more information on outlines, see Chapter 10, "Organizing Your Document with Outlining."
show style bar	No	Choose **Yes** to display the key codes of style sheet formats that you attached to the paragraphs in your document. The codes appear in the style bar just to the left of your text. This option is useful when you work with style sheets, as explained in Chapter 20, "Using Style Sheets."

Table 9.1—Continued

Option	Default	Description
paginate	Auto	Choose **No** to turn off the display of active page breaks. If you turn off the display, page breaks do not appear unless you use the Print Repaginate command.
mute	No	Choose **Yes** to silence the rather irritating "be-dap" sound Word emits when you make a mistake.
summary sheet	Yes	Choose **No** if you don't want a summary sheet to appear when you save your documents. (If you plan to use Library Document-retrieval, as described in Chapter 8, "Finding and Managing Documents," fill out the summary sheets).
date format	MDY	Choose **DMY** for non-U.S. date formats. When you insert the date slug from the standard glossary, Word displays the date in the format selected in this field. For more information about the standard glossary and the date slug, see Chapter 12, "Using Glossaries and Bookmarks."
time format	12	If you choose **24**, Word displays times in 24-hour format when you insert the time slug from the standard glossary. Otherwise, times are displayed in 12-hour format. For more information about the standard glossary and the time slug, see Chapter 12, "Using Glossaries and Bookmarks."

Table 9.1—Continued

Option	Default	Description
decimal character	.	Choose **,** (comma) to use the European decimal character. For more information on how Word handles numbers, see Chapter 11, "Creating Tables and Lists with Tabs, Autosort, and Math."
line numbers	No	Choose **Y**es to turn on a line number indicator on the status line. Word counts line numbers from page breaks. If you want Word to skip blank lines as it counts, choose Yes in the **skip blank lines** field.
count blank space	No	Choose **Y**es to tell Word to count blank lines and spaces when counting lines.
cursor speed	3	Choose a higher number to speed up the cursor, a lower one to slow it down. Caution: At a speed of **9**, the cursor really races around; before you know it, you can wipe out a whole screen of text while holding the Backspace key.
linedraw character			Press F1 to display a list of the characters you can use in Word's linedraw mode. For more information on this mode, see Chapter 17, "Creating Forms and Illustrations."
speller path		Word automatically updates this field when you install Word and the Spell program using SETUP. For more information, see the appendix, "Word and Your Computer."

Using Multiple Windows

A window is a frame through which you view a document. Think of the document window as if it were suspended just above the text, showing you about one-third page at a time. When you scroll your document, you move it up or down past the stationary window.

By default, Word displays a single window; you can open additional windows if you want—up to eight of them at a time. In these windows, you can display the following:

❏ Different parts of the same document. You can look at two parts of a single document, each in its own window, and scroll one, leaving the other stationary. This feature takes a little getting used to, but is very useful—especially when you copy or move text from one part of a document to another.

❏ Different documents. You can work with up to eight different documents at a time with Word, each in its own window. This feature makes it exceptionally easy to copy or move text from one document to another.

When you open a new window, the other windows shrink to make room (see fig. 9.6). You can zoom any window to full size at a keystroke (or mouse click). In this way, you can work with several parts of a document (or several different documents) and switch to full-screen views in seconds! Word's windowing capabilities put it at the top of its class. Get to know them and use them often!

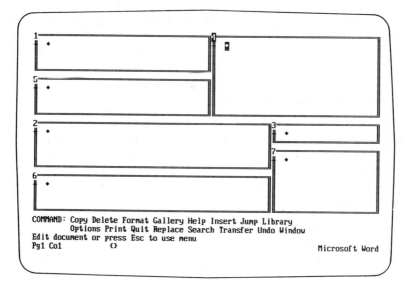

Fig. 9.6.

Multiple window display (unzoomed).

Note: You can display a special window that shows footnotes and annotations. This window is discussed in Chapter 14, "The Legal and Scholarly Word."

The following sections explain how to open a window, make a window active, size a window, move text between windows, zoom windows, and close windows.

One of several good reasons for using the mouse is the ease with which you can split, zoom, size, and close windows. You can accomplish all these tasks with the keyboard, but the mouse makes it easier and faster, as explained in the following sections.

Opening Windows

When you open a new window, you can split the screen horizontally or vertically. For most purposes, horizontal splits are best because you can see a whole line of text. You can split the screen with the keyboard or the mouse.

To split the screen with the keyboard, do the following:

1. Choose the **W**indow **S**plit command.

2. Choose the **H**orizontal or **V**ertical option.

3. When the Window Split Horizontal (shown in fig. 9.7) or Window Split Vertical command menu appears, press F1 in the **at line** field to activate a special cursor on the left window border (shown in fig. 9.8). Use the arrow keys to move the special cursor to the place you want the window split. Alternatively, just type in the **at line** field the line number where you want the window to split.

4. To clear the new window so that it displays a new blank document, choose the **Y**es option in the **clear new window** field. By default, this option is set to **N**o. If you split the screen without changing the **clear new window** field, Word displays an additional window on the document that is already open.

5. Carry out the command by pressing Enter or clicking the command name.

```
WINDOW SPLIT HORIZONTAL at line: 🯁   clear new window: Yes(No)

Enter number
Pg1 Co1            {}                   ?                   Microsoft Word
```

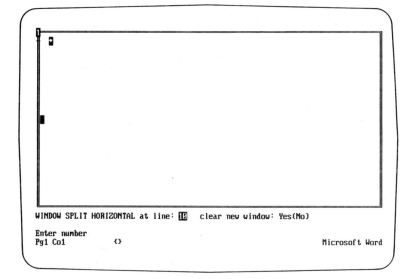

Fig. 9.7.

The Window Split Horizontal command menu.

Fig. 9.8.

Special cursor used to choose the window split location.

```
WINDOW SPLIT HORIZONTAL at line: 🯰🯱   clear new window: Yes(No)

Enter number
Pg1 Co1            {}                                       Microsoft Word
```

To split the screen with the mouse, do the following:

1. To split the screen vertically, point to the place on the top border where you want the split to occur. To split the screen horizontally, point to the right border.

2. When the mouse pointer changes shape (a big rectangle in text mode or a square outline in graphics mode), click the left button to split the screen without clearing the new window. To split the screen and clear the new window, click the right button.

Note: If the ruler is displayed, hold the Alt key before clicking the top border.

If you forgot to clear the new window when you split the screen, make it active (as described in the following section) and choose the **T**ransfer **C**lear **W**indow command.

To load an existing document into a new blank window, make it active (as described in the following section) and choose the **T**ransfer **L**oad command.

Making Windows Active

Only one window can be active at a time. When a window is active, the cursor appears in it, as does any text you type. In addition, the window number at the top left of the window is highlighted. To work in another window, you must move the cursor and make the other window active. You can make another window active with the keyboard, but by far the easiest and most convenient technique involves the mouse.

To make another window active with the keyboard, do the following:

1. Make sure that Word is in edit mode, not command mode. Word is in edit mode when no command on the command menu is highlighted.

2. Press F1 to make the next window in the number sequence active. Each window is numbered (1 through 8). When you press F1, the cursor moves through the windows in sequence.

When several windows are open on the screen, moving through all the preceding windows to get to the window you want can be somewhat tedious. With a mouse, however, you can select a new window immediately just by clicking the mouse cursor within the new window, as explained in the following steps.

Caution: In previous versions of Word, you could press Shift-F1 to move backward through the sequence of windows. Since Version 4, however, this key has been a speed-key shortcut for the Undo command. If you press Shift-F1, you could undo your previous text entry, editing, or formatting without realizing it.

To make another window active with the mouse, do the following:

1. Point at the character (or any other unit of text) you want to select in the window you want to activate.

2. Click the left or right button.

If you previously selected a block of text in the window you want to activate, you can make the window active without changing the selection. Just activate the window by pointing to the window number.

Sizing Windows

When more than one window is open on the screen, you can change the size of a window by using the keyboard or the mouse.

To size a window with the keyboard, do the following:

1. Activate the window you want to resize.

2. Choose the **W**indow **M**ove command.

3. When the Window Move command menu appears (see fig. 9.9), select the **to row** field and press F1. Use the arrow keys to move the special cursor to the row where you want the window's lower right corner. Alternatively, type in this field the row number where you want the lower right corner of the window.

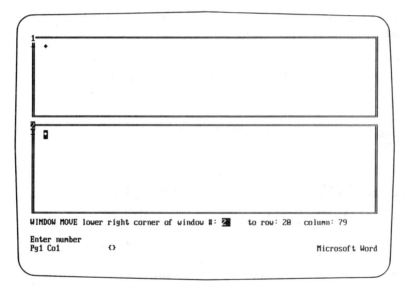

Fig. 9.9.

Sizing a window with the Window Move command.

```
1
  ◆


2
  ▯



WINDOW MOVE lower right corner of window #: 2    to row: 20    column: 79

Enter number
Pg1 Co1          {}                              Microsoft Word
```

4. Select the **column** field and press F1. Use the arrow keys to move the special cursor to the column where you want the window's lower right corner. Alternatively, type in this field the column number where you want the lower right corner of the window.

5. Carry out the command by pressing Enter or clicking the command name.

Note: You cannot change the lower right corner of the lower right window. To change its size, size one of the windows above or below it. Also, you cannot shrink a window if no other window can take its place. If you split the screen horizontally into two windows, for example, you cannot specify a new column location for either window's lower right corner. Nothing is "under" the windows; Word insists that the whole document display area be filled with one or more windows.

When sizing windows, you most often adjust the row dividing two horizontally split windows. Remember to make the top window active before using Window Move; adjust the split by typing a new number in the **to row** field. Just ignore the **column** field.

To size windows with the mouse, do the following:

1. Move the pointer to the lower right corner of the window you want to resize.

2. When the mouse pointer changes shape (a large rectangle in text mode or an arrow pointing four ways in graphics mode), click either button and drag the window to its new proportions.

3. Release the button when you are satisfied with the size of the window.

Moving and Copying Text with Multiple Windows

A major reason for splitting the screen is the ease with which you can copy and move text. You can use the split-screen technique to copy or move text from one part of a document to another. You can also use it to copy or move text between documents.

To copy or move text between two parts of the same document, do the following:

1. Split the screen horizontally and do not clear the new window. Two windows are open on the same document.

2. Scroll the bottom screen to the place where you want to copy or move text.

3. Make the top window active and select the text to be copied or moved. Use the **C**opy command (or Alt-F3) to copy the text to the scrap. Alternatively, use the **D**elete command (or the Del key) to delete the text to the scrap.

4. Make the bottom window active and position the cursor where you want the text stored in the scrap to appear. Then choose the **I**nsert command (or press Ins).

To copy or move text between two documents, do the following:

1. Split the screen horizontally and clear the new window. The top screen shows your document but the bottom screen is blank.

2. Use the **T**ransfer **L**oad command to load the second document into the bottom window.

3. Activate the window from which you want to copy or move text and select the text to be copied or moved. Use the **C**opy command (or Alt-F3) to copy the text to the scrap. Alternatively, use the **D**elete command (or the Del key) to delete the text to the scrap.

4. Activate the window in which you want to insert the text. Position the cursor where you want the text stored in the scrap to appear. Choose the **I**nsert command (or press Ins).

If you have a mouse, you can use the super-fast mouse copying and moving techniques (described in Chapter 3, "Word 5 Editing Strategies") to copy or move text between windows.

Zooming Windows

When you open three or more windows, it becomes difficult to work with the text displayed in the windows. To solve this problem, Word allows you to zoom any window to full size at a keystroke (or mouse click).

When you zoom a window, it expands to fill the whole document display area, hiding all other windows. (To remind you that you zoomed a window and other windows are hidden "underneath," the code ZM appears in the status line.) You don't need to save the hidden documents before zooming; they're still open, and Word prompts you to save them if you use the Quit command without doing so.

You can "unzoom" a window just as quickly. Even better, once in zoom mode, you can press F1 to move through the sequence of windows—and all the windows are zoomed as you move through them. Using this technique, you can display full views of up to eight different documents, and move among them with just one keystroke!

Ctrl-F1

To zoom a window with the keyboard, do the following:

1. Activate the window you want to zoom.

2. Press Ctrl-F1 to toggle on the zoom mode. The code ZM appears in the key status indicator on the status line.

To move to the next window in sequence while in zoom mode, just press F1.

To unzoom a window, press Ctrl-F1 again.

To zoom a window with the mouse, do the following:

1. Point to the window number of the window you want to zoom.

2. Click the right button.

To move to the next window in zoom mode, do the following:

1. Point to the window number of the displayed window.

2. Click the left button. The next window in sequence is displayed, zoomed to full size.

To unzoom a window, do the following:

1. Point to the window number of the zoomed window.

2. Click the right button.

Closing Windows

You can close windows one at a time by using the keyboard or mouse. When you close a window, Word loses the window's contents (unless you save them to disk). You can save the text in all the windows by at once using **T**ransfer **A**llsave, and you can close all of them (and clear the screen) by using the **T**ransfer **C**lear **A**ll command.

To close windows with the keyboard, do the following:

1. Activate the window you want to close. If you want to save the text in it, use the **T**ransfer **S**ave command.

2. Choose the **W**indow **C**lose command. Make sure that the correct window number is displayed.

3. Carry out the command by pressing Enter or clicking the command name.

If you see the message Enter Y to save changes to document, N to lose changes, or Esc to cancel, you did not save the text of the window. Press Y to save or N to abandon the changes to that window.

To close windows with the mouse, do the following:

1. Position the pointer on the top or right window border.

2. When the mouse changes shape (to an arrow pointing four ways), click both buttons.

If you see the message Enter Y to save changes to document, N to lose changes, or Esc to cancel, you did not save the text of the window. Press Y to save or N to abandon the changes to that window.

Chapter Summary

Experienced Word users like to hide the command menu when using Word. After all, it can be distracting to have all those command names in front of you as you grope for words while writing! When you press Esc, the menu jumps back on the screen. If you do not use the mouse, you may want to display a "clean screen" by hiding the window borders. Users of color systems are doubly lucky with Word 5's much-improved color customization features. Not only can you indulge in a computer-based form of interior decorating (dusky rose borders! burnt ocher background! orange command names!), you can also see font sizes on the screen.

By all means, make full use of multiple windows. Multiple windows are useful, of course, when copying or moving text from one part of a document (or one file) to another. With Word's zoom mode, you can load up to eight separate documents, each in its own full-size window, and move among them at a keystroke. As you learn in the next chapter, you can set up windows so that you can see a dynamically updated outline of your document's overall structure in one window while you write in the other! Windows aren't just a special little-used feature of Word; for anyone who wants to write productively and well with the computer, windows are part of the repertoire of basic techniques.

10

Organizing Your Document with Outlining

Word processing doesn't automatically improve writing. Because the display window allows only a limited view of the document, writers sometimes find it difficult to retain a grasp of the overall structure of the document. The problem is worsened with the penalties imposed by scrolling, which moves text only one-third of a page at a time. What's more, putting a document through a major reorganization is tedious and difficult, and as you move big blocks of text around, you can lose sight of how the change relates to the overall plan. The result, all too often, is that lengthy documents created on computers show signs of poor organization. And that's too bad—especially because writing teachers consider the quality of a document's organization to be the single most important factor in good writing.

Microsoft Word solves this problem by offering an outline mode, a remarkable feature that, for anyone who writes documents longer than letters, should make Word the program of choice in personal computer word processing. Word's outlining mode differs from an outline created on paper or even with a separate outlining program. The outline isn't separate from the document it outlines: it's part of the document, another way of looking at the document you're writing. In one view, you see the document's body text, the text that appears when you print. In the outlining view, you see the same document as an outline (with the body text hidden so that you see the document's overall structure). The headings and subheadings in the outline correspond to headings and subheadings in the document. When you shift to outline mode, the body text "collapses," or disappears, leaving the patterns of headings and subheadings you have created. At a keystroke, you can remind yourself how you have organized a lengthy and complex report, chapter, or essay.

And that's not all. When you rearrange headings or subheadings in the outline mode, Word actually restructures your document. Word moves the body text as well as the headings. What this means, in short, is that you can put a document through a major reorganization in just a few keystrokes. If you think the section entitled "The Meaning of Scouting" should come before "The Founder of Scouting: Baden-Powell," simply rearrange the headings on the outline, and Presto! Word moves the body text too. That's power editing, and once you appreciate what it means, you may never be satisfied with another word processing program.

You find a complete approach to creating and editing outlines, as well as restructuring complex documents, in this chapter. It covers all the basic commands, of course, but it does something more, too: this chapter shows you how to apply this wonderful feature to the creation, organization, and editing of lengthy, complex documents. Specifically, it covers the following:

- ❑ Creating an outline by typing headings and assigning heading levels

- ❑ Viewing your outline's structure by collapsing and expanding headings and body text

- ❑ Editing and restructuring your outline in the outline-organize mode

- ❑ Numbering an outline automatically

- ❑ Printing your outline

- ❑ Outlining an existing document so that you can see its structure in the outline mode

Note: In this chapter, K+, K−, and K* refer, respectively, to the plus, minus, and asterisk keys on the numeric keypad. Pressing the keyboard keys does not produce the same results. When a command uses a number, for example Alt-9 and Alt-0, you must use the numbers on the top row of the main keyboard.

If you have used Word 4, incidentally, you won't find any new outlining features or commands in Version 5—outlining is one of the few features that survived the Version 5 revision without changes.

Creating an Outline

Outlines can be created before you write your document, while you write it, or even after you write it. This section covers the creation of an outline in a blank document window. For information on outlining while or after you write text, see "Outlining an Existing Document," later in this chapter.

When you create an outline with Word, you work in the program's outline-edit mode. In this mode, you can type, correct, indent, and change the level of outline headings.

To shift to the outline-edit mode and enter a Level 1 heading, do the following:

Shift-F2

1. Choose the **O**ptions command.

2. When the Options Command menu appears, choose **Yes** in the **show outline** command field. Alternatively, use the Shift-F2 keyboard shortcut.

   After you return to the document window, the page and column number indicator changes to read Level 1. This message tells you that the text you type is entered as a first-level heading.

3. Type the title of your document. If you make a mistake, use the Backspace or Del key to correct your mistake and retype the heading. Press Enter.

The title becomes a Level 1 heading in the outline, as shown in figure 10.1.

Learn to use the Shift-F2 keyboard shortcut to toggle back and forth between document and outline mode. Because Shift-F2 is a toggle key, use it to shift from the document mode to the outline mode at a keystroke; another keystroke returns the screen to the document mode.

Fig. 10.1.

Level 1 heading (document title).

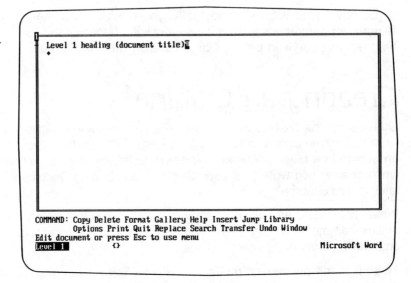

```
┌─────────────────────────────────────────────────────┐
│  Level 1 heading (document title)▌                   │
│  ◆                                                    │
│                                                       │
│                                                       │
│                                                       │
│                                                       │
│                                                       │
│                                                       │
│ COMMAND: Copy Delete Format Gallery Help Insert Jump Library │
│          Options Print Quit Replace Search Transfer Undo Window │
│ Edit document or press Esc to use menu                │
│ ▐Level 1▌         {}                    Microsoft Word │
└─────────────────────────────────────────────────────┘
```

Note: Because the **outline** field is in the Window Options part of the Options menu, the choice you make for outline mode applies only to the active window. Shift-F2 works only with the active window as well. If two or more window are open on the screen, only the active window shifts to the outline mode when you press Shift-F2.

Assigning Heading Levels

Every outline uses subheadings, or indented headings. If Level 1 is used for the document's title, Level 2 corresponds to major section titles.

To create a subheading, do the following:

1. Place the cursor at the end of the Level 1 heading and press Enter.

2. Press Alt-0 to indicate that you want to type a subheading.

   The cursor jumps one default tab stop to the right. The status line displays Level 2.

3. Type the subheading (see fig. 10.2).

To continue typing Level-2 headings, just press Enter. When you press Enter in outline-edit mode, Word starts a new heading or subheading at the same level. In this way, you can rapidly type all your document's major section titles.

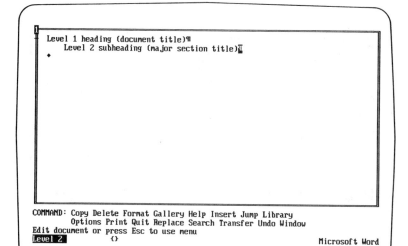

```
┌─────────────────────────────────────────────────────────┐
│ Level 1 heading (document title)¶                        │
│     Level 2 subheading (major section title)⌐            │
│   •                                                      │
│                                                          │
│                                                          │
│                                                          │
│                                                          │
│                                                          │
│                                                          │
│                                                          │
│                                                          │
│                                                          │
│ COMMAND: Copy Delete Format Gallery Help Insert Jump Library│
│          Options Print Quit Replace Search Transfer Undo Window│
│ Edit document or press Esc to use menu                   │
│ Level 2            {}                    Microsoft Word   │
└─────────────────────────────────────────────────────────┘
```

Fig. 10.2.

Adding a Level 2 subheading.

Use this procedure to insert Level 3 subheadings within the existing Level 2 subheadings:

1. Position the cursor at the beginning of the Level 2 subheading below the place where you want to insert the new subheading.

   Use the arrow keys or the mouse to move around the outline, just as you do with ordinary text.

2. Press Enter.

3. Press Alt-0 to indicate that you want to type a subheading.

   The status line displays Level 3.

4. Type the Level 3 subheading (see fig. 10.3).

Caution: If your document has body text, be sure to create a new line only as suggested in step 1 above: press Enter at the beginning of the heading below the place where you want to insert a new heading. Otherwise, Word links the existing heading's body text with the new heading.

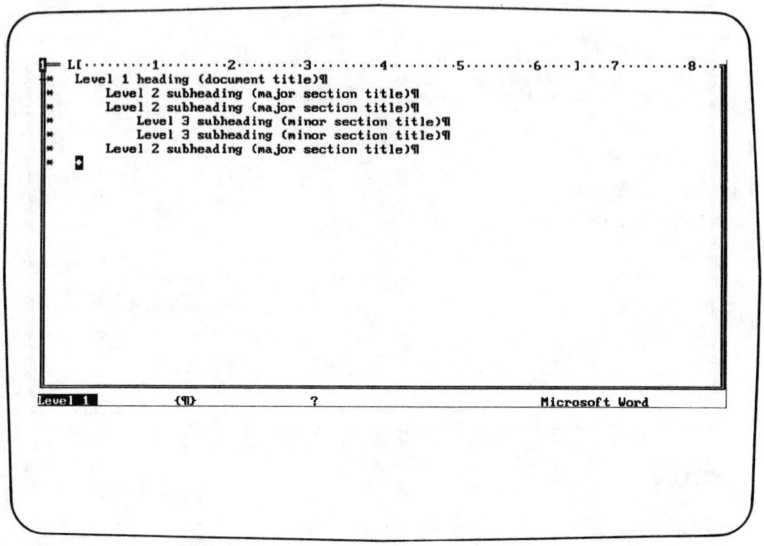

Fig. 10.3.

Inserting a Level 3
subheading.

```
  L[·········1·········2·········3·········4·········5·········6····]····7·········8···
    Level 1 heading (document title)¶
        Level 2 subheading (major section title)¶
        Level 2 subheading (major section title)¶
            Level 3 subheading (minor section title)¶
            Level 3 subheading (minor section title)¶
        Level 2 subheading (major section title)¶

        ▯



 Level 1              {¶}              ?                    Microsoft Word
```

Changing a Subheading's Indentation

If you change your mind about a heading's level, you can move it left
(raise its level) or move it right (lower its level).

To move a subheading left (raise its level), do the following:

1. Position the cursor anywhere within the heading you want to
   move.

2. Press Alt-9.

To move a subheading right (lower its level), do the following:

1. Position the cursor anywhere within the heading you want to
   move.

2. Press Alt-0.

Note: You cannot indent a subheading more than one tab stop farther
than the preceding heading. Doing so is illogical, anyway; every
subheading has a preceding heading indented one tab stop less than
itself.

Collapsing and Expanding Headings

Once you fill out your outline with headings and subheadings at several levels, it may be large enough to exceed the size of the screen (see fig. 10.4). If you cannot see the outline's overall structure, the outline mode's usefulness is lessened. For this reason, you can collapse subheadings—that is, hide them so that they are temporarily out of view. You can expand or reveal them later.

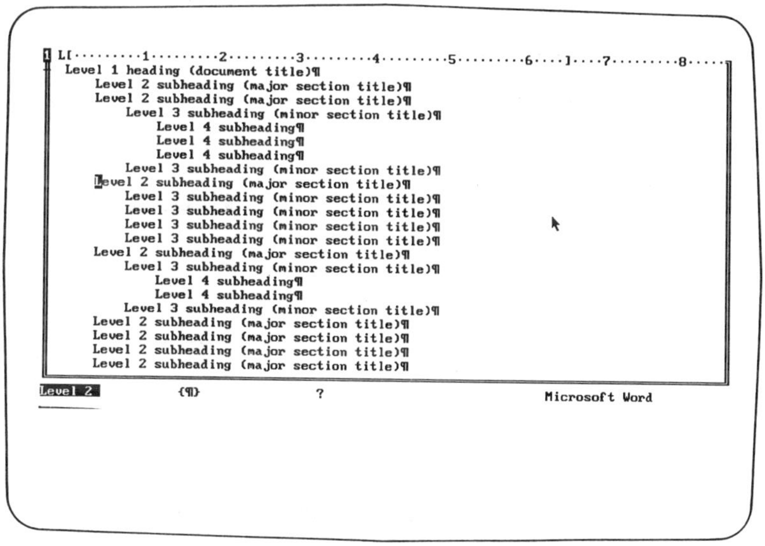

Fig. 10.4.

An outline filling more than one screen loses some effectiveness.

Collapsing Headings

You can collapse all the subheadings that fall under a single heading if you want. Alternatively, you can collapse all the subheadings down to a specific level. After you collapse subheadings, a plus sign (+) appears in the status bar next to the heading to remind you that something is hidden.

To collapse the subheadings under a heading with the keyboard, do the following:

1. Place the cursor on the heading above the subheadings you want to collapse.

2. Press K –.

The subheadings disappear from view and a plus sign appears in the status bar (see fig. 10.5).

Note: If you use a laptop computer without a numeric keypad, press Alt-8 instead of K−.

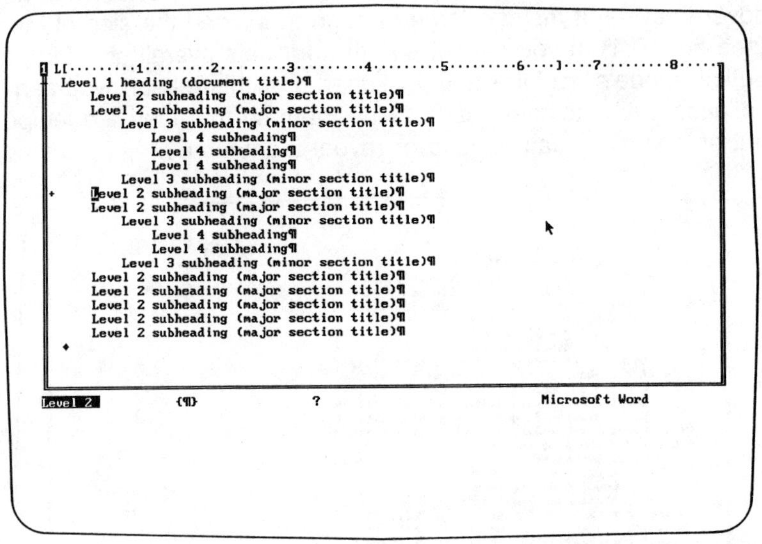

Fig. 10.5.

The plus sign in the status bar indicates collapsed subheadings.

```
█ L[········1·········2·········3·········4·········5·········6····]···7·········8·····│
  █ Level 1 heading (document title)¶
        Level 2 subheading (major section title)¶
        Level 2 subheading (major section title)¶
            Level 3 subheading (minor section title)¶
                Level 4 subheading¶
                Level 4 subheading¶
                Level 4 subheading¶
            Level 3 subheading (minor section title)¶
    ·   █evel 2 subheading (major section title)¶
        Level 2 subheading (major section title)¶
            Level 3 subheading (minor section title)¶
                Level 4 subheading¶
                Level 4 subheading¶
            Level 3 subheading (minor section title)¶
        Level 2 subheading (major section title)¶
        Level 2 subheading (major section title)¶
        Level 2 subheading (major section title)¶
        Level 2 subheading (major section title)¶
        Level 2 subheading (major section title)¶
    ·

  Level 2          {¶}              ?                        Microsoft Word
```

To collapse the subheadings under a heading with the mouse, do the following:

1. Point to the heading above the subheadings you want to collapse.

2. Click both buttons.

To collapse all the subheadings down to a level you specify, do the following:

1. With the cursor anywhere in the outline, press Ctrl-K+.

2. When the message Enter a number between 1 and 7 appears, press the number of the lowest level you want to see.

To display Levels 1, 2, and 3, for instance, press 3.

Note: If you use a laptop computer without a numeric keypad, you can press Alt-7 instead of Ctrl-K+.

Expanding Headings

You can expand the collapsed subheadings one level below a heading, or, if you want, you can expand all the subheadings, no matter what level, beneath a heading.

To expand the collapsed subheadings one level below a heading with the keyboard, do the following:

1. Select the heading below which you want to expand the subheadings one level.

2. Press K+.

To expand the collapsed subheadings one level below a heading with the mouse, do the following:

1. Point to the heading below which you want to expand the subheadings one level.

2. Click the right button.

To expand all the subheadings under a heading with the keyboard, do the following:

1. Select the heading below which you want to expand all the subheadings.

2. Press K*.

Note: If you use a laptop computer without a numeric keypad, you can press the PrtSc key instead of K*.

Adding and Managing Body Text

When you finish roughing out your outline, you add body text, the ordinary text of your document. To add body text to the outline, shift to the document mode, format the titles and headings as you want them to look in your final document, and type the text under each heading. To view your document's structure, return to the outline mode, collapse the body text, and adjust the outline as you want.

The following sections explain how to do each step of this procedure.

Formatting the Headings

When you press Shift-F2 to return to document mode, the indentations created in outline mode disappear (see fig. 10.6). But don't worry! They're not lost. Just toggle Shift-F2 again to return to the outline-edit mode, and the indentations return. At this point, however, you want to format the headings, so return to document mode. Add character formatting as you want, and use the **F**ormat **P**aragraph command to add blank lines, indentations, and other paragraph formats (see fig. 10.7).

 Caution: Don't add blank lines or indentations to headings by pressing Enter or Tab. If you do, your outline is more difficult to work with—extraneous "empty" headings and indents appear where they don't belong. If you want indentations and blank lines, use the **F**ormat **P**aragraph command to add these characteristics to the headings.

Fig. 10.6.

The appearance of the outline in document mode.

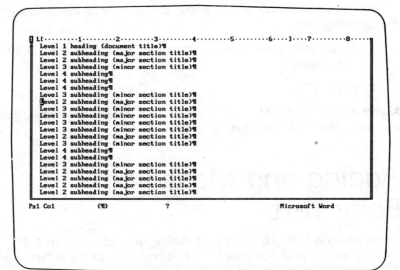

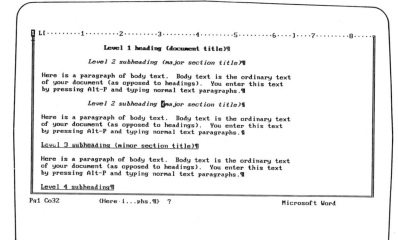

Fig. 10.7.

Formatting the headings.

Adding Body Text

To add body text to your document, do the following:

1. Place the cursor at the end of the heading to which you want to add body text.

2. Press Enter.

3. Press Alt-P to define the new paragraph as a body text paragraph. If you don't, Word defines the body text you enter as a heading, and the text appears as such in outline mode.

4. Add the desired paragraph formats you want and type the text.

Important: Whenever you start a new paragraph, remember to press Alt-P to define the paragraph as body text.

Shifting Back to the Outline-Edit Mode and Collapsing Body Text

Once you add body text to the headings, press Shift-F2 to return to the outline-edit mode. When you do, you find that the body text you added is visible (see fig. 10.8). Each body text paragraph is marked with a capital T in the style bar. To see only the outline, collapse the body text. You can collapse the body text under a single heading or, better, you can collapse all the body text in one command.

Fig. 10.8.

The appearance of the outline in outline-edit mode after adding body text.

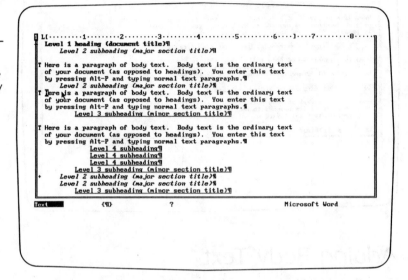

To collapse the body text under a single heading, do the following:

1. Select the heading for which you want to collapse the body text.

2. Press Shift- − (minus sign).

An uppercase T appears in the style bar to warn you that body text is hidden under the heading (see fig. 10.9).

You can expand the body text under a single heading by using Shift- +, but you probably will do so rarely. Body text is more of a nuisance than an asset in outline-edit mode. You always can see body text by pressing Shift-F2 to return to the document mode.

Note: If you use a laptop computer without a numeric keypad, you can press Shift-Alt-8 instead of Shift- − . You can press Shift-Alt-7 instead of Shift- + .

To collapse all the body text at once, do the following:

1. Press Shift-F10 to select the whole outline.

   Word automatically shifts to the outline-organize mode when you press Shift-F10.

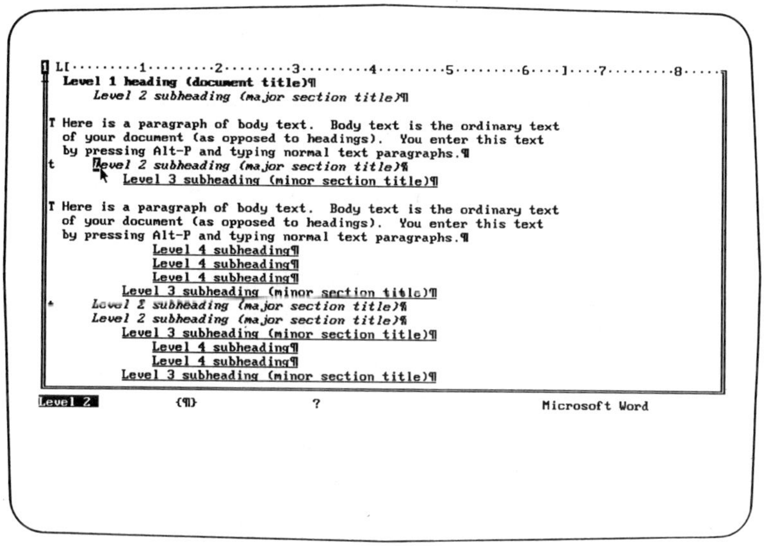

Fig. 10.9.

Outline with some body text hidden (lowercase t in style bar) and some displayed (uppercase T).

2. Press Shift- − .

3. Press Shift-F5 to exit the outline-organize mode.

You learn more about the outline-organize mode later in this chapter. For now, be sure that you exit this mode after hiding all the body text.

As you toggle back and forth between document and outline, you quickly realize that it would be nice if you could select a mode that hides body text automatically. (Microsoft, how about making this change for Version 6?) Currently, every time you add body text in the document mode, the new text appears in the outline after you toggle Shift-F2. To see the structure of the outline, you must hide the body text by pressing Shift-F10 and Shift- − . If you tire of pressing these keys, however, here is a dandy little macro that does the job in one keystroke:

<Shift F2><Shift F10><Shift minus><Shift F5>

For more information on creating, saving, and using macros, see Chapter 21, "Creating and Using Word 5 Macros."

Table 10.1 sums up the outlining keys you have learned so far.

Table 10.1
Keys and Commands for Outlining

Key(s)	Effect
Shift-F2	Toggle between document view and outline view
Alt-0	Lower the selected heading's level
Alt-9	Raise the selected heading's level
K− or Alt-7	Collapse subheadings and body text below selected heading
K+ or Alt-8	Expand subheadings (not body text) below selected heading
Shift-K+ or Shift-Alt-7	Expand body text below selected heading
Shift-K− or Shift-Alt-8	Collapse body text below selected heading
K* or PrtSc	Expand all headings below the selected heading
Ctrl-K+	Display headings to the specified level
Shift-F5	Toggle between outline-edit and outline-organize mode

You can display a document in outline mode in one window while showing the document mode in another. Try zooming the windows to full size. Then you can move from document to outline and back just by pressing F1! For more information on using windows, see Chapter 9, "Customizing the Screen and Using Windows."

Using Outlining To Move Around in a Lengthy Document

Toggling between the document mode and the outline mode, as you have learned, is a wonderful way to keep your document's overall structure in mind as you write. This capability can be useful for another reason as well. In a lengthy document, it can be tedious to scroll using PgUp or PgDn, and if you don't know on which page a section starts, the Jump Page command isn't much help either. But you can scroll with great precision using the outline mode.

To scroll through a lengthy document using the outline mode, do the following:

1. Press Shift-F2 to enter the outline mode.

2. Hide the body text so that you can see the outline's structure by pressing Shift-F10 and then Shift- − .

3. Place the cursor on the heading to which you want to scroll.

4. Press Shift-F2 again to return to the document mode.

Easy, isn't it?

Restructuring an Outline

As you have already learned, you can edit the text within a heading in the outline-edit mode. To restructure your outline by moving headings around, however, shift to the outline-organize mode by pressing Shift-F5. After you do, the word ORGANIZE appears on the status line. When in outline-organize mode, you will find that the cursor keys change their functions (see table 10.2 for a list of the cursor keys and their new functions). The smallest unit of text you can select in the outline-organize mode is an entire heading (with its paragraph mark).

Note: Shift-F5 has no effect in document mode. To use the outline-organize mode, press Shift-F2 to switch to the outline-edit mode. Then press Shift-F5. To leave the outline-edit mode, press Shift-F5 again. To return to your document, press Shift-F2 again.

The following sections explain how to restructure an outline by moving and deleting headings.

Table 10.2
The Keyboard in Outline-Organize Mode

Key	Effect
Up arrow	Selects preceding heading at current level (skips headings at lower levels)
Down arrow	Selects next heading at current level (skips headings at lower levels)
Left arrow or F9	Selects the next heading up, regardless of level
Right arrow or F10	Selects next heading down, regardless of level
Home	Selects nearest heading at next higher level above the selected heading
End	Selects last heading at next lower level below the selected heading
F6	Selects the current heading and all subheadings and/or body text below it
F6-down arrow	Selects the current heading and following headings at the same level
Del	Deletes the selected heading to scrap
Ins	Inserts heading from scrap

Restructuring Your Document by Copying and Moving Headings

Now here's the fun part. When you select a heading and press Del to cut it to the scrap, Word doesn't just delete the heading. The program also deletes the subheadings and body text under the heading. To move the whole package (heading, subheadings, and text) to a new location, simply position the cursor where you want the heading to appear and press Ins. Presto! You have just restructured your whole document.

As just suggested, you may use any of the standard text copying and moving techniques in outline-organize mode to restructure your outline and body text. You can even use speed-key shortcuts and the super-fast mouse copying an moving techniques described in Chapter 3, "Word 5 Editing Strategies."

Deleting Headings

If you want to remove a heading and everything under it, select the heading in the outline-organize mode and press Del. If you delete the wrong heading, use **U**ndo immediately.

Caution: The editing capabilities in the outline mode are very powerful. If you are not careful, you can delete body text you want to save. Before deleting a heading, remember that Word deletes not only the heading, but also all the subheadings and body text under it. So if you want to remove just the heading (but not the subheadings or body text stored under it), delete the heading's text in the document mode, not the outline mode.

Outlining an Existing Document

You can use all the techniques discussed in this chapter even if you didn't start your document with an outline. Following is the procedure to do so.

1. Load the document. If the document lacks a title and headings, add them.

2. Press Shift-F2 to go to the outline-edit mode.

3. Place the cursor in the first heading.

4. Press Alt-9 to define the paragraph as an outline heading. Word defines the paragraph as a Level 1 heading.

5. Press Alt-0 to lower the heading's level if you want. Keep pressing Alt-0 to lower the heading still further. If you lower the heading too many levels, press Alt-9 to raise the level.

6. Repeat steps 4 and 5 until you define all the document headings as outline headings.

7. Hide the body text by press Shift-F10 and Shift- – .

8. Exit the outline-edit mode by pressing Shift-F5.

Now your document is outlined! You can use the outline as a guide to the structure of your document while editing and writing, or you can restructure large text units by restructuring the outline.

Numbering an Outline Automatically

If you want Word to number your outline automatically, follow these steps. Word uses the outline numbering scheme suggested in *The Chicago Manual of Style* (University of Chicago Press).

1. In the outline-edit mode, select the first character in the outline.

2. Choose the **L**ibrary **N**umber command (see fig. 10.10).

Fig. 10.10.

The Library Number Command menu.

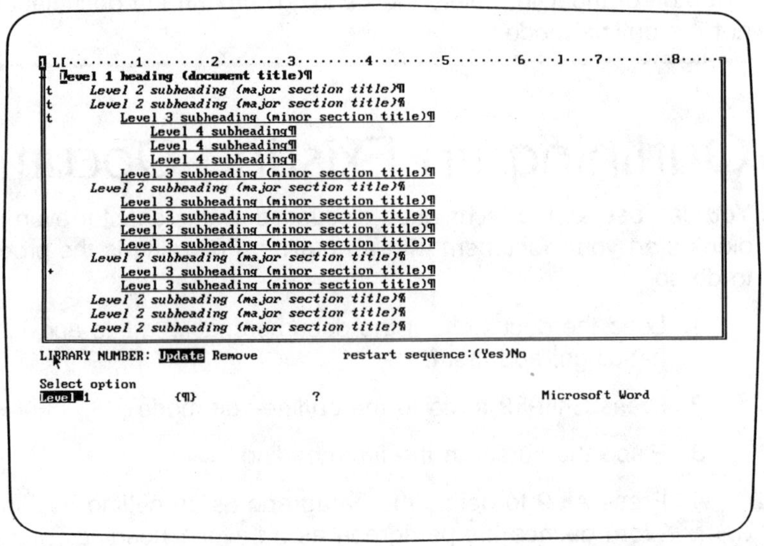

```
[] L[·······1·······2·······3·······4·······5·······6···]···7·······8···]
[Level 1 heading (document title)¶
t     Level 2 subheading (major section title)¶
t     Level 2 subheading (major section title)¶
t        Level 3 subheading (minor section title)¶
            Level 4 subheading¶
            Level 4 subheading¶
            Level 4 subheading¶
        Level 3 subheading (minor section title)¶
  Level 2 subheading (major section title)¶
        Level 3 subheading (minor section title)¶
        Level 3 subheading (minor section title)¶
        Level 3 subheading (minor section title)¶
        Level 3 subheading (minor section title)¶
  Level 2 subheading (major section title)¶
+       Level 3 subheading (minor section title)¶
        Level 3 subheading (minor section title)¶
  Level 2 subheading (major section title)¶
  Level 2 subheading (major section title)¶
  Level 2 subheading (major section title)¶


LIBRARY NUMBER: Update Remove          restart sequence:(Yes)No

Select option
Level 1           {¶}           ?                    Microsoft Word
```

3. Choose **U**pdate and make sure that the **Y**es option is selected in the **restart sequence** field.

4. Press Enter to carry out the command.

Numbers appear in the outline, as shown in figure 10.11, as well as in the document, as shown in figure 10.12.

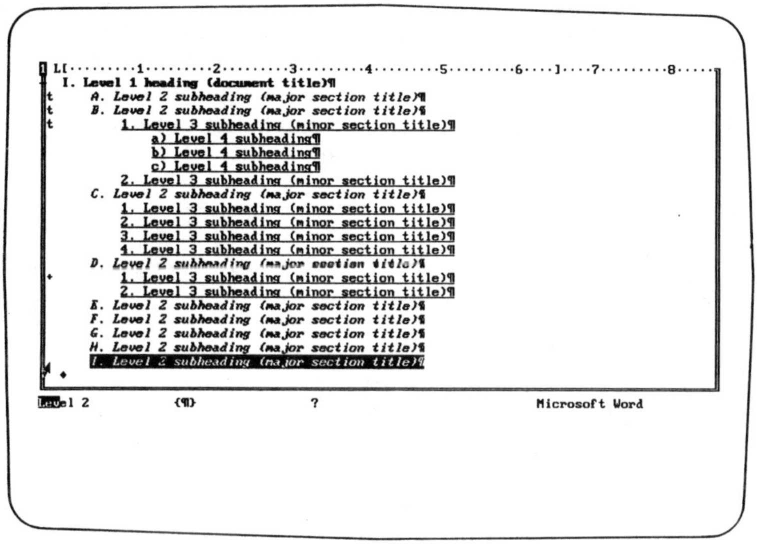

Fig. 10.11.

An automatically-numbered outline (outline mode).

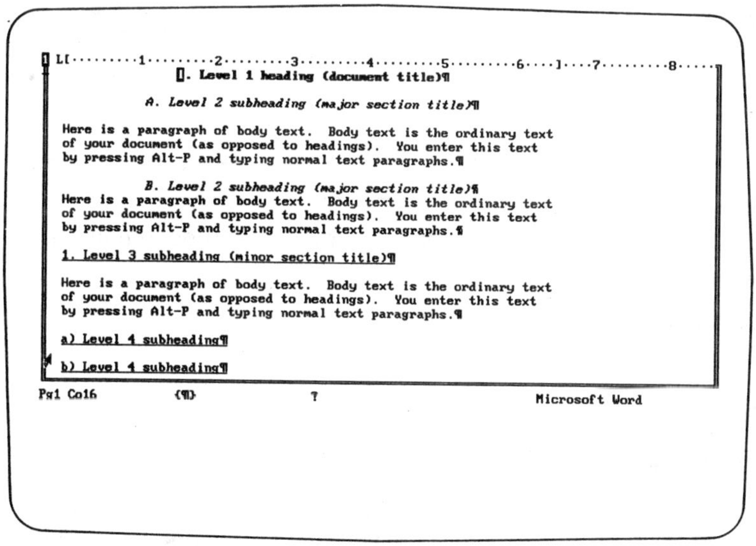

Fig. 10.12.

An automatically-numbered outline (document mode).

To outline a document using the numbering format used in legal documents, switch to the outline-edit mode. Then type *1.* (the number 1 and a period) followed by a space at the beginning of the first heading. Then use the **L**ibrary **N**umber command. The outline is numbered in the legal format (see fig. 10.13).

Fig. 10.13.

Legal numbering format for outlines.

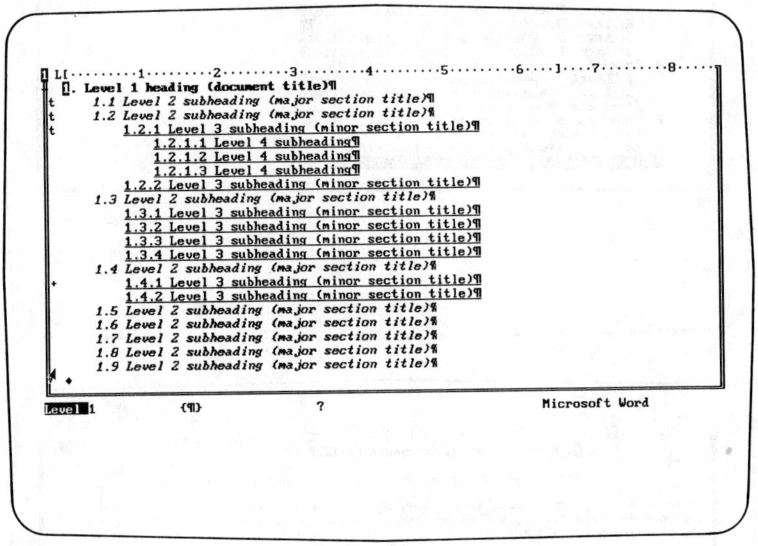

To remove automatic numbering from your outline and document, do the following:

1. Select the first character of the first heading.
2. Choose the **L**ibrary **N**umber command.
3. Choose the **R**emove option.
4. Press Enter to carry out the command.

Word removes all the numbers it added and also removes the first number you typed. The command removes legal numbers as well as the default outline numbers.

Printing Your Outline

You can print your outline without printing body text if you want. To print only the outline, do the following:

1. Press Shift-F2 to enter the outline mode.

2. Hide the body text, if any is showing, by pressing Shift-F10, Shift- − , and Shift-F5.

3. Collapse subheadings to a level you specify, if you want, by pressing Ctrl-K + .

4. Choose the **P**rint **P**rinter command.

Chapter Summary

Word's outlining capabilities are unparalleled in the world of personal computing software. They are so unusual, in fact, that many users probably don't have the slightest idea how to use them! For most people, writing an outline brings back yucky memories of autocratic grade-school teachers, rigid outlines printed out laboriously on lined paper, and other horrors. With Word, however, outlining isn't just a good idea for getting organized before writing; it's also a way of intelligently adapting to the computer as a writing medium, a medium that narrows the overall view of your document's structure. What's more, Word's outlining mode is a way to move around in a large document, and even to restructure large text domains at a keystroke. If you frequently write lengthy or complex documents, such as business reports, journal articles, or funding proposals, make Word's outlining features part of your daily repertoire of Word 5 techniques.

11

Creating Tables and Lists with Tabs, Autosort, and Math

Common features of most business documents, especially reports and proposals, are tables (such as a table of expenses for a quarter) and lists (such as a bibliography). With Word, creating and formatting tables and lists are easy tasks for the reasons you expect: Word's text entry, editing, and formatting capabilities, which you are already familiar with, make typing tables and lists a snap. With Version 5 of Word, creating tables and lists is even easier than with previous versions; when you change tabs with the Format Tab Set command, Word repositions the aligned text right on the screen, before you carry out the command. You can get your table just right before pressing Enter. If you have a mouse, you can skip the Format Tab Set command completely and just click the tabs you want right on the ruler.

If you frequently prepare documents with more than one or two tables, you're in for a very special treat when you use Word 5. Just imagine how much time you can save when Word 5 does these tasks automatically:

❏ Numbers all the tables in your report and renumbers them if you restructure your text

287

❏ Fills in the page and table numbers of tables cross-referenced in the text and corrects the numbers if you rearrange the tables

❏ Adds precisely drawn horizontal and vertical rules (straight lines) so that your tables appear as if they were professionally typeset

❏ Adds a column of numbers and performs other arithmetic operations right on the screen

❏ Sorts columns or lists of numerical or alphabetical data in descending or ascending order

❏ Imports spreadsheets from Lotus 1-2-3, Microsoft Excel, or Multiplan directly into your Word documents so that the spreadsheet appears as a table

These features aren't just for advanced users of Word; they're for anyone who prepares tables and lists regularly in everyday writing situations. This chapter surveys these useful Word 5 features, beginning with a survey of Word 5's much-improved commands for setting, moving, and deleting custom tab stops. The next section presents a table tutorial that opens the door to Word's powerhouse of table-related features. If you want to create high-quality tables and improve your table-crunching productivity, don't skip this tutorial. Also covered in this chapter are Word 5's math and list-sorting features.

Using Custom Tabs

When you open a new document with Word, the document's tab stops conform to the measurement entered in the **default tab width** field of the Options menu. The preset measurement in this field is **0.5″**. With this setting, tab stops appear every half inch across the screen.

To set new tabs for an entire document, change the Options menu **default tab width** by typing a new measurement in this field. Most often, however, you want to set up special custom tabs for a section of your document, such as a table or list. To create custom tabs, use the Format Tab Set command.

Before starting on custom tabs, however, note a very important fact about custom tabs: they're a paragraph format. When you use the Format Tab Set command to create custom tabs, the command affects the currently selected paragraph (or paragraphs, if more than one is selected). Remember that a paragraph in Word is all the text between two paragraph marks. A paragraph can be a single line or can refer to dozens of lines. Because custom tabs are paragraph formats, you can create a document with many different tab configurations, each assigned to a particular paragraph.

When you set a tab, you can specify its alignment and leader as well as its position. *Alignment* refers to the way Word lines up the text at the tab. The default alignment is **L**eft flush, but you can choose **R**ight flush, **C**enter, or **D**ecimal alignment (numbers are lined up at the decimal point). You can also choose **V**ertical alignment, which enters a vertical line at the tab stop. A *leader* is a row of characters before the tab stop. Word sets no default leader, but you can choose dots, dashes, or underscore leaders. If you choose dots, Word enters a row of dots automatically. Figure 11.1 shows the custom tab options.

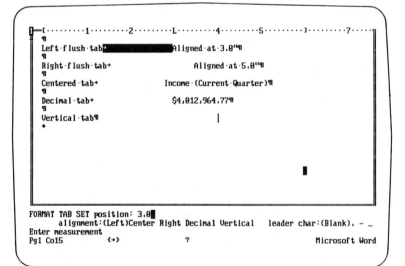

Fig. 11.1.

Custom tab options.

When you use custom tabs, choose the **Y**es option in the **ruler** field of the Options menu. As you will learn, Word displays codes on the ruler that show where you set custom tabs. Also, choose the **A**ll option in the **show non-printing symbols** field of the same command menu. Word displays right-facing arrows whenever you press the Tab key. You will find the display of tab keystrokes valuable when you edit tables and align text.

> **Caution:** Remember to avoid aligning text with spaces. If you use spaces to align text, Word may not print the text aligned properly—even if the text looks fine on the screen. Always use tabs to align text in columns on the screen.

Setting Custom Tabs

When you set a custom tab, Word cancels the default tab stops to the left of the first custom tab (but not to the right). Remember that the tab you set applies only to the paragraph or paragraphs selected.

Alt-F1

To set a custom tab, do the following:

1. Select the paragraph or paragraphs to which you would like to apply the custom tabs.

2. Choose the **F**ormat **T**ab **S**et command. Alternatively, use the Alt-F1 keyboard shortcut.

3. When the Format Tab Set menu appears (again see fig. 11.1), press F1. Then use the arrow keys to move the highlight along the ruler to the location of the first tab you want to set. Alternatively, type a measurement (such as *6.2*) in the **position** field.

   Use the right- and left-arrow keys to move the highlight one space at a time. If you press PgUp or PgDn, Word moves the highlight one inch at a time. Press End to go to the right indent mark, and Home to go to the left indent mark.

4. When the cursor is positioned where you want the tab stop, choose **L**eft, **R**ight, **C**enter, **D**ecimal, or **V**ertical to create a custom tab with the alignment you want.

   If you want to create a tab stop with a leader, type the leader character before the alignment letter. To create a flush-right stop with a dot leader, for instance, type *.R*.

5. If you want to set another custom tab for the same paragraph, repeat steps 2 and 3.

6. Press Enter to carry out the command.

After you carry out the command, Word places codes—L(eft), R(ight), C(enter), or D(ecimal)—in the ruler to show the tab alignments set (for an example of a left-tab marker, see fig. 11.1). If you chose a leader character, Word also displays the leader character (a period, dash, or underscore) in front of the tab alignment code.

A marvelous and welcome Word 5 change makes it even easier to set tabs with the mouse. In preceding versions, you had to use the Format Tab Set command and then click the ruler. Now you can skip the command entirely! Following is the procedure to set tabs with the mouse:

1. With the ruler displayed, select the paragraph or paragraphs to which the tab stops are to apply.

2. If you want an alignment other than flush left, click the L next to the left indent marker on the ruler (see fig. 11.2) until it displays the alignment code you want. Skip this step if you want flush-left alignment.

3. To select a leader character, click the space left of the L on the ruler line until the alignment you want appears.

4. To set the tab, click the ruler where you want the tab stop.

5. To set additional tabs, repeat steps 2 through 4.

Easy, isn't it? Kudos, Microsoft.

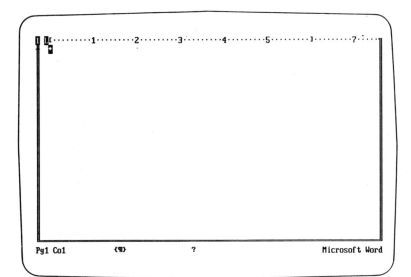

Fig. 11.2.

Setting tabs from the ruler.

Moving Custom Tabs

Once you have set custom tabs and typed some text, you may find that the aligned text doesn't please your eye. If so, it's very easy to move custom tabs. A very welcome new Word 5 feature lets you see on-screen the effect of moving a tab, even before you carry out the command. When you move the tab, Word keeps the alignment and leader choices made for it. Mouse users find it just as easy to move tabs as to set them; you can bypass Format Tab Set completely.

To move a custom tab stop with the keyboard, use the following procedure:

1. Select the paragraph or paragraphs containing the tab you want to move.

2. Choose the **F**ormat **T**ab **S**et command or press Alt-F1.

3. Press F1. Then press the down- or up-arrow keys to select the tab you want to move.

   Word highlights the tab code on the ruler (see fig. 11.3).

4. Press Ctrl-left arrow to move the tab stop to the left, or press Ctrl-right arrow to move the tab stop to the right. Word realigns the text right on the screen!

   Note: If you "run over" another tab stop, Word deletes the one you run over.

5. To move other tabs, repeat steps 3 and 4.

6. Press Enter to carry out the command.

It's even easier to move custom tabs with the mouse. Just position the cursor in the paragraph containing the tab stop you want to move. With the ruler displayed, point to the tab stop code you want to move, click the right button, and drag the tab to its new position.

To change a tab's alignment width with the mouse, do the following:

1. Click the left tab mark on the ruler until it displays the alignment you want.

2. Point to the tab you want to change and click the left button.

Deleting Custom Tabs

You can delete custom tab stops one at a time or restore the default tabs in just one command.

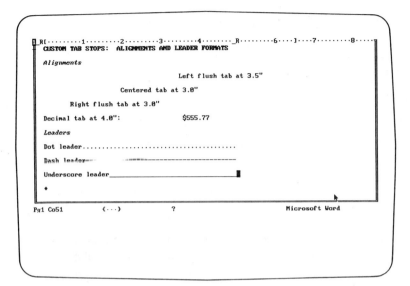

Fig. 11.3.

Moving tabs with the keyboard.

To delete custom tabs one at a time, use the following steps:

1. Select the paragraph or paragraphs containing the custom tab that you want to delete. Choose Format Tab Set or press Alt-F1.

2. Press the down-arrow key to select the tab you want to delete.

3. Press Del to erase the tab. Alternatively, press Ctrl-Del to erase the selected tab and all the custom tabs to the right of the selected tab.

4. To delete additional individual tabs, repeat steps 2 and 3.

5. Press Enter to carry out the command.

To help you remember the special keys used when creating, moving, and deleting tabs with the keyboard, see table 11.1.

Table 11.1
Special Keys when Using Format Tab Set

Key	Effect with Format Tab Set
F1	Select tab stops on ruler
Down arrow	Select next tab stop right (after pressing F1)
Up arrow	Select next tab stop left (after pressing F1)

Table 11.1—Continued

Key	Effect with Format Tab Set
Right arrow	Move highlight right on ruler
Left arrow	Move highlight left on ruler
PgUp	Move highlight one inch left on ruler
PgDn	Move highlight one inch right on ruler
Del	Delete custom tab stop
Ctrl-Del	Delete custom tab stop and all custom tab stops to right of cursor

Deleting custom tab stops with the mouse is easy. Just position the cursor in the paragraph containing the stop and, with the ruler displayed, click both buttons on the tab stop code. Presto! It's gone.

Creating and Editing Tables

Now that you have surveyed the essentials of creating, moving, and deleting tabs, it's time to tackle tables. Running through this section is an extended tutorial to guide you through many seemingly advanced Word commands, most of which you haven't used before. As you will surely agree, however, it's easy to use these powerful features. Once you see what they can do for you, chances are good that you will make them part of your everyday Word working routine.

Creating the Table Header

The table header contains the table number, the title, the column headings, and the *stub* (the heading for the left column). In the following tutorial, you create a simple ruled table with two column headings.

Numbering the Table Automatically

To have Word number your tables automatically, enter a series code name (a new Word 5 feature) instead of the table number when you type the table's header. (A series code name can contain up to 31 characters, including hyphens, periods, and underscore characters, but it must begin and end with a letter or number.)

To number tables automatically, use the following steps:

1. Press Alt-C to create a centered paragraph format.

2. Type *Table* and press the space bar.

3. Type *tablenumber:* (don't forget the colon). Figure 11.4 shows how your document should look.

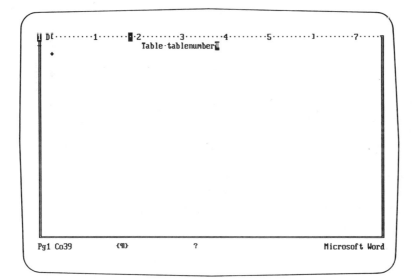

Fig. 11.4.

Typing the series code name.

4. With the cursor positioned just after the colon, press F3. Word places parentheses around the series code name that you just typed (see fig. 11.5).

5. Repeat steps 1 through 4 for all the tables in your document.

When you print your document, Word removes the series code name and inserts a number. If this table is the first table in your document, it reads *Table 1.*

Typing the Table Title and Entering a Double Ruled Line

Now add the table's title and a double-ruled line under it by working through the following instructions:

1. Type the title of the table and press Enter three times to leave two blank lines under the title (see fig. 11.6).

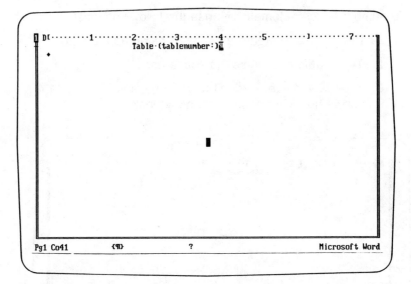

Fig. 11.5.

The series code name after you press F3.

Normally, it's best to use the **space after** field in the Format Paragraph command menu to create blank lines. As you see later, though, the whole table is to be formatted so that Word keeps it together on the page.

Fig. 11.6.

Typing the table title.

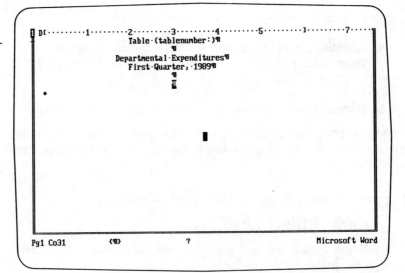

2. Select the **F**ormat **B**order command. When the command menu appears, as shown in figure 11.7, choose the **L**ines option in the **type** field. Don't carry out the command yet. You must choose additional options first.

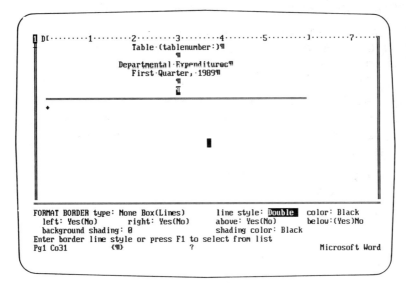

Fig. 11.7.

Adding a double-ruled line with the Format Border command.

3. Choose the **line style** field and press F1. Select the **Double** option from the list presented.

4. Choose **Y**es in the **below** field.

5. Carry out the command by pressing Enter or clicking the command name.

Adding Column and Stub Headings

A column heading, positioned above the columns of data, describes the data to be enumerated in the table. The stub heading describes the categories or items listed and is positioned flush left (and usually one or two lines below the column headings). Use the following instructions to create simple column headings for a table.

1. Select the end mark under the double-ruled line and choose the **F**ormat **T**ab **S**et command.

2. Set custom tabs, with centered alignment, for the columns in your table. If the table has two columns of data and you use a 6.0-inch line length, try setting tabs at 3.0 inches and 4.5 inches.

3. Type the column headings.

   To type the two-line column headings shown in figure 11.8, press Tab and type *Project*. Press Tab again and type *Project*. Then press Shift-Enter. Press Tab and type *"Cantaloupe"*. Press Tab again and type *"Apricot"*.

4. When you finish typing the column headings, press Enter. If your table will have a stub head, type it flush to the left margin. (The stub head is the heading positioned over the left column.)

5. With the cursor positioned on the last line you typed, use the **Format Border** command. Choose **Lines** in the **type** field, **Normal** in the **line style** field, and **Yes** in the **below** field. Press Enter to carry out the command.

   Word creates a single-ruled line under the stub head, as shown in figure 11.8.

Fig. 11.8.

The column headings with a single-ruled line.

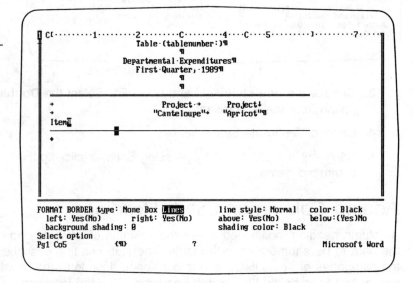

Getting Fancy: Using Decked Heads and Vertical Lines

A *decked head* is a header that spans two or more column headers, as shown in figure 11.9. Use the following instructions to create a table using decked heads.

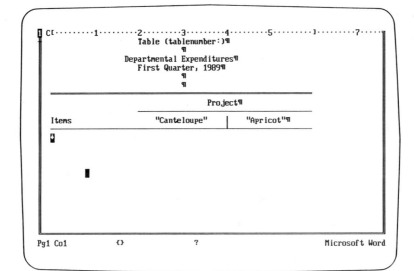

Fig. 11.9.

A decked head
for a table.

1. In a new Word document, type the table header, following the instructions just given.

2. Position the cursor on the end mark just below the double line that separates the table header from the table body.

3. Determine the center point of the columns.

   If you have columns centered at 3.0 and 5.0 inches, for example, the center point between them is 4.0 inches.

4. Set a centered tab for the decked head at the center point.

5. Type the decked head.

6. Use the **F**ormat **B**order command. Choose the **L**ines option in the **type** field, the **N**ormal option in the **line style** field, and the **Y**es option in the **below** field. Press Enter to carry out the command.

   After using this command, notice that the line spans the whole screen; it is shortened in the next step.

7. With the cursor positioned in the decked-head paragraph, use the **F**ormat **P**aragraph command (see fig. 11.10). To shorten the line under the decked head, type a value in the **left indent** field and press Enter to carry out the command.

   To indent the line two inches, for example, type 2 in the **left indent** field.

Fig. 11.10.

Creating the first line of a decked head.

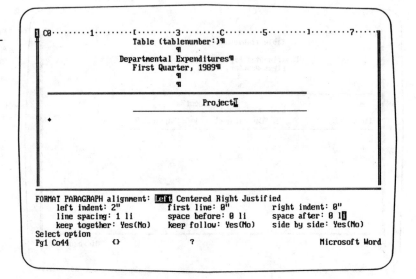

```
 C0········1········[·······3·······C········5········]········7·····
                    Table (tablenumber:)¶
                               ¶
                   Departmental Expenditures¶
                     First Quarter, 1989¶
                               ¶
                               ¶
         _____
                            Project

    ◆

FORMAT PARAGRAPH alignment: Left Centered Right Justified
        left indent: 2"           first line: 0"        right indent: 0"
        line spacing: 1 li        space before: 0 li    space after: 0 li
        keep together: Yes(No)    keep follow: Yes(No)  side by side: Yes(No)
Select option
Pg1 Co44          {}              ?                    Microsoft Word
```

8. Now select the end mark, which is right under the line you just entered. Use the **Format Tab Set** command.

9. Set a vertical tab using the same measurement you used to center the decked head.

10. Set centered tabs to the left and right of the vertical tab you just set. (If you're using Word's default margins, try setting tabs at 3 inches and 5 inches).

11. Type the column headings (see fig. 11.11).

12. Type the stub head on the same line, and add a line under the table header using the **Format Border** command (again see fig. 11.9).

With a little experimentation, you can create more complex headings with boxed heads (column headers enclosed fully in boxes). You may find Word's line-drawing mode helpful to complete the boxes. For more information on the line-drawing mode, see Chapter 17, "Creating Forms and Illustrations."

Creating the Table Body

Now that you have created the table header, it's time to create the table body—the part of the table containing the columns of data. Use the following steps to duplicate the table shown in figure 11.12.

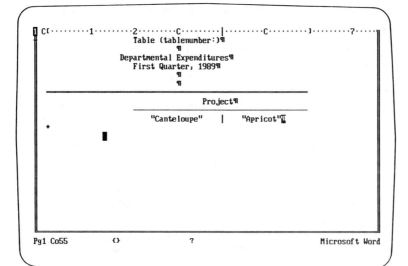

Fig. 11.11.

Creating the second line of a decked head.

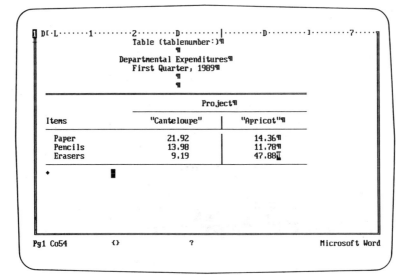

Fig. 11.12.

Entering body copy for the table.

1. Position the cursor below the table header and use the **F**ormat **T**ab **S**et command.

2. Set a flush-left tab at 0.2 inches if you want to indent text in the left column (as shown in fig. 11.12).

3. Set decimal tabs at precisely the same places you entered centered tabs in the heading.

4. Set a vertical tab at precisely the same place you entered a vertical tab below the decked head.

5. Press Enter or click the command name to carry out the command.

6. Type the items and the expenditures. Do not use the space bar to align text; press Tab once between each item. Press Enter at the end of each line.

7. When you come to the end of the table, place the cursor on the last line and use the **Format Border** command to create a single-ruled line below the table.

As you can see, it's easy to create very handsome tables with Word 5!

Adjusting the Column's Position

One of Word's best improvements is the ease with which you can adjust the position of columns in a table. To change the position of a table, follow these instructions:

1. Select the lines that contain the table's body text (see fig. 11.13).

Fig. 11.13.

Selecting the table in order to adjust the position of the column.

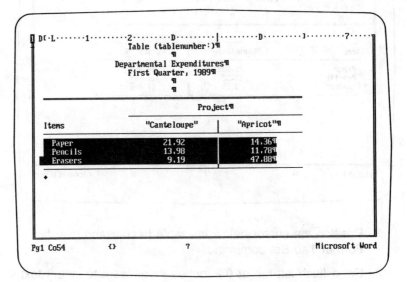

2. Move the tab of the column you want to adjust.

   If you're using the keyboard, choose the **Format Tab Set** command, press F1, select the tab you want to adjust, and press Ctrl-right arrow or Ctrl-left arrow. If you're using the mouse, point to the tab you want to move, hold down the right button, and drag right or left.

As you move the tab, you see the column move on-screen. If you're using the keyboard method, carry out the **Format Tab Set** command by pressing Enter after you have adjusted the position to your satisfaction.

Cross-Referencing a Table in the Text

When you create a report or proposal with many tables, deleting a table or restructuring your document causes havoc with the cross-references entered in the text. You can avoid renumbering the tables by using a series code name instead of numbers when you create the tables. But even if you automatically renumber the tables, the cross-references in the text may not be accurate. Suppose that you delete table 15; the old table 16 becomes the new table 15. If you mention table 16 in your text, the cross-reference is no longer accurate.

You can avoid such problems by cross-referencing tables in such a way that Word 5 fills in the correct table number automatically when you print your document. While you're at it, you can also have Word tell your reader precisely where the table is located. The following procedures explain how to cross-reference a table in your text.

To mark the table for cross-referencing, do the following:

1. Select the table series code name (see fig. 11.14).

2. Choose the **Format bookmarK** command. When the command menu appears (see fig. 11.15), type a name that reminds you of the table's contents.

   Like series code names, bookmark names can be up to 31 characters in length, and can include periods, dashes, and underscore characters.

3. Press Enter to carry out the command.

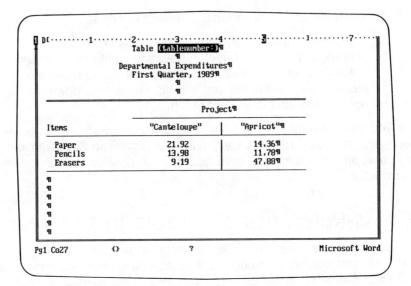

Fig. 11.14.

Selecting the table series code name for cross-referencing.

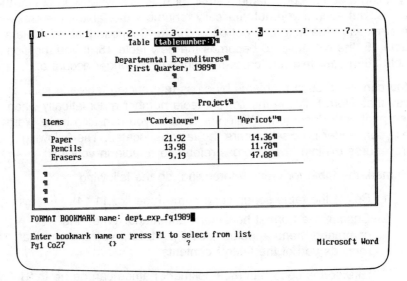

Fig. 11.15.

Entering a bookmark name for the table.

To refer to the table in the text, do the following:

1. When you want to refer to the table in the text, type *Table* and press the space bar. Then type the table series code name (such as *tablenumber*), a colon, and the bookmark name you assigned to the table in the preceding steps.

2. With the cursor positioned just after the bookmark name, press F3. Word encloses the cross-reference in parentheses (see fig. 11.16).

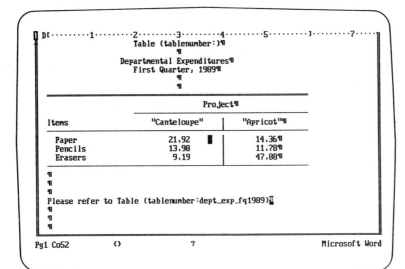

Fig. 11.16.

Cross-referencing a table number in the text.

3. To have Word automatically insert the page on which the table appears, type *Page* and press the space bar. Then type *page*, a colon, and the bookmark name assigned to the table. To create a cross-reference to the page on which the departmental expenditures table is located, for instance, type *Page page:departmental expenditures.*

4. With the cursor positioned just after the bookmark name, press F3.

You have just made use of a wonderful Word 5 feature called bookmarks. This feature lets you name a range of text (like you name a range of cells in a spreadsheet). Bookmarks have many applications, and you learn more about them in Chapter 15, "Enhancing Group Productivity: Using Annotations and Redlining."

Editing Tables with Column Selection

Suppose that you just created the table described in the preceding sections, but your boss says, "This won't do. *Apricot* comes before *Canteloupe* in alphabetical order—and besides, my favorite protege is in charge of the Apricot project. So put those expenditures in the left column!" With some programs, it might be wiser to delete most of the table and type it over. But Word's column-select mode lets you select columns of data and move them laterally, just as you cut and paste with paragraphs of text.

To switch columns in a two-column table, do the following steps:

1. Select the character at the upper left corner of the column you want to move. For this example, begin with the column on the left.

2. Press Shift-F6 to turn on the column-select mode.

3. Extend the selection to the right and down to encompass the column (see fig. 11.17). Be sure to include all the tab stops that come after the text in the column.

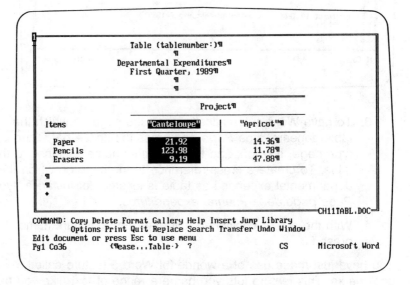

Fig. 11.17.

Selecting a
column to move.

4. Press Del to cut the column to the scrap (see fig. 11.18). The right column shifts to the left to fill up the blank space left when you pressed Del.

5. Make sure that each line of data in the new left column ends with a tab character before the newline or paragraph mark (see fig. 11.19). If a line doesn't end with a tab character, select the newline character and press Tab. You must set up the tab marks so that Word can "receive" the column insertion properly.

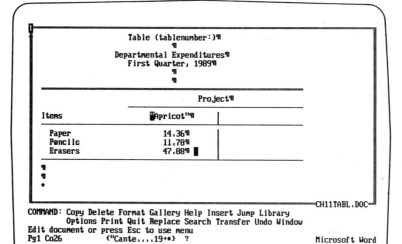

Fig. 11.18.

Deleting one column causes the other to shift.

```
                Table (tablenumber:)¶
                            ¶
                Departmental Expenditures¶
                First Quarter, 1989¶
                            ¶
                            ¶
  ─────────────────────────────────────────────
                            Project¶
  Items              ▓Apricot"¶           │
                                          │
    Paper              14.36¶             │
    Pencils            11.78¶             │
    Erasers            47.88¶ █           │
  ─────────────────────────────────────────────
  ¶
  ¶
  •

                                              ─CH11TABL.DOC─
COMMAND: Copy Delete Format Gallery Help Insert Jump Library
         Options Print Quit Replace Search Transfer Undo Window
Edit document or press Esc to use menu
Pg1 Co26         {"Cante....19→■}  ?                Microsoft Word
```

Fig. 11.19.

Ensuring that tabs appear at end of each line.

```
                Table·(tablenumber:)¶
                            ¶
                Departmental·Expenditures¶
                First·Quarter,·1989¶
                            ¶
                            ¶
  ─────────────────────────────────────────────
                →       Project¶
  Items→              "Apricot"→        │    ▓
                                        │
    → Paper→            14.36→          │    ¶
    → Pencils→          11.78→          │    ¶
    → Erasers→          47.88→          │    ¶
  ─────────────────────────────────────────────
  ¶
  ¶                          █
  •

                                              ─CH11TABL.DOC─
COMMAND: Copy Delete Format Gallery Help Insert Jump Library
         Options Print Quit Replace Search Transfer Undo Window
Edit document or press Esc to use menu
Pg1 Co51         {"Cante....19→■}  ?                Microsoft Word
```

6. Select the character at the upper left corner where you want the column to be inserted and press Ins. Word inserts the column at the cursor's location (see fig. 11.20).

Fig. 11.20.

The new position of a column.

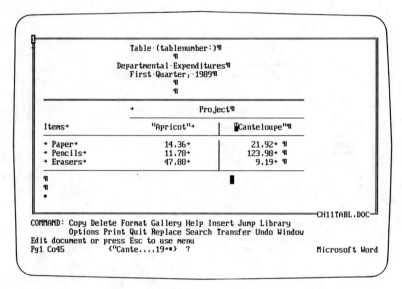

Performing Calculations on Tabular Data: Using Math

Word isn't a spreadsheet program, but you can perform simple arithmetic operations right on the screen. With Word's column-select mode, you can add columns of numbers in a few keystrokes! Use the following instructions to do so.

1. Select the upper right corner of the column of data you want to add.

2. Press Shift-F6 to turn on the column-select mode.

3. Expand the selection to the right and down to encompass just the numbers in the column (see fig. 11.21).

4. Press F2. Word adds the data and enters the sum in the scrap.

5. To insert the sum into your text, place the cursor where you want the sum to appear and press Ins (see fig. 11.22).

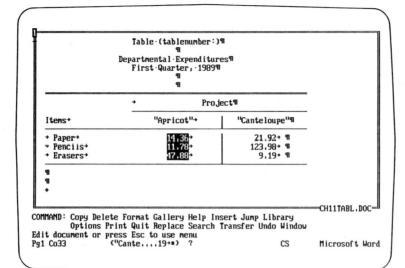

Fig. 11.21.

Selecting the column of numbers.

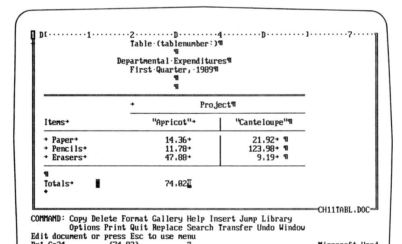

Fig. 11.22.

Inserting the sum from the scrap.

More about Math

As you just learned, you can add a column of numbers by selecting them and pressing F2. You can use the F2 (calculate) key in other ways, as well. There's no need to run for a calculator when you're working with Word! In most cases, you can perform a simple computation right on the screen, such as 4,564 * 11.65% ("What's 11.65% of 4,564?"). You even can add numbers by selecting a sentence that contains them, such as "Included in the survey were 11,983 volunteers and 12,891 salaried personnel," pressing F2, and getting the sum—24,874—in an instant!

To use the calculate key, follow these steps:

1. Type an arithmetic expression anywhere in your document using one of the arithmetic symbols, called *operators*, listed in table 11.2.

2. Select the expression and press F2. The answer appears in the scrap.

3. Press Shift-Insert. Word replaces the selected expression with the result in the scrap.

Table 11.2
Word's Arithmetic Operators

Operator	Arithmetic Function	Example
+ (or no operator)	Addition	8 + 5 or 8 5
− (or parentheses)	Subtraction	8 − 5 or 8 (5)
*	Multiplication	8 * 5
/	Division	8 / 5
%	Percent	10%

Normally, Word evaluates percentages first, followed by multiplication and division operations, and finally addition and subtraction operations. You can alter the order of evaluation using parentheses. If you place an expression in parentheses, Word evaluates the expression in parentheses first. Without parentheses, 2 * 2 + 4 = 8, but with parentheses, 2 * (2 + 4) = 12.

Caution: Keep the order of evaluation in mind if you create complex expressions.

Importing Spreadsheet Data

If Word's math capabilities aren't sufficient for your number-crunching purposes, prepare your tables in a Lotus 1-2-3, Multiplan, or Excel spreadsheet. Then use the Library Link Spreadsheet command to import the spreadsheet into your Word document. After you import the table, you can format it, using any of the techniques discussed in this chapter.

This technique is extremely useful for two reasons. First, if you commonly use a spreadsheet program to prepare and manipulate tables of data, this method saves you the trouble of retyping the spreadsheet (or importing it after saving it as an ASCII file). Second, and most important, Word makes a record of the table's origin after you import the spreadsheet. With just one command, you can update the link so that your table contains the latest information in your spreadsheet. In this way, you can keep the authoritative version of a spreadsheet table in your Word document. Once you import the table into your Word document, you can update the Word table easily after you make changes to the spreadsheet table.

Keep in mind that Word imports a range of cells; you must specify a cell range to import a table from a spreadsheet. Word can import named ranges, or ranges of cells to which you apply a name (such as PROFITS or EXPENSES). Typing a name is much easier than typing a range of cells. When you create your spreadsheet, therefore, be sure to name the range that you import into your Word document.

Hint: identify all the cells that you want to appear in your Word table and create a range called TABLE.

Importing a Table from a Spreadsheet Program

To import a table, do the following procedure:

1. Place the cursor where you want the table to appear.

2. Choose the **Li**brary **L**ink **S**preadsheet command.

3. When the command menu appears, type the name of the spreadsheet. If you can't remember the name, press F1 to see a list (see fig. 11.23).

If the desired spreadsheet isn't in the default directory, use path information in addition to the file name.

Hint: When you press F1, Word displays a list of all the files in the directory. To see a list of just the Lotus files, type *.wks or *.wk1 before pressing F1.

Fig. 11.23.

The Library Link
Spreadsheet
command menu
with file names
listed.

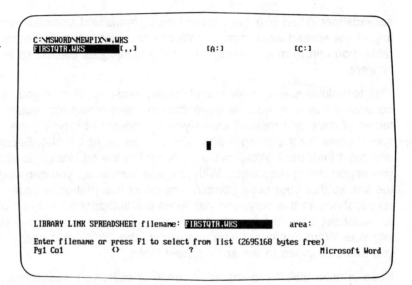

4. Press Tab or click the **area** field and type the name of the range you want to import. If you can't remember the name, press F1 to see a list (see fig. 11.24). Alternatively, type the cell range, using the same format your spreadsheet program does.

Fig. 11.24.

Viewing a list of
spreadsheet
ranges.

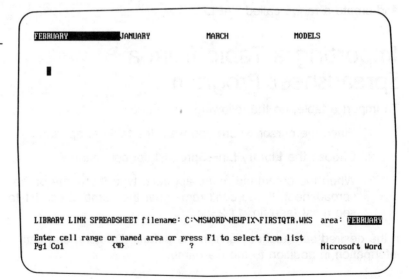

5. Press Enter to carry out the command. Word imports the file according to the specifications given in the Library Link Spreadsheet command.

After the table appears, it may not be formatted attractively (see fig. 11.25). During the import, however, Word ends each line with a newline character and places a tab keystroke between each column. Use the **F**ormat **T**ab **S**et command to create tabs and move them until you're satisfied with the results (see fig. 11.26).

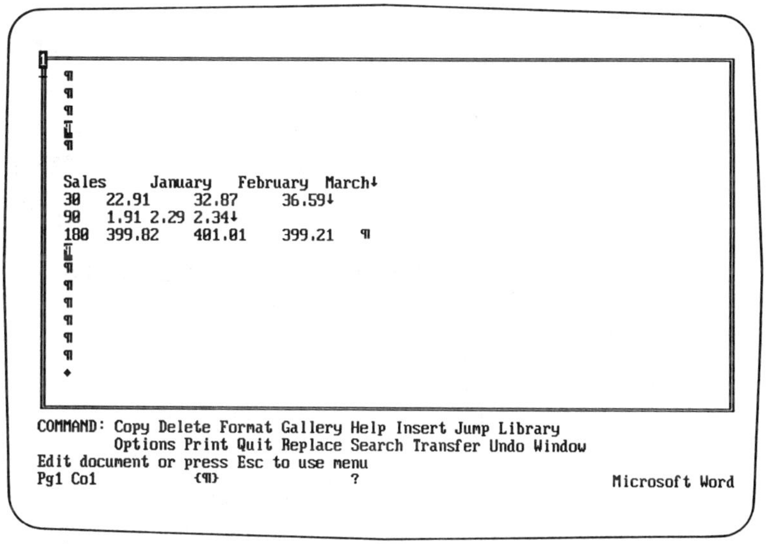

¶
¶
¶
¶
¶

Sales   January   February March↓
30   22.91   32.87   36.59↓
90   1.91 2.29 2.34↓
100 399.82   401.01   399.21   ¶
¶
¶
¶
¶
¶
¶
¶
♦

COMMAND: Copy Delete Format Gallery Help Insert Jump Library
        Options Print Quit Replace Search Transfer Undo Window
Edit document or press Esc to use menu
Pg1 Co1   {¶}   ?   Microsoft Word

Fig. 11.25.

The imported spreadsheet before tab formatting.

Caution: Word places codes before and after the table. These codes are formatted as hidden text and tell Word where the spreadsheet came from. ***Don't delete them***. If you do, Word can't update the spreadsheet. To avoid deleting the codes, choose the **Y**es option in the **show hidden text** field of the Options menu.

Updating the Table

If you discover an error in the spreadsheet or add new data to it, you can easily update the table that Word has imported. Use the following instructions to update the spreadsheet table in your Word document:

Fig. 11.26.

The imported spreadsheet after tab formatting.

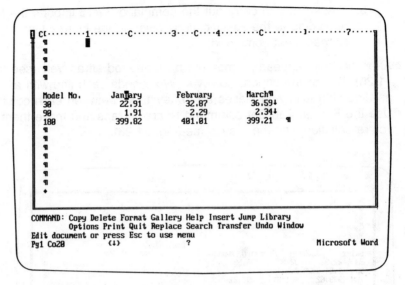

```
C[· · · · · · · · · 1 · · · · · · · ·C· · · · · · · ·3· · · C· · · ·4· · · · · · ·C· · · · · · · · ·]· · · · · · · ·7· · · · ·

    Model No.      January        February       March¶
    30              22.91          32.87          36.59↓
    90               1.91           2.29           2.34↓
    180            399.82         401.01         399.21    ¶
```

```
COMMAND: Copy Delete Format Gallery Help Insert Jump Library
         Options Print Quit Replace Search Transfer Undo Window
Edit document or press Esc to use menu
Pg1 Co20          {↓}                    ?                      Microsoft Word
```

1. Select the table to be updated. If you want to update all the tables in your document at one time, press Shift-F10 to select the entire document.

2. Choose the **L**ibrary **L**ink **S**preadsheet command. Press Enter to carry out the command without typing anything in the command fields.

3. Word highlights the table and displays the message, Enter Y to update or Esc to cancel. Press Y to update the table.

Word erases the old imported table, but does not erase the paragraph mark at the end of the table. For this reason, Word does not lose the tab formatting assigned to the table. Word then imports the new spreadsheet. The new version of the spreadsheet appears and takes the tab formatting preserved by the paragraph mark.

This is a great feature and is easy to use. By all means give it a try!

Sorting Lists

Word's Library Autosort command is your ticket to sorting lists in alphabetical or numerical order. This command has its limitations—it's a memory hog. If you try to sort a lengthy list, the insufficient memory message appears. Try saving your document before using Library Autosort; if that doesn't work, consider adding expanded memory to your system.

In general, Library Autosort sorts paragraphs of text. A paragraph in Word, as you know, can be as short as a single line, or as long as several pages. The key point is that paragraphs are units for sorting as far as Word is concerned. Word sorts each paragraph according to the first few characters in it. If a paragraph starts with "Zelda's zebras were known by a variety of affectionate names," it is likely to wind up last in an alphabetical sort.

Word keeps all the text of a paragraph together when it sorts. When you create a list, therefore, keep the items you want sorted in their own separate paragraphs.

To sort a list, follow these steps:

1. Create the list. Type each unit of data as a separate paragraph (see fig. 11.27).

2. Select the list and choose the **Library Autosort** command.

3. Choose the options you want in the Library Autosort command menu (see fig. 11.28).

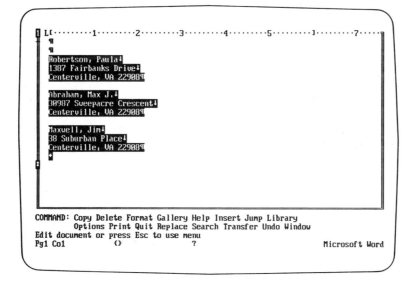

Fig. 11.27.

Creating and formatting the list.

To sort alphabetically, choose **A**lphanumeric in the **by** field. To sort numerically, choose **N**umeric in the same field. To sort in ascending order (A,B,C or 1,2,3), choose **A**scending in the **sequence** field. To sort in descending order (C,B,A or 3,2,1), choose **D**escending. To take case into account as you sort, choose **Y**es in the **case** field.

4. Press Enter to carry out the command. The sorted text appears highlighted (see fig. 11.29).

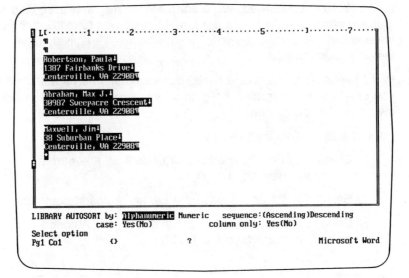

Fig. 11.28.

The Library
Autosort
command menu.

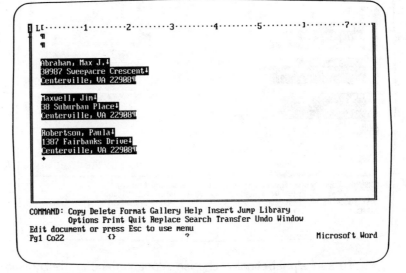

Fig. 11.29.

The sorted list
(highlighted).

Important: If the sort produces erroneous results, use the **Undo** command *immediately*. Undo can't undo the sort if you use another command or add more text after sorting.

Sorting Columns of Data in a Table

When you create tables of numerical data, create new lines with Shift-Enter (newline). That way, you can reformat the tabs easily—the whole table is a single paragraph as far as Word is concerned. Setting up tables as a single paragraph, however, causes problems for sorting. When the entire table is one big paragraph, you cannot sort the data using the techniques described for lists. If you try, nothing happens: Word thinks there's just one paragraph to sort.

Happily, an easy way around this problem exists. Before you sort, select one column of data (called the sort-key column). Word treats the sort-key column as if it were the first few characters of separate paragraphs and keeps all the lines of data together without mixing them up when it sorts.

When is it useful to sort data in a table? Whenever it makes sense to organize the data in some way. If you list items in the left column under the stub, you can sort them alphabetically. You can sort the data numerically, too. You can sort the table in descending numerical order, for example, so that the largest figures are at the top of the column.

To sort a table, follow these instructions:

1. Place the cursor in the upper left corner of the column you want to use as the sort key and press Shift-F6. Select the column. In figure 11.30, the expenditures of the Apricot Project are highlighted.

2. Choose the **L**ibrary **A**utosort command and select the desired options from the menu.

Important: Be sure to choose the **No** option in the **column only** field.

In figure 11.30, the menu is set to perform a numerical sort in descending order (3,2,1 etc.). If you choose **Yes** in the **column only** field, Word sorts only the column selected, leaving the text to the left and right the way it is. In other words, it scrambles your data. If this happens, use the **Undo** command immediately.

3. Press Enter to carry out the command. Word performs the sort, keeping all the lines together (see fig. 11.31). You can now see that the Apricot group has consumed an inordinate number of erasers this quarter.

Fig. 11.30.

Selecting a
column for sorting
the table in
descending order.

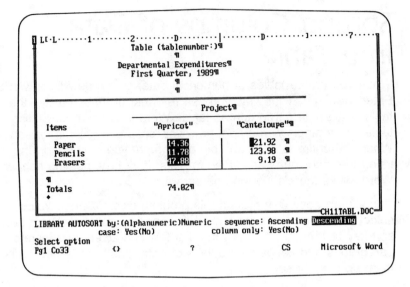

Fig. 11.31.

The table with
the sorted list
(highlighted).

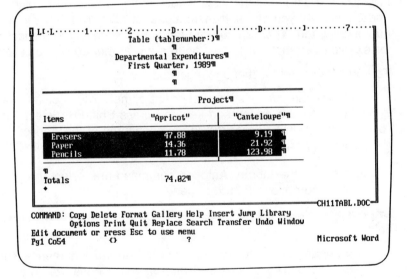

Chapter Summary

In this chapter you learned how Word 5 makes it easy to create great-
looking tables and lists. Version 5's much-improved features for setting
and moving tabs make it a snap to set and alter custom tab stops for
any paragraph in your document. Mouse users are especially fortunate

when it comes to setting tabs; as long as you work with the ruler displayed, you can set and move tabs on the ruler without the Format Tab Set command. Remember to use tabs, not spaces, to align text with Word at all times.

You also learned how you can type arithmetic expressions on the screen and get answers right away. Word's Library Autosort command sorts paragraphs alphabetically or numerically and can sort in ascending (A,B,C or 1,2,3) or descending (C,B,A or 3,2,1) order.

The next chapter tells you how to use two of Word's versatile features: glossaries and bookmarks. They are especially useful for boilerplate text.

12

Using Glossaries and Bookmarks

The big productivity benefits of word processing aren't automatic; you must understand enough about a program like Word 5 to put its productivity-enhancing features to work. If you ever find yourself typing the same passage of text over and over, read on, because you're about to learn how you can store dozens of passages of repeatedly used text, called boilerplate, and recall each of them with a few keystrokes.

The keys to this time-saving feature are Word's *glossaries*, which are named storage spaces for text, and a new Word 5 feature called *bookmarks*, which are named sections of text in a document. To retrieve text from a glossary, you simply type the document name and press F3. To retrieve text from another Word document that contains bookmarks, you use the Library Link Document command. Either way, the boilerplate text you have stored is just a few keystrokes away.

Will you find uses for boilerplate? The answer depends on the kind of writing you're planning to do, but almost surely it's "Yes." Just ask yourself whether you frequently find yourself typing the same text over and over again. Here's a brief list of some examples of repeatedly used text:

❑ A memo header that includes a lengthy distribution list

❑ Your return address

❑ The addresses of people with whom you frequently correspond

321

❑ Standard responses to letters of inquiry or complaint

❑ Frequently used text with complex formatting

❑ Commonly used forms

❑ Bibliographic citations you use repeatedly

In short, if you type something repeatedly, it's a candidate for storage and retrieval in a glossary. Use your imagination! An English teacher has created glossaries for grading papers on disk; if he runs across a dangling phrase in a student's paper, he inserts an entry called DANGLE, which explains why the construction is wrong and shows how to repair it.

Even if you don't think you will ever use a glossary or bookmark, the material in this chapter is essential reading: As you will learn in Chapter 21, "Creating and Using Word 5 Macros," knowledge of Word's glossaries is a prerequisite for creating, storing, and retrieving Word 5 macros. Word stores and retrieves macros the same way it stores and retrieves glossary entries—you use the same commands, and you will face the same challenges of glossary file management. Bookmarks, too, are essential for the cross-referencing operations discussed in Chapter 14, "The Legal and Scholarly Word."

In this chapter, you will learn to do the following:

❑ Create a glossary entry and store it so that you can retrieve it with the Insert command or the F3 key

❑ Assign a glossary entry to a keyboard shortcut for even faster retrieval

❑ Edit and erase glossary entries

❑ Create and manage new glossary files to store and retrieve related glossary entries

❑ Use glossaries to store text safely while editing

❑ Mark text as a bookmark

❑ Move around in a lengthy document by using bookmarks

❑ Import bookmark text by using document-linking commands

Creating and Managing a Glossary Entry

Word's glossaries are very much like the scrap, except that there is more than one glossary, and each has a name. It's exceptionally easy to create, retrieve, edit, and delete glossary entries, as you will see in this section, which outlines the basic procedures.

Creating a Glossary Entry

To create a glossary entry, follow these steps:

1. Type the text you want the entry to contain. You can include character and paragraph formatting.

2. Select the text.

   If you want the paragraph's formatting to be part of the entry, be sure to select the paragraph mark at the end of the paragraph. If you added division formats, also select the division mark (see fig. 12.1). To switch on paragraph marks, choose the **P**artial or **A**ll options in the **show non-printing symbols** field of the **O**ptions menu.

3. Choose either the **C**opy or **D**elete command.

4. When the **to** command field appears, type the name you want to give the glossary (see fig. 12.2).

   Glossary names must be one word, and cannot exceed 31 characters. You can use underscores, periods, and hyphens, although a glossary entry's name *cannot begin or end* with these characters. You cannot use other punctuation or spaces.

5. Carry out the command.

Caution: If you see the message, Enter Y to overwrite glossary or Esc to cancel, you have tried to use a name that has already been used for another entry. Retype the name and try again.

Fig. 12.1.

Selecting the text to be copied or cut to a glossary.

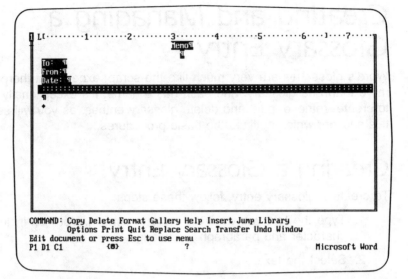

Fig. 12.2.

Creating the glossary entry.

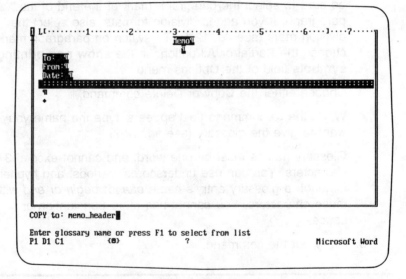

Word 5 provides a way to create glossary entries so that you can retrieve them by using a Ctrl-key code. When you name the entry, type a caret (^) right after the glossary name, and then press the key code you want to use. If you want to retrieve the entry using Ctrl-S, for instance, hold down the Ctrl key and press S. Word will insert the code in brackets. Carry out the command.

Note: Be careful to use a key code that Word is not using for some other purpose. If you assign the glossary entry to Shift-F10, for instance, Word will not select your whole document when you press this key code—you will get your glossary entry instead. Don't use function keys or the Alt key; Word makes extensive use of these. The Ctrl key is best. For more information on saving glossary entries with key codes, see Chapter 21, "Creating and Using Word 5 Macros."

Retrieving a Glossary Entry

You can retrieve a glossary entry by using the Insert command or the F3 key. (If you saved your entry with a key code, just press the key code to retrieve it.)

To retrieve a glossary entry, follow this procedure:

1. Choose the Insert command.

2. When the **from** field appears, type the glossary name. If you cannot remember it, press F1 and choose from the list.

3. Carry out the command.

To retrieve a glossary entry using the F3 shortcut, do the following:

1. Type the glossary name. Position the cursor immediately after the name you have just typed.

2. Press F3. Word erases the name and inserts the glossary text.

F3

Editing a Glossary Entry

If you have created a glossary entry that contains an error, such as a spelling mistake, you can fix it easily by following these steps:

1. Insert the entry with the Insert command or F3.

2. Edit the text.

3. Select the text and use either the Copy or Delete command. Give the glossary entry the same name you used before, and carry out the command.

4. When the message Enter Y to overwrite glossary or Esc to cancel appears, press Y.

Deleting a Glossary Entry

If a glossary entry is no longer needed, delete it as follows:

1. Choose the **T**ransfer **G**lossary **C**lear command.

2. Press F1 to display the list of glossary names.

3. Highlight the name of the entry you want to delete and carry out the command. To delete all the glossary entries you have created, leave the field blank and carry out the command.

   Note: You cannot delete the entries called page, date, time, footnote, nextpage, dateprint, and timeprint. These entries are permanent. Their functions are discussed in the section titled "Using the Supplied Glossary Entries."

4. When the message Enter Y to confirm appears, press Y.

Abandoning All the Entries You Have Created in a Session

Sometimes during a session you will create one or more entries for temporary purposes. If you don't want to save any of the entries, just quit Word as you would normally. When you see the message Enter Y to save glossary changes, N to lose changes, or Esc to cancel, just press N.

Managing Glossary Files

When you start Word, the program loads the default glossary, a file called NORMAL.GLY. This file isn't like a DOC file, a file that contains a document. NORMAL.GLY is a special file for storing and retrieving glossary entries on disk. As you will learn in this section, you can save your glossary entries in glossary files so that they will be available the next time you use Word. You can even create your own glossary files to contain special-purpose glossary entries.

Saving Glossary Files

As you create glossary entries during an editing session, Word adds them to the NORMAL.GLY file. Like all the work you do with Word, however, these entries will be erased if you do not save them to disk. You can save them to NORMAL.GLY—or to a new glossary file, if you want.

Saving to NORMAL.GLY

Because NORMAL.GLY is the default glossary file, the one Word uses by default every time you start the program, use this file to save glossary entries you are likely to use in every editing session.

To save your entries to NORMAL.GLY, follow these instructions:

1. Choose the **T**ransfer **G**lossary **S**ave command.

2. When the command menu appears (see fig. 12.3), you will see that Word has proposed NORMAL.GLY as the destination for your entries. Just carry out the command to save your entries to NORMAL.GLY.

```
TRANSFER GLOSSARY SAVE filename: C:\MSWORD\NORMAL.GLY

Enter filename
Pg1 Co1          {Memo¶...e: ⬛¶}    ?                    Microsoft Word
```

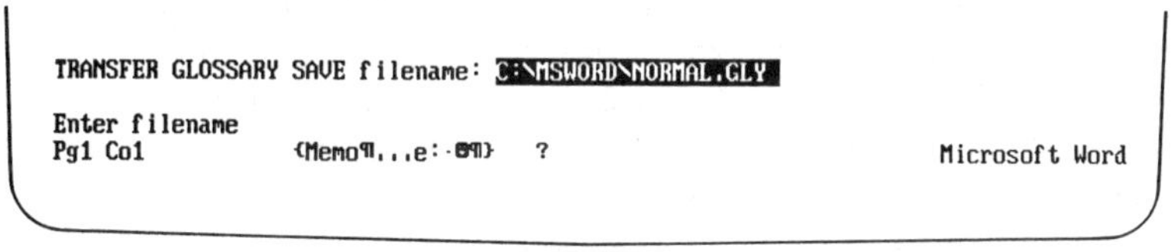

Fig. 12.3.

The Transfer Glossary Save menu.

Once you learn about Word 5's fantastic macro capabilities and realize how easily you can create and use macros, you will doubtless create dozens of them. Remember, though, that you must store macros in glossary files. Because you will want to use many of these macros every day, many of them should be stored in NORMAL.GLY so that Word will load them at the start of every editing session. For this reason, don't save too many glossaries to NORMAL.GLY. Save room for all those handy macros you will create.

Creating a New Glossary File

If the entries you have created are for special-purpose writing tasks, save them to a glossary file other than NORMAL.GLY. If you pack too many entries into NORMAL.GLY, the file's large size will reduce the amount of memory available for other operations, such as sorting. Furthermore, if you create and save more than 46 glossary entries, you will not be able to see the whole list of entries on the screen when you press F1 on the Insert command menu. For both reasons, it's best to save special-purpose entries to their own glossary file. Suppose, for instance, that you have created some glossary entries to use in response to complaint letters, a job you must handle occasionally. Because you don't use these entries every day, save them to COMPLAINT.GLY.

To save the entries in a new glossary file, follow these steps:

1. Choose the **T**ransfer **G**lossary **S**ave command.

2. When the command menu appears, type a new glossary file name.

The file name must conform to DOS rules (no more than 8 letters or numbers). Omit the period and extension; Word will supply the GLY extension automatically.

Be sure to use a file name that will remind you of the file's contents.

If you plan to create many glossaries for boilerplating and each will have several paragraphs to several pages of text, store and retrieve the boilerplate text with bookmarks. Using bookmarks, you can store boilerplate text in an ordinary Word file on disk, leaving your memory free. See the section called "Using Bookmarks" for details.

Loading Glossary Files

Here's a helpful new Word 5 feature: You can load a glossary file you have created so that it completely replaces the one that's already in memory. Believe it or not, in previous versions the only way you could load a glossary file was to merge it with the file already in memory. The result, all too often, was that glossary files inexorably grew beyond reasonable proportions.

To load a glossary file, simply do this:

1. Choose the **T**ransfer **G**lossary **L**oad command.

2. When the command menu appears, type the name of the glossary file you want to load and carry out the command.

If the glossary file you want isn't in the default directory, include path information as needed. If you cannot remember the name of the file or the directory in which it's stored, press F1 to search for the file. When you find it, highlight its name and press Enter.

Merging Glossary Files

You still can combine glossary files, if you want, although keeping special-purpose glossary files separate from your everyday, default glossary (NORMAL.GLY) is preferable. Just use the **T**ransfer **G**lossary **M**erge command to load a glossary file from disk and merge the glossary file with the one currently in memory.

Printing Glossaries

To print the contents of the glossary file currently in memory, choose the **P**rint **G**lossary command. If you want to print another glossary file, load it first using the **T**ransfer **G**lossary **L**oad command.

Using the Supplied Glossary Entries

As you have already learned, NORMAL.GLY—and even the special-purpose glossary files you create—contains seven supplied glossary entries, which you cannot erase. These entries are useful for certain purposes. In Chapter 5, for instance, you learned how to insert a page slug in running heads by using the page entry.

After you insert one of these supplied glossary entries into your text, the glossary entry appears in your document surrounded by parentheses (page), which tell you that the word is a glossary entry, not ordinary text. As you will see if you move the cursor over the glossary entry, Word treats the whole entry as if it were a single character. You can delete the entry, if you want; just press Backspace or Del to rub it out.

Briefly, the supplied glossary entries are as follows:

- ❏ page. When you insert this entry into your document, Word prints the current page number at the entry's location.

- ❏ nextpage. This entry prints the next page number at the entry's location. This entry is very useful for forward references such as "See Figure 4, on page (nextpage)."

- ❏ date. Word prints the current DOS system date at the entry's location. Word uses the date format you have selected in the **date format** field of the Options menu.

❑ dateprint. At the time of printing, Word prints the DOS system date at the entry's location. Word uses the date format you have selected in the **date format** field of the Options menu.

❑ time. Word prints the current DOS system time at the entry's location. Word uses the time format you have selected in the **time format** field of the Options menu.

❑ timeprint. At the time of printing, Word prints the DOS system time at the entry's location. Word uses the time format you have selected in the **time format** field of the Options menu.

❑ footnote. This entry is used only when you have inadvertently deleted a footnote reference mark. For more information on this entry, see Chapter 14, "The Legal and Scholarly Word."

Of all these entries, the most useful are page and dateprint. The chief uses of page are in running heads, as you have already learned. In the following quick tutorial, which illustrates the use of dateprint, you will create and save a letter header that automatically enters your return address and inserts the date you print the letter.

1. Press Alt-C and type your return address. Use character formatting if you want.

2. Press Enter two or three times to leave some blank space under the return address.

3. Type *dateprint* and press F3. Word inserts the code (dateprint) into your document (see fig. 12.4).

4. Select all the text, including the glossary entry and all paragraph marks.

5. Choose the **D**elete command or the **C**opy command. When the command menu appears, type *RETURNADDRESS*, press the caret (^) key, and press Ctrl-R. The Copy command menu should look like the one shown in figure 12.5.

6. Carry out the command.

Every time you press Ctrl-R, Word will enter your return address and the dateprint glossary. The letters you write will never lack the current date.

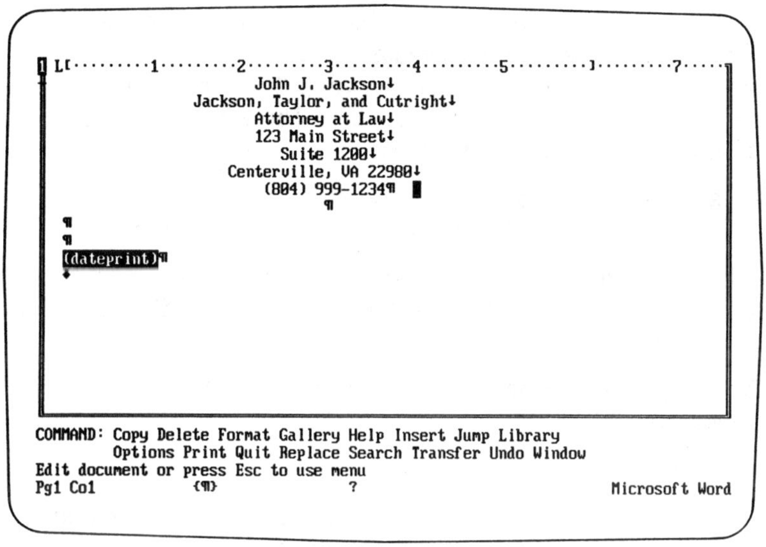

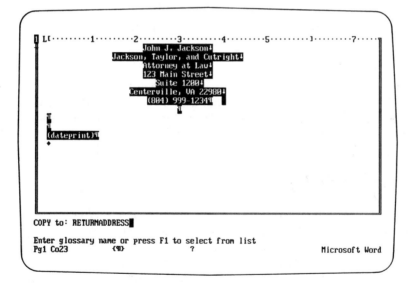

Fig. 12.4.

Return address with dateprint glossary entry.

Fig. 12.5.

Cutting the text to a glossary.

Editing with Glossaries

Glossaries are useful for purposes other than inserting boilerplate text. For super-safe block moves, they're much to be preferred over the scrap. When you're doing a block move by cutting text to the scrap, you may be distracted by some error you find while scrolling to the text's new location. If you delete this error, however, you will wipe out the scrap's contents. If this happens, to be sure, you can restore the scrap's contents by using **U**ndo immediately. But if you don't, you could lose permanently the text you're moving. If the text being moved is just one or two words, that's no major loss. But what if you're moving several pages of deathless prose?

The best way to avoid this problem is to move text by using glossaries instead of the scrap. To use this method, follow these steps:

1. Select the text to be moved and choose the **D**elete command. Don't press the Del key; you need the **D**elete command proper.

2. Type a glossary name for the text to be moved, such as *blockmove*.

3. Scroll to the text's new location.

4. Choose the **I**nsert command, and when the command menu appears, type the glossary's name. Alternatively, type the glossary's name in the text and press F3.

5. At the end of the editing session, press N when Word displays the message Enter Y to save changes to glossary, N to lose changes, or Esc to cancel.

If you want to save some of the entries you have created, however, use the **T**ransfer **G**lossary **C**lear command to delete the block-move glossaries and then save the glossary file by using **T**ransfer **G**lossary **S**ave.

Using Bookmarks

A new Word 5 feature called *bookmarks* greatly expands Word's boilerplate capabilities—and as you will see, bookmarks have many other applications as well. A bookmark is simply a named unit of text. If you have ever used a spreadsheet, you will notice a bookmark's similarity to a named range of cells. With spreadsheets, after you have named the range, you can refer to the range by its name rather than type the cell references. A bookmark is much the same. After you have named the unit of text, you can refer to it by name. Once you have created bookmarks, you can use them in three ways:

❏ You can jump immediately to any bookmark in your document using the Jump bookmarK command.

❏ You can cross-reference bookmarks so that, when Word prints your document, the program automatically fills in the correct page number on which the bookmark appears.

❏ You can import bookmarks from other Word documents by using the Library Link Document command.

As you can see, bookmarks have more than one use, but a common one is to mark boilerplate passages for inclusion in other documents. What's the difference between a glossary and a bookmark for boilerplate purposes? A glossary stores text in Word's memory, while a bookmark stores text on disk. If you like to create large numbers of boilerplate passages, or if your boilerplate text is lengthy, the best way to store and retrieve it is to use bookmarks. This method enables you to keep your memory space free for sorting, indexing, and other memory-intensive operations.

This section discusses techniques for creating and canceling bookmark designations, moving around in a complex document using bookmarks, and applying bookmarks to boilerplate applications. Chapter 14 discusses cross-referencing with bookmarks.

Marking Text as a Bookmark

To mark text as a bookmark, do the following:

1. Select the text you want to include in the bookmark.

   If you want the bookmark text to include its paragraph formatting, be sure to include the paragraph mark in the selection.

2. Choose the **F**ormat bookmar**K** command. When the command menu appears (see fig. 12.6), type a name for the bookmark and carry out the command.

Every bookmark's name must be unique, and it must be one word. You can use up to 31 letters or numbers, and within the word, you can use underscore characters, periods, and hyphens. Do not use colons, semicolons, or spaces.

If you make a mistake when selecting the text or don't like the name you have chosen, choose the **U**ndo command immediately after using the **F**ormat bookmar**K** command.

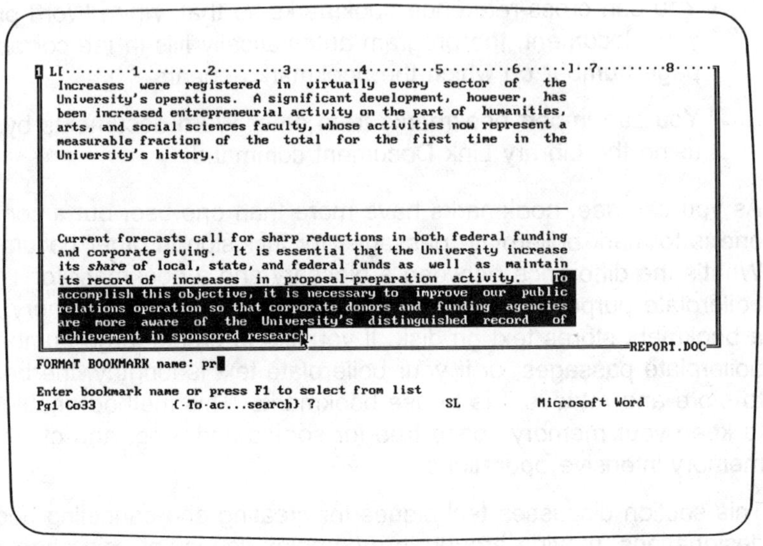

Fig. 12.6.

Creating a bookmark.

```
L[·······1·······2·······3·······4·······5·······6·····]·7·······8·····
  Increases were registered in virtually every sector of  the
  University's operations. A significant development, however, has
  been increased entrepreneurial activity on the part of  humanities,
  arts, and social sciences faculty, whose activities now represent a
  measurable fraction of the total for the first time in the
  University's history.


  Current forecasts call for sharp reductions in both federal funding
  and corporate giving.  It is essential that the University increase
  its share of local, state, and federal funds as well as maintain
  its record of increases in proposal-preparation activity.  To
  accomplish this objective, it is necessary to improve our public
  relations operation so that corporate donors and  funding agencies
  are more aware of the University's distinguished record  of
  achievement in sponsored research.
                                                      REPORT.DOC

FORMAT BOOKMARK name: pr

Enter bookmark name or press F1 to select from list
Pg1 Co33          {·To·ac...search} ?              SL      Microsoft Word
```

Jumping to a Bookmark

One advantage of creating bookmarks is that you can use them to navigate in a lengthy, complex document. If you have ever thought, "I wish I could find that section where I discuss the social effects of irrigation," then bookmarks may prove useful. When you have finished typing an important section that you think you will come back to for further editing, format it as bookmark text. Be sure to give it a distinctive name. Remember, you can use up to 31 characters when you assign a name to a bookmark. Use underscore characters to separate words, as in "soc_impact_of_irrigation."

To jump to a bookmark, follow this procedure:

1. Choose the **J**ump bookmar**K** command.

2. When the command menu appears, type the bookmark name. Alternatively, press F1 to choose from a list of all the bookmarks you have created for a document (see fig. 12.7). Choose the bookmark from the list.

3. Carry out the command.

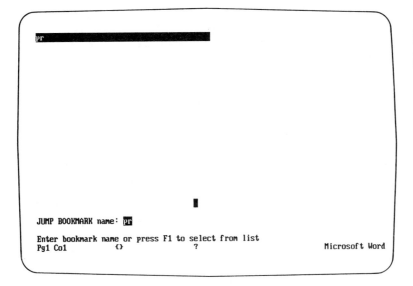

Fig. 12.7.

Jumping to a bookmark.

Removing a Bookmark

If you want, you can cancel a bookmark assignment by doing the following:

1. Use the **J**ump bookmar**K** command to find and select the bookmark you want to cancel.

2. Choose **F**ormat bookmar**K**.

3. Leave the **name** field blank and carry out the command.

4. Press Y to confirm that you want to cancel the bookmark.

Boilerplate Applications with Bookmarks

As already discussed, bookmarks can be used like glossary entries. You can store bookmark text in a special Word file that contains boilerplate text, and any time you like, you can insert the bookmark text into a document you're writing. The advantage of this technique over using glossaries is that the text is stored on disk, not in Word's memory. What's more, it's easier to edit text on disk than to edit glossaries. If you plan to make extensive use of boilerplate applications, you would be well advised to store boilerplate text as bookmarks rather than as glossaries.

As you will see, storing boilerplate text in glossaries has another advantage as well: Word maintains an active connection between the bookmark and the copy of its text that you enter into your document. The significance of this fact is best grasped by comparing bookmarks to glossaries.

When you import text from a glossary into your document, Word simply copies the glossary text into your document and that's the end of the connection. The copied text becomes part of the document you're creating. But what happens if you discover that the glossary contains an error? You may have copied it several times. You will have to search for all the copies and correct them manually.

When you import text from a bookmark into your document by using the Library Link Document command, however, Word keeps a record of the bookmark's source. If you change the bookmark text, you can update the text you have imported by using a simple command. In fact, you can update all the bookmarks in your document with just one command. In this way, you can make sure that all the boilerplate in your document is up-to-the-minute correct before you print the document. This feature is of great value, for example, for businesses whose reputation and legal liability may depend on using a single authoritative version of a critical passage of text.

To create the file containing the boilerplate text, place all the boilerplate passages in a single Word document. Format each unit of boilerplate text as a bookmark, using the techniques just introduced. Then save the document.

Importing Bookmarks

To import bookmark text from another document into the one you're writing, follow these instructions:

1. Place the cursor where you want the imported text to appear.

2. Choose the **L**ibrary **L**ink **D**ocument command.

3. When the command menu appears (see fig. 12.8), type the name of the file that contains the boilerplate text stored as bookmarks.

4. Press Tab or click the **bookmark** field.

5. Type the name of the bookmark. If you don't remember the name, press F1 to see a menu (see fig. 12.9). Highlight the name of the bookmark you want to import.

6. Carry out the command.

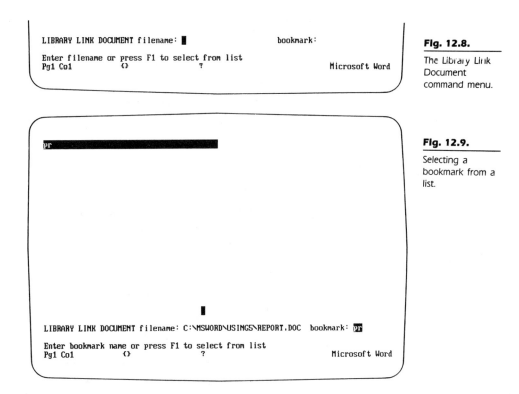

Fig. 12.8.

The Library Link Document command menu.

Fig. 12.9.

Selecting a bookmark from a list.

After you use the Library Link Document command, Word inserts the bookmark text at the cursor's location. Above the text, Word inserts a coded line formatted as hidden text. Do not remove this coded line. Because it's formatted as hidden text, it will not print. But Word needs this information to tell where the bookmark came from. If you delete the code, Word will not be able to update the bookmark.

Updating a Document's Bookmarks

To update the bookmarks you have imported into a document, do the following:

1. Select the bookmark you want to update. Alternatively, select the whole file by pressing Shift-F10.

2. Choose the **Li**brary **L**ink **D**ocument command, and carry it out without typing anything in the command fields.

3. When you see the prompt Enter Y to update, N to skip, or Esc to cancel, press Y to update the bookmark.

Word deletes the existing bookmark text and imports the updated bookmark.

If several people are using a single computer in a business setting, or if you're using Word on a network, a manager can maintain an authoritative version of the boilerplate file. Everyone else should get into the habit of updating bookmarks before printing. This practice helps ensure that every document will always contain up-to-the-minute versions of the boilerplate text.

Linking Files

You can use the Library Link Document command to import all the text from a file, even if it does not contain bookmarks. Word will import the whole file and insert it at the cursor's location. Like imported bookmarks, the imported file is marked with a hidden line of text, and you can update the link.

Chapter Summary

Creating and retrieving glossary entries is easy. You have no reason to retype text again and again when Word can do it for you. Examine your day-to-day working habits. If you find yourself typing the same text over and over again in many or most editing sessions, save it to Word's default glossary, NORMAL.GLY. For text for special-purpose writing applications, create a new glossary file to hold the boilerplate entries. And don't forget that glossaries are useful for purposes other than boilerplate. Explore the supplied glossary entries and use them. If you're moving large chunks of text around, consider using glossaries instead of the scrap.

If you use numerous or lengthy boilerplate passages, or if it's important to maintain a single, authoritative version of each boilerplate passage, create a file containing boilerplate passages marked as bookmarks. Import the bookmarks using the Library Link Document command. Like glossaries, bookmarks can be used in other ways as well.

You can use bookmarks to move around in a lengthy, complex document. In Chapter 14, you will learn how to use bookmarks for cross-referencing purposes.

13

Creating Indexes and Tables of Contents

Today's businesses must cope with a phenomenal amount of paperwork. The British firm Marks and Spencer recently estimated that its employees crank out more than 30 million pages of paperwork per year. American firms generate enough paperwork each day to circle the globe many times over. In 1984 alone, more than 14 million file cabinets were manufactured so that an estimated 200 billion pieces of paper would have some place to go!

Much of this amazing output of paperwork involves the production of business reports and proposals. Just to cope with new regulations, the oil company Exxon had to submit a report to the Department of Energy that ran just shy of 500,000 pages. And to deal with the documentation for just one government contract, RCA's Missile and Surface Radar facility had to crank out more than 100,000 pages of technical manuals a year. Cutting down the labor involved in producing all these reports and proposals can produce a handsome payoff.

Word comes in handy for anyone faced with the job of creating a report or proposal. Previous chapters already have discussed some of the reasons for Word's usefulness (for instance, Word's wonderful outline mode, which greatly aids the tasks of planning, organizing, and restructuring complex documents). Covered here, however, are two features that are sure to save you huge amounts of time if your report or proposal must have an accurate index and table of contents. As you learn in this chapter, Word can compile an index and table of contents, insert the correct page numbers, and print both tables for you

339

automatically! And if you make changes to your document, Word makes all the necessary corrections to the tables without any intervention on your part. This feature alone can save you big chunks of time as you struggle to meet deadlines.

In this chapter, you learn how to do the following:

❏ Insert into your text codes that Word will read as index entries

❏ Compile the index automatically after you have finished coding your document

❏ Code headings so that Word treats them as table of contents entries

❏ Compile the table of contents automatically after you have finished coding your document

❏ Create a table of contents from an outline of your document, without any coding

❏ Create additional tables you may need, such as tables of figures and tables of tables

Note: This chapter will prove most useful for those of you whose reports and proposals will be reproduced directly from Word printouts, because the index references and tables of contents refer to the pages Word creates. If you're preparing a document to be typeset, you need to prepare the table of contents and index from the page proofs the printer gives you. In such circumstances, Word isn't much help.

Creating an Index

To create an index with Word, you begin by marking in your document those terms you want included in the index. Then you compile the index, using the Library Index command. Finally, you format the index to suit your tastes or style guidelines.

You may be wondering why Word's indexing command isn't completely automatic (you must mark the terms to be indexed manually). The answer is that an automatically generated index using every word in your document would run many times the length of the document itself! A good index begins with a working idea of who the reader will be and what terms the reader is likely to consider when searching for information. No computer program yet devised is capable of approaching this level of analytical ability.

Types of Index Entries: An Overview

You can create two different kinds of index entries with Word: concordance entries and conceptual entries.

A *concordance entry* is a word in your document that you mark for indexing. Word prints the concordance entry in your document and prints the entry again in the index. Use concordance entries to mark words that actually appear in your text.

A *conceptual entry* is a word that you embed in the text (formatted as hidden text so that the word doesn't print) and mark for indexing. Word prints the conceptual entry only in the index, not in the text. Use conceptual entries when the words in your document aren't quite right for indexing. For example, if a passage you want to index contains the word *industrialization,* but you think *industry* is a better term for the index, use *industry* as a conceptual entry.

You can use either technique to create main entries or subentries. A main entry is printed flush to the margin in the index, and Word alphabetizes these terms. A subentry is indented and appears beneath an entry. You can create up to five levels of subentries, although one or two is usually sufficient.

Marking Concordance Entries the Easy Way

As you will quickly discover, marking every index entry by hand is a tedious job. But you can use the easy way—a partially automated way—to get Word to mark concordance entries. You should begin your index with this technique and then use the manual methods to expand the index and to include conceptual entries.

To mark concordance entries automatically, follow these steps:

1. Open a new, blank Word document, and make a list of the words you want Word to mark as concordance entries. Refer to a draft printout of your document, or display the document in a second window. Type each word on its own line, ending each line with a paragraph mark. The list need not be in alphabetical order.

2. Save the file.

3. Load the document you want indexed.

4. Place the Word Utilities disk in the disk drive, and use the **T**ransfer **G**lossary **L**oad command. When the `filename` prompt appears, type *macro.gly* and carry out the command.

   MACRO.GLY contains Word's supplied macros, the ones that come with the program. When you type the file name, be sure to include path information if the file isn't in the default directory.

5. After Word loads the glossary, use the **I**nsert command and choose **index.mac** from the list.

6. When you are prompted to do so, type the name of the file that contains your list of words. Be sure to include path information if the file isn't in the default directory.

The macro called index.mac goes through your document, marking each word that matches the list you made. Starting the indexing process with this macro makes excellent sense because index.mac does much of the tedious coding for you. You then can expand the index by manually marking additional concordance entries and the conceptual entries you want in your index.

Marking Index Entries Manually

Even if you begin your index with index.mac, you will need to mark some entries manually. You surely will find some concordance entries other than those in your list, and you have no choice but to mark conceptual entries manually. In addition, manual techniques provide the only means by which you can mark an entry that spans a range of pages or that refers the reader to another index term.

To mark index entries manually, you need to know that every index entry has three parts:

❑ *Index code (.i.)*. You must format this code, a lowercase *i* surrounded by periods, as hidden text. The code tells Word that the text to follow should be treated as an index entry.

❑ *Index entry*. The index entry is the text you want indexed (normally one or two words). If you do not format the entry as hidden text, Word treats it as a concordance entry; that is, Word prints the term in the text *and* in the index. If you do format the entry as hidden text, Word treats it as a conceptual entry. The word doesn't appear in the text but does appear in the index.

❏ *Index end mark (;)*. This code, a semicolon formatted as hidden text, tells Word where the index entry stops. If you don't insert the code, Word considers all the text to the end of the paragraph as part of the index entry.

You can mark index entries as or after you type. In most cases, you will probably mark index entries only after you have completed your document. Indexing is usually one of the last steps in document production. The tutorials in this chapter, therefore, were designed to be used after you have typed the text.

Before you begin marking index entries, choose the **Options** command. Make sure that you have chosen the **Yes** option in the **show hidden text** field. You need to see hidden text on-screen if you want to mark index entries correctly.

Caution: If you fail to mark the index code and end mark as hidden text, Word will not remove them from your document or print the entry in the index. You must exercise special care when indexing to make sure that all the codes and end marks are properly formatted as hidden text.

Marking Concordance Entries

To mark a concordance entry, use the following procedure:

1. Place the cursor on the first character of the word you want to index.

2. Press Alt-E to enter hidden text, and type the index code (.*i.*).

3. Now place the cursor directly after the word.

4. Press Alt-E again and type the end mark (;).

Figure 13.1 shows two concordance entries (.i.information; and .i.knowledge;).

Fig. 13.1.

Two terms marked as concordance entries.

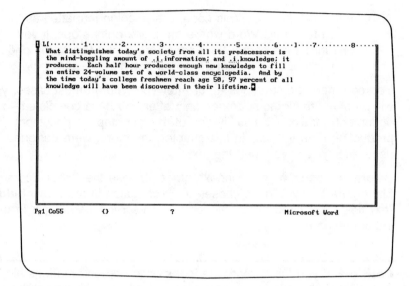

```
L[········1········2········3········4········5········6····]···7·········8·····
  What distinguishes today's society from all its predecessors is
  the mind-boggling amount of .i.information; and .i.knowledge; it
  produces.  Each half hour produces enough new knowledge to fill
  an entire 24-volume set of a world-class encyclopedia.  And by
  the time today's college freshmen reach age 50, 97 percent of all
  knowledge will have been discovered in their lifetime.

Pg1 Co55          {}              ?                    Microsoft Word
```

Caution: If the entry you're marking contains punctuation (commas, quotation marks, or colons), surround the entry with quotation marks so that Word doesn't get confused. The following entry, for example, is marked correctly:

.i."Los Angeles, California";

Be sure to format the quotation marks as hidden text so that they don't print in your document.

If you have loaded the glossary called MACRO.GLY, you can use a supplied macro called *index_entry.mac* to mark concordance entries. To use index_entry.mac, select the term you want to index. (Important: you *must* select the word.) Then choose the Insert command, and select **index_entry.mac** from the list.

Marking Conceptual Entries

To mark a conceptual entry, follow these steps:

1. Place the cursor just before the text that discusses the concept you want to index.

2. Press Alt-E.

3. Type *.i.* followed by the conceptual entry and the semicolon. Everything you have just typed should be formatted as hidden text.

Figure 13.2 shows a conceptual entry (`.i.growth of knowledge;`).

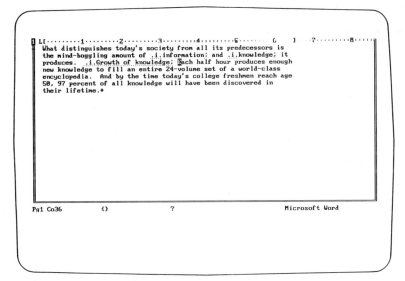

```
L[·········1·········2·········3·········4·········5·······  [    ]   ·7·········8·····]
What distinguishes today's society from all its predecessors is
the mind-boggling amount of .i.information; and .i.knowledge; it
produces.  .i.Growth of knowledge; Each half hour produces enough
new knowledge to fill an entire 24-volume set of a world-class
encyclopedia.  And by the time today's college freshmen reach age
50, 97 percent of all knowledge will have been discovered in
their lifetime.◆




Pg1 Co36          {}            ?                Microsoft Word
```

Fig. 13.2.

A conceptual entry formatted as hidden text.

Marking Subentries

Subentries are preferred when an entry otherwise would be followed by a long list of page numbers. In such cases, subentries help the reader locate the correct information. Here's an example:

Industrial ventures
    aluminum cookware 60
    graphite processing 32
    luxury goods 59
    matches 38
    textiles 23

Subentries are like conceptual entries in that the whole entry is formatted as hidden text—you don't want the subentry code to appear in your document.

To create a subentry, follow these instructions:

1. Place the cursor just before the text you want to index.

2. Press Alt-E.

3. Type the index code (*.i.*) followed by the main entry, a colon, the subentry, and the end code (;).

A properly formatted subentry appears as follows:

.i.industrial ventures:textiles;

Figure 13.3 shows an example of a subentry

(`.i.knowledge:growth;`).

Fig. 13.3.

A subentry
formatted as
hidden text.

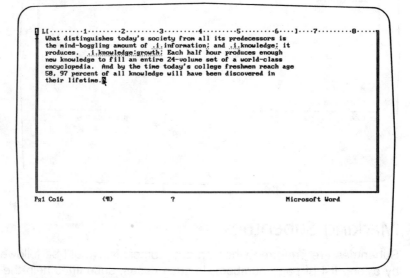

Marking a Range of Pages

Often you will need to index a topic that's discussed on more than one page, such as

Industry 19-43

To create an entry that marks a range of pages, follow these steps:

1. At the beginning of the discussion of the topic, insert an entry, using the following coding scheme:

.i.subject;

The word *subject* here refers to the topic you're indexing. If you're indexing the topic "industry," the beginning code would be .i.industry;. Format the whole entry as hidden text.

2. At the end of the discussion of the topic, insert exactly the same entry.

3. After Word compiles your index, the page range will be indicated with a comma and a space, as in

Industry 19, 43

You must edit the entry manually so that the page range is expressed correctly, as in

Industry 19-43

Creating Cross-References

You can create an entry that directs the reader to another entry, such as

Manufacturing
See Industry 26

To create such an entry, use the following coding scheme:

.i.manufacturing:See Industry;

and format the whole code as hidden text.

Table 13.1 sums up your index coding options.

Table 13.1
Summary of Options for Coding Index Entries

Appearance in Index	Coding in Text
Capital investment 11	.i.capital investment;
Industry	.i.industry;
Industry capital goods 60	.i.industry:capital goods;
Graphite 19-26	.i.graphite; [text] .i.graphite;
Graphite 19-26 mining 20	i.graphite:mining;

Table 13.1—Continued

Appearance in Index	Coding in Text

Graphite 19-26
  mining 20
    capital 22
	.i.graphite:mining:capital;

Manufacturing See Industry	.i.manufacturing:See Industry;

Compiling and Formatting the Index

When you are certain that your document is in its final form, and you have marked all the index entries, you need to compile the index. Use these steps:

1. Choose the Library Index command (see fig. 13.4). If you want a comma and a space to separate the entry and page number, type a comma and a space in the **entry/page # separated by** field. Modify the other options if necessary. The default settings call for Word to capitalize the first word of main entries and to indent subentries 0.2 inch.

2. Carry out the command.

Fig. 13.4.

The Library Index menu.

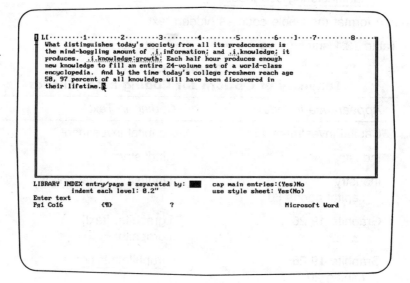

```
 L[········1·········2·········3·········4·········5·········6···]····7·········8···
   What distinguishes today's society from all its predecessors is
   the mind-boggling amount of .i.information; and .i.knowledge; it
   produces.  .i.knowledge:growth: Each half hour produces enough
   new knowledge to fill an entire 24-volume set of a world-class
   encyclopedia.  And by the time today's college freshmen reach age
   58, 97 percent of all knowledge will have been discovered in
   their lifetime.
```

```
LIBRARY INDEX entry/page # separated by: ███   cap main entries:(Yes)No
              indent each level: 0.2"            use style sheet: Yes(No)
Enter text
Pg1 Co16          {¶}               ?                    Microsoft Word
```

Word then compiles the index. For a lengthy document, the process can take several minutes. Word places the index at the end of your document, beneath a division mark. The index begins with a hidden text code (.Begin Index.) and ends with another one (.End Index.). Do not delete these codes unless you are sure that the index is complete. If you delete the codes, Word can't erase the index automatically when it creates a revised version.

If you find that terms are missing from your index or that the index contains errors, insert or correct the codes in your document. Then use **L**ibrary **I**ndex again to recompile the index.

After Word has compiled your index and you're satisfied with it, you can format it as you would any text. Because the index is in its own division at the end of your document, you need to turn page numbering on if you want the index's pages numbered. Add character emphasis, multiple-column formatting, and other formats as you prefer.

Creating a Table of Contents

By far the easiest way to generate a table of contents for your document is to outline the document, using the techniques discussed in Chapter 10, "Organizing Your Document with Outlining." If you haven't used an outline, you still can create a table of contents. But you have to mark the headings in your document so that Word can compile a table of contents from them.

Using an Outline

To create a table of contents from an outlined document, follow these instructions:

1. Turn off the display of hidden text by choosing the **No** option in the **show hidden text** field of the Options menu. This step helps you make sure that pagination is correct.

2. Switch to the outline mode by pressing Shift-F2.

3. Collapse all the body text, and display all the headings you want to use in the table of contents. If you want only the major section headings to appear, for instance, use the Ctrl-K+ command to specify Level 2 headings.

4. Use the **L**ibrary **T**able command.

5. When the command menu appears, as shown in figure 13.5, choose the **O**utline option in the **from** field.

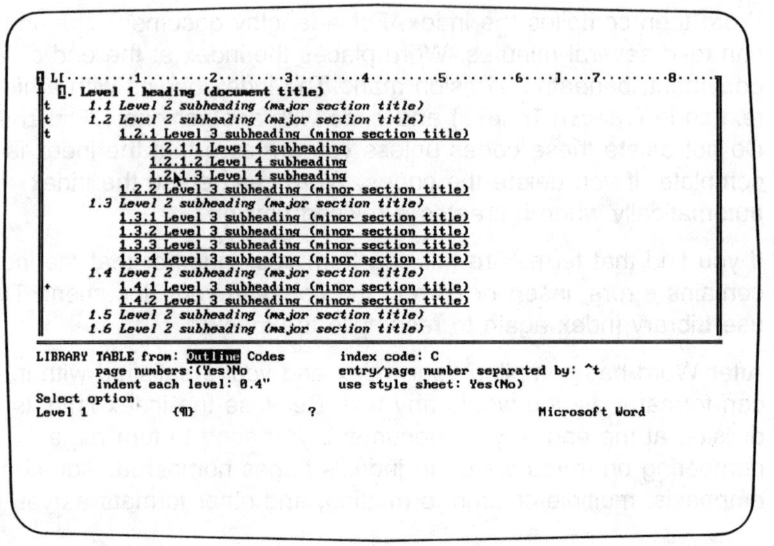

Fig. 13.5.

Using the Library
Table command.

```
L[········1·········2·········3·········4·········5·········6···]···7·········8·····
[]. Level 1 heading (document title)
   1.1 Level 2 subheading (major section title)
   1.2 Level 2 subheading (major section title)
      1.2.1 Level 3 subheading (minor section title)
         1.2.1.1 Level 4 subheading
         1.2.1.2 Level 4 subheading
         1.2.1.3 Level 4 subheading
      1.2.2 Level 3 subheading (minor section title)
   1.3 Level 2 subheading (major section title)
      1.3.1 Level 3 subheading (minor section title)
      1.3.2 Level 3 subheading (minor section title)
      1.3.3 Level 3 subheading (minor section title)
      1.3.4 Level 3 subheading (minor section title)
   1.4 Level 2 subheading (major section title)
      1.4.1 Level 3 subheading (minor section title)
      1.4.2 Level 3 subheading (minor section title)
   1.5 Level 2 subheading (major section title)
   1.6 Level 2 subheading (major section title)

LIBRARY TABLE from: Outline Codes          index code: C
            page numbers:(Yes)No            entry/page number separated by: ^t
            indent each level: 0.4"         use style sheet: Yes(No)
Select option
Level 1           {¶}                ?              Microsoft Word
```

Word then compiles the table of contents and places it at the end of
your document (see fig. 13.6). Like the indexes Word compiles, the
table of contents begins and ends with codes. Do not delete these
codes. They're formatted as hidden text, so they won't print. Word
needs the codes to locate the table in case you decide to recompile it.

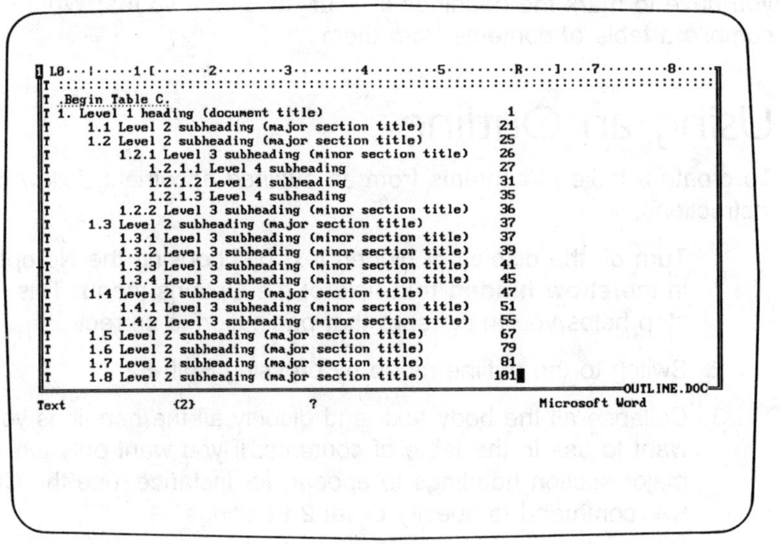

Fig. 13.6.

The table of
contents.

```
L0···!······1·[·····2·········3·········4·········5······R···]···7·········8···:
:::::::::::::::::::::::::::::::::::::::::::::::::::::::::::::::::::::::::::::::::::::
.Begin Table C.
1. Level 1 heading (document title)                                    1
   1.1 Level 2 subheading (major section title)                       21
   1.2 Level 2 subheading (major section title)                       25
      1.2.1 Level 3 subheading (minor section title)                  26
         1.2.1.1 Level 4 subheading                                   27
         1.2.1.2 Level 4 subheading                                   31
         1.2.1.3 Level 4 subheading                                   35
      1.2.2 Level 3 subheading (minor section title)                  36
   1.3 Level 2 subheading (major section title)                       37
      1.3.1 Level 3 subheading (minor section title)                  37
      1.3.2 Level 3 subheading (minor section title)                  39
      1.3.3 Level 3 subheading (minor section title)                  41
      1.3.4 Level 3 subheading (minor section title)                  45
   1.4 Level 2 subheading (major section title)                       47
      1.4.1 Level 3 subheading (minor section title)                  51
      1.4.2 Level 3 subheading (minor section title)                  55
   1.5 Level 2 subheading (major section title)                       67
   1.6 Level 2 subheading (major section title)                       79
   1.7 Level 2 subheading (major section title)                       81
   1.8 Level 2 subheading (major section title)                      101
                                                            OUTLINE.DOC
Text              {2}                ?              Microsoft Word
```

You can format the table of contents by adding character emphases, indentations, blank lines, and other formats to suit your tastes and style guidelines.

When you print your document, the table of contents appears at the end. Because the table is in its own division, no page numbers will print (unless you turn them on deliberately). You therefore can place at the beginning of your document the page or pages containing the table of contents.

Coding Entries

Marking headings for inclusion in a table of contents is much like creating concordance entries for an index. You must distinguish between three parts of each marked heading:

❑ *Table of contents code (.c.).* You must format this code, a lowercase *c* surrounded by periods, as hidden text. The code tells Word that the text to follow should be treated as a table of contents entry.

❑ *The heading.* So that the heading will print in your document, you should not format the heading as hidden text.

❑ *End mark (;).* This code, a semicolon formatted as hidden text, tells Word where the table of contents entry stops.

You can mark table of contents entries as you type or after you are finished typing. In most cases, you will probably mark the headings only after you have completed your document. The tutorial in the next section assumes that you're marking your headings after you have typed the text.

Before you begin marking index entries, choose the **O**ptions command and make sure that you have chosen the **Y**es option in the **show hidden text** field. You need to see hidden text on-screen if you want to mark table of contents entries correctly. And make sure that you have formatted the .c. code and end mark as hidden text!

Marking Major Headings

Word prints major headings (or first-level headings) flush to the left margin. These headings are chapter titles in a book, or major section headings in an article or proposal.

To code a major heading, follow these steps:

1. Place the cursor at the beginning of the heading and press Alt-E.

2. Type the table of contents code (.c.).

3. Place the cursor on the space following the heading and press Alt-E.

4. Type a semicolon (;).

Your heading should conform to this coding scheme:

.c.First Level of Heading;

Make sure that the table of contents code (.c.) and end mark (;) are formatted as hidden text. If the heading contains a colon, semicolon, or quotation marks, enclose the whole heading in quotation marks (formatted as hidden text), as in the following example:

.c."The "Tiger Panic" of 1983: An Interpretation";

Coding Headings at Lower Levels

To code headings at second and other subordinate levels, use the codes listed in table 13.2. Use second-level codes for subject headings within chapters, third-level codes for sections within the second-level units, and so on.

Table 13.2
Table of Contents Codes

Level	Code
First	.c.
Second	.c.:
Third	.c.::
Fourth	.c.:::
Fifth	.c.::::

The following is an example of a second-level table of contents entry:

.c.: Analysis of Data;

Compiling the Table of Contents from Codes

To compile the table of contents after you have coded your headings, choose the **L**ibrary **T**able command and select the **C**odes option in the **from** field.

Using Shortcuts

Coding headings is as tedious as coding index entries. But here are some shortcuts:

❏ *Create glossary entries for the table of contents code and end mark.* Type the code and mark as hidden text. Then save the code (*.c.*) to a glossary called *c* and the mark (*;*) to a glossary called *e*. When you insert the glossaries called *c* and *e*, Word inserts not only the code but also the hidden text formatting. As suggested in the preceding chapter, you can assign these glossaries to control keys when you name them; use Ctrl-C and Ctrl-E.

❏ *Use Word's indexing macros.* The macro toc_entry.mac, supplied with Word 5, may prove useful. This macro automatically enters table of contents codes and end marks around a heading. For more information on the macros supplied with Word, see Chapter 21, "Creating and Using Word 5 Macros."

Chapter Summary

In this chapter you learned how to use Word to automate two tedious tasks: indexing your document and compiling a table of contents. You learned how to begin your index with the supplied macro called index.mac (which marks concordance entries from a list of terms you create), how to mark concordance entries and conceptual entries manually, and how to use the Library Index command to compile the index. Remember: If you make changes to your document, you can rerun Library Index. You can use the command as many times as you need.

This chapter demonstrates that the easiest way to generate a table of contents is to create an outline for your document. Word then can generate a table of contents from the outline and print the table at the end of your document. If you're not using an outline, you can code the headings the same way you code the index entries.

Word can generate more tables than just the two discussed in this chapter. In fact, you can create up to 24 separate tables for a single document. As you learn in the next chapter, you can put this capability to work to generate a table of authorities for legal documents.

14

The Legal and
Scholarly Word

One good way to make a claim stick is to credit it to a
dependable authority. Doing so says, in effect, "Don't mess with
me; if you do, you're messing with all these other folks, too!" Making
claims stick is crucial in many professions but especially in academics,
scientific or business research, and law. If you're writing a dissertation,
a major marketing report, or a court brief, you had better have your
ducks in a row—and that means using footnotes, endnotes, or tables
of authorities to document the claims you're making. If you're using
Word in a legal context, you need to number the lines in the printout.
And you had better be ready to refer the reader to important
discussions of critical points.

As you'll discover in this chapter, Word is an excellent program for
anyone who needs to incorporate these kinds of references. Word's
footnoting capabilities rank among the best in the word processing
world—a fact that's obvious to anyone who has used the program.
Word can position notes at the bottom of the page or at the end of a
division, and if the footnote text is too long, Word "floats" the text to
the next page. Word automatically numbers footnotes, and you can
even display a special footnote window that shows the footnotes
whose reference marks are currently displayed in the document
window.

Not so obvious are Word's capabilities for handling tables of legal
authorities. But as you'll see, you can use Word 5's supplied macros to
tackle that job with speed and style. And Word 5's new bookmark

feature makes in-text cross-references a breeze. You can easily print a document with cross-references such as "See the discussion of Peters vs. Smith on page 19," and have Word fill in the correct page references.

This chapter covers the following topics:

❑ Creating, numbering, editing, and deleting footnotes and endnotes

❑ Using Word's supplied macros to create a table of authorities for legal documents

❑ Printing line numbers in your document and displaying the cursor's line position in the status line

❑ Using bookmarks to create automatically paginated cross-references in your printed document

Using Footnotes and Endnotes

A variety of commands control footnotes and endnotes. You use the Format Division Layout command to choose whether to place footnotes at the bottom of the page or at the end of the division. You use the Format Footnote command to create footnotes and type footnote text. And you use the Jump Footnote command to move between footnote text and your document.

A note, whether a footnote or endnote, has two parts:

❑ The *footnote reference mark* is the mark (a number or a symbol such as an asterisk) that appears in the text where you insert a footnote. If you choose numbers, Word automatically inserts the correct number—and updates it automatically if your editing makes changes necessary.

❑ The *footnote text* is the text of the footnote itself. In your document, this text is positioned in the special footnote area after the end mark in your document. When you print, you choose between printing your notes at the end of a division (endnotes) or the bottom of each page (footnotes).

Choosing the Position for Notes

You may choose between footnotes and endnotes for each division you create.

By default, Word prints footnotes at the bottom of the page, automatically "floating" excess footnote text to the bottom of the next page if the text cannot fit on one page. The program inserts a 2-inch rule to separate the text of the document from the text of the notes.

To place notes at the end of a division (endnotes), choose the **End** option in the **footnotes** field of the Format Division Layout menu. If your document has only one division, which is normally the case, the notes appear at the end of your document, positioned just below the last line of text.

If you have chosen endnotes and want footnotes instead, choose the **Same-page** option in the **footnotes** field of the Format Division Layout menu.

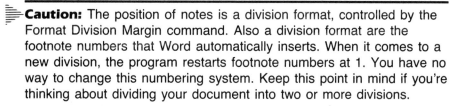

Caution: The position of notes is a division format, controlled by the Format Division Margin command. Also a division format are the footnote numbers that Word automatically inserts. When it comes to a new division, the program restarts footnote numbers at 1. You have no way to change this numbering system. Keep this point in mind if you're thinking about dividing your document into two or more divisions.

Inserting a Note

You use the Format Footnote command to insert a footnote or endnote in your document.

Note: This command's name is misleading. It doesn't *format* the note; it *inserts* the note. To format your footnote, you use other commands, as explained in the section called "Formatting Notes."

To insert a footnote, follow these instructions:

1. Position the cursor where you want the footnote reference mark to appear.

2. Choose the **Format Footnote** command. The **reference mark** command field appears, as shown in figure 14.1. If you want Word to number your notes automatically, leave the field blank and just press Enter.

   If you type any character, such as an asterisk or a number, Word uses that character as the footnote reference mark. You can type up to 28 characters in the **reference mark** field, but relying on Word's automatic numbering is best.

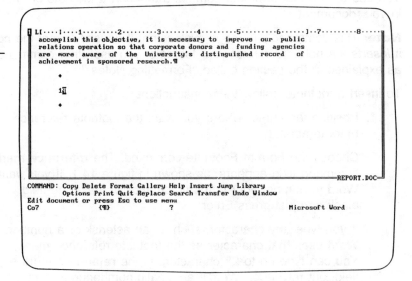

Fig. 14.1.

Inserting a
footnote.

```
┌─────────────────────────────────────────────────────┐
│                Is Advertising a Form of Poetry?¶      │
│                         ¶                             │
│   Advertising pelts us every day with a variety of messages,│
│   and some of them, to be sure, are manipulative, duplicitous,│
│   or exploitive.█ Yet it cannot be denied that the best│
│   advertisements are mythic images; they are the images of│
│   popular consciousness, and we can resist then no more than│
│   we can resist our sense of pride in our cultural identity.│
│   And the slogans or message advertisements use, particularly│
│   the ones printed in large type in magazine or newspaper ads,│
│   are often superb examples of poetic diction.  They│
│   deliberately exploit ambiguity, double meanings, and other│
│   poetic devices.  In the end, a well-crafted ad draws us into│
│   its meaning space, inviting us to draw the connections among│
│   the images and the clever dual meanings of the text,│
│   experiencing our culture and language in a way that is│
│   aesthetically pleasing.¶                            │
│   ◆                                                   │
│                                                       │
│ FORMAT FOOTNOTE reference mark: █                     │
│                                                       │
│ Enter text                                            │
│ Pg1 Co15          {?}            ?         Microsoft Word│
└─────────────────────────────────────────────────────┘
```

3. Carry out the command by pressing Enter or clicking the
   command name.

   Word echoes the footnote number in the special footnote
   area beyond the end mark and positions the cursor there so
   that you can type the note (see fig. 14.2). You can use
   character and paragraph formatting as you type the note.

Fig. 14.2.

The footnote
number repeated
in the footnote
area.

```
┌─────────────────────────────────────────────────────┐
│ L[····¦····1·········2·········3·········4·········5·········6······]·7·········8·····│
│ accomplish this objective, it is necessary to  improve  our  public│
│ relations operation so that corporate donors and  funding  agencies│
│ are  more  aware  of  the  University's  distinguished  record  of│
│ achievement in sponsored research.¶                   │
│     ◆                                                 │
│                                                       │
│   1█¶                                                 │
│     ◆                                                 │
│                                                       │
│                                          ═REPORT.DOC═ │
│ COMMAND: Copy Delete Format Gallery Help Insert Jump Library│
│          Options Print Quit Replace Search Transfer Undo Window│
│ Edit document or press Esc to use menu                │
│ Co7          {¶}            ?         Microsoft Word  │
└─────────────────────────────────────────────────────┘
```

4. Type the footnote text.

5. To move back to the footnote reference mark, choose the **J**ump **F**ootnote command (see fig. 14.3). You can press PgUp or use other scrolling techniques to return to the reference mark, but Jump Footnote takes you to the exact spot where you used the Format Footnote command.

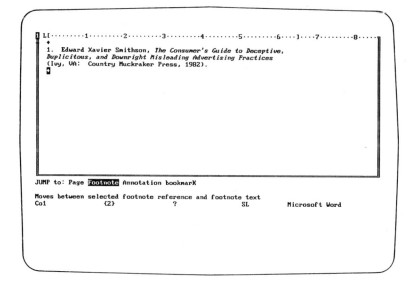

Fig. 14.3.

Using the Jump Footnote command.

6. Word enters the reference mark as ordinary text. If you want the reference mark to appear superscripted, as shown in figure 14.4, you must format the reference mark with the Alt-+ (plus) keyboard shortcut (or the **F**ormat **C**haracter command). To superscript the footnote reference mark, make sure that the cursor is positioned on the mark. Then press Alt-+ twice.

Many Word users are annoyed by the fact that Word does not superscript the footnote reference mark automatically. But remember that many style guidelines, particularly in technical fields, call for reference marks to be created as ordinary text enclosed in brackets or parentheses. Programs that superscript reference marks automatically—and don't allow users to change this format—are unusable in such fields.

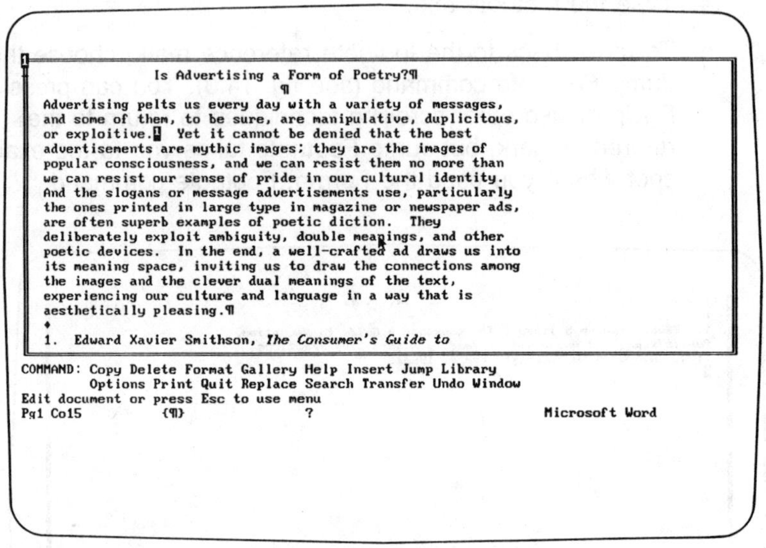

Fig. 14.4.

A superscripted footnote reference mark.

```
┌─────────────────────────────────────────────────┐
│ ▌         Is Advertising a Form of Poetry?¶      │
│                         ¶                         │
│ Advertising pelts us every day with a variety of messages, │
│ and some of them, to be sure, are manipulative, duplicitous, │
│ or exploitive.▌  Yet it cannot be denied that the best │
│ advertisements are mythic images; they are the images of │
│ popular consciousness, and we can resist them no more than │
│ we can resist our sense of pride in our cultural identity. │
│ And the slogans or message advertisements use, particularly │
│ the ones printed in large type in magazine or newspaper ads, │
│ are often superb examples of poetic diction.  They │
│ deliberately exploit ambiguity, double meanings, and other │
│ poetic devices.  In the end, a well-crafted ad draws us into │
│ its meaning space, inviting us to draw the connections among │
│ the images and the clever dual meanings of the text, │
│ experiencing our culture and language in a way that is │
│ aesthetically pleasing.¶ │
│ ◆ │
│ 1.  Edward Xavier Smithson, The Consumer's Guide to │
│                                                   │
│ COMMAND: Copy Delete Format Gallery Help Insert Jump Library │
│         Options Print Quit Replace Search Transfer Undo Window │
│ Edit document or press Esc to use menu │
│ Pg1 Co15          {¶}              ?              Microsoft Word │
└─────────────────────────────────────────────────┘
```

One of the many good reasons for creating your own custom style sheets is that you can define a new default character style for footnote reference marks. If you normally use 12-point Helvetica, for instance, you can set up a style sheet that formats footnote reference marks automatically with 8-point Helvetica. And after you create the style sheet, Word automatically enters the style whenever you create a footnote. Creating style sheets obviously pays off if you plan to use footnotes extensively and need to superscript your reference marks. For more information, see Chapter 20, "Using Style Sheets."

Formatting Notes

As you have just learned, Word formats reference marks with the standard style for characters. Also formatted in a standard style, the standard paragraph style, is the footnote or endnote text. If you want to change the paragraph formatting, you must do so deliberately, using the Format Paragraph command.

You can format each note as you enter it. An easier method, however, is to format all the notes at once when you have finished typing your document and have inserted all your notes. Follow these steps to format notes all at once after you have typed them:

1. Press Ctrl-PgDn to move the cursor to the end mark.

2. Press the down-arrow key to select the first character of the first footnote. (Be careful to exclude the end mark from the selection. This procedure doesn't work if you include the end mark in the highlight.)

3. Press F6 (Extend).

4. Press the down-arrow key to move the highlight to the last line.

   Note: Ctrl-PgDn takes you only to the end mark, not to the end of the footnotes.

5. Press the End key to expand the highlight to the last character of the last footnote.

6. Choose the **F**ormat **P**aragraph command and select the formats you want (see fig. 14.5). For example, you may want to specify *1* in the **space before** field, and select the **L**eft option in the **alignment** field. After you have selected your formats, carry out the command.

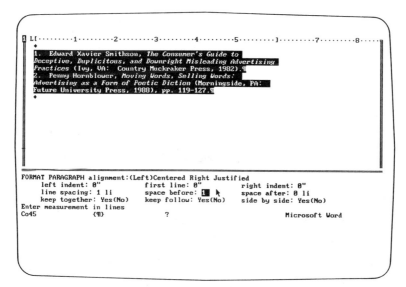

Fig. 14.5.

Using the Format Paragraph command.

7. Choose the **F**ormat **C**haracter command and select the formats you want, if any. Use this command if you are using a font other than the default font for your printer.

The footnotes should now be formatted the way you want. Figure 14.6 shows footnotes left-justified, with one line before each paragraph, and with the book titles in italics. If you add additional footnotes, you have to format the new notes to match the old ones.

Fig. 14.6.

An example of formatted footnotes.

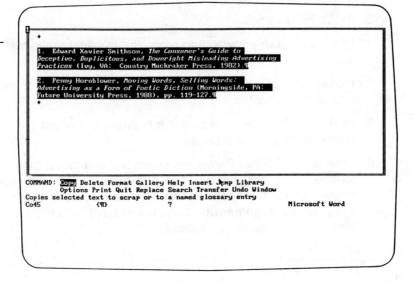

To make sure that you have formatted your footnotes correctly, preview the formatting you have chosen, using the Print preView command.

Editing Notes

Editing notes is easy once you have inserted them. Here's how to revise the text of a note:

1. Select the reference mark of the note you want to edit.

2. Choose the **Jump Footnote** command. Word automatically scrolls to the text of the footnote you have selected.

3. Revise the footnote as you would edit ordinary text.

4. Choose the **Jump Footnote** command to return to the footnote reference mark.

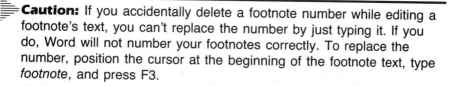

Caution: If you accidentally delete a footnote number while editing a footnote's text, you can't replace the number by just typing it. If you do, Word will not number your footnotes correctly. To replace the number, position the cursor at the beginning of the footnote text, type *footnote*, and press F3.

Searching for the Next Reference Mark

The Jump Footnote command, as you have just seen, performs different tasks depending on where you use it. If you position the cursor on a footnote reference mark, the command takes the cursor to the footnote text. If the cursor is in the footnote text when you use the Jump Footnote command, Word moves the cursor back to the reference mark.

Word offers still another way to use the Jump Footnote command. If the cursor is positioned in ordinary text when you use this command, Word scrolls to the next footnote reference mark in the document. Remember this use of the command when you need to search for your next footnote reference mark.

If you want to browse through your list of footnotes, press Ctrl-PgDn to move the cursor to the end mark. Then you can scroll through the list.

Deleting a Note

Don't try to delete a note by deleting all the footnote text in the footnote area. If you do, Word gives you the message, Not a valid action for footnotes. To delete a note, simply position the cursor on the reference mark and press Del. Word cuts the footnote to the scrap and removes the footnote text from the footnote area. (You can tell when you have cut a footnote to the scrap. Word indicates the note's presence there with two cloverleaf characters, as shown in fig. 14.7.) To cancel the deletion, choose the **U**ndo command immediately.

Moving a Note

Word makes moving notes easy. When you rearrange the notes, Word automatically renumbers the sequence. To move a note, do the following:

Fig. 14.7.

A footnote stored
in the scrap.

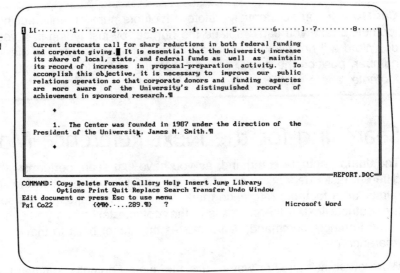

```
 L[········1········2········3········4········5········6····]·7········8····]

    Current forecasts call for sharp reductions in both federal funding
    and corporate giving.█ It is essential that the University increase
    its share of local, state, and federal funds as  well  as  maintain
    its record of  increases  in  proposal-preparation  activity.      To
    accomplish this objective, it is necessary to  improve  our  public
    relations operation so that corporate donors and  funding  agencies
    are  more  aware  of  the  University's  distinguished  record    of
    achievement in sponsored research.¶

        ◆

        1.  The Center was founded in 1987 under the direction of  the
    President of the University, James N. Smith.¶

        ◆


                                                           REPORT.DOC
COMMAND: Copy Delete Format Gallery Help Insert Jump Library
         Options Print Quit Replace Search Transfer Undo Window
Edit document or press Esc to use menu
Pg1 Co22          {◊¶◊.····289.¶}    ?                       Microsoft Word
```

1. Place the cursor on the reference mark and press Del. Word
   places the reference mark and the footnote text in the scrap.

2. Move the cursor to the footnote's new location.

3. Press Ins or use the Insert command.

Using the Footnote Window

One handy Word feature is the footnote window, a special window that
displays the text of footnotes whose reference marks are currently
displayed in the document window. The footnote window is wonderful
to use while you're editing. As you scroll through your document, the
program automatically displays the notes relevant to the text you're
editing. You can move to the notes and edit or format them just by
switching windows. Note, too, that you can open a footnote window
even if you have zoomed a window to full size—something you can't
do with other windows.

To open the footnote window, follow these steps:

1. Choose the **W**indow **S**plit **F**ootnote command.

2. When the **at line** field appears, type the number of the line
   at which you want the window to split. Alternatively, press F1
   to activate the special cursor, and then press the down-arrow
   key until you have selected the line you want (see fig. 14.8).

3. Carry out the command.

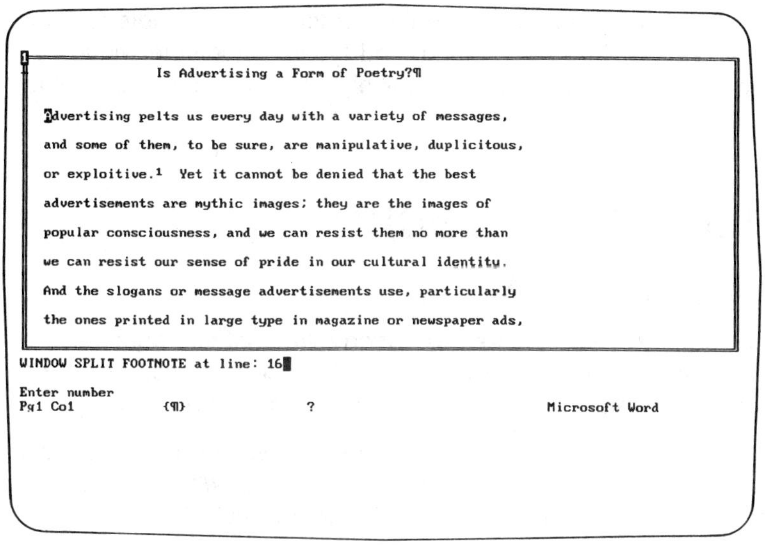

Fig. 14.8.

Opening the footnote window.

Word splits the screen with a line of dashes and, if a footnote reference mark is in the document window, displays the footnote text in the footnote window (see fig. 14.9). If the document window does not contain a reference mark, the footnote window is blank.

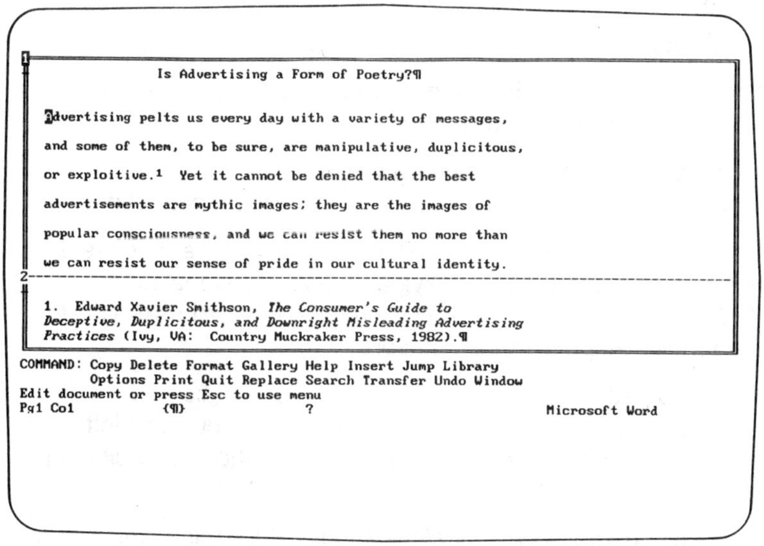

Fig. 14.9.

Displaying a footnote in the footnote window.

To close the footnote window, place the cursor in the footnote window, choose the **Window Close** command, and type the footnote window's number in the **command** field. Alternatively, click both buttons on the right border.

Generating a Table of Authorities

Legal scholars, legal secretaries, and attorneys must cite authorities by appending to the end of the document a list of the statutes, cases, or other authorities cited. This list usually includes page references.

To assist legal personnel with tables of authorities, Word supplies two macros, authority_entry.mac and authority_table.mac, which you can use to mark authorities and to generate a table of authorities.

Marking a Citation

To mark a citation the first time you type it, use this method:

1. Use the **Transfer Glossary Load** command to load the glossary called MACRO.GLY from the Word Utilities disk.

2. Place the cursor where you plan to type the citation.

3. Choose the **Insert** command and press F1. Then choose authority_entry.mac from the list.

4. When you see the message Type the new citation, highlight it, and press Enter, follow those instructions.

5. When you see the message What is the source, choose a number from the list (1 = Previous Case, 2 = Constitution, 3 = Statute, or 4 = Other). If you choose 4, Word asks you to name the category of this citation.

6. When you see the message Move the cursor to the character before this citation, press the up- and left-arrow keys to expand the highlight so that the whole citation is selected. Then press Enter.

7. Choose a name by which Word should store this citation in a glossary. If you don't plan to use this citation again in the document, just press Enter.

Word stores the citation, complete with all the formatting needed for the table of authorities, in the glossary you have just created. When you refer to the case or statute the second and subsequent times, you needn't retype the citation; simply insert its glossary entry.

Compiling the Table

When you are finished typing and revising the document, follow these steps to compile the table of authorities:

1. Use the **Insert** command and choose the authority_table.mac entry from the list.

2. If you see the message Search text not found, ignore it.

Word creates a table of authorities and places it at the end of your document in a separate division. You can format this table as needed.

Note: Do not delete the hidden text codes Word places before and after the table. If you do, Word won't delete the existing table if you revise your document and want to recompile the table.

If you don't like the way Word categorizes authorities or prints the table, you can modify the authority_entry.mac and authority_table.mac macros until they work just the way you want. For information on using and modifying macros, see Chapter 21, "Creating and Using Word 5 Macros."

Printing Line Numbers

Legal documents frequently include line numbers in the left margin. With the Format Division line-Numbers command, you can print documents with line numbers for each page, each division, or the whole document. Line numbering ignores any blank lines entered with the Format Paragraph command's **space before** or **space after** field. This factor is yet another reason to add blank lines with this command rather than just press Enter. Similarly, Word's line-numbering scheme ignores blank lines entered when you have chosen double-line spacing (or other line spacing options).

Using the Format Division line-Numbers Command

To add line numbers to your document, follow these steps:

1. Choose the **Format Division** line-**Numbers** command (see fig. 14.10).

2. Choose the **Yes** option.

   Choose other options as you please. Choose **D**ivision to number lines throughout a division, or **C**ontinuous to number them throughout your entire document. Type a new measurement in the **from text** field to change the line numbers' distance from the left side of the page. Type 2 in the **increments** field to print line numbers on every other line, type 5 to print numbers on every fifth line, and so on.

3. Carry out the command.

Fig. 14.10.

The Format Division line-Numbers menu.

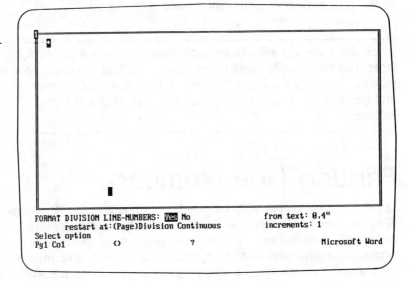

```
FORMAT DIVISION LINE-NUMBERS: Yes No          from text: 0.4"
         restart at:(Page)Division Continuous  increments: 1
Select option
Pg1 Co1              {}              ?                    Microsoft Word
```

To preview your line numbers before printing, choose the **P**rint pre**V**iew command.

Displaying the Cursor's Line Number Position

To display on the status line the cursor's present line number position, follow these steps:

1. Choose the **O**ptions command.

2. Select the **Y**es options in the **show line breaks** and **line numbers** fields. Choose **No** in the **count blank space** field.

3. Carry out the command.

Note: Word displays line numbers on the status line exactly the way you set them to print with the Format Division line-Numbers command. For example, if you choose **P**age in the **restart at** field of the Format Division line-Numbers menu, Word restarts the line numbers at 1 after a page break. If you choose the **C**ontinuous option in the **restart at** field, Word numbers lines continuously throughout your document. The status line reflects these numbering schemes.

Creating Cross-References

A cross-reference is an in-text reference to another part of the same document, as in "See the discussion of artichokes on page 16." If you define text as a bookmark, you can cross-reference a certain portion of text elsewhere in the document. And when you print your document, Word automatically fills in the page number for the cross-reference.

To designate text as a bookmark and then cross-reference the page number on which the bookmark appears, follow these steps:

1. Select the text you want to cross-reference.

2. Choose the **F**ormat bookmar**K** command and type a name for the bookmark. In figure 14.11, the text has been named `poetry_defined`.

3. Carry out the command.

4. Move the cursor to the place you want the cross-reference to appear.

5. Type the cross-reference code *page:* (don't forget the colon) and type the bookmark name.

6. Press F3.

Fig. 14.11.

Naming a
bookmark.

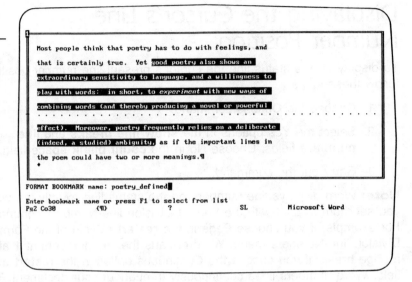

Word encloses the cross-reference code in parentheses. If you don't
press F3, Word doesn't print the page number.

In figure 14.12, the complete cross-reference is shown as it looks in
your document. Word doesn't insert the page number until you print
the document.

For more information on bookmarks, see Chapter 12, "Using
Glossaries and Bookmarks."

Fig. 14.12.

A cross-reference
in the text.

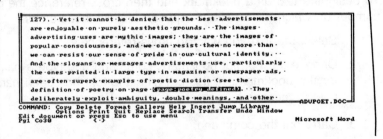

Chapter Summary

You will undoubtedly have occasions when you need to include
footnotes, endnotes, tables of authorities, line numbering, or cross-

references in your documents. This chapter showed you how easily you can access Word's referencing features. You learned how to choose between footnotes or endnotes and how to insert, format, edit, and delete a note. You learned how to use Word's supplied macros to create and compile a table of legal authorities. Also included in this chapter was a step-by-step explanation of printing line numbers in your document and displaying them in the status line. Finally, you learned an easy method for cross-referencing passages of text.

Now that you have all your ducks in a row, you can move on to the next chapter, which surveys Word's many wonderful features for collaborative writing.

15

Enhancing Group Productivity: Using Annotations and Redlining

Much professional and business writing is collaborative—and for good reason. Two (or more) heads are better than one. When your future is riding on the success of a proposal, for instance, it makes sense to assemble a team of experts, each with his or her distinctive strengths. No wonder approximately one in every five professional documents stems from collaborative efforts; the figure is as high as three in five in some fields.

Collaborative writing poses special challenges, especially when word processing comes into the picture. Every word processing program, Word included, is designed to maintain a single authoritative version of a document. The older versions disappear into the void when you save changes to disk. (Each of Word's BAK files always contains the preceding version of a file; but if you save to disk several times during a session, as you should, the BAK file closely resembles the DOC file by the end of the session.) What this arrangement means, in principle, is that one reviewer can make major changes to a document, leaving no trace of what's been changed or omitted. But what happens if the other reviewers, or the document's original author, don't like the changes?

373

Word's solution to this problem is a nifty feature called *redlining*, a special editing mode that displays editing changes and allows reviewers to confirm them. The key to the redlining mode is the Format revision-Marks command. When you turn on this command, the text you insert appears in a special typeface, the text you delete is marked with strikethrough characters, and a symbol—a vertical bar—appears in the style bar.

Redlining solves the problem of how to handle editing changes in collaborative writing, but leaves one question unanswered: How should collaborative writers make comments to one another in the text? You can enter a comment with some special marking phrase, such as *!!!Hey, these figures aren't correct!!!*, but doing so makes your document even harder to read and edit. Worse, someone has to go through the document manually and remove the comments.

To solve this problem, Word 5 includes an extremely useful new feature called *annotations*. Annotations closely resemble footnotes (see Chapter 14) except that the reference mark can include text—such as your initials—as well as a number. Each reviewer can use his or her own initials to insert personalized annotations. And Word can display all the annotations in the footnote window as you scroll through the document.

These two features—redlining and annotating—facilitate collaborative writing as no other currently available program can. If you frequently write with teams, you'll want to read this chapter with special care. It covers the following topics:

- ❑ Toggling the redlining mode on and off with Word's Format revision-Marks command

- ❑ Accepting or undoing a reviewer's changes, using the Format revision-Marks command

- ❑ Creating annotations and using them in collaborative writing situations

Using Redlining

Think of redlining as a mode, like the overtype mode, in which Word's characteristics change. When Word is in the redlining mode, the text you enter appears in a distinctive character emphasis of your choice, such as uppercase, boldface, or double-underlined. The text you delete does not disappear but displays as strike-through characters. You (or other reviewers) have the option of then accepting the changes or undoing them.

Redlining *is* like a mode, but with one exception. If more than one document is on the screen, Word uses the mode only for the active document, the one in which the cursor is positioned. Furthermore, if you turn on redlining, save a document, and quit Word, redlining still will be in effect the next time you load the document. In other words, Word stores your redlining toggle choice with each specific document.

Turning On Redlining

To turn on redlining,

1. Choose the **F**ormat revision-**M**arks **O**ptions command.

2. When the command menu appears (see fig. 15.1), choose **Y**es in the **add revision marks** field.

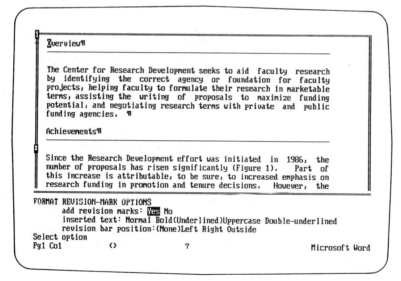

Fig. 15.1.

The Format revision-Marks menu.

3. Choose the format for marking new text in the **inserted text** field. You can choose normal, bold, underlined, uppercase, or double-underlined. Choose an emphasis you're not using for other purposes.

4. If you want to use revision bars, choose a position (**L**eft, **R**ight, or **O**utside) in the **revision bar position** field.

5. Carry out the command.

Note that the code MR appears in the status line.

If you have a color monitor, use the **colors** field in the **O**ptions menu to give a distinctive color to strike-through characters and to the emphasis you're using to mark inserted text.

Revising a document with redlining differs from the usual editing practice. You can see all the changes you have made right on the screen. Figures 15.2 and 15.3 show how a document looks when you have edited in redlining mode. In figure 15.2, a new clause has been marked with double-underlining, and a revision bar appears in the left margin. Figure 15.3 shows an example of deleted text formatted with strike-through characters.

Searching for a Reviewer's Changes

Suppose that a reviewer has given you a document which has been edited in redlining mode. Rather than scroll through the document manually, looking for each new change, let Word automatically search for your reviewer's changes. Here's how:

1. Position the highlight at the beginning of the file. (Press Ctrl-PgUp to move to the beginning of the file in one keystroke.)

2. Choose the **F**ormat revision-**M**arks **S**earch command.

After Word finds and highlights the first unit of text that has been changed, the program continues to display the Format revision-Marks menu. You can accept or undo the changes. (For more information, see the next two sections.) To continue the search without accepting or undoing a change, press *S*.

Accepting a Reviewer's Revisions

If you approve of the changes a reviewer has made, here's how to remove the marks and accept the changes:

1. Use the **F**ormat revision-**M**arks **S**earch command to search for the next revision.

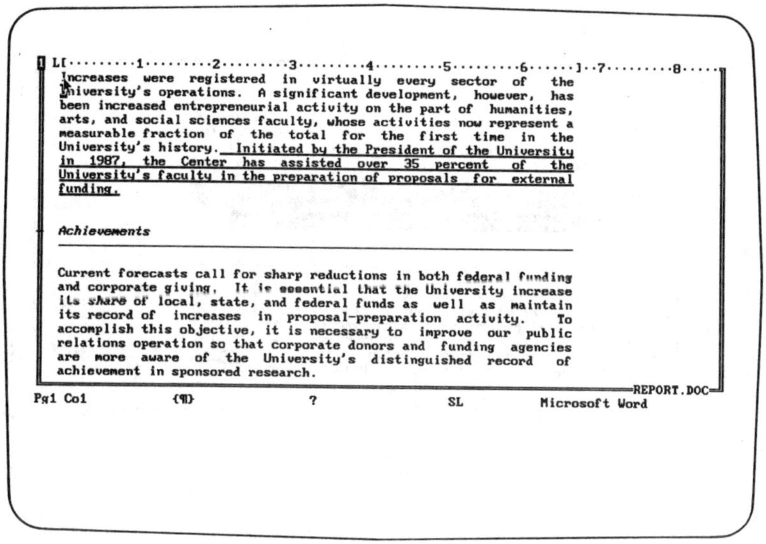

```
L[········1········2·······3·······4·······5·······6······]·7·······8·····
Increases were registered in virtually every sector of  the
University's operations.  A significant development, however, has
been increased entrepreneurial activity on the part of  humanities,
arts, and social sciences faculty, whose activities now represent a
measurable fraction of  the  total for  the  first  time  in  the
University's history.  Initiated by the President of the University
in 1987, the Center has assisted over 35 percent  of  the
University's faculty in the preparation of proposals  for  external
funding.

Achievements


Current forecasts call for sharp reductions in both federal funding
and corporate giving.  It is essential that the University increase
its share of local, state, and federal funds as well as maintain
its record of increases in proposal-preparation activity.    To
accomplish this objective, it is necessary to improve our public
relations operation so that corporate donors and funding agencies
are more aware of the University's distinguished record of
achievement in sponsored research.
                                                  REPORT.DOC
Pg1 Co1          {¶}            ?            SL       Microsoft Word
```

Fig. 15.2.

Inserting text in the redlining mode.

```
L[········1········2·······3·······4·······5·······6······]·7·······8·····
Achievements


Since the Research Development effort was initiated  in  1986,  the
number of proposals has risen significantly (Figure 1).   Part of
this increase is attributable, to be sure, to increased emphasis on
research funding in promotion and tenure decisions.   However,  the
rate of increase parallels the rate of increase in faculty visits
to the Center for Research Development.  It is therefore  plausible
to conclude that the Center's activities have played a key role  in
fostering this healthy increase  in  research  development  at  the
University.

Increases  were  registered  in  virtually  every  sector  of  the
University's operations.  A significant development, however,  has
been increased entrepreneurial activity on the part of  humanities,
arts, and social sciences faculty, whose activities now represent a
measurable fraction  of  the  total for  the  first  time  in  the
University's history.  Initiated by the President of the University
in 1987,  the  Center  has  assisted  over  35  percent  of  the
University's faculty in the preparation of proposals  for  external
                                                  REPORT.DOC
Pg1 Co12         {¶}            ?            SL  MR   Microsoft Word
```

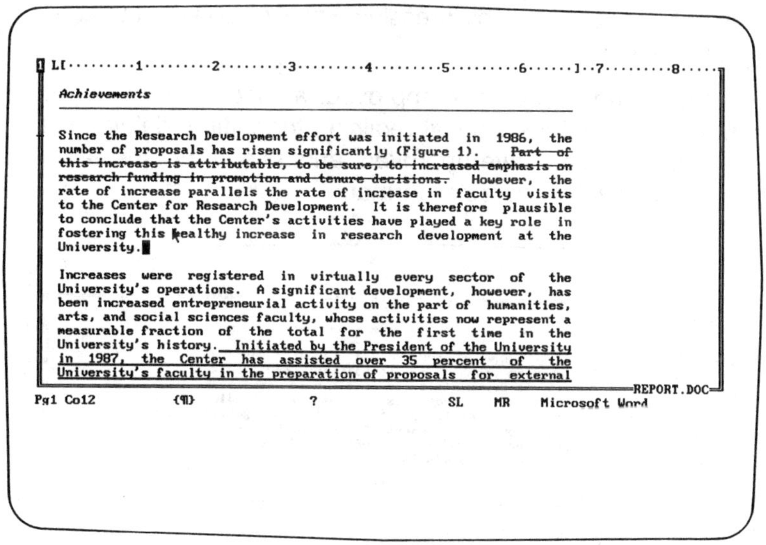

Fig. 15.3.

Deleting text in the redlining mode.

2. Select the text you want to accept (see fig. 15.4). To accept all changes in the document, select the entire document by pressing Shift-F10.

3. Choose **F**ormat revision-**M**arks accept-**R**evisions. (In Version 4 of Word, this command was named Remove-marks, which didn't adequately describe its function.

Fig. 15.4.

Accepting your
reviewer's
changes.

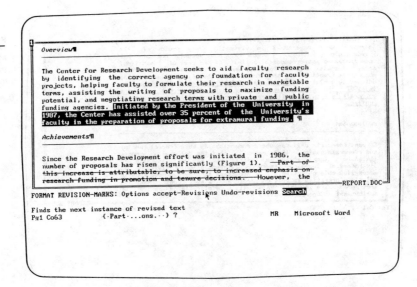

4. Carry out the command by pressing Enter or clicking the
   command name.

   Word makes the changes you have approved, as shown in figure 15.5.
   The program takes out all the special redlining formatting, deletes the
   strike-through changes you have approved, and inserts the specially
   emphasized text in regular character format.

Fig. 15.5.

The text after you
have accepted
the changes.

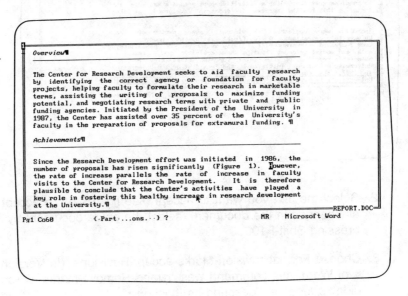

If you see the message Revised text not found, you have forgotten to select the text you want to accept. Highlight the appropriate changes and use the **F**ormat revision-**M**arks accept-**R**evisions command again.

Undoing a Reviewer's Changes

If you don't like the changes a reviewer has made, follow these steps:

1. Use the **F**ormat revision-**M**arks **S**earch command to search for the next revision.

2. Highlight the changes you don't want to accept. To undo changes throughout the whole document, press Shift-F10.

3. Choose the **F**ormat revision-**M**arks **U**ndo-revisions command.

Word restores the original version of the text. The program deletes the strike-through formatting, the text your reviewer inserted, and the revision bar in the highlighted text.

Using Annotations

One of Word 5's many useful innovations is the Format Annotation command, which works much like the Format Footnote command does (see Chapter 14). An annotation is like a footnote, except that the annotation's reference mark can contain up to 28 characters of text in addition to the number that Word automatically inserts. Moreover, you can use macros that are supplied with Word 5 to collect all the annotations on various copies of a document into one of the copies, or into a separate file if you prefer. And when the revisions are complete, you can remove all the annotations from the document.

An annotation has the following two parts:

❑ The *annotation reference mark* is the mark (or marks) that appear in the text where you insert an annotation. You can enter up to 28 characters in the reference mark. For example, you can use your name or initials to identify yourself as the person who's inserting the annotation. Word also numbers the annotations, and renumbers them automatically if you insert or delete annotations. The numbers used are in the same series as footnotes. In other words, if your documents include footnotes as well as annotations, both are numbered in the same sequence.

❏ The *annotation text* is the text of the annotation itself, which is positioned in the special footnote area after the end mark in your document.

You can use annotations in collaborative writing in two ways. As an author, you can add annotations to ask your reviewers to comment on or revise specific passages in your text. As a reviewer, you can add annotations to explain changes you have made or to comment on specific passages. For reviewers, Format Annotation is the perfect complement to Format revision-Marks; you can add an annotation explaining why you have revised a passage.

Inserting an Annotation

To add an annotation to your document, follow these steps:

1. Place the cursor where you want the annotation's reference mark to appear.

2. Choose the **F**ormat **A**nnotation command.

3. When the command menu appears (see fig. 15.6), type your initials or your name in the **mark** field. You can type up to 28 characters.

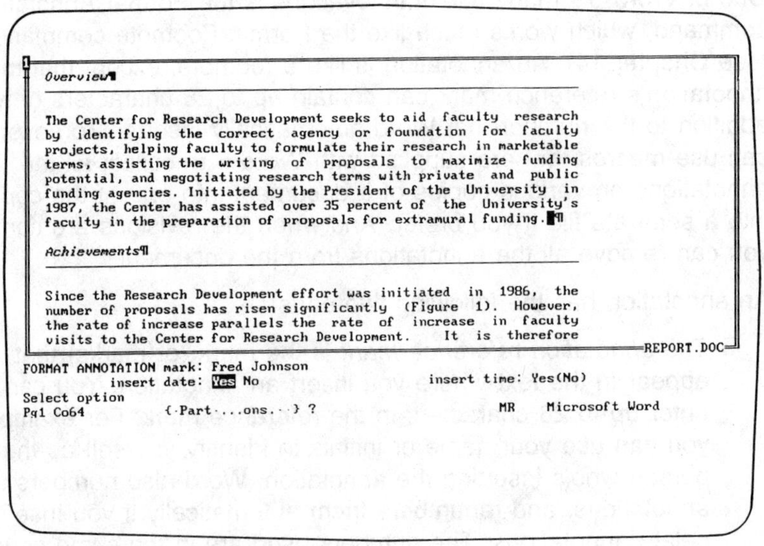

Fig. 15.6.

The Format Annotation menu.

```
┌─┐
│ Overview¶
│
│ The Center for Research Development seeks to aid  faculty  research
│ by  identifying  the  correct  agency  or  foundation  for  faculty
│ projects, helping faculty to formulate their research in marketable
│ terms, assisting  the  writing  of  proposals  to  maximize funding
│ potential, and  negotiating  research  terms with private  and  public
│ funding  agencies.  Initiated  by  the  President  of  the  University  in
│ 1987, the  Center  has  assisted  over 35 percent  of  the  University's
│ faculty in the preparation of proposals for extramural funding.█¶
│
│ Achievements¶
│
│ Since  the  Research  Development  effort  was  initiated  in  1986,  the
│ number of proposals  has  risen  significantly  (Figure  1).  However,
│ the rate of  increase  parallels  the  rate  of  increase  in  faculty
│ visits to the Center for Research Development.   It  is  therefore
│                                                          ═REPORT.DOC═
│ FORMAT ANNOTATION mark: Fred Johnson
│        insert date: Yes No                      insert time: Yes(No)
│ Select option
│ Pg1 Co64          {·Part·...ons.·} ?              MR   Microsoft Word
└─┘
```

4. Choose **Yes** in the **insert date** and **insert time** fields so that Word inserts the system date and time.

   If you're not using a clock/calendar board, you should set the system date and time correctly before starting Word. If you forgot, press Esc to exit the Format Annotation command. Then use the **Library Run** command to run the built-in DOS programs called DATE and TIME.

5. Carry out the Format Annotation command. Word inserts the annotation number and the characters you typed as the annotation reference mark. The program echoes the number and text in the footnote area after the document's end mark, and includes the date and time (if you selected these options).

6. Type your comments where Word has positioned the cursor (in the footnote area), as shown in figure 15.7.

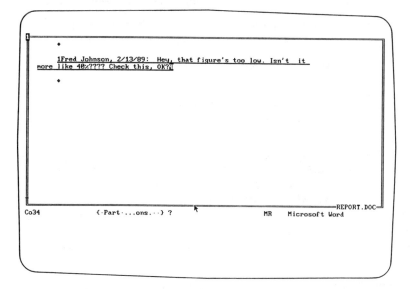

Fig. 15.7.

Typing the annotation text.

7. To return to the reference mark's location in the text, choose the **Jump Annotation** command.

When you use the Format Annotation command again, you will find that Word displays the text you have used (such as your initials) as its proposed response to the **mark** command field.

Word uses the standard character and paragraph formats when entering annotation reference marks and text. If you want to give annotations a distinctive style, you can create style sheet entries, that uses the automatic character style called *annotation ref* and the automatic paragraph style called *annotation*. Once you have created these entries and attached the style sheet to your document, Word automatically uses the styles you have chosen. For more information on style sheets, see Chapter 20, "Using Style Sheets."

Editing Annotations

Editing annotations is easy once you have inserted them. (See the section on "Deleting an Annotation" if you want to remove an annotation entirely.) Here's how to revise the text of an annotation:

1. Select the reference mark of the annotation you want to edit.

2. Choose the **J**ump **A**nnotation command. Word automatically scrolls to the text of the annotation you have selected.

3. Revise the annotation the same way you would edit ordinary text.

4. Choose the **J**ump **A**nnotation command again to return to the annotation reference mark.

 Caution: If you accidentally delete an annotation reference mark while editing an annotation's text, you can't replace the number by simply typing it. If you do, Word will not number your annotations correctly. To replace the number, position the cursor at the beginning of the annotation text, type *footnote*, and press F3.

Searching for the Next Annotation Reference Mark

The Jump Annotation command, like the Jump Footnote command, performs different tasks depending on where you use it. If you position the cursor on an annotation reference mark, the command takes the cursor to the annotation text. If the cursor is in the annotation text when you choose Jump Annotation, Word moves the cursor back to the reference mark.

Word offers still another way to use the command. If the cursor is positioned in ordinary text when you use Jump Annotation, Word scrolls to the next annotation reference mark in your document. Remember this use of the command when you need to find the next annotation reference mark.

Deleting an Annotation

Don't try to delete an annotation by deleting all its text in the annotation area. If you do, Word displays this message: Not a valid action for footnotes or annotations.

To delete an annotation, simply position the cursor on the reference mark and press Del. Word cuts the annotation to the scrap and removes the annotation text from the annotation area. To cancel the deletion, choose the Undo command immediately.

Moving an Annotation

To move an annotation, follow these steps:

1. Place the cursor on the reference mark and press Del. Word places the reference mark and the annotation text in the scrap.

2. Move the cursor to the annotation's new location.

3. Press Ins or use the Insert command.

Whenever you rearrange your annotations, Word automatically renumbers them as needed.

Using the Footnote Window To Display Annotations

The footnote window, as you learned in Chapter 14, is a special window that automatically displays the text of the footnotes whose reference marks are currently displayed in the document window. The footnote window displays annotations too. For more information, refer to the section in Chapter 14 on "Using the Footnote Window."

If you're reviewing a document to which others have added annotations, you will find the footnote window especially useful. As you scroll through your document, the program automatically displays the annotations relevant to the text you're displaying. You can read the annotations just by glancing at the footnote window.

Consolidating Annotations

After you have created a document, you may need to distribute it to other individuals. The best way to do so is to circulate only one authoritative version of a document, which each reviewer can examine in sequence. Save the document with redlining turned on so that the insertions and deletions the reviewers make will be highlighted. And tell them to explain their changes or make comments by using annotations.

Although this method is the easiest one, deadlines often prevent reviewers from waiting their turns to examine the file. In such cases, you should give each reviewer a disk containing a copy of the file. This way, the reviewers can all work simultaneously, and much time is saved. (When you distribute copies of a file in this way, be sure that each copy has its own unique file name, such as COPY1.DOC, COPY2.DOC, and so on.) But when you, the document's author, get these disks back, you're faced with a problem. Must you load each separate file, one after the other, to read each reviewer's annotations? That method would be tedious, to say the least.

To solve this problem, Word 5 is supplied with macros that consolidate annotations from several copies of a file. Word 5 consolidates annotations in the following two ways:

❑ By merging the annotations from several copies of a file into a master copy. This approach works best when the reviewers haven't altered the file in any way other than inserting annotations.

❑ By collecting all the annotations into a separate file and listing the annotations by page number. This technique is best if the reviewers have altered their copies by inserting or deleting text.

Merging Annotations

You probably want to use this procedure if the various copies of the document are identical except for their annotations. If the reviewers have changed the sentences on which they have made annotations, you need to collect the annotations in a separate file or print them, as described in the next section.

To merge annotations into one copy of a document, follow this procedure:

1. Start Word or use the **T**ransfer **C**lear **A**ll command to display a new, blank document.

2. Insert the Word Utilities disk into the disk drive, and use the **T**ransfer **G**lossary **L**oad command. Load the file called MACRO.GLY, which contains Word's supplied macros. If you're not loading a file from your current hard disk directory, be sure to specify the drive and/or path name before file name.

3. Use the **I**nsert command and choose the macro called annot_merge.mac. Alternatively, use the Ctrl-AM shortcut.

4. When you are prompted to type the name of the destination document, type the file name of the master copy of the document. Don't forget to use path information if the document isn't in the default directory.

5. After the macro splits the screen, type the name of the first source document, the document from which the macro will copy annotations. Use the name of the file in which the first reviewer included comments.

Having loaded both files, the macro then compares them. If the two files are identical, the process is automatic. If the two files are not identical, however, the macro pauses and asks for instructions on where to insert the annotations.

When the macro finishes the first source file, Word prompts you for the name of another source document. Type the name of the second source document, or if you don't have another one, quit the macro by pressing Esc.

The annot_merge.mac macro doesn't delete the annotations from the source documents but simply copies them from all the source documents and consolidates them into a single authoritative version of the file.

Collecting Annotations

Word uses annot_collect.mac to collect the annotations from a series of identical or nearly identical documents, and to generate a new file containing all the annotations listed by page number. This technique doesn't require the copies of the document to be identical, but it works best if all the copies have the same pagination. You can "freeze" the pagination you have given the master document by turning off Word 5's auto pagination feature before you distribute copies of the file. That way, the page breaks remain the same even if reviewers insert or delete text. Collect annotations with the following method:

1. Tell all the reviewers to choose the **N**o option in the **paginate** field of the Options menu before editing a file copy. This step will ensure that, even if the reviewers add or delete text, pagination does not change.

2. Start Word or use the **T**ransfer **C**lear **A**ll command to display a new, blank document.

3. Insert the Word Utilities disk into the disk drive, and use the **T**ransfer **G**lossary **L**oad command. Load the file called MACRO.GLY, which contains Word's supplied macros.

4. Use the **I**nsert command and choose the macro called annot_collect.mac. Alternatively, use the Ctrl-AC shortcut.

5. When you are prompted to do so, type the name of the file that will receive all the annotations. This file should be a new Word document. Choose a file name you haven't used previously.

6. When the macro asks whether you want to be prompted for the file names of the source documents, press Y and type the name of the source file—the file from which the macro copies the reviewer's annotations. If you type *N*, the macro displays the Library Document-retrieval menu, which you can use to retrieve the source files by stating criteria in the Query menu. For information on Library Document-retrieval, see Chapter 8, "Finding and Managing Documents."

When the macro finishes compiling the annotations, it saves them to disk, using the file name you have chosen. You can print this file or examine it on-screen.

Removing All the Annotations from a Document

Once you have finished reviewing all the annotations and have responded to them, you can delete all of them at once by using the macro called annot_remove.mac. Follow these steps:

1. Start Word or use the **T**ransfer **C**lear **A**ll command to display a new, blank document.

2. Insert the Word Utilities disk into the disk drive, and use the **T**ransfer **G**lossary **L**oad command. Load the file called MACRO.GLY.

3. Use the **I**nsert command and choose the macro called annot_remove.mac. Alternatively, use the Ctrl-AR shortcut.

4. When the macro finishes running, it prompts you to save the document with a new file name (thus preserving the old copy with the annotations intact). Type a file name and press Enter.

Chapter Summary

Word 5's Format revision-Marks and Format Annotation commands make Word the program of choice for collaborative writing. With Format revision-Marks, a reviewer can insert or delete text but let the document's original author (or other reviewers) decide whether to accept the changes or undo them. With Format Annotation, reviewers can enter queries or comments right into the document without disturbing the flow of text. And the annotations can be removed from the entire document with just one command. If you collaborate even occasionally, Word 5's features can help your team communicate effectively and produce a top-notch document.

16

Creating Form Letters

Surely you have received a letter that begins "Dear Mr. or Ms. So-and-So, here's great news for you and the So-and-So family! You have definitely won at least one of the following fantastic prizes: a Lincoln Continental Town Car, a six-month trip to the South Seas, $30,000 in cash, or a cheap digital wrist watch! To claim your prize, all you have to do is visit our fine new recreational center, the Happy Acres Landfill and Hazardous Waste Repository, and listen to six hours of grueling cross-examination by our sadistic sales staff!" More than likely, your name is printed slightly out of register, betraying the ploy: everyone in your neighborhood is getting the same letter. You have received, in other words, a personalized form letter—a letter that is sent to many people but personalized by a computer so that the letter appears as if it is sent only to you.

Letters of this sort are irritating, but personalized form letters have many legitimate uses in business and the professions. Whenever you want to send the same message to many people, but with a personal touch, consider sending a personalized form letter. And when you do, remember that Word offers one of the most powerful form-letter features you will find in any word processing package.

Unfortunately, these form-letter features also are among the most challenging Word features to use, for it can be difficult to get a form letter application working correctly with Word. To be fair to Microsoft, similar features in other programs are not easy to use, either.

However, even a novice Word user can develop and use a simple form-letter application. This chapter does not cover every aspect of Word's powerful form letter capabilities. By means of the extended tutorial in this chapter you will learn how to create a form letter for an application many Word users will need to use sooner or later: maintaining a mailing list for a small organization. You can build on what you learn in this tutorial to take full advantage of Word's form-letter features.

You will learn to do the following in this chapter:

❑ Design a form-letter application, specifying in advance what kinds of information you will need to list in your letter

❑ Create the data document, a Word file containing the information you want Word to insert into your form letters

❑ Create the main document, the file containing the text of your letter

❑ Use simple conditional statements, which insert additional text in the letter if the data meets specified criteria

❑ Use the Print Merge command, a special print command that generates form letters

❑ Cope with error messages, which you most likely will get when you try to print your first form-letter application with Word

The rest of this chapter is a form-letter tutorial. The application described is a mailing list to generate form letters for members of a small neighborhood organization formed out of concern for local environmental and public safety issues. Although tutorials are not always fun, they are helpful, and you should follow along. Getting form-letter applications to work with Word is tricky, to say the least. This tutorial introduces several time-saving (and frustration-avoiding) techniques born out of much experience with this powerful feature.

Creating a Form-Letter Application

A form-letter application takes information from a mailing list and, one by one, cranks out copies of a letter personalized with each individual's name, address, city, state, ZIP code, and other information. These applications require two Word documents:

❑ *Data document*. This document contains the personalized information you want Word to insert into each copy of the letter. The data document begins with a header record, which lists the types of information you will use (such as LASTNAME, FIRSTNAME, ADDRESS, CITY, STATE, ZIP, and so on). Each of these types of information has a name (such as LASTNAME), which is called a *field name*. After the header record, you enter information about each individual in data records, each on its own line. A complete data record contains entries for each of the fields you have named in the header record, and each data record ends with a paragraph mark.

❑ *Main document*. This document contains the text you want to send to everyone—the text of the letter. In place of the information you want to personalize, however, you type the field names, enclosed by chevron codes that tell Word to interpret the word within them as a field name. So instead of writing *Dear Mr. Smith:* in your letter, you write *Dear «SALUTATION» «LASTNAME»:*. When you print your letter, Word automatically substitutes the information in your data document for the field names in the main document.

The basic concept is simple enough, but making the application work correctly is a challenge. Note well: You're not a failure at personal computing if your form-letter application doesn't work the first time—or the second or third. Just follow the tutorial carefully, and you will be in good shape.

Creating the Data Document

We begin by creating the data document, the Word file that contains the information you want Word to insert into your form letter. Most experienced Word users probably would agree that the data document is the weakest part of Word's form-letter capabilities; it's difficult to enter data in a way that's amenable to updating or error correcting. In the tutorial that follows, you will learn how to separate field entries using tabs, and how to use lines and borders to differentiate records. These steps will make it easier to fix the problems that inevitably arise the first time you run a form-letter application.

Creating the Header Record

The data document begins with a header record, a special record that lists the field names you plan to use. Without the header record, Word would not know the field names you have chosen for the data you enter. Create the header record by following these steps:

1. Choose the **O**ptions command and select the **A**ll in the **show non-printing symbols** field. You will need to see where you have placed tabs.

2. Choose the **F**ormat **D**ivision **M**argins command and, when the command menu appears, type *15"* in the **page width** field.

   Each record must be contained on one line ending with a paragraph mark. In order to get all the information on one line, you need to widen the "page" to make sufficient room.

3. Press Enter and, when the paragraph mark appears, press the up-arrow key to select the mark.

   You're going to format this paragraph, and as you probably already have discovered, you cannot format the end mark. This step creates a paragraph mark that is differentiated from the end mark so that it can be formatted.

4. Use the **F**ormat **T**abs **S**et command, and type the following tab settings:

       0.5"
       2.0"
       3.5"
       5.0"
       8.0"
       10.0"
       10.6"
       11.3"

   These tab settings set up a format that enables you to enter the data in neat columns.

5. Choose the **F**ormat **B**order command and select the **B**ox option. This command encloses the header record in a box, thus distinguishing the header from the rest of the data document.

6. Select the paragraph mark inside the box and type the following field names, pressing Tab after each one (except for the last one):

   NO
   LASTNAME
   FIRSTNAME
   SALUTATION
   ADDRESS
   CITY
   STATE
   ZIP
   DUES1989

Make sure that you have spelled each of these field names correctly and that each is followed by a tab keystroke, except the last one.

Your header record should look like the one shown in figure 16.1.

Adding Data

Now that you have created the header record, you need to add the data. Don't worry about adding the data in alphabetical order; Word will sort the list automatically.

Caution: Do not use commas anywhere in a field entry. If you do, the form-letter application will not work unless you enclose the entry in quotation marks. To be on the safe side, get into the habit of avoiding commas entirely when you create data documents.

You can add the data by following these steps:

1. Position the cursor on the paragraph mark at the end of the header record and press Enter. This step copies the tab and border formats to the next paragraph.

2. Use the **F**ormat **B**order command again. When the command menu appears, choose the **L**ines option in the **type** field, the **double** option in the **line style** field, and the **Y**es option in the **below** field.

   These choices will insert double lines between the data records, helping to differentiate them. If you prefer, you can leave the lines out by skipping step 2.

Fig. 16.1.

Scrolling the
header record for
a form-letter
application.

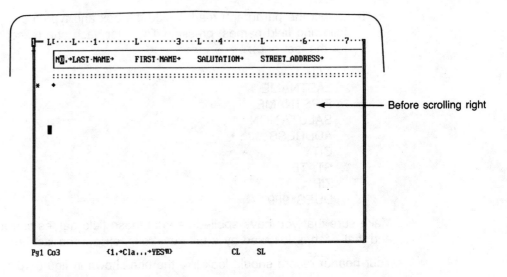

← Before scrolling right

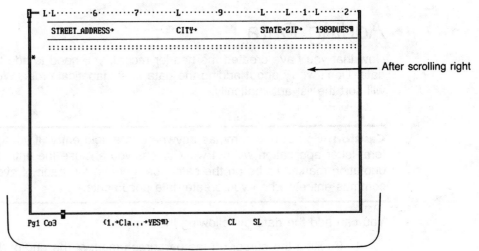

← After scrolling right

3. Select the first blank line under the header record and add a record, as shown in figure 16.2. Begin by typing the number *1*, and press Tab. Then type the last name, and press Tab. Continue in this way, pressing Tab after each field entry. When you reach the end of the line, do not press Tab. Press Enter instead.

4. Continue typing the data records as shown in figure 16.2.

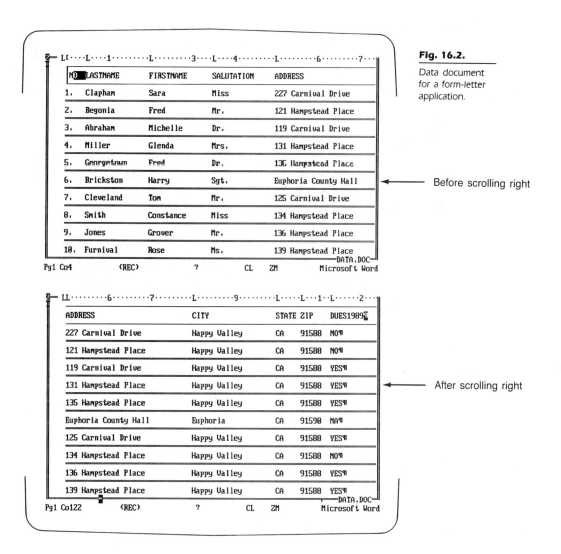

Fig. 16.2.

Data document for a form-letter application.

NO	LASTNAME	FIRSTNAME	SALUTATION	ADDRESS
1.	Clapham	Sara	Miss	227 Carnival Drive
2.	Begonia	Fred	Mr.	121 Hampstead Place
3.	Abraham	Michelle	Dr.	119 Carnival Drive
4.	Miller	Glenda	Mrs.	131 Hampstead Place
5.	Georgetown	Fred	Dr.	135 Hampstead Place
6.	Brickston	Harry	Sgt.	Euphoria County Hall
7.	Cleveland	Tom	Mr.	125 Carnival Drive
8.	Smith	Constance	Miss	134 Hampstead Place
9.	Jones	Grover	Mr.	136 Hampstead Place
10.	Furnival	Rose	Ms.	139 Hampstead Place

Before scrolling right

Pg1 Co4   {REC}   ?   CL   ZM   DATA.DOC Microsoft Word

ADDRESS	CITY	STATE	ZIP	DUES1989
227 Carnival Drive	Happy Valley	CA	91588	NO¶
121 Hampstead Place	Happy Valley	CA	91588	NO¶
119 Carnival Drive	Happy Valley	CA	91588	YES¶
131 Hampstead Place	Happy Valley	CA	91588	YES¶
135 Hampstead Place	Happy Valley	CA	91588	YES¶
Euphoria County Hall	Euphoria	CA	91590	NA¶
125 Carnival Drive	Happy Valley	CA	91588	YES¶
134 Hampstead Place	Happy Valley	CA	91588	NO¶
136 Hampstead Place	Happy Valley	CA	91588	YES¶
139 Hampstead Place	Happy Valley	CA	91588	YES¶

After scrolling right

Pg1 Co122   {REC}   ?   CL   ZM   DATA.DOC Microsoft Word

5. When you have finished typing the data, check to make sure that every field entry is followed by a tab keystroke, except the last entry on each line.

6. Save the document.

Your data document should look exactly like the one shown in Figure 16.2.

> **Caution:** If any record has more tab keystrokes or fewer tab keystrokes than the header record, the application will not work. Check your data document carefully.

Creating the Main Document

Now you need to create the main document. You will enter several commands surrounded by chevrons. These commands tell Word where to find the data and which data to insert. To create the main document, follow these steps:

1. In a new, blank Word document, hold down the Ctrl key and press the left bracket (Ctrl-[). This command enters the left chevron. Then type the word *data* and press the space bar. Next, type the name of your data document. Finally, press Ctrl-] (right bracket) to enter the right chevron. This expression (see fig. 16.3) tells Word where to find the data you want inserted.

Fig. 16.3.

Inserting the DATA instruction.

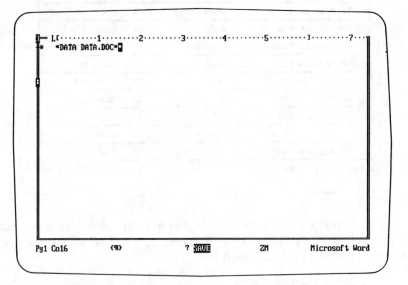

2. Type a return address, and insert the dateprint glossary by typing *dateprint* and pressing F3 (see fig. 16.4.).

3. Type the field names as shown in figure 16.5.

   Note: Each field name must be surrounded by chevrons.

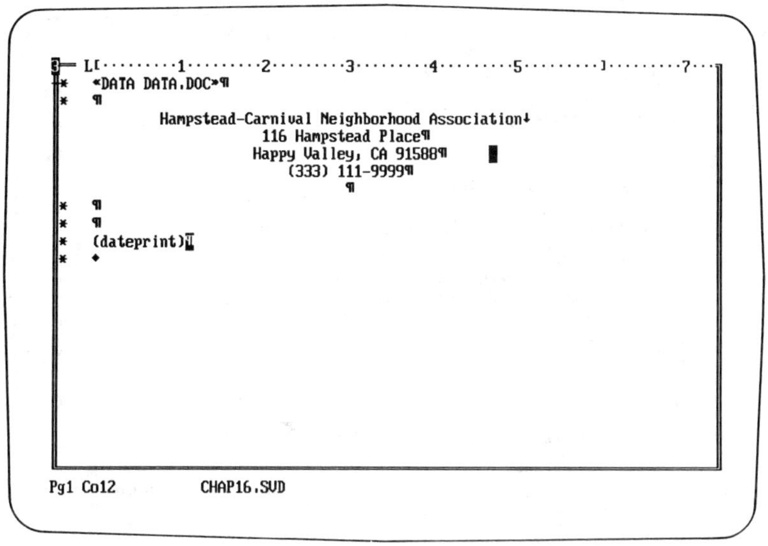

Fig. 16.4.

The main document with the return address and the dateprint glossary item.

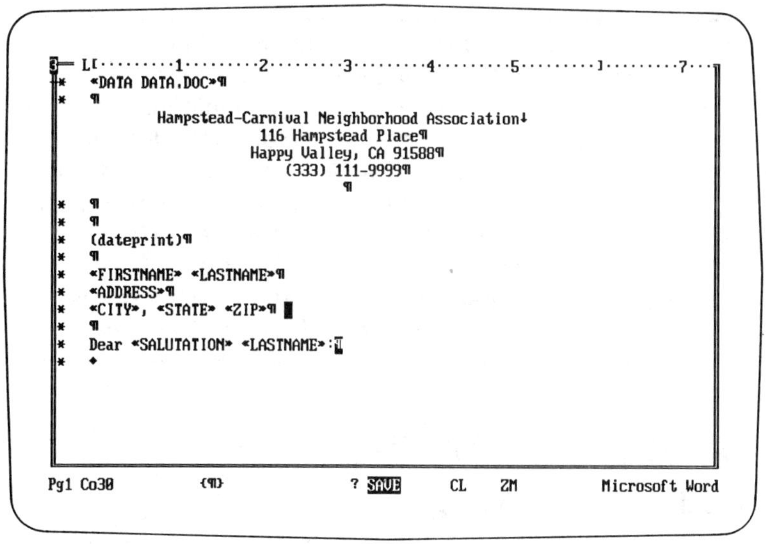

```
L[········1·········2·········3·········4·········5·········]·········7···
* «DATA DATA.DOC»¶
*  ¶
              Hampstead-Carnival Neighborhood Association↓
                      116 Hampstead Place¶
                    Happy Valley, CA 91588¶        █
                       (333) 111-9999¶
                             ¶
*  ¶
*  ¶
* (dateprint)▯
*  ♦
```

Pg1 Co12   CHAP16.SVD

Fig. 16.5.

Adding field names to the main document.

```
L[········1·········2·········3·········4·········5·········]·········7···
* «DATA DATA.DOC»¶
*  ¶
              Hampstead-Carnival Neighborhood Association↓
                      116 Hampstead Place¶
                    Happy Valley, CA 91588¶
                       (333) 111-9999¶
                             ¶
*  ¶
*  ¶
* (dateprint)¶
*  ¶
* «FIRSTNAME» «LASTNAME»¶
* «ADDRESS»¶
* «CITY», «STATE» «ZIP»¶ █
*  ¶
* Dear «SALUTATION» «LASTNAME»:▯
*  ♦
```

Pg1 Co30   {¶}   ? SAVE   CL   ZM   Microsoft Word

As you can see, you need not enter the field names in the order the data document lists them. You simply place them where you want the information to appear.

4. Type the text of the letter, as shown in figure 16.6.

5. Save the main document to disk.

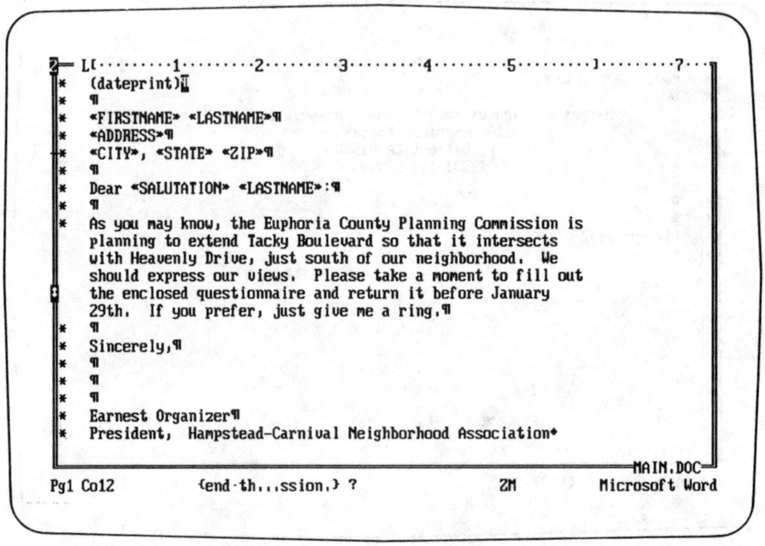

Fig. 16.6.

Adding text to the main document.

```
┌─────────────────────────────────────────────────────────┐
│  2─ L[·······1·······2·······3·······4·······5·····]·····7··· │
│  * (dateprint)▌                                              │
│  *  ¶                                                        │
│  * «FIRSTNAME» «LASTNAME»¶                                   │
│  * «ADDRESS»¶                                                │
│  * «CITY», «STATE» «ZIP»¶                                    │
│  *  ¶                                                        │
│  * Dear «SALUTATION» «LASTNAME»:¶                            │
│  *  ¶                                                        │
│  * As you may know, the Euphoria County Planning Commission is │
│    planning to extend Tacky Boulevard so that it intersects │
│    with Heavenly Drive, just south of our neighborhood. We  │
│    should express our views. Please take a moment to fill out │
│    the enclosed questionnaire and return it before January  │
│    29th. If you prefer, just give me a ring.¶               │
│  *  ¶                                                        │
│  * Sincerely,¶                                               │
│  *  ¶                                                        │
│  *  ¶                                                        │
│  *  ¶                                                        │
│  * Earnest Organizer¶                                        │
│  * President, Hampstead-Carnival Neighborhood Association♦   │
│                                              ┌MAIN.DOC┐      │
│  Pg1 Co12      {end·th...ssion.} ?      2M    Microsoft Word │
└─────────────────────────────────────────────────────────┘
```

Caution: Before proceeding, double-check your work. The main document should begin with a DATA statement, which correctly identifies the data document. Be sure to include path information if the data document is located on a drive or in a directory other than the default directory. Be sure, too, that the DATA statement is surrounded by chevrons. (Note that you cannot enter the chevrons by typing less-than or greater-than symbols—you must use the Ctrl-[and Ctrl-] commands.) Check the field names to make sure that each is surrounded by chevrons. And make sure that you have spelled the field names exactly the way they're spelled in the data document.

Sorting and Renumbering the Data Document

The sorting techniques introduced in Chapter 11 are very useful for putting your data document into order, alphabetized by last name. And you can use the Library Number command to number the records accurately. Sorting and numbering your data document aren't luxury operations; they're very important steps to take if you want to troubleshoot your application quickly and effectively. You will learn why in the section titled "Printing Just the Records You Specify."

The following procedure shows how to sort your data document and update the numbering:

1. Position the cursor at the upper right corner of the LASTNAME column, and press Shift-F6 to toggle on the column-select mode.

2. Select the entire column of last names (see fig. 16.7). Don't select the header record.

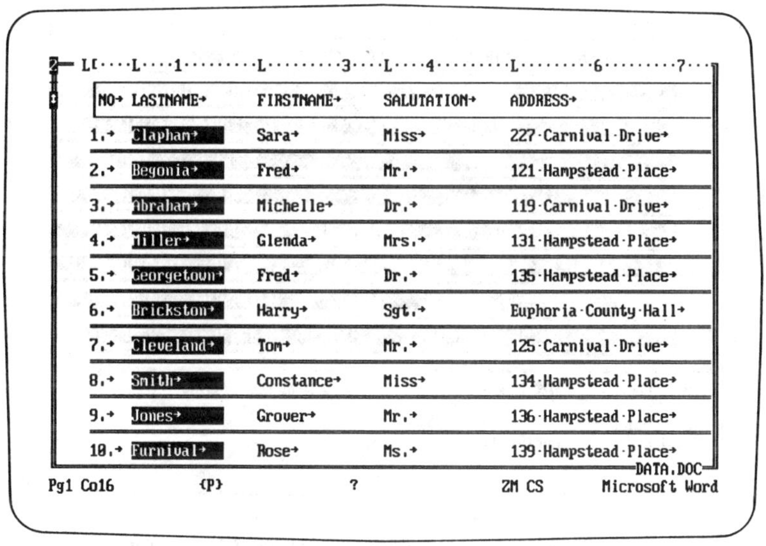

Fig. 16.7.

Selecting the column of last names (column-select mode).

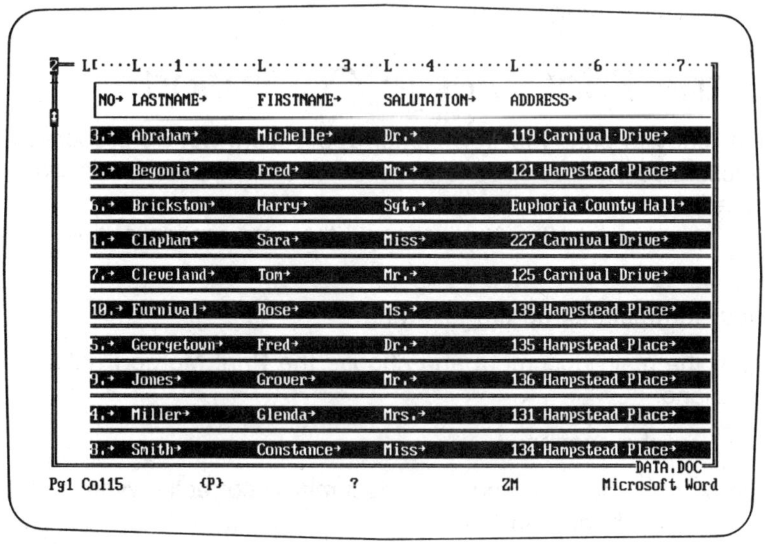

Fig. 16.8.

Data document sorted by last name (but with numbers out of order).

3. Choose the **L**ibrary **A**utosort command and press Enter. Word will sort the list using the last names as the key.

4. When the list has been sorted (see fig. 16.8), you will notice that the numbers aren't in order. Choose the **L**ibrary **N**umber command (see fig. 16.9). Highlight the **U**pdate option and carry out the command.

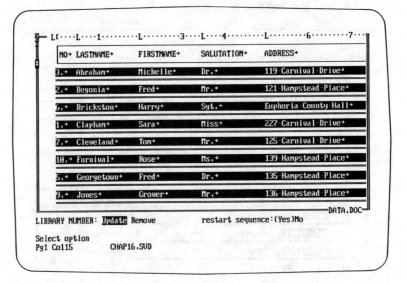

Word automatically renumbers the records to reflect the new alphabetical order (see fig. 16.10).

Using the Print Merge Command

Now you're ready to print your form-letter application. But be prepared for error messages—it isn't easy to get a form-letter application to work correctly the first time. If you see an error message, see "Troubleshooting Form-Letter Applications," the next section of this chapter.

To print your form letters, do the following:

1. Open the main document and choose the **P**rint **M**erge **P**rinter command.

2. Carry out the command.

If you have created the data and main documents correctly, Word will format and print each letter in turn.

```
 ┌─ L[····L···1·········L····3··L····4·········L·······6·········7···┐
 │  ┌──────────────────────────────────────────────────────────────┐
 │  │ NO→ LASTNAME→     FIRSTNAME→    SALUTATION→   ADDRESS→         │
 │  │ 1.→  Abraham→     Michelle→     Dr.→          119·Carnival·Drive→ │
 │  │ 2.→  Begonia→     Fred→         Mr.→          121·Hampstead·Place→ │
 │  │ 3.→  Brickston→   Harry→        Sgt.→         Euphoria·County·Hall→ │
 │  │ 4.→  Clapham→     Sara→         Miss→         227·Carnival·Drive→ │
 │  │ 5.→  Cleveland·   Tum→          Mr.→          125·Carnival·Drive→ │
 │  │ 6.→  Furnival→    Rose→         Ms.→          139·Hampstead·Place→ │
 │  │ 7.→  Georgetown→  Fred→         Dr.→          135·Hampstead·Place→ │
 │  │ 8.→  Jones→       Grover→       Mr.→          136·Hampstead·Place→ │
 │  │ 9.→  Miller→      Glenda→       Mrs.→         131·Hampstead·Place→ │
 │  │ 10.→ Smith→       Constance→    Miss→         134·Hampstead·Place→ │
 │  └──────────────────────────────────────────────────DATA.DOC──┘
 │ Pg1 Co1        {P}            ?            2M       Microsoft Word
```

Fig. 16.10.

Data document sorted and numbers updated.

Troubleshooting Form-Letter Applications

If you see error messages while trying to print your form-letter application, you have probably made a simple error that is easily corrected. The following are the most common error messages users see:

❑ Not a valid field name. The field names in your data document's header record must begin with an alphabetical character (not a number). They must be 64 characters or less, and the only punctuation you can include is the underscore character. A field name must not contain spaces.

❑ Too few fields in data record. One of the records in your data document contains fewer tab keytrokes than the header record. Check your data document and fix the mistake.

❑ Too many fields in data or header record. One of the records contains more tab keystrokes than the header record. Check your data document and fix the mistake. You will see this message, too, if you attempt to use more than 256 fields.

❏ Unknown field name. Your main document contains a field name that doesn't match the field names used in the data document's header record. Make sure that you have spelled the field names correctly in your main document.

As you can see from this troubleshooting guide, every record must have exactly the same number of tab keystrokes, and the field names in the main document must be consistent with the ones in the data document. If you're having problems, they almost surely stem from one of these two common difficulties.

Printing Just the Records You Specify

If you get the message Too many fields in data or header record or Too few fields in data record after several records have printed, it means that Word has encountered a record that contains more or fewer tab keystrokes than the header record. The trouble in such cases is that Word very well may have printed many, or even most, of the data records in your data document. You need to fix the mistake in the data document and resume printing the rest of the data records.

If you have numbered your data records as suggested in this chapter's tutorial, you will not have any trouble coping with this problem. Just determine the number of the last record that was successfully printed, and then go to the next record in the data document to find the error. After you fix the record that contains too many or too few fields, choose the **P**rint **M**erge **O**ptions command and the **R**ecords option in the range field. Then type a record range (such as *15-99*) in the **record numbers** field, and choose the **P**rint **M**erge **P**rinter command.

If you didn't number your records, however, you must count them yourself to determine where printing should resume. You can see why it's a good idea to number the records. If you don't use numbers, Word also displays line numbers of cursor positions. These numbers help you count records and locate specific records.

Getting Fancy: Using a Conditional Instruction

Now that you have successfully printed a simple form-letter application, try including a conditional instruction. A conditional instruction includes additional text in a letter if a condition you specify is met. A glance at your data document reveals that you have kept track of who has paid dues and who hasn't. In the following tutorial, you will learn how to admonish those who haven't paid their dues and praise those who have.

1. Load the main document and add the following after the body of the letter (but before the closing):

   «IF DUES1989 = "no"»By the way, my records show that you haven't paid your dues for the year. Won't you send us a check for $5.00 today?«ENDIF»
   «IF DUES1989 = "yes"»Incidentally, thanks for paying your 1989 dues. Everyone in the Association appreciates your support and community spirit!«ENDIF».

   Be sure to enclose the IF expressions with chevrons, entered (as usual) with Ctrl-[and Ctrl-]. See figure 16.11 for the correct appearance of the letter after this text has been added.

```
 L[········1·········2·········3·········4·········5········]·········7···
* «ADDRESS»¶
* «CITY», ·«STATE»·«ZIP»¶
 ¶
* Dear·«SALUTATION»·«LASTNAME»:¶
 ¶
* As·you·may·know, ·the·Euphoria·County·Planning·Commission·is·
  planning·to·extend·Tacky·Boulevard·so·that·it·intersects·
  with·Heavenly·Drive, ·just·south·of·our·neighborhood.··We·
  should·express·our·views.··Please·take·a·moment·to·fill·out·
  the·enclosed·questionnaire·and·return·it·before·January·
  29th.··If·you·prefer, ·just·give·me·a·ring.¶
* ¶
* «IF·DUES1989="no"»By·the·way, ·my·records·show·that·you·
  haven't·paid·your·dues·for·the·year.··Won't·you·send·us·a·
  check·for·$5.00·today?«ENDIF»«IF·
  DUES1989="yes"»Incidentally, ·thanks·for·paying·your·1989·
  dues.··Everyone·in·the·Association·appreciates·your·support·
  and·community·spirit!«ENDIF»↓
 ¶
* Sincerely,¶
* ¶
* ¶
                                                    ┌MAIN.DOC┐
Pg1 Co1           {¶}          ?  SAVE        2M     Microsoft Word
```

Fig. 16.11.

Letter with conditional instruction.

2. Print the main document using the **P**rint **M**erge **P**rinter command.

The first part of this IF instruction says, in English, "If the DUES1989 field matches 'no,' then print 'By the way, my records show that you haven't paid your dues for the year. Won't you send us a check for $5.00 today?'" An example of a letter generated by this instruction is shown in figure 16.12.

Fig. 16.12.

Letter containing conditionally inserted text (asking member to pay dues immediately).

```
              Hampstead-Carnival Neighborhood Association
                          116 Hampstead Place
                        Happy Valley, CA 91588
                           (333) 111-9999




          December 14, 1988

          Fred Begonia
          121 Hampstead Place
          Happy Valley, CA 91588

          Dear Mr. Begonia:

          As you may know, the Euphoria County Planning Commission is
          planning to extend Tacky Boulevard so that it intersects
          with Heavenly Drive, just south of our neighborhood.  We
          should express our views.  Please take a moment to fill out
          the enclosed questionnaire and return it before January
          29th.  If you prefer, just give me a ring.

          By the way, my records show that you haven't paid your dues
          for the year.  Won't you send us a check for $5.00 today?

          Sincerely,



          Earnest Organizer
          President, Hampstead-Carnival Neighborhood Association
```

The second part of this instruction says, in effect, "If the DUES1989 field matches 'yes,' then print 'Incidentally, thanks for paying your 1989 dues. Everyone in the Association appreciates your support and community spirit!'" See figure 16.13 for an example of a letter containing this text.

Fig. 16.13.

Letter containing conditionally inserted text (thanking member for paying dues).

```
              Hampstead-Carnival Neighborhood Association
                        116 Hampstead Place
                       Happy Valley, CA 91588
                          (333) 111-9999




  December 14, 1988

  Michelle Abraham
  119 Carnival Drive
  Happy Valley, CA 91588

  Dear Dr. Abraham:

  As you may know, the Euphoria County Planning Commission is
  planning to extend Tacky Boulevard so that it intersects
  with Heavenly Drive, just south of our neighborhood.  We
  should express our views.  Please take a moment to fill out
  the enclosed questionnaire and return it before January
  29th.  If you prefer, just give me a ring.

  Incidentally, thanks for paying your 1989 dues.  Everyone in
  the Association appreciates your support and community
  spirit!

  Sincerely,


  Earnest Organizer
  President, Hampstead-Carnival Neighborhood Association
```

By implication, the instruction also says that if the DUES1989 field contains something other than "yes" or "no," such as "na" (not applicable), do nothing.

Chapter Summary

This chapter explains how to create a form-letter application, which requires a data document and a main document. The data document contains field names, separated by tabs, and the data, with each data record occupying its own line. The main document begins with the DATA instruction that tells Word where to find the data to insert. The text of the letter is contained also in the main document, with field names inserted wherever you want Word to fill in the information automatically. You should always double-check the field names before printing your form letter with the Print Merge Printer command. This chapter also talks about error messages and what to do to fix the problems.

This chapter concludes Part II, "Word 5's Features and Applications." The next section of the book covers what are perhaps the most exciting features of Word 5: its graphics and desktop publishing capabilities.

Desktop
Publishing with
Microsoft Word

Includes

Creating Forms and Illustrations

Integrating Text and Graphics

Creating Multiple-Column Text and Newsletters

17

Creating Forms and Illustrations

When people think of desktop publishing, they frequently think of its more glamorous and exciting applications, such as creating newsletters that win design awards or experimenting with handsome or exotic fonts. The bread and butter of desktop publishing, however, comes from much more mundane applications, such as creating and printing business forms: invoices, employee pay sheets, or quarterly report forms, to give a few examples.

Common though they may be, forms represent a big expense for most organizations. And they're necessary. A well-designed form prompts an individual to provide precisely the information an organization needs in order to accomplish some important task (like paying employees on time). Organizations pay a great deal of money to have printers design and print custom forms to suit the way the organization does its business. If you have a copy of Word 5 and a reasonably good printer, however, you may be able to save your organization the expense of paying a professional to design a custom form, because Word 5's tools for designing forms are very good indeed.

Since Version 4.0, Word has included some useful tools for designing forms—as well as filling them in. The Format Border command makes it easy to create boxes and lines, and the Format Tab Set command includes a vertical tab, which creates vertical lines within boxes. You can add finishing touches with Word's Line Draw mode, which turns the cursor into a "pen" capable of drawing straight vertical and horizontal lines wherever you want. And once you have finished your

409

form, you can set up a Print Merge application with the SET and ASK commands so that you're automatically prompted to supply the needed information. With the addition of a few simple math expressions, you can create a form that will automatically total the figures you supply. You can use the Line Draw mode, too, to create simple illustrations for reports and proposals. All these tools are useful in business and professional settings, and it's well worth your time to investigate them.

Version 5 adds only minor improvements to this useful set of tools for creating forms and illustrations. Because it's so much easier to set tabs with Word 5, you can add vertical lines to forms and tables quite easily by setting vertical tabs. New to the Format Border command, too, are fields to add and control background, for shading paragraphs.

This chapter covers the following subjects:

❏ Creating a good-looking form with the Format Border and Format Tab Set (vertical tab) commands

❏ Adding data entry marks to your form, which give you a way to move the cursor around your form without disturbing the text or the tab keystrokes

❏ Creating an automated form application with Print Merge, which prompts you to type the information to be printed on the form

❏ Using the Line Draw mode to create simple illustrations with Word

Note: To make full use of the material in this chapter, your printer must be capable of printing the IBM extended character set. If you're not sure that your printer can print these characters, check your manual or call your dealer before proceeding. Sometimes it's necessary to set a switch before your printer can handle these characters.

This chapter presupposes some knowledge of tab formatting, math, and the Print Merge command, so you might find it helpful to read or skim Chapter 11 ("Creating Tables and Lists with Tabs, Autosort, and Math") and Chapter 16 ("Creating Form Letters") before proceeding.

Creating the Form

Using Word 5's wonderful new tab-setting features, as well as the Format Border command, you can create a form in short order. Once you have created your form, you can print it and duplicate it so that people can fill it out by hand. If you prefer to keep the form application completely automated, however, you will learn in subsequent sections how you can fill out the form using Word.

Like the preceding chapter, this chapter includes several tutorials. Although it's tedious to follow keystroke-by-keystroke tutorials, they are worth following when you're dealing with difficult or complicated material. You will find that these tutorials illustrate many important Word 5 techniques besides cranking out forms, so you get a double benefit.

 Caution: Use a 12-point, fixed-space font, such as Courier or Pica, for this exercise. If you use a proportionally spaced font or a font larger or smaller than 12-point type, your printer may not print the form the way it looks on the screen.

To create your first form, follow these steps:

1. In a new, blank Word document, use the **O**ptions command and choose **A**ll in the **show non-printing symbols** field. Then choose **Y**es in the **show ruler** field, and carry out the command. You will need to see tab keystrokes and the ruler for this tutorial.

2. Use the **F**ormat **D**ivision **M**argins command to set new left and right margins of 0.75 inches. This form requires a 7-inch line length.

3. Press Alt-C to center the cursor; then type the heading shown in figure 17.1.

4. Press Enter after you type the heading. If you don't have a mouse, choose the **F**ormat **T**ab **S**et command. Click the **C**enter option in the **alignment** field, and set centered tabs at the following locations:

        0.5″
        1.5″
        2.5″
        3.5″
        4.5″
        5.5″
        6.5″

Fig. 17.1.

Heading for a
business form.

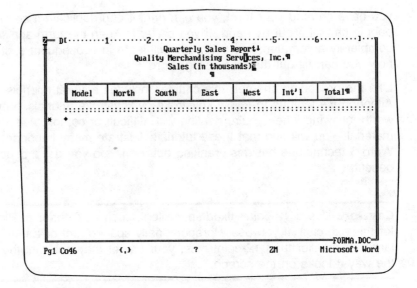

Choose the **V**ertical option in the **alignment** field, and set
vertical tabs at the following locations:

1.0″
2.0″
3.0″
4.0″
5.0″
6.0″

If you have a mouse, click the **L** at the left of the ruler until C
is displayed. Then click centered tabs at the following
locations:

0.5″
1.5″
2.5″
3.5″
4.5″
5.5″
6.5″

Click the **C** at the left of the ruler until the vertical line character is displayed, and click vertical tabs at the following locations:

1.0"
2.0"
3.0"
4.0"
5.0"
6.0"

5. Type *Model*, and press Tab. Continue typing the rest of the headings shown in figure 17.1, pressing Tab after each, until you get to the last heading (*Total*). Don't press Enter or Tab after you type *Total*.

6. Choose the **F**ormat **B**order command and when the command menu appears, choose the **B**ox option in the **type** field and type *double* in the **line style** field. Carry out the command. Your form's heading should look exactly like the one shown in figure 17.1.

7. With the cursor placed on the paragraph mark at the end of the header, press Enter. Word copies all the formats you have chosen, including the vertical tabs and the border, to the next paragraph.

8. Now use the **F**ormat **B**order command. Type *normal* in the **line style** field and choose Box in the **type** field. Carry out the command.

9. Change the centered tabs at 1.5", 2.5", 3.5", 4.5", 5.5", and 6.5" to decimal tabs.

   When you are finished, your screen should look like that shown in figure 17.2.

10. Press Enter two times to copy down the screen the format you have just created.

When you are finished, your form should look like that shown in figure 17.3.

As you can see, setting up a handsome form with Microsoft Word is easy. You can print this form and duplicate it if you want. In the next sections, however, you will learn how to use Word to fill in the form at the keyboard. You can do so manually, using a special command that moves the cursor from one data entry field to the next. If you want,

Fig. 17.2.

Border and tab formats for the body of the form.

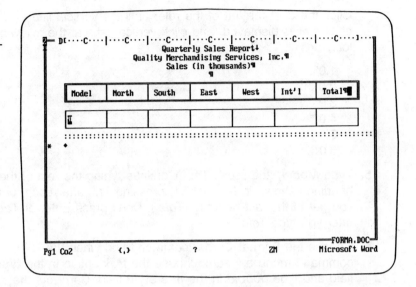

Fig. 17.3.

Business form with completed body.

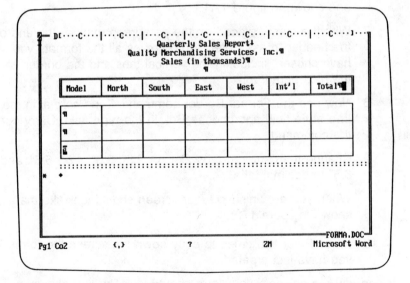

however, you can set up an application with Print Merge that prompts you to fill in the information you need. This feature is easy to set up, and it makes filling out a periodic form as easy as loading the document, choosing Print Merge, answering a series of questions, and sitting back while Word does all the work for you.

Filling In the Form with Word

If you want to fill in the forms you create with Word, you have two choices. First, you can fill in the forms manually. If you choose this route, add data entry marks to your form so that you can move around the form easily (using the Ctrl-> and Ctrl-< commands) without effacing or disturbing existing tabs or text. Second, you can set up a Print Merge application so that Word prompts you to supply the needed information. If you produce weekly, monthly, or quarterly reports that require you to list information in a form, you may find this technique very valuable indeed.

Filling In the Form Manually

In the following tutorial, you will add data entry marks to the form you created earlier in this chapter. Then you will use the Ctrl-> and Ctrl-< commands to add the data. Finally, you will learn how you can obtain totals quickly using Word's built-in math capabilities.

Adding the Data Entry Marks

The form you created needs to have data entry marks added to it so that information is inserted in the appropriate place. Follow these steps to insert the data entry marks:

1. Type model names in the first column as shown in figure 17.4. In order for the names to align correctly in their column, be sure to press Tab before typing the numbers.

2. Position the cursor after the first model name, and press Tab.

3. Press Ctrl-] to enter the first data entry mark (a right chevron).

4. Press Alt-E twice to format the mark as hidden text.

5. Select the mark.

Rather than formatting each mark individually, you will copy the formatted mark to the scrap and insert it repeatedly.

6. Copy the mark to the scrap.

7. Press Tab. The cursor moves to the next decimal tab stop. The highlight is placed after the tab stop, but the mark appears in the correct place.

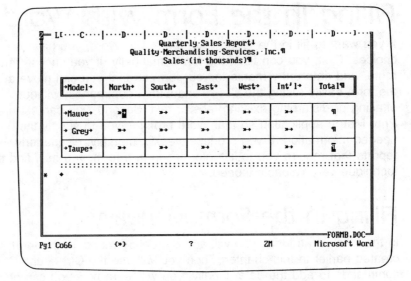

Fig. 17.4.

Typing the model names in the first column.

8. Press Ins to insert the formatted mark from the scrap.

9. Continue in this way until you have added data entry marks throughout the form, as shown in figure 17.4. *Don't* add marks to the *Total* column.

10. Save the form to disk and clear Word.

Now that you have added data entry marks to your form, you use a special command, Ctrl->, to jump to the next data entry mark. This command makes it very easy to fill in the data without disturbing the headings or tab settings in the form. And after you have filled in the data, you can use Word's built-in math capabilities to obtain totals.

Caution: For the rest of this tutorial, make sure that you have chosen the **No** option in the **hidden text** field of the Print Options menu, and the **Yes** option in the **show hidden text** field of the Options menu. You want to see hidden text on the screen, but you don't want it to print.

Adding the Data

Now that you have the data entry marks inserted, you need to know how to put them to use. Follow these steps to add data to your form:

1. Use the **T**ransfer **S**ave command to load the blank form you created. Choose the **Y**es option in the **read only** command field.

   You want to preserve your blank form for use at another time. By loading the file in read-only mode, you ensure that you cannot overwrite the blank form; you can save your work, but you must do so using a new file name.

2. Press Ctrl-PgUp to position the cursor at the beginning of the form.

3. Press Ctrl-> to move to the next data entry mark.

4. Type the first sales figure shown in figure 17.5.

5. Press Ctrl-> to move to the next data entry mark.

   Don't press Tab; if you do, you will disturb the tab settings. If you press Tab accidentally, be sure to delete the extra tab keystroke symbol. (Delete the extra tab keystroke symbol by pressing Del once.)

6. Continue in this way until you have added data to the whole form, as shown in figure 17.5.

If you want to go back to a previous data entry mark, use the Ctrl-< command.

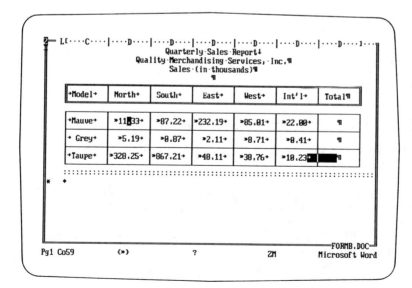

Fig. 17.5.

Adding the data with Ctrl->.

Obtaining Totals with Math

You can use Word 5's built-in math capabilities to total figures. Follow these instructions to use math in your form:

1. Carefully select all the numbers in the the first row of the form, except the model name (see fig. 17.6). If you accidentally select the model name, Word will not include it in the total because it's composed of letters, not numbers.

Fig. 17.6.

Obtaining totals for a row.

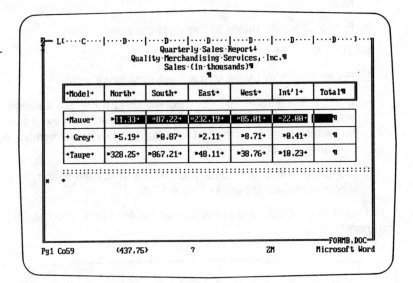

2. Press F2. The total appears in the scrap (see fig. 17.6).

3. Position the cursor on the paragraph mark in the *Total* column.

4. Press Ins. Word inserts the total at the cursor's location.

5. Continue in this way until all the rows are totaled (see fig. 17.7.)

If you want, you can total the *Total* column by selecting the column in the column-select mode (Shift-F6) and pressing F2 (see fig. 17.8).

Print the form. After you do, save it to disk using a new file name, thus preserving the original.

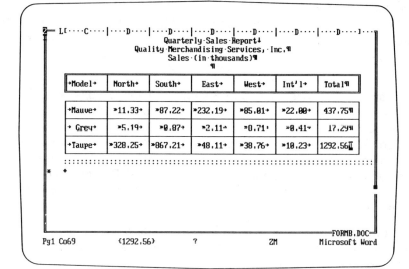

Fig. 17.7.

Totaling all the rows.

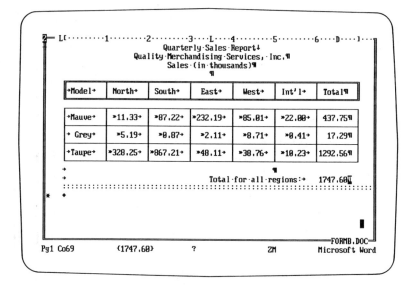

Fig. 17.8.

Totaling the totals column.

Creating a Form Application with Print Merge

Using the Ctrl-> command, you can fill in a form manually quite easily. However, an even easier way is to set up a form that automatically prompts you to supply the required information. The key here is to use some of the same commands you use to create a form-letter application and to print your form using Print Merge. The goal isn't to print many copies of the form; you will print just one copy. But the use of these commands, as you will see, helps to automate what could be a tedious task.

The keys to this application are the ASK and SET instructions. When you add the ASK instruction to your document and print it with Print Merge, Word pauses and asks you to type in a certain type of information. After you do, Word links the information you have supplied to a field name and prints the information wherever you have inserted the field name in your document. You can use the SET instruction, moreover, to perform computations on the information you have linked to field names.

In the following tutorial, you will learn how to create a Print Merge version of the form document you just created. Follow the instructions outlined in the following steps:

1. Create a blank form like the one shown in figure 17.9. Don't add data entry marks; you will use a different approach to get the data into the form.

Fig. 17.9.

Blank form for a
Print Merge
application.

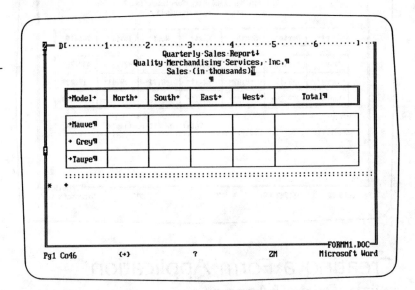

2. Add the line *Sales for month of «month», «year»* below the title (see fig. 17.10). Add chevrons by using the Ctrl-[and Ctrl-] commands.

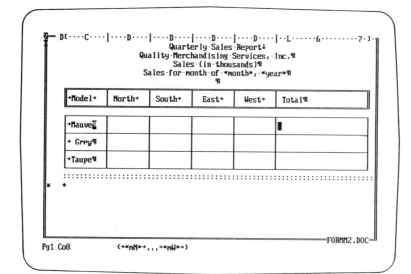

Fig. 17.10.

Adding field names to print the month and date.

3. Add field names to each cell in the form, using a distinctive (but brief) name for each, as suggested in figure 17.11. Enter the chevrons with the Ctrl-[and Ctrl-] commands. The field names are succinct but identify the information to be supplied.

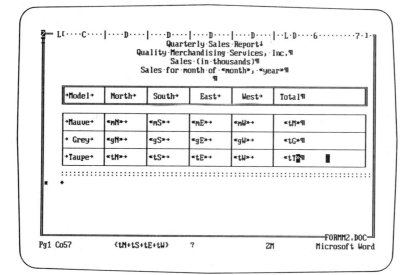

Fig. 17.11.

Adding field names to the cells in the form.

Now add the ASK and SET instructions.

4. Press Ctrl-PgUp to move the cursor to the beginning of the document, press Enter to create a blank line, press the up arrow to highlight the new line, and press Alt-P to cancel the centered paragraph formatting.

5. Now enter the ASK and SET commands precisely as they are shown in figure 17.12. Enter the chevrons by using the Ctrl-[and Ctrl-] commands.

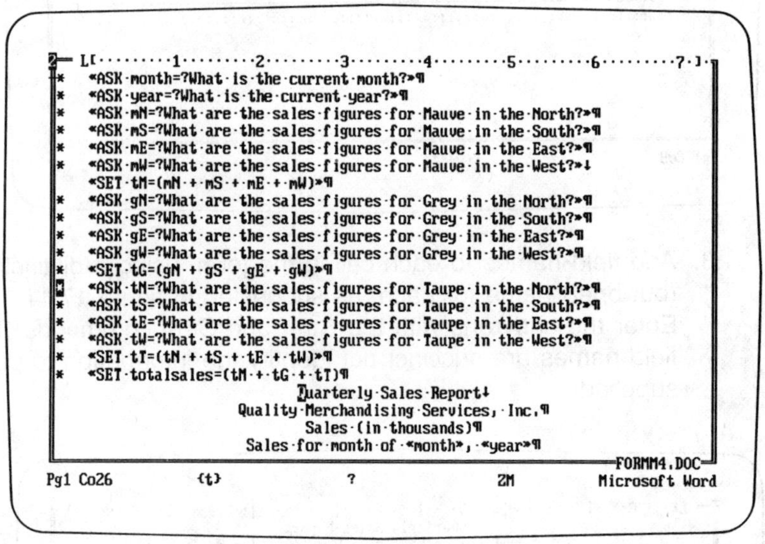

Fig. 17.12.

ASK and SET instructions for a form application using Print Merge.

```
L[·········1·········2·········3·········4·········5·········6·········7·]·
* «ASK·month=?What·is·the·current·month?»¶
* «ASK·year=?What·is·the·current·year?»¶
* «ASK·mN=?What·are·the·sales·figures·for·Mauve·in·the·North?»¶
* «ASK·mS=?What·are·the·sales·figures·for·Mauve·in·the·South?»¶
* «ASK·mE=?What·are·the·sales·figures·for·Mauve·in·the·East?»¶
* «ASK·mW=?What·are·the·sales·figures·for·Mauve·in·the·West?»↓
  «SET·tM=(mN·+·mS·+·mE·+·mW)»¶
* «ASK·gN=?What·are·the·sales·figures·for·Grey·in·the·North?»¶
* «ASK·gS=?What·are·the·sales·figures·for·Grey·in·the·South?»¶
* «ASK·gE=?What·are·the·sales·figures·for·Grey·in·the·East?»¶
* «ASK·gW=?What·are·the·sales·figures·for·Grey·in·the·West?»¶
  «SET·tG=(gN·+·gS·+·gE·+·gW)»¶
  «ASK·tN=?What·are·the·sales·figures·for·Taupe·in·the·North?»¶
* «ASK·tS=?What·are·the·sales·figures·for·Taupe·in·the·South?»¶
* «ASK·tE=?What·are·the·sales·figures·for·Taupe·in·the·East?»¶
* «ASK·tW=?What·are·the·sales·figures·for·Taupe·in·the·West?»¶
* «SET·tI=(tN·+·tS·+·tE·+·tW)»¶
* «SET·totalsales=(tM·+·tG·+·tI)»¶
                    Quarterly·Sales·Report↓
              Quality·Merchandising·Services,·Inc.¶
                    Sales·(in·thousands)¶
              Sales·for·month·of·«month»,·«year»¶
                                                    ═FORMM4.DOC═
Pg1 Co26        {t}           ?              2M      Microsoft Word
```

Be sure to double-check the field names. If you enter one of them improperly, the application will not work correctly.

Enter all the equal signs and question marks carefully, too. Each ASK and SET instruction must be surrounded by chevrons.

6. To run your application, choose the **Print Merge Printer** command. You will be asked to respond to prompts that appear in the command area (see fig. 17.13).

When you supply information to a response command menu, Word links the information you type to the field name you included in the ASK instruction. When you're asked to name the current month, for instance, Word links what you type with the field name called month. Wherever you have inserted that field name in your form, Word prints what you have typed.

```
─ L[·······1·······2·······3·······4·······5·······6·······7·]
* «ASK·month=?What·is·the·current·month?»¶
* «ASK·year=?What·is·the·current·year?»¶
* «ASK·mN=?What·are·the·sales·figures·for·Mauve·in·the·North?»¶
* «ASK·mS=?What·are·the·sales·figures·for·Mauve·in·the·South?»¶
* «ASK·mE=?What·are·the·sales·figures·for·Mauve·in·the·East?»¶
* «ASK·mW=?What·are·the·sales·figures·for·Mauve·in·the·West?»↓
* «SET·tM=(mN·+·mS·+·mE·+·mW)»¶
* «ASK·gN=?What·are·the·sales·figures·for·Grey·in·the·North?»¶
* «ASK·gS=?What·are·the·sales·figures·for·Grey·in·the·South?»¶
* «ASK·gE=?What·are·the·sales·figures·for·Grey·in·the·East?»¶
* «ASK·gW=?What·are·the·sales·figures·for·Grey·in·the·West?»¶
* «SET·tG=(gN·+·gS·+·gE·+·gW)»¶
* «ASK·tN=?What·are·the·sales·figures·for·Taupe·in·the·North?»¶
* «ASK·tS=?What·are·the·sales·figures·for·Taupe·in·the·South?»¶
* «ASK·tE=?What·are·the·sales·figures·for·Taupe·in·the·East?»¶
* «ASK·tW=?What·are·the·sales·figures·for·Taupe·in·the·West?»¶
* «SET·tT=(tN·+·tS·+·tE·+·tW)»¶
* «SET·totalsales=(tM·+·tG·+·tT)»¶
                    Quarterly·Sales·Report↓
                                              ─FORMM4.DOC─
RESPONSE: █

What is the current month?
Pg1 Co26          {?}              ?              2M          Microsoft Word
```

Fig. 17.13.

Print Merge prompt to supply information.

To test the application, enter simple figures (enter 10 for all the Mauve sales, 20 for all the Gray sales, and 30 for the Taupe) to check whether the application is working properly. If it is, you should obtain a printout like the one shown in figure 17.14.

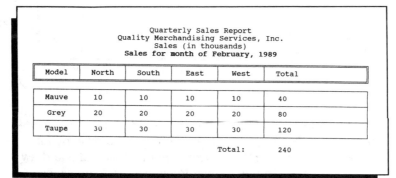

Quarterly Sales Report
Quality Merchandising Services, Inc.
Sales (in thousands)
Sales for month of February, 1989

Model	North	South	East	West	Total
Mauve	10	10	10	10	40
Grey	20	20	20	20	80
Taupe	30	30	30	30	120

Total: 240

Fig. 17.14.

A form generated by Print Merge.

If your application doesn't work properly, make sure that you have spelled all the field names correctly. Make sure, too, that each field name, as well as each ASK and SET instruction, is surrounded by chevrons. Check what you see on your screen carefully against the figures in this chapter.

Creating Illustrations with Cursor Line Draw

If your printer can print the IBM extended character set, you can create simple illustrations with Word's Cursor Line Draw mode (toggled on and off with Ctrl-F5). Cursor Line Draw turns the cursor into a "pen" that draws vertical and horizontal lines by using graphics characters from the extended character set. You can use Cursor Line Draw to create an illustration, such as an organizational chart, using boxes, rectangles, and lines (see fig. 17.15).

Fig. 17.15.

A simple organizational chart created using Cursor Line Draw.

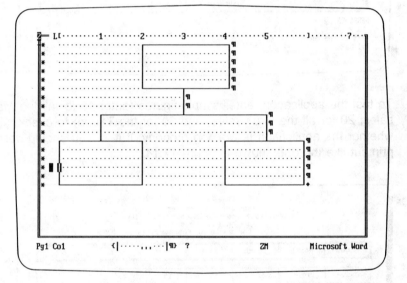

Cursor Line Draw is lots of fun, but it does have limitations. This mode enters characters that, like any other characters, can be disturbed if you enter or delete text. Generally speaking, mixing text and line draw characters is challenging—and often very frustrating. (Adding simple labels or headings is less difficult, as you will see.) You should try to avoid the Line Draw mode when you're creating tables and forms. Keep the following suggestions in mind:

❑ Using the Format Border command to add horizontal lines to tables and forms is almost always better. The lines you create with this command are paragraph formats, so you can type and tab over them without disturbing them. Moreover, if you change the paragraph format, the lines change too.

❏ Using the vertical tab option in the Format Tab Set command to add vertical lines to tables and forms is almost always better. These lines, like the lines you enter with the Format Border command, are paragraph formats, so you will not disturb them if you type or tab over them.

❏ Don't try drawing over existing text. If you want to use Cursor Line Draw, create the drawing in a blank part of your document. Add the text after you make the drawing.

❏ If you want to add text to your drawing, keep the text to a minimum, and be sure to use a fixed-width (monospace) font such as Courier or Pica. Add the text in the overtype mode (press F5) so that you don't delete the spaces Word has inserted.

To use Cursor Line Draw, do the following:

1. Position the cursor where you want to start drawing, and press Ctrl-F5.

   Word displays the LD code in the key status indicator. Be sure to draw in a blank section of your document.

2. Press the right, left, down, and up arrows to "draw" with the cursor. Press Home to draw a line quickly to the left margin, and press End to draw a line quickly to the right margin.

   As you can see, Word automatically enters spaces and paragraph marks to make room for the characters you're entering. When you join lines, the program automatically smooths the junctions.

3. To move the "pen" elsewhere on the screen, exit the Line Draw mode by pressing Ctrl-F5 and reposition the cursor. Then use Ctrl-F5 again.

4. To correct mistakes, exit Line Draw by pressing Ctrl-F5 and delete the unwanted characters as you would delete any text.

You can change the linedraw character if you want. The default character is a single line. To choose among the other options, use the **O**ptions command and select the **linedraw character** field. Then press F1 to see your options (see fig. 17.16).

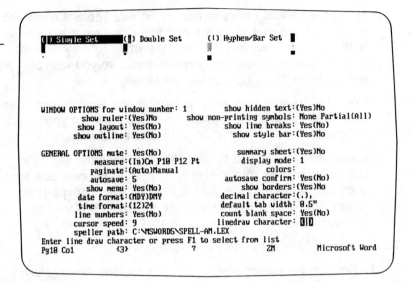

Fig. 17.16.

Linedraw
character options
(Options menu).

Chapter Summary

Forms are a big part of a bureaucratic society. Creating them and filling them out are big nuisances for many organizations. This chapter told you how to use Word 5 to reduce the cost and tedium of creating forms by making it easy to design and print attractive-looking forms. You also learned how to use Word to fill in the forms automatically.

Now that you have dealt with what is surely the most mundane of Word's desktop publishing applications, turn to the most glamorous—integrating the text you create with Word 5 with graphics created in other programs.

18

Integrating Text
and Graphics

Graphics are all the rage these days, and many users are now
pondering such questions as, "Do I need a desktop publishing
program?" in addition to the usual imponderables, such as "Must I
have more RAM?" or "Is a 40M drive big enough, or do I need 80?"
A real desktop publishing program, such as Aldus PageMaker® or
Ventura Publisher®, is capable of displaying and editing text and
graphics simultaneously. Such programs are handy, especially if your
job responsibilities require you to lay out newsletters, brochures, and
camera-ready copy for your organization's publications.

Most of us, however, aren't in that league. And what's more, desktop
publishing programs are for desktop publishing, not word processing.
You cannot beat a top-notch word processing program, such as Word
5, for creating, editing, and printing text. What the typical user needs is
a high-quality word processing program that can incorporate everyday
graphics images, such as graphs generated from spreadsheet
programs, into document files, with a minimum of fuss and bother (for
an example, see fig. 18.1).

Fig. 18.1.

Spreadsheet-generated graphics incorporated into a Word document.

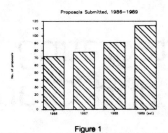

Overview

The Center for Research Development seeks to aid faculty research by identifying the correct agency or foundation for faculty projects, helping faculty to formulate their research in marketable terms, assisting the writing of proposals to maximize funding potential, and negotiating research terms with private and public funding agencies.

Achievements

Since the Research Development effort was initiated in 1986, the number of proposals has risen significantly (Figure 1). Part of this increase is attributable, to be sure, to increased emphasis on research funding in promotion and tenure decisions. However, the rate of increase parallels the rate of increase in faculty visits to the Center for Research Development. It is therefore plausible to conclude that the Center's activities have played a key role in fostering this healthy increase in research development at the University.

Increases were registered in virtually every sector of the University's operations. A significant development, however, has been increased entrepreneurial activity on the part of humanities, arts, and social sciences faculty, whose activities now represent a measurable fraction of the total for the first time in the University's history (Figure 2).

Figure 1

Objectives

Current forecasts call for sharp reductions in both federal funding and corporate giving. It is essential that the University increase its *share* of local, state, and federal funds as well as maintain its record of increases in proposal-preparation activity. To accomplish this objective, it is necessary to improve our public relations operation so that corporate donors and funding agencies are more aware of the University's distinguished record of achievement in sponsored research.

Figure 2

For such purposes, Word 5's graphics capabilities are ideal. To be sure, Word—unlike a real desktop publishing program—doesn't let you view and edit text and graphics simultaneously. To incorporate graphics into your Word files, you use the Library Link Graphics command, and Word inserts a line of information about the graphic into your document. When you print your document, this information tells Word where to find the graphic image and how to size it. You don't see the integration of text and graphics until you print or you use the Print preView command.

The Library Link Graphics command is easy to learn to use. And what's more, new Word 5 features enable you to "anchor" the imported graphic so that it stays put; text "flows" around the graphic to the left or right, if there is space, and all these steps are done automatically. Furthermore, you can box the graphic and shade it, if you want. All in all, Word 5's graphics features make it easy to integrate text and graphics in a way that's businesslike and straightforward. You're sure to be impressed with the handsome results you will get.

This chapter covers the following subjects:

❏ Importing graphics into Word documents from a variety of programs

❏ Sizing and positioning the graphic within the Word document

❏ Adding borders and captions to the graphic

❏ Capturing graphics screens from graphics programs using the program CAPTURE.COM, which is on Utilities Disk #3

❏ Anchoring graphics so that text "flows" around the anchored image

About Graphics Files

The world of graphics files has little standardization. Many competing file formats exist, and some programs use their own unique format. Fortunately, Word can read several important graphics formats directly. And for those it cannot read, you can use the CAPTURE.COM utility on Utilities Disk #3. This utility "captures" any graphics screen image to a Word-readable file format. In short, if you can display it on your computer's screen, you can print it in a Word document.

You will learn more about CAPTURE.COM elsewhere in this chapter. The following is a brief overview of the graphics files Word 5 can read directly:

❏ Hewlett-Packard® Graphics Language (HPGL) format. Many programs support the HPGL standard, which initially was devised for Hewlett-Packard plotters. Word can read files printed to disk using this format. Programs capable of producing HPGL plotter files include ChartMaster, Diagram-Master™, Generic CAD, Harvard™ Graphics, Microsoft® Chart, and Versacad.

❑ Lotus® and Symphony® PIC files. Word can read Lotus and Symphony graphics files directly.

   Note: Many Lotus-compatible spreadsheet programs produce files that Word can read; among such programs are VP-Planner®, Quattro®, and SuperCalc®4.

❑ Microsoft Clipboard images. If you're running Word within Windows, here's some very good news: anything you can get into the Clipboard in bit-mapped format can be imported into Word, including the charts you create with Microsoft® Excel.

❑ PC Paintbrush® PCX or PCC files. Word reads the files created by this program, which Microsoft distributes with the Microsoft® Mouse.

❑ PostScript® files. You can import any graphics image generated by the PostScript printer control language, but you will not be able to view the image in Print preView.

❑ Tagged Image File Format (TIFF) files. Scanners, such as the DFI Handy Scanner, produce images conforming to this format. Word can read TIFF B (monochrome) files in compressed or uncompressed form, as well as uncompressed TIFF G (gray scale) files.

Importing and Sizing Graphics

When you import a graphics file, you can use Word's default sizing settings; or you can specify the width and height of the image, the amount of space above and below the image, the placement of the image within its frame, or the space that Word allots for the image. If you want, you can add borders and a caption.

Importing the Graphic

When you import a graphic image into Word, the program assumes, by default, that you want the image to print with the same width as the margins you're using. When you name the file, Word examines its format and proposes for the image a height that's proportional to the width you have chosen. The whole process is automatic.

To import an image into a Word document, using automatic sizing, follow this procedure:

1. Place the cursor where you want the image to appear.

2. Choose **L**ibrary **L**ink **G**raphics. When the command menu appears (see fig. 18.2), type the graphic's file name in the **filename** field.

   If you're not sure what the file name is, press F1 to see a list of files. If you're using Windows, choose **C**lipboard to import a bit-mapped image from the Clipboard.

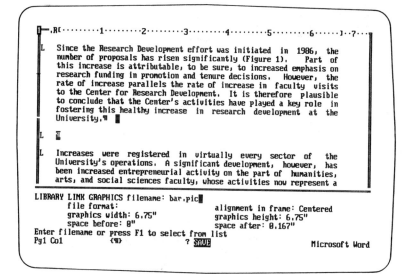

Fig. 18.2.

Importing a Lotus .PIC file with Library Link Graphics command.

3. Carry out the command.

Word adds a message to your file at the cursor's location (see fig. 18.3). The message, which begins with a hidden text command (.G.), specifies the file's name and location, the width and height of the image, and the file's format.

To preview the image's appearance and location before printing, choose the **P**rint pre**V**iew command (see fig 18.4).

Fig. 18.3.

Message
containing
information about
the imported
graphic file.

this increase is attributable, to be sure, to increased emphasis on
research funding in promotion and tenure decisions. However, the
rate of increase parallels the rate of increase in faculty visits
to the Center for Research Development. It is therefore plausible
to conclude that the Center's activities have played a key role in
fostering this healthy increase in research development at the
University.¶

.G.C:\MSWORD\BAR.PIC;4";2.888";Lotus P█C¶

Increases were registered in virtually every sector of the
University's operations. A significant development, however, has
been increased entrepreneurial activity on the part of humanities,
arts, and social sciences faculty, whose activities now represent a
measurable fraction of the total for the first time in the
University's history.¶

```
LIBRARY LINK GRAPHICS filename: bar.pic
           file format: Lotus PIC          alignment in frame: Centered
           graphics width: 6.75"           graphics height: 4.874"
           space before: 0"                space after: 0.167"
Enter graphics file format or press F1 to select from list
Pg1 Co52            {¶}              ?                    Microsoft Word
```

Fig. 18.4.

Previewing the
graphic's
appearance.

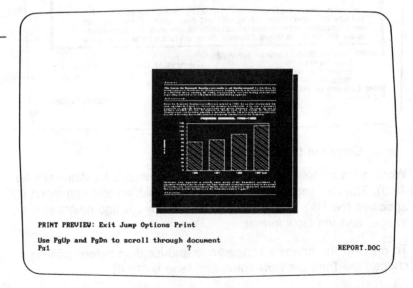

```
PRINT PREVIEW: Exit Jump Options Print

Use PgUp and PgDn to scroll through document
Pg1                              ?                       REPORT.DOC
```

Sizing and Positioning the Graphic

Word's automatic sizing capabilities provide a quick way to import a
graphic without worrying about its size or position. But if you would like
to control the size, you can specify the image's height and width by
typing measurements in the **graphics width** and **graphics height**

command fields. In addition, you can add white space before and after the graphic. By default, Word leaves very little space—just 1/16 inch—between the graphic and the text that comes before and after it, so you may want to add more.

You also can specify how the image is to be placed within its *frame*, a term that requires a little explanation. By default, Word creates for the image a special space, or frame, that's as wide as the column in which the cursor is positioned. If you're working with single-column text, the column width is the same as the line length, which is determined by the settings you have chosen in the Format Division Margins command menu.

If you choose an image width that's smaller than the frame, you can position the image within the frame by making choices in the **alignment in frame** field of the Library Link Graphics command menu. Press F1 in this field to see a list of options (centered, left, or right alignment).

If you would like to see the actual size and position of the frame in which the graphic will print without using Print preView, toggle on the Show Layout mode, using Alt-F4. Although you will not see the graphic itself, its frame will be displayed in the correct position, and you can judge quickly whether you have sized and placed the graphic correctly.

Resizing the Graphic

After using the Library Link Graphics command and checking your sizing and white space choices with Print preView, you may decide to change the graphic's size or increase the white space around it. To do so, simply position the cursor within the information about the graphic, and choose the **Library Link Graphics** command again. Change the settings in the command menus, and carry out the command.

Adding Borders or Shading

To enhance your graphic image, you may want to add borders or shading. You can add them by following these steps:

1. Position the cursor within the information about the graphic image, that was inserted by the **Library Link Graphics** command.

2. Choose the **F**ormat **B**order command (see fig. 18.5), and choose lines, boxes, or shading as you want.

3. Carry out the command. To preview the effect you have chosen, use the **P**rint pre**V**iew command (see fig. 18.6).

Fig. 18.5.

The Format Border command menu.

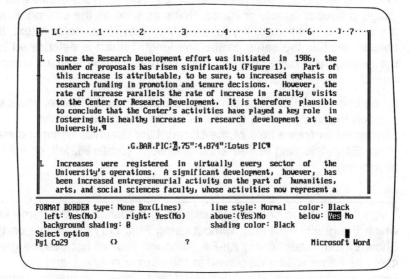

Fig. 18.6.

Previewing the borders.

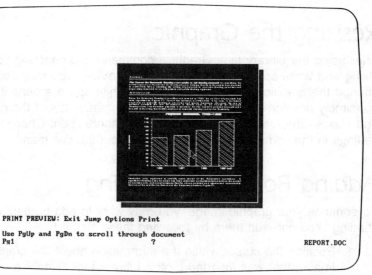

Adding Captions

You can add captions that print within the borders you have created simply by typing the caption's text within the graphic image's paragraph.

To add a caption, do the following:

1. Position the cursor on the paragraph mark that ends the information about the graphic, and press Ctrl-Enter to start a new line. Press Ctrl-Enter again.

2. Type the caption (see fig. 18.7).

3. Press Alt-C to center the caption. Preview the caption with **P**rint pre**V**iew before printing (see fig. 18.8).

Moving the Graphic

Once you have imported a graphic into a Word document with the Library Link Graphics command, you can move the image to another part of the document if you want. Simply move the paragraph containing the information about the graphic that the Library Link Graphics command inserted.

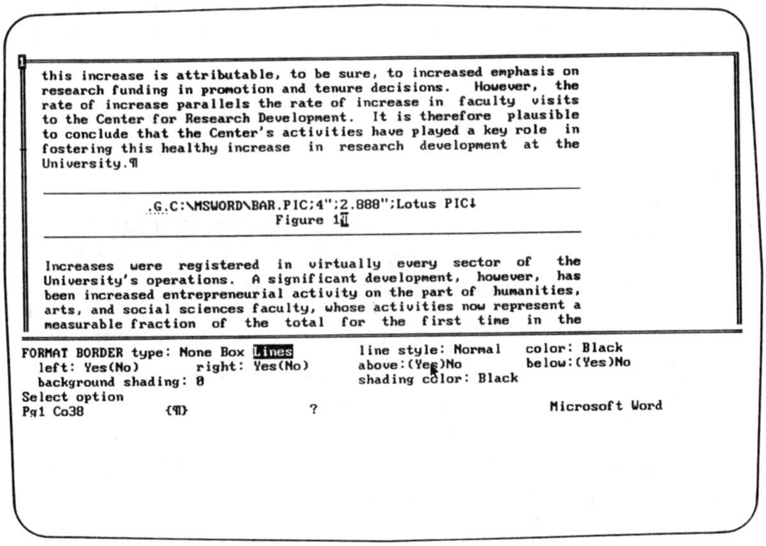

Fig. 18.7.

Adding a caption.

Fig. 18.8.

Previewing the caption.

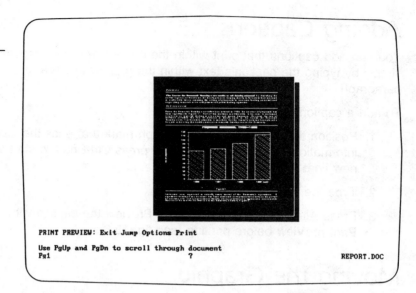

Anchoring Graphics

A major new addition to the Format Command submenu is the Format pOsition command, which "nails down" a graphic (or text paragraph) at a fixed place on the screen. Once you have used this command to fix the location of a graphic image or a paragraph of text, it stays put, even in Word's insert mode. Text that doesn't fit above the fixed frame flows around it.

In figure 18.9, for example, a graph, sized to be 4.0 inches wide, has been anchored to the center of the page (vertically) and to the right (horizontally).

The Format pOsition command provides many options for positioning the graphic's or text's frame on the page. You specify the frame's alignment by choosing horizontal and vertical frame positions.

When you choose the horizontal frame position, you select from **Left**, **Centered**, **Right**, **Outside** (outside on facing pages of a bound document), or **Inside** (inside on facing pages of a bound document). Any of these frame alignments can be applied to the column in which the frame is positioned, measured from the left to the right margin, or the entire page, measured from the page's edges. In figure 18.9, for instance, the graphic is positioned flush right horizontally, relative to the left and right margins.

Overview

The Center for Research Development seeks to aid faculty research by identifying the correct agency or foundation for faculty projects, helping faculty to formulate their research in marketable terms, assisting the writing of proposals to maximize funding potential, and negotiating research terms with private and public funding agencies.

Achievements

Since the Research Development effort was initiated in 1986, the number of proposals has risen significantly (Figure 1). Part of this increase is attributable, to be sure, to increased emphasis on research funding in promotion and tenure decisions. However, the rate of increase parallels the rate of increase in faculty visits to the Center for Research Development. It is therefore plausible to conclude that the Center's activities have played a key role in fostering this healthy increase in research development at the University.

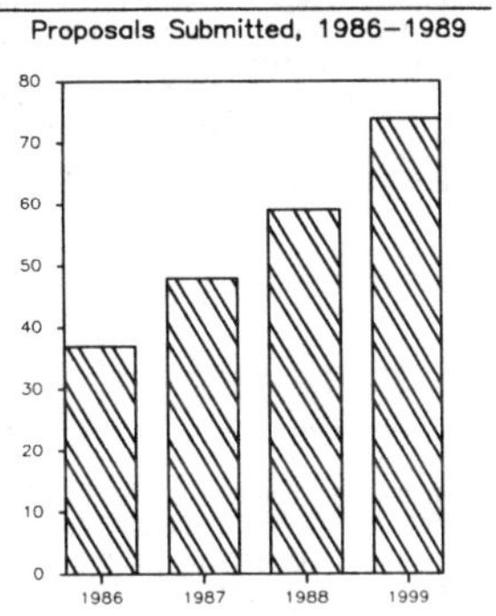

Proposals Submitted, 1986–1989

Increases were registered in virtually every sector of the University's operations. A significant development, however, has been increased entrepreneurial activity on the part of humanities, arts, and social sciences faculty, whose activities now represent a measurable fraction of the total for the first time in the University's history.

Objectives

Current forecasts call for sharp reductions in both federal funding and corporate giving. It is essential that the University increase its share of local, state, and federal funds as well as maintain its record of increases in proposal-preparation activity. To accomplish this objective, it is necessary to improve our public relations operation so that corporate donors and funding agencies are more aware of the University's distinguished record of achievement in sponsored research.

Fig. 18.9.

A graph anchored with Format pOsition.

When you choose the vertical frame position, you select from **In line**, **Top**, **Centered**, or **Bottom**. Any of these frame alignments can be applied to the area between the top or bottom margins, or if you want, the entire page, measured from the top edge of the page to the bottom edge. In figure 18.9, for instance, the graphic is positioned in the center of the page vertically, relative to the top and bottom margins.

To anchor a graphic image, follow these instructions:

1. Place the cursor within the information about the graphic you want to position.

2. Choose the Format pOsition command (see fig. 18.10).

3. In the **horizontal frame position** field, press F1 to choose a horizontal alignment for the frame (see fig. 18.11). You also can type a measurement if you want.

Fig. 18.10.

The Format pOsition command menu.

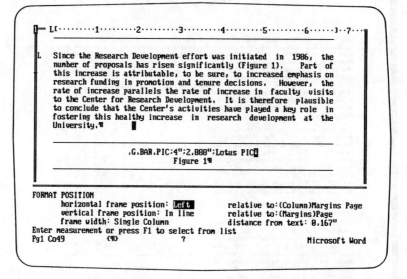

Fig. 18.11.

Horizontal alignment options.

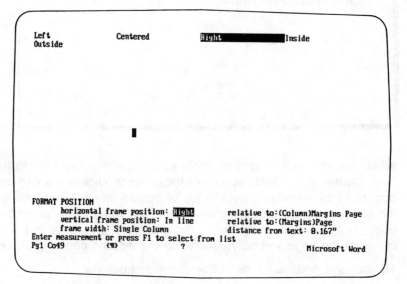

4. In the **relative to** field, press F1 to choose from the **Page**, **Column**, or **Margins** options.

5. In the **vertical frame position** field, press F1 to choose from a list of alignment options (see fig. 18.12). If you want, you can type a measurement.

6. In the **relative to** field, choose from the top and bottom of the page or the top and bottom margins.

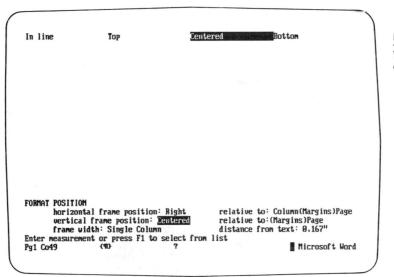

```
In line            Top              Centered            Bottom


















FORMAT POSITION
       horizontal frame position: Right      relative to: Column(Margins)Page
       vertical frame position: Centered     relative to:(Margins)Page
       frame width: Single Column            distance from text: 0.167"
Enter measurement or press F1 to select from list
Pg1 Co49             {¶}             ?                    ▌Microsoft Word
```

Fig. 18.12.

Vertical alignment options.

7. If you're positioning a graphic, press F1 to choose the **Width of Graphic** option in the **frame width** field (see fig. 18.13). Word will use the graphic width you chose in the Library Link Graphics command menu. If you're positioning a paragraph of text, however, type a measurement for the paragraph's frame width.

8. If you would like to add additional white space around the frame—and you probably will, considering that Word leaves only 1/16 inch of white space—type a measurement in the **distance from text** field.

9. Carry out the command.

10. Check your work using **P**rint pre**V**iew (see fig. 18.14).

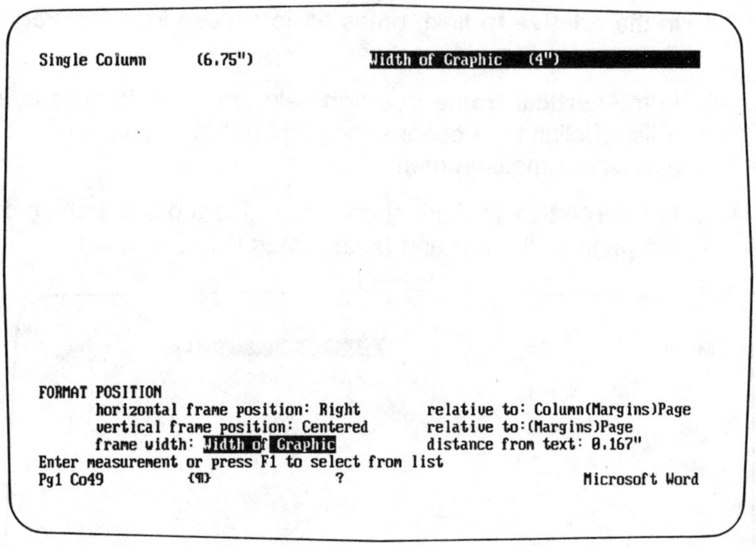

Fig. 18.13.

Setting the frame width to the width of the graphic.

```
Single Column      (6.75")            Width of Graphic   (4")




















FORMAT POSITION
        horizontal frame position: Right        relative to: Column(Margins)Page
        vertical frame position: Centered       relative to:(Margins)Page
        frame width: Width of Graphic           distance from text: 0.167"
Enter measurement or press F1 to select from list
Pg1 Co49              {¶}               ?                      Microsoft Word
```

Fig. 18.14.

Previewing the graphic's location after anchoring.

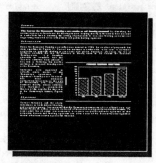

```
PRINT PREVIEW: Exit Jump Options Print

Use PgUp and PgDn to scroll through document
Pg1                                     ?                      REPORT.DOC
```

Experiment with Format pOsition until you understand the effects of the various options.

Capturing Graphics with CAPTURE.COM

If Word cannot read the graphics file format created by a graphics program, you still can print the program's graphics in your Word documents. The key is to use CAPTURE.COM, a program included on Utilities Disk #3. CAPTURE.COM is a memory-resident program. You load it before starting your graphics program. When you see the screen you want to capture, you press Shift-PrtSc, type the name of the file to which you would like to save the screen, and press Enter to size the image using the arrow keys. When you have identified the part of the image you want to save, press Enter again, and CAPTURE.COM saves the screen to a file, using the extension SCR.

To include an image saved with CAPTURE.COM in a Word document, use the **L**ibrary **L**ink **G**raphics command and name the file. Word automatically detects the CAPTURE file format.

Chapter Summary

Word 5's new graphics features will satisfy fully the needs of most users whose graphics needs are limited to including graphs, charts, and other everyday illustrations in reports and proposals. Unlike a true desktop publishing program, Word doesn't display graphics and text simultaneously, except in Print preView mode, which doesn't let you change the position of the elements you see or edit. Even so, you can easily use Word 5's graphics features to integrate charts, graphs, and pictures into your text. Once you choose the graphic's width, Word sizes the graphic's height automatically. With a simple command, you can control the amount of white space around the graphic and, if you want, add boxes or lines to set it off from the text.

To gain even more control over the position of graphics in your document, try anchoring them with the Format pOsition command. With this command, you can fix a graphic's location relative to the edges of the page or the margins, both horizontally and vertically. If the graphic is narrower than the text column, text flows around it automatically, producing a handsome result.

In the next chapter, you will learn how you can add to the desktop publishing knowledge you already have gained by creating multiple-column text. With surprisingly little effort, you can produce handsomely formatted newsletters—and if you combine this expertise with the formatting control provided by the Format pOsition command, you can produce some stunning effects.

19

Creating Multiple-Column Text and Newsletters

Among the many endearing habits of North Americans is their propensity to publish newsletters on virtually every subject known to humanity. One recent estimate is that well over 100,000 newsletters now course their way through our continent's postal systems. At that rate, a modest-sized rural county of 100,000 people may well be responsible for more than 40 newsletters. The newsletters published range in tone from the frivolous (such as *The Pigeon Fancier's Digest*) to the serious (*The Millionaire's Guide to Investment Bonanzas*). Considering that most of these newsletters traditionally have been produced on primitive equipment, one conclusion is certain: The desktop publishing revolution is sure to fuel an explosion in the sheer bulk of newsletters produced.

If you're among the teeming thousands who see a newsletter in your future, you have come to the right place. Although Word 5 isn't a desktop publishing program in the strict sense (because it doesn't let you simultaneously display and edit graphics), you will find that it's a great program for producing a straightforward, but handsome, newsletter. Your newsletter can be complete with multiple-text columns and, if you want, graphics positioned just where you want them. True, you could do an even better job with a genuine desktop publishing program. But with Word 5, it doesn't take much effort to produce a newsletter that will win the respect of your audience; and, as you have already seen, Word 5 can do much more than a desktop publishing program can.

Best of all, with Word 5 you can produce a newsletter with surprisingly little effort. Most of the people who produce newsletters, after all, aren't doing it because they enjoy the experience of blending text and graphics. They do it because they want to get their message to people, quickly, cheaply, and professionally. Their graphics aims are modest: they simply want to get their messages across in a way that's clean, professional, and attractive (for an example, see fig. 19.1). Word 5 is an outstanding choice for persons with these goals.

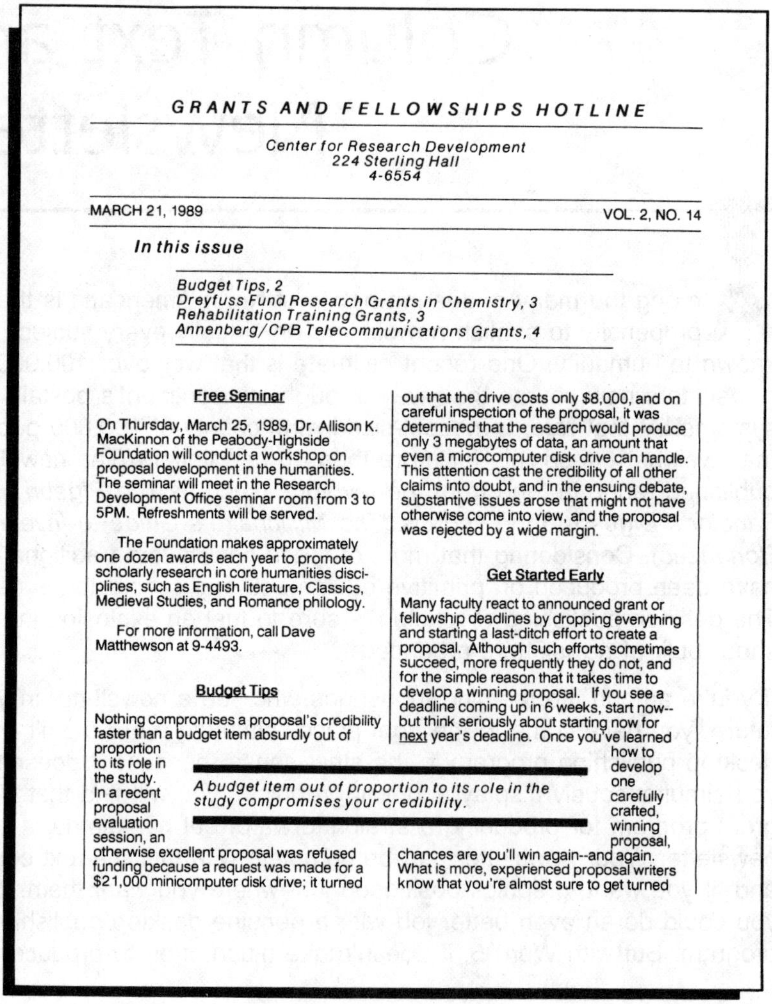

Fig. 19.1.

A simple but attractive newsletter created with Word 5.

GRANTS AND FELLOWSHIPS HOTLINE

Center for Research Development
224 Sterling Hall
4-6554

MARCH 21, 1989   VOL. 2, NO. 14

In this issue

Budget Tips, 2
Dreyfuss Fund Research Grants in Chemistry, 3
Rehabilitation Training Grants, 3
Annenberg/CPB Telecommunications Grants, 4

Free Seminar

On Thursday, March 25, 1989, Dr. Allison K. MacKinnon of the Peabody-Highside Foundation will conduct a workshop on proposal development in the humanities. The seminar will meet in the Research Development Office seminar room from 3 to 5PM. Refreshments will be served.

The Foundation makes approximately one dozen awards each year to promote scholarly research in core humanities disciplines, such as English literature, Classics, Medieval Studies, and Romance philology.

For more information, call Dave Matthewson at 9-4493.

Budget Tips

Nothing compromises a proposal's credibility faster than a budget item absurdly out of proportion to its role in the study. In a recent proposal evaluation session, an otherwise excellent proposal was refused funding because a request was made for a $21,000 minicomputer disk drive; it turned

A budget item out of proportion to its role in the study compromises your credibility.

out that the drive costs only $8,000, and on careful inspection of the proposal, it was determined that the research would produce only 3 megabytes of data, an amount that even a microcomputer disk drive can handle. This attention cast the credibility of all other claims into doubt, and in the ensuing debate, substantive issues arose that might not have otherwise come into view, and the proposal was rejected by a wide margin.

Get Started Early

Many faculty react to announced grant or fellowship deadlines by dropping everything and starting a last-ditch effort to create a proposal. Although such efforts sometimes succeed, more frequently they do not, and for the simple reason that it takes time to develop a winning proposal. If you see a deadline coming up in 6 weeks, start now-- but think seriously about starting now for next year's deadline. Once you've learned how to develop one carefully crafted, winning proposal, chances are you'll win again--and again. What is more, experienced proposal writers know that you're almost sure to get turned

Word 5's newsletter-producing capabilities far outstrip those of its predecessor, which saddled would-be newsletter editors and authors with a host of vexing problems. Chief among the problems was Word 4's inability to blend single-column and multiple-column text on a page. To create a single-column banner over double-column text, for example, one was forced to create the banner as running-head text—an awkward solution at best. But all that's history. With Word 5, you easily can blend single-column and multiple-column text on a page. Creating newsletters now is so much easier that, if you tried to do so with previous versions of Word, you simply will not believe the difference. And with the Show Layout mode, you even can display multiple-column text and edit the text simultaneously.

Additional Word 5 features enable you to create a much more attractive newsletter. Using the Format pOsition command discussed in the last chapter, for instance, you can "anchor" headlines, graphics, and text anywhere you like on the page, and the text—even if it's formatted in multiple columns—will float around the anchored material. With this technique, you can highlight important passages of text by placing them in sidebars, like the ones you frequently see in magazines.

By any standard, Word 5 equips you with a formidable tool chest for producing eye-catching newsletters. This program alone is sure to help launch thousands of new newsletters—*The Pigeon Fancier's Digest* is sure to have competition.

Creating Side-by-Side Paragraphs

Word creates multiple-column text in two very different ways, and you must understand the difference. The first way, side-by-side paragraphs, creates two-column text in which the paragraphs printed side-by-side are linked so that the paragraph on the left is always printed adjacent to the paragraph on the right. The second way, multiple-column formatting, doesn't link paragraphs in that way. The columns are completely independent of each another.

Side-by-side paragraphs are of greatest use when you need to link the two paragraphs. An example would be a product list, in which the left column describes the product while the right column describes its many merits.

Creating side-by-side paragraphs with Word is, unfortunately, something of a trick. (Multiple columns are much easier to create.) The following steps introduce the basic procedure for creating side-by-side paragraphs:

1. In a new, blank Word document, choose the **Format Paragraph** command. Type *3.5"* in the **right indent** command field, type *1 li* in the **space after** field, choose **Yes** in the **side by side** field, and carry out the command.

   The left-hand paragraph must be indented 3.5 inches from the right margin to allow room for the right-hand paragraph.

2. Type the left-hand paragraph and press Enter.

3. Choose the **Format Paragraph** command again and type *3.5"* in the **left indent** command field. Choose **Yes** in the **side by side** field, and type *1 li* in the **space after** field. Carry out the command.

   The right-hand paragraph must be indented 3.5 inches from the left margin to allow room for the left-hand paragraph.

4. Type the right-hand paragraph and press Enter.

As you create the paragraphs on the screen, they're not shown side-by-side (see fig. 19.2). But you can see the effect by choosing the Show Layout mode (toggled on and off using Shift-F4), which slows down Word's speed considerably, or **P**rint pre**V**iew (see fig. 19.3).

Fig. 19.2.

Creating side-by-side paragraphs.

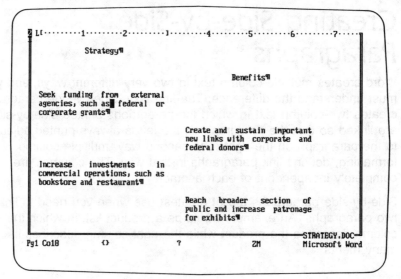

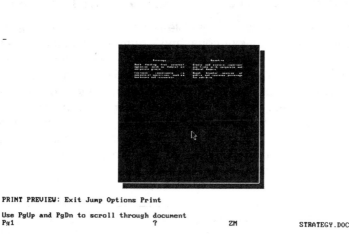

Fig. 19.3.

Side-by-side
paragraphs in the
Print preView
mode.

To create additional side-by-side paragraphs, copy the paragraph
formats. If you're using the keyboard, copy the left-hand paragraph's
formats by selecting its paragraph mark and copying it to the scrap.
Then position the cursor below the last paragraph you typed and press
Enter. Use the same technique to copy the right-hand paragraph's
formatting. If you're using a mouse, you can copy paragraph formatting
by selecting the paragraph you want to format, moving the pointer to
the selection bar beside the paragraph that has the format you want to
copy, holding down the Alt key, and clicking the right button.

Caution: You can create only 16 pairs of continuous side-by-side
paragraphs. Although you can create another 16 pairs by inserting a
paragraph that's not formatted side-by-side, you should reserve this
application for short lists. If you want to create a longer list, and the
right-hand paragraph will consist only of one or a few words, try
creating ordinary paragraphs, formatted with a hanging indentation of
3.0 inches and a flush left tab of 3.0 inches.

Creating Multiple-Column Text

The second way you can create multiple-column text with Word is to use the Format Division Layout command's **number of columns** field. Far easier than creating side-by-side paragraphs, this technique produces vertical columns of text in which the adjacent paragraphs are unrelated; they're positioned next to each other owing to the accidents of formatting. The effect, in other words, is similar to the multiple-column text found in newspapers or magazines. You can create up to 22 columns, although in practice choosing more than 3 or 4 columns of text produces unattractive results. You can format an unlimited number of pages or paragraphs in this way.

When you create narrow text columns, use the **L**ibrary **H**yphenate command to insert optional hyphens in your document. Word will not use these hyphens unless they are needed to even the right margin. You can hide the display of optional hyphens by choosing **N**one in the **show non-printing symbols** field of the Options menu.

Using the Format Division Layout Command To Create Multiple-Column Text

To create multiple-column text, follow these steps:

1. Position the cursor in the division you want to format with multiple columns.

    Note: Multiple-column text is a division format, so the whole division will be formatted with the number of columns you specify. If your document has no division breaks, the whole document will have multiple-column text.

2. Type a number greater than 1 in the **number of columns** field of the **F**ormat **D**ivision **L**ayout command menu (see fig. 19.4). Use the default **space between columns** measurement (0.5 inch).

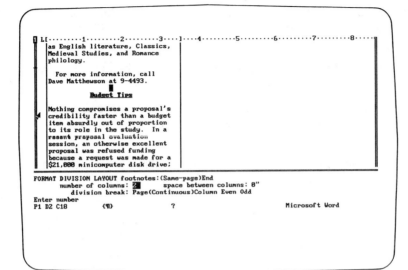

Fig. 19.4.

Creating multiple-column text.

As you can see from figure 19.4, you don't see the multiple-column text on the screen in the default display mode. However, you can view—and edit—multiple columns on the screen in the Show Layout mode. To use this mode, press Shift-F4.

In Show Layout mode, you can use two new commands to move from one column to the next. Ctrl-K 5-right arrow moves the cursor to the next column right, and Ctrl-K 5-left arrow moves the cursor to the next column left.

The narrower the column, the better the chance that Word will leave unsightly gaps between words as it tries to justify lines. You will improve your document's appearance significantly if you use flush-left alignment rather than right-margin justification. Use the **L**ibrary **H**yphenate command, moreover, to place optional hyphens in your text. Both these methods will assist Word as it tries to even out the right margin in narrow text columns.

Blending Single- and Multiple-Column Text on a Page: Printing a Banner

A most welcome feature of Word 5 is that you can blend single- and multiple-column text on one page with a minimum of hassle. To change the number of columns on a page, you press Ctrl-Enter to create a new division. Then you format the new division for multiple-column text.

You can use this technique to print a single-column headline, followed by multiple-column text. This procedure is the one to use:

1. In a new, blank Word document, type a headline or banner and center it by pressing Alt-C. Add blank lines under the headline (see fig. 19.5).

2. Place the cursor where you want the multiple-column text to start, and press Ctrl-Enter to create a division break (see fig. 19.6).

3. With the cursor under the division break, choose the **F**ormat **D**ivision **L**ayout command. In the **division break** field, choose the **C**ontinuous option. (This option prevents Word from inserting a page break at the division break.) Then type *2* in the **number of columns** field and carry out the command (see fig. 19.7).

The division break now separates the single- and multiple-column text (see fig. 19.8).

Fig. 19.5.

Creating a banner.

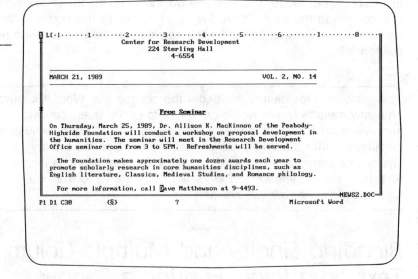

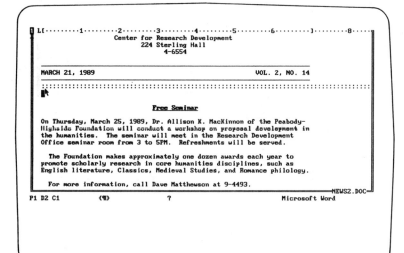

Fig. 19.6.

Entering a division break.

```
| L[·······1·······2·······3·······4·······5·······6·······]·······8··]
                    Center for Research Development
                         224 Sterling Hall
                              4-6554
      ─────────────────────────────────────────────────────────────
      MARCH 21, 1989                              VOL. 2, NO. 14
      ::::::::::::::::::::::::::::::::::::::::::::::::::::::::::::::::::::::
      ▮
                              Free Seminar

      On Thursday, March 25, 1989, Dr. Allison K. MacKinnon of the Peabody-
      Highside Foundation will conduct a workshop on proposal development in
      the humanities.  The seminar will meet in the Research Development
      Office seminar room from 3 to 5PM.  Refreshments will be served.

         The Foundation makes approximately one dozen awards each year to
      promote scholarly research in core humanities disciplines, such as
      English literature, Classics, Medieval Studies, and Romance philology.

         For more information, call Dave Matthewson at 9-4493.
                                                            ─NEWS2.DOC─
      P1 D2 C1          {¶}              ?              Microsoft Word
```

Fig. 19.7.

Formatting the second division for multiple-column text.

```
?─ L[········1········2········3·]··4········5········6········7···]
                  Center for Research Development¶
                       224 Sterling Hall¶
                            4-6554¶
      ───────────────────────────────────────────────────────────
      MARCH 21, 1989                           VOL. 2, NO. 14¶
      ::::::::::::::::::::::::::::::::::::::::::::::::::::::::::::::::::
    * ¶
                   Free Seminar¶
           ¶
      On Thursday, March 25, 1989, Dr.
      Allison K. MacKinnon of the
      Peabody-Highside Foundation will
      conduct a workshop on proposal
      development in the humanities.
      The seminar will meet in the

      FORMAT DIVISION LAYOUT footnotes:(Same-page)End
               number of columns: 2        space between columns: 0.5"
                  division break: Page Continuous Column Even Odd
      Select option
      P1 D2 C1          {Place·}      ?  ▮           2M     Microsoft Word
```

> **Caution:** If Word inserts a page break at the division break, you forgot to choose the Continuous option in the Format Division Layout command menu's **division break** field when you formatted the second division. Place the cursor within the second division and use the command again.

Fig. 19.8.

Division break separating single- and multiple-column text.

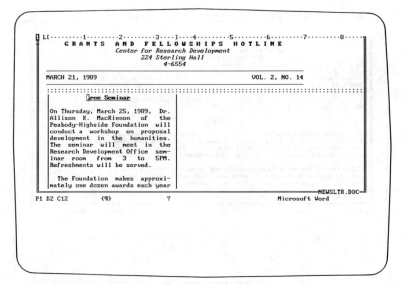

```
L[·······1·······2·······3···]···4·······5·······6·······7·······8··]
  GRANTS  AND  FELLOWSHIPS  HOTLINE
            Center for Research Development
                  224 Sterling Hall
                       4-6554

MARCH 21, 1989                          VOL. 2, NO. 14

:::::::::::::::::::::::::::::::::::::::::::::::::::::::::::::::::::::::::::
  Free Seminar

On Thursday, March 25, 1989,  Dr.
Allison K. MacKinnon  of   the
Peabody-Highside Foundation  will
conduct  a  workshop  on  proposal
development  in  the  humanities.
The  seminar  will  meet  in  the
Research Development Office  sem-
inar  room  from   3  to  5PM.
Refreshments will be served.

   The  Foundation  makes  approxi-
mately one dozen awards each year

                                    ─NEWSLTR.DOC─
P1 D2 C12        {¶}          ?          Microsoft Word
```

Adding Running Heads to a Document with Single- and Multiple-Column Text

You probably will use running heads for your newsletter. If you do, bear in mind that division breaks cancel running heads. The place to enter the running heads for your newsletter is right after the division break that separates the single- and multiple-column text on page 1. Putting the running heads there may look unattractive and peculiar on the screen (see fig. 19.9), but don't worry—they will not print there.

For more information on running heads, see Chapter 5, "Word 5 Formatting Strategies: Page Formatting."

Forcing a Column Break

Just as you can force a page break by pressing Ctrl-Shift-Enter, so too can you force a column break by pressing Alt-Ctrl-Enter. To force a column break, place the cursor where you want the column break to occur and use this command. Word will move the next paragraph to the top of the next column, leaving white space if necessary.

This command, new to Word 5, is a significant addition to your keyboard arsenal. Without it, you would have to create a column break by entering a division break, thereby canceling all your running heads.

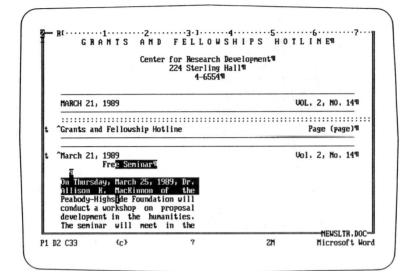

Fig. 19.9.

Running heads positioned after the division break.

Adding Vertical Lines to Multiple-Column Text

The opening figure of this chapter shows a newsletter with vertical lines separating and enclosing the columns. You can duplicate this effect in the following way:

1. Select all the multiple-column text paragraphs, headings, and blank lines (see fig. 19.10). Use any of the extend-selection techniques to highlight any text or blank lines within the multiple-column region.

2. Choose the **Format Border** command. When the menu appears, choose **Lines** in the **type** command field, **Yes** in the **right** field, and **Yes** in the **left** field (see fig. 19.11).

3. Choose the **Format Division Layout** command. Type *0* (zero) in the **space between columns** field (see fig. 19.12). This choice forces the borders of the two contiguous columns to overlap.

When you carry out the command, the columns will appear somewhat wider, and the borders will appear on the screen (see fig. 19.13).

Fig. 19.10.

Selecting all the multiple-column text.

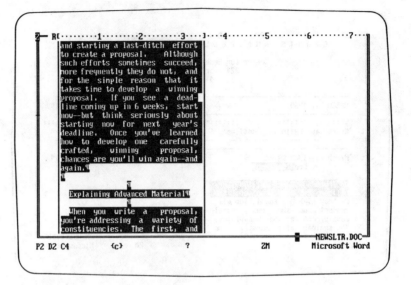

Fig. 19.11.

Using the Format Border command.

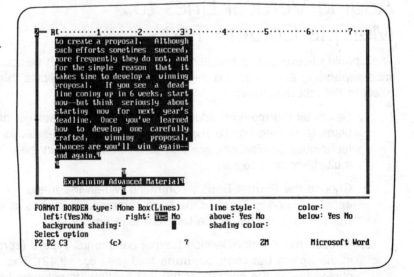

 Caution: Do not insert blank lines using the **space before** and **space after** fields of the Format Paragraph command if you want to add vertical lines this way. Word will not print the left and right borders adjacent to such blank lines. Add blank lines using the Enter key.

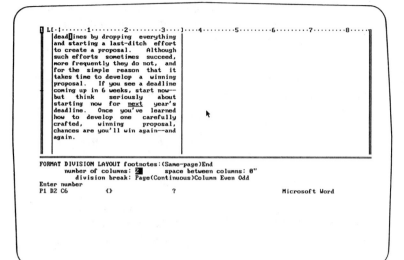

Fig. 19.12.

Using the Format Division Layout command.

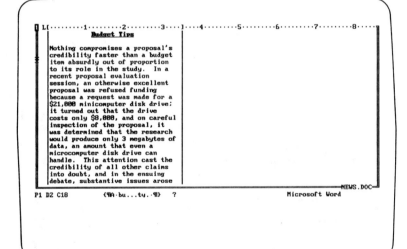

Fig. 19.13.

Text columns after adding left and right borders (normal display mode).

Using Format pOsition
To Anchor Text

One of the most exciting Word 5 features for newsletters is the Format pOsition command, which "anchors" a frame—a graphic or a paragraph of text—at a location you specify. Text floats around the anchored frame automatically when you print your document. You simply specify where you want the frame to appear, and Word does the rest.

This technique is very useful for adding sidebars, such as the one in figure 19.1, that highlight important passages of text in your document.

To add a sidebar to a newsletter, do the following:

1. Type the sidebar text in its own paragraph within the page on which you want the sidebar to appear (see fig. 19.14).

2. Add lines or borders if you want (see fig. 19.15).

3. Choose the **F**ormat p**O**sition command. Choose positions in the **horizontal** and **vertical frame placement** fields. Be sure to specify a frame width in the **frame width** field (see fig. 19.16).

   For more information on the Format pOsition command fields, see Chapter 18, "Integrating Text and Graphics."

4. Carry out the command.

Before printing, check the sidebar's position with **P**rint pre**V**iew (see fig. 19.17).

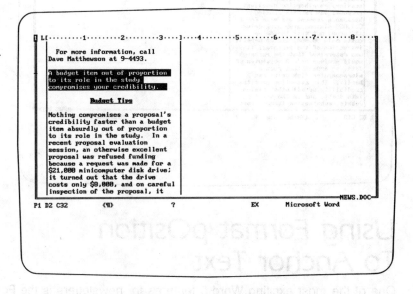

Fig. 19.14.

Typing the sidebar text.

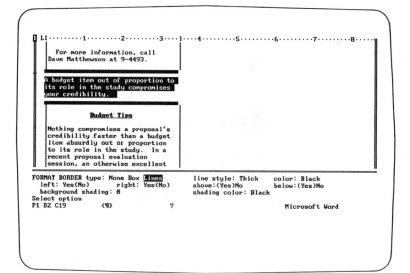

Fig. 19.15.

Adding thick lines above and below the sidebar text.

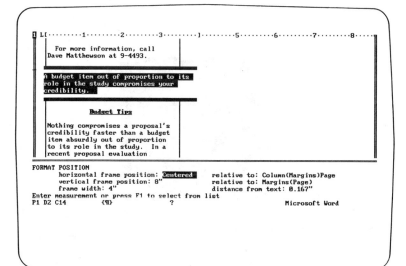

Fig. 19.16.

Using the Format pOsition command.

Adding Graphics to Newsletters

Using the techniques discussed in Chapter 18, "Integrating Text and Graphics," you easily can add graphics to your newsletters. Anchor the graphic images with the Format pOsition command so that text flows around the picture (see fig. 19.18).

Fig. 19.17.

Checking the sidebar's position with Print preView.

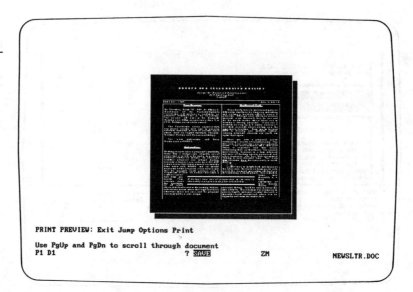

Fig. 19.18.

Print preView of graphic inserted into newsletter and anchored at center of page.

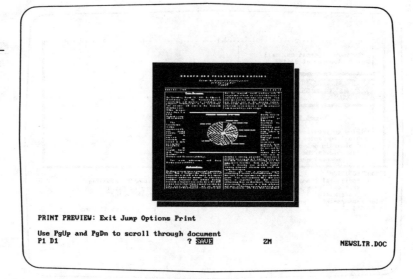

Chapter Summary

The significant Word 5 revisions of the program's multiple-column capabilities make it much easier to create newsletters. With Word 5, you can mix single- and multiple-column text on the screen, and you easily can enter column breaks without starting a new division (and thus canceling all your running heads). The Format pOsition command, moreover, provides flexible tools for anchoring text and graphics on the page so that text floats around them automatically. Using these techniques, you can produce handsome, professional-looking newsletters quickly and easily.

With this chapter, you have come to the end of Part III, "Desktop Publishing with Microsoft Word." In the next section of this book, you will learn how to put two of Word 5's most powerful features, style sheets and macros, to work for you. And even if you're a beginner in personal computing, word processing, and Word, you will find that the material is comprehensible—and useful. Indeed, if you aren't putting style sheets and macros to work, you haven't come close to seeing Word's maximum potential to increase your productivity at the keyboard.

IV

Word 5's
Style Sheets
and Macros

Includes

Using Style Sheets
Creating and Using Word 5 Macros

20

Using Style Sheets

For most Word users, style sheets are unknown territory, something like the northern reaches of Greenland. But Word offers plenty of reasons to put style sheets on more familiar ground. As you quickly discover, style-sheet formatting is easy to grasp, easy to use, and virtually a precondition for using Word at the highest levels of productivity and efficiency. As you see in this chapter, you can modify Word's default style sheet, NORMAL.STY, to cure the deficiencies in Word's default formats. What's more, you can create your own custom Alt-key formatting commands to enter several formatting commands in one keystroke! If you do not use style sheets now, you should: you're not only missing out on some of Word's most elegant and impressive features, you're also depriving yourself of a technique that can save you no end of time and formatting aggravation.

Many users consider style sheets an "advanced" feature of Word and shy away from them. Part of the problem is Microsoft's documentation; the subject inspires some especially murky prose. But the underlying concepts are really quite simple—you already possess 90 percent of the knowledge you need to use style sheets effectively. When you create style sheets, you make choices from menus, and you're already an expert on that subject. Some of the menus used in creating style sheets are old friends, such as the Format Character and Format Paragraph menus in the Gallery, which is Word's style-sheet workshop.

The concept of style-sheet formatting is really quite simple. As you already know, you use Alt-key codes (such as Alt-B or Alt-J) to define character and paragraph formats in your document. You can modify these key codes so that they enter different formats, or several formats at once, and you can add new key codes. With style sheets, in short, you can reconfigure Word's formatting keys to suit your writing needs precisely.

Why bother creating your own key codes? What's wrong with the Alt-key codes Microsoft provides? These codes are useful, but they are "plain vanilla" key codes intended to appeal to the "average" user. They're aimed, therefore, at the lowest common denominator, and as you have doubtlessly discovered, you must frequently modify them or add additional formats after using them.

To illustrate the deficiencies of the default formatting key codes, consider this example. I start a proposal by modifying the default paragraph format to include double-line spacing, right-margin justification, and a 0.5-inch first-line indent. Also, I use the Format Character command to override the default character font so that my paragraphs print in the Times Roman font. To enter all these formats, I must press Alt-J, Alt-2, Alt-F, Esc **F**ormat **C**haracter (Tab, Tab, Tab...)—that's too many keystrokes. What a hassle! And there's more to come. Suppose I use Alt-Q to indent a quotation. When I press Alt-P to resume the normal paragraph format, I'm back to the lowest common denominator again—flush left, single spacing. And if I press Alt-space bar to cancel a character emphasis, I'm back to the Courier font. I have to enter all the formatting commands over again or scroll up and copy the previous formats.

In the midst of tedious formatting operations of this sort, any user is likely to start thinking, with a gleam in the eye, "What if I had my own, private Alt-P, an Alt-P that would enter precisely the formats I want? An Alt-P that would simultaneously enter double-spacing, right-margin justification, a 0.5-inch first-line indent, and Times Roman character formatting?"

If you have ever wanted Alt-key formatting codes of your very own, this is the place to learn how to do it. That's what style sheets are all about. Other reasons exist, too, for creating style sheets. As you learn in this chapter, style sheets provide the best way to overcome the deficiencies of many of Word's default formats. If you don't like the way Word prints footnote reference marks for example, or if you want page numbers to print at the bottom of the page automatically in every document you create, style sheets provide the key. What's more, style sheets are essential if you use your printer's multiple-font capabilities. Style sheets can even help you get maximum performance from Word's outlining capabilities!

This chapter shows you, using a series of tutorials, how to make style sheets work for you. It covers the following:

❏ Modifying Word's default style sheet, NORMAL.STY, so that Word automatically uses your preferences in formatting page numbers, footnote reference marks, and other styles

❏ Creating and defining new standard paragraph and division formats, which Word can use automatically every time you start the program

❏ Modifying the default Alt-key formatting commands so that they work precisely the way you want

❏ Creating and defining new key codes for special formatting jobs

❏ Creating style-sheet entries automatically from formats already inserted in your documents

❏ Formatting document heading styles so that your headings automatically appear at the correct level as headings in the outline mode

❏ Editing style sheets and using style sheets to maximum advantage on hard disk systems

❏ Using style sheets to create a new standard character format

❏ Coping with command style sheet errors

A word of encouragement for beginners: there isn't a thing in this chapter that you cannot handle, even as a novice in personal computing. This chapter is a series of tutorials, each designed to put you in complete control of Word's style-sheet capabilities. The results place you among those who know how to obtain peak performance from this wonderful program.

Experienced personal computer users, especially spreadsheet mavens, see the similarity between style sheets and keyboard macros, which define the keyboard so that several commands can be entered at once. After all, style sheets define Alt-key formatting commands, and keyboard macros define the keyboard to enter several commands with one keystroke. As you see in Chapter 21, Word 5 includes one of the niftiest keyboard macro utilities ever seen in a personal computer program; you can use it, if you want, to create keyboard formatting commands. But you quickly discover that style-sheet key codes are significantly faster than macros. Style-sheet key codes are stored in memory; macros are (unfortunately) read from disk. So use style sheets to define super-fast key codes for formatting purposes.

About Style Sheets

Before beginning, you may profit from understanding a few of the following basic facts about style sheets.

❑ You have already used a style sheet. ("What? Me? Using a style sheet?") Yes, you have. The style sheet is called NORMAL.STY and contains the default Alt-key formatting codes. When you start Word, it looks for a file called NORMAL.STY in the default directory. If Word finds the file, the program loads the file and applies it to the displayed document.

❑ You can modify NORMAL.STY, and if you want, you can add new Alt-key formatting codes to it. Thanks to a wonderful new Word 5 feature, you don't lose the default NORMAL.STY key codes when you modify NORMAL.STY. In previous versions of Word, when you modified NORMAL.STY, all the default key codes went bye-bye, occasioning no small frustration, foul language, and wasted time. Although you could still use the key codes if you pressed X before the letter, as in Alt-XB, this unfortunate fact really raised the cost of creating custom style sheets. If you did create your own style sheets, you had to manually insert the character emphases (boldface, italic, and underlining) and other default key codes desired. A tedious business at best. Because NORMAL.STY is easy to modify now, you easily can change Word's formatting defaults to suit your needs.

❑ A style sheet isn't an ordinary Word file. It's a special file, always stored with the extension STY, that you cannot edit like a normal document. To create and edit style sheets, use the Gallery command.

❑ Most of a style sheet is concerned with Alt-key codes. But you should grasp one other important and wonderful feature of style-sheet formatting. With a style sheet, you can define Word's automatic styles, the styles the program uses automatically (without your having to use an Alt-key command).

These styles include footnote references, footnote text, page numbers, the standard division format, the standard paragraph format, headings, index and table of contents entries, and more. One of the best reasons for creating a style sheet is to define these formats so that they print exactly the way you want—without your having to do anything except attach the style sheet to your document.

With the new Version 5 features, the best way to take advantage of style sheets is to modify NORMAL.STY. To be sure, you can use the techniques discussed in this chapter to create style sheets with other file names—style sheets you can use for special-purpose applications, such as creating a report in a little-used format. For most users, however, creating a modified version of NORMAL.STY is the royal road to style-sheet mastery—and to complete customization of Word so that it fits your needs. By customizing NORMAL.STY, you can define the automatic styles the way you want them, create new standard paragraph and division formats, modify existing key codes, and perhaps add a new key code or two; and all these changes become the new formatting defaults for the program! This chapter begins, therefore, with a tutorial that shows you how to modify NORMAL.STY.

Modifying NORMAL.STY

In the tutorial that follows, you learn how to modify Word's default formats so that they precisely suit your needs. You begin by defining Word's automatic styles, such as footnote reference marks and page numbers, so that they print the way you want.

Next, you create new standard formats for paragraphs and divisions. Then, you modify existing key codes and, if you want, add new key codes of your own. Finally, you learn how to copy complex formats to your style sheet using the Format Stylesheet Record command. The result is a default style sheet that truly makes Word your own professional productivity tool.

In case you're worried about how permanent these changes are, relax. When you modify NORMAL.STY, you save the style sheet to disk. As long as this file is in the default directory, Word uses it. But if you decide not to use your customized version of NORMAL.STY, just move it to another directory, erase it, or change it to a different file name. The old defaults will be in effect the next time you start the program. Word re-creates the original NORMAL.STY if it can't find a file by that name.

Defining Automatic Styles

As you have already learned, style sheets store information that tells Word what to do when you use an Alt-key formatting command. But style sheets also store information about Word's automatic styles, such as the styles for footnote reference marks, page numbers, standard paragraphs, running heads, and more. You don't use an Alt-key command to enter these styles; Word applies them automatically. In the default version of NORMAL.STY, for instance, footnote reference marks are defined as normal characters, positioned flush with the baseline of the text. You can deliberately format each occurrence with the Format Character command—or better, modify NORMAL.STY to apply superscripting automatically. The following tutorial teaches you how to do that.

1. Start Word with a new, blank document. Then choose the **G**allery command.

   When the Gallery screen appears (see fig. 20.1), you're in a special section of the Word program devoted to creating, editing, and saving style sheets. The window you see isn't a document window. You cannot enter text into it directly. You must use commands to insert, edit, or delete style-sheet entries.

Fig. 20.1.

The Gallery menu and style sheet window.

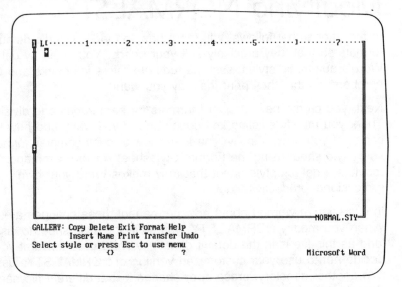

```
 L[········1········2········3········4········5········]········7····]

                                                      NORMAL.STY
GALLERY: Copy Delete Exit Format Help
         Insert Name Print Transfer Undo
Select style or press Esc to use menu
                    {}              ?              Microsoft Word
```

2. Choose the Insert command. When the Insert menu appears, leave the **key code** field blank, and choose Character from the **usage** field. Next, place the cursor in the **variant** field and press F1. When the menu appears, choose **Footnote ref**.

You leave the **key code** field blank because you are defining an automatic style. You need not press an Alt-key code to apply the style; Word applies it automatically when you attach the style sheet to the document.

Finally, type *SUPERSCRIPTED REF MARK* in the **remarks** field. Check figure 20.2 to make sure that your choices are correct, and press Enter to carry out the command. You need not type the remark in capital letters, but it helps to make your style sheet more readable. If you want, you can leave this field blank or type some other remark.

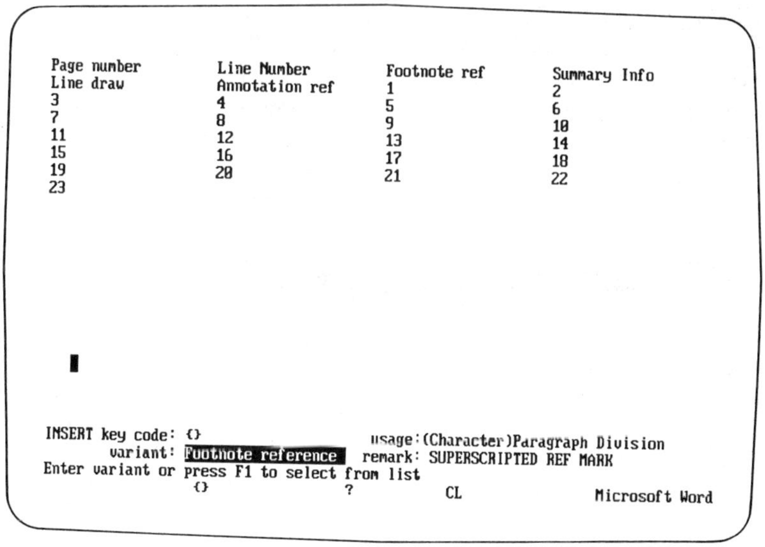

```
Page number      Line Number      Footnote ref     Summary Info
Line draw        Annotation ref   1                2
3                4                5                6
7                8                9                10
11               12               13               14
15               16               17               18
19               20               21               22
23




▌



INSERT key code: {}                        usage:(Character)Paragraph Division
        variant: Footnote reference        remark: SUPERSCRIPTED REF MARK
Enter variant or press F1 to select from list
             {}                  ?         CL          Microsoft Word
```

Fig. 20.2.

Inserting an entry to format footnote reference marks automatically.

The Insert command in the Gallery menu, as you have just seen, doesn't function like the Insert command in the Edit command menu. The Gallery Insert command creates style-sheet entries. After you use Gallery Insert, Word inserts an entry into the style sheet (see fig. 20.3). The entry you just made, however, is not formatted yet—it doesn't include any formatting instructions. After inserting an entry with Insert, you must use the Format command to format the entry.

Fig. 20.3.

An unformatted style sheet entry.

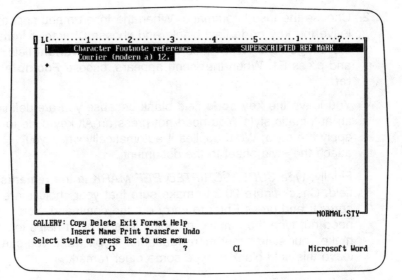

3. Choose the **G**allery **F**ormat command (the Format Character menu comes up automatically). Choose the **S**uperscript option in the **position** field. Press Enter to carry out the command. Word adds the formatting instructions you chose to the entry (see fig. 20.4).

Fig. 20.4.

A style sheet entry with formatting instructions.

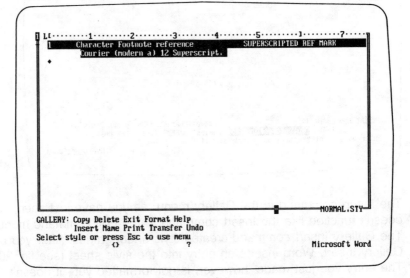

Why wait any longer to see the results of your work? The next step explains how to do a test.

4. Choose the **E**xit command to leave the Gallery. Type some text on the blank document screen and choose **F**ormat **F**ootnote to create a footnote. Type some footnote text and print your document. (If you use graphics mode, you can see the superscript right on the screen.)

Congratulations! You have just changed what many users find one of Word's most irritating default formats. If you save this style sheet using the **T**ransfer **S**ave command in the Gallery menu, the new defaults are in effect every time you use Word.

Continue the tutorial by creating a new default paragraph format for footnote text.

5. Choose the **G**allery command to return to the style sheet. Then choose Insert again, and leave the **key code** field blank. Choose **P**aragraph from the **usage** field. Then place the cursor in the **variant** field and press F1. When the menu appears, choose **footnote**. Finally, type *FOOTNOTE TEXT* in the **remarks** field. Check your choices against figure 20.5 and press Enter to carry out the command.

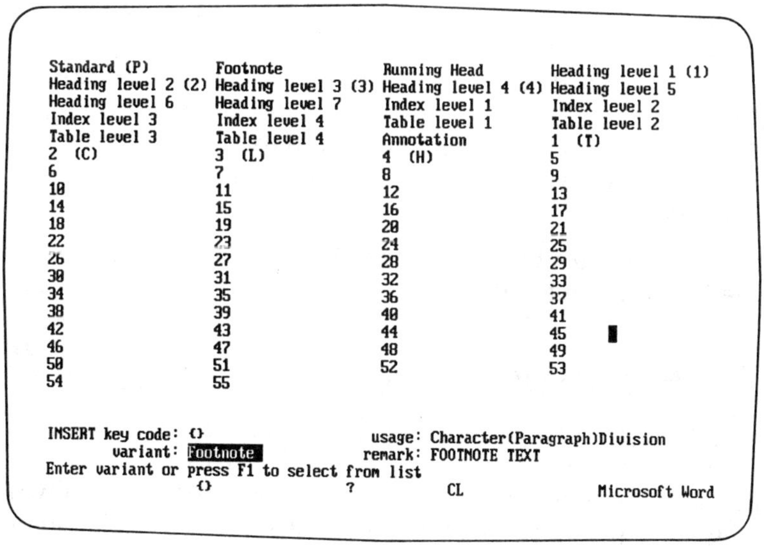

```
Standard (P)        Footnote         Running Head       Heading level 1 (1)
Heading level 2 (2) Heading level 3 (3) Heading level 4 (4) Heading level 5
Heading level 6     Heading level 7  Index level 1      Index level 2
Index level 3       Index level 4    Table level 1      Table level 2
Table level 3       Table level 4    Annotation         1  (T)
2  (C)              3  (L)           4  (H)             5
6                   7                8                  9
10                  11               12                 13
14                  15               16                 17
18                  19               20                 21
22                  23               24                 25
26                  27               28                 29
30                  31               32                 33
34                  35               36                 37
38                  39               40                 41
42                  43               44                 45   ▮
46                  47               48                 49
50                  51               52                 53
54                  55


INSERT key code: {}                    usage: Character(Paragraph)Division
         variant: Footnote             remark: FOOTNOTE TEXT
Enter variant or press F1 to select from list
                  {}             ?           CL          Microsoft Word
```

Fig. 20.5.

Inserting an entry to format footnote text automatically.

6. Choose the **F**ormat **P**aragraph command from the Gallery menu. When the menu appears, choose **J**ustified from the **alignment** field and type *1 li* in the **space before** field. Press Enter to carry out the command. Word adds the formatting instructions you specified to the entry (see fig. 20.6).

Fig. 20.6.

Another formatted entry.

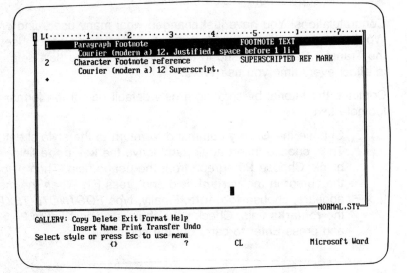

7. Save the modified style sheet by using the Gallery menu's **T**ransfer **S**ave command. Use Word's proposed response (NORMAL.STY) for the file name, and press Enter. If you don't save the style sheet now, you'll be prompted to do so when you choose the **Q**uit command.

Test the entry as you did before. (Choose **E**xit to leave the Gallery and inspect the formatting of the footnote text you just entered.) Neat, no?

A Brief Excursus: Usages and Variants

Many would-be style sheet artists are panicked into retreat by the murky terms *usage* and *variant* that appear in the Gallery Insert command menu. Frankly, these terms—like Gallery itself—are not well chosen; the terms poorly describe their functions. This digression from the tutorial is intended to make sure that you grasp what these terms mean.

As you have already learned by doing, every style-sheet entry must fall into one of three usage categories—that is, you can create a character-format entry, a paragraph-format entry, or a division-format entry. Think of the term *usage* as synonymous with *type of format*, and you are on the right track. The first entry you created was a character format (footnote reference mark); the second one was a paragraph format (footnote text). You also can create division formats with the division usage.

Every entry must have its own unique variant, which is either numbered or has a name (like footnote ref or footnote). The named variants are automatic styles. The numbered ones are for you to define. Use the numbered variants to create your own Alt-key formatting commands or to modify existing ones. You select the variants from a list displayed when you position the cursor in the **variant** field and press F1. A different list appears for each of the three usages available.

One more point before continuing: When you create a character variant, you can format it using only character styles. (That's why the Format Character menu comes up automatically when you choose Gallery Format.) When you create a division variant, you can format it using only division styles. (When you choose Gallery Format after selecting a division usage, you go directly to the Format Division menu.) When you create a paragraph variant, however, you can use character, tab, and border styles as well as paragraph styles. For this reason, you can create a single key code to enter a dozen or more formatting commands simultaneously! Later in this chapter, for instance, you learn how to create a key code (Alt-L) that, with one keystroke, enters a hanging indentation with the first line flush to the left margin, a flush-left tab at 3.0 inches, second and subsequent line indents at 3.0 inches, right-margin justification, and Helvetica 10 character formatting.

One of the reasons that style-sheet formatting is virtually indispensable for anyone working with multiple fonts is that you can combine character and paragraph formatting in one style-sheet entry. As you see in "Style Sheets and Laser Printers" later in this chapter, you can set up standard and other paragraph formats to enter the fonts you want. You can set up headings that print in 14-point Helvetica bold, standard paragraphs that print in 10-point Times Roman, and footnotes that print in 8-point Times Roman. All you have to do is add character formats to the paragraph usages you create.

In the next part of the tutorial, you learn how to create new standard paragraph and division formats, which are also automatic styles. Before going on, however, take a look at table 20.1, which lists all the automatic styles (sorted by usage). You may want to modify some of them now, while the technique is still fresh in your mind. Be sure to save the new entries using the Gallery menu's Transfer Save command.

Table 20.1
Word 5's Automatic Styles

Variant	Affects
Character Usages	
Annotation ref	Character format for annotation reference mark
Footnote ref	Character format for footnote reference mark
Line draw	Character format for line draw character in Cursor Line Draw mode
Line number	Character format for line numbers inserted with Format Division line-Numbers
Page number	Character format for page numbers inserted by Format Division Page-numbers
Summary info	Character format for summary sheets
Paragraph Usages	
Annotation	Paragraph format for annotations
Footnote	Paragraph format for footnote or endnote text
Heading level 1–7	Paragraph format for outline and document headings
Index level 1–4	Paragraph format for index entries
Running head	Paragraph format for running heads
Standard	Standard (default) paragraph format (entered with Alt-P)

Table 20.1 — Continued

Variant	Affects
Table level 1–4	Paragraph format for table of contents entries
Division Usages	
Standard	Standard (default) division formats, including margins, page layout, footnote location, and page numbers

Creating New Standard Paragraph and Division Formats

If you aren't happy with the default paragraph and division formats, read on. You can create new defaults to be available every time you use the program. In this tutorial, you further modify the NORMAL.STY style sheet created in the preceding section.

1. Start Word with a new, blank document and choose the **G**allery command.

2. Choose **I**nsert. When the command menu appears, press P in the **key code** field. Choose **P**aragraph in the **usage** field. Position the cursor in the **variant** field, press F1, and choose **S**tandard from the list. Type *STANDARD PARAGRAPH* in the **remark** field. Press Enter to carry out the command.

3. Choose the **G**allery **F**ormat **P**aragraph command. When the command menu appears, specify justified alignment, double-line spacing, and 0.5-inch first-line indentation. Then press Enter to carry out the command.

4. Choose the **G**allery **I**nsert command. When the command menu appears, leave the **key code** field blank. Choose **D**ivision in the **usage** field. Position the cursor in the **variant** field, press F1, and choose **S**tandard from the list. Type *STANDARD DIVISION* in the **remark** field and press Enter to carry out the command.

5. Choose the **G**allery **F**ormat command. When the Format Division menu appears, choose **M**argins. Type *1.0″* in the **left** and **right** fields and press Enter to carry out the command. Then use the **G**allery **F**ormat **D**ivision command again and choose the **P**age-numbers option. Choose **Y**es to turn on page numbering, type *10.5″* in the **From top** field, and *4.5″* in the **from left** field. Press Enter to carry out the command.

Your style sheet should look like the one in figure 20.7.

Fig. 20.7.

Style sheet with
new standard
paragraph and
division formats.

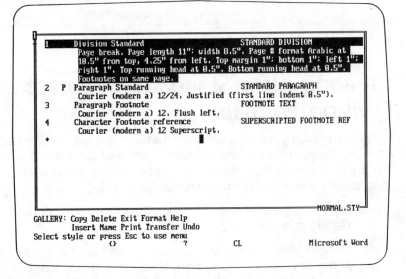

Fig. 20.7.

Style sheet with new standard paragraph and division formats.

In figure 20.7, note that double-line spacing is indicated with the characters *12/24*. These figures mean "12-point font with a line height of 24 points."

Modifying Existing Key Codes

Because the new style sheet you created uses right-justified margins as its default, you should modify some of the existing key codes to include right-margin justification. This tutorial modifies existing key codes using an assembly-line approach. As you follow the steps, you learn a great deal about how style sheets work.

1. Choose the **I**nsert command. Press N in the **key code** field, choose the **P**aragraph usage, tab over the **variant** field, and type *INDENTED PARAGRAPH* in the **remark** field. Then press Enter to carry out the command.

Note that when you tab over the **variant** field, Word selects an unoccupied number automatically. Each entry that doesn't use an automatic style must have its own unique variant number.

2. Use the Insert command to create the following key codes. Fill out the command fields as indicated:

> **key code:** T
> **usage:** Paragraph
> **variant:** (tab over this field)
> **remark:** HANGING INDENT

> **key code:** Q
> **usage:** Paragraph
> **variant:** (tab over this field)
> **remark:** QUOTATION

3. Select all the key codes you just inserted. Use any of the extended-selection techniques you have learned to select the three entries.

4. Press Alt-P to cancel any extraneous formatting that may have crept into these entries.

Sometimes Word adds the standard paragraph format to new entries you create, and sometimes it doesn't. If you have changed the standard paragraph format, you may get formats you don't want in these entries, such as 0.5-inch first-line indentation. Pressing Alt-P cancels any special paragraph formats that may have been assigned to these entries. (This technique works, incidentally, even if you have redefined Alt-P with a new standard paragraph format.)

5. Press Alt-2 to double-space all three entries.

6. Press Alt-J to justify all three entries. Your entries should look like the ones in figure 20.8.

7. Now select the Q entry you just created and press Alt-Q. You just added the default Alt-Q formats to your entry. Alt-Q is the default keyboard shortcut for a quotation format.

8. Select the T entry you just created and press Alt-T to add the default Alt-T formats. Alt-T is the default keyboard shortcut for a hanging-indent format.

Fig. 20.8.

Three entries
formatted in
assembly-line
fashion.

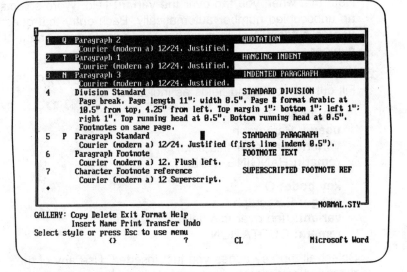

9. Select the N entry you just created and press Alt-N to add
   the default Alt-N formats. Alt-N is the default keyboard
   shortcut for a paragraph indented from the left margin.
   Compare your entries to figure 20.9.

10. Save the modified style sheet using the Gallery menu
    Transfer **S**ave command. Use Word's proposed response
    (NORMAL.STY) for the file name.

Fig. 20.9.

The completed
entries.

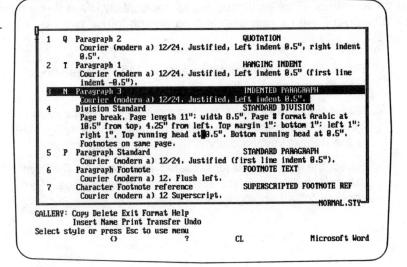

You have just learned how to modify existing Alt-key codes by using a true-blue, 14-karat, undocumented feature of Word. Just remember, you read it here first!

Defining New Key Codes

This section explains how to add a new custom key code to the style sheet you have been modifying. This key code creates a list format suitable for defining words or explaining product features. The first line of the format is to be flush left with the margin and include a flush-left tab at 3.0 inches. Turnover lines (second and subsequent lines) are to be indented 3.0 inches. All text is to be double-spaced and justified. This procedure steps you through the creation of such a key code.

1. In the NORMAL.STY style sheet modified in the preceding tutorials, choose the **G**allery menu **I**nsert command.

2. Press L in the **key code** field, choose **P**aragraph in the **usage** field, tab over the **variant** field, and type *LIST* in the **remark** field. Press Enter to carry out the command.

3. Press Alt-P to cancel any unwanted paragraph formats.

4. Choose the **G**allery menu **F**ormat **T**ab **S**et command and set a flush-left tab at 3.0 inches.

5. Choose the **G**allery menu **F**ormat **P**aragraph command. Choose justified alignment, type *2 li* in the **line spacing** field, type *3.0"* in the **left indent** field, and type *-3.0"* (minus 3.0") in the **first line** field. Then press Enter to carry out the command. Compare your entry with the one in figure 20.10.

6. If you like, you can add character formatting to this entry. Make sure that the entry is selected and then use the **F**ormat **C**haracter command. Choose a font and font size appropriate for your printer and press Enter to carry out the command.

Use the **P**rint **O**ptions command to name your printer before choosing a font. With many printers, moreover, you must make an entry in the **model** field of the Print Options menu before you can use fonts other than the printer's default character font. For more information on printers and fonts, refer to the section entitled "Creating a Standard Character Format" later in this chapter.

7. Save the style sheet using the **G**allery **T**ransfer **S**ave command.

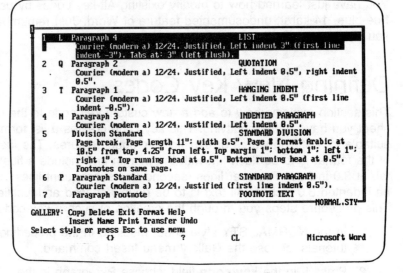

Fig. 20.10.

Adding a list
entry.

Modifying NORMAL.STY by Recording Styles

The Format Stylesheet Record command, much improved over its Version 4 counterpart, provides yet another way to create a style-sheet entry. This command is easy to use, provided you understand the components of a style-sheet entry (such as usage and variant). Following is a brief tutorial illustrating this technique.

1. In the edit mode (not the Gallery), use the **T**ransfer **C**lear **A**ll command to clear the screen.

2. Type a two-word or three-word heading and press Alt-C to center the paragraph.

3. Select the heading and make it boldface by pressing Alt-B.

4. Choose the **F**ormat **P**aragraph command. When the command menu appears, type *1 li* in the **space before** and **space after** fields. Choose **Y**es in the **keep follow** field. Then press Enter to carry out the command.

5. Choose **F**ormat **S**tylesheet **R**ecord. When the command menu appears, type *1* in the **key code** field, and choose **P**aragraph in the **usage** field. Position the cursor in the

variant field, press F1, and choose **Heading level** 1 from the list. Type *FIRST-LEVEL HEADING* in the **remark** field (as shown in fig. 20.11). Then press Enter to carry out the command.

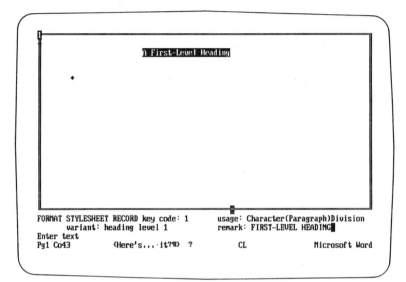

Fig. 20.11.

Using Format Stylesheet Record.

6. Choose the **G**allery command and look at the new key code you have created (see fig. 20.12).

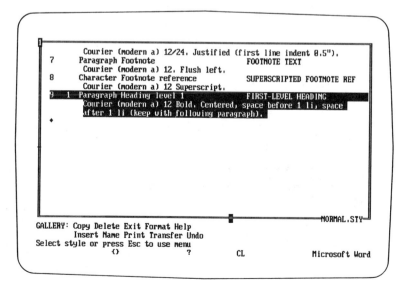

Fig. 20.12.

A recorded style sheet entry in the Gallery.

As you can see, this technique is convenient because it saves you the trouble of keying in the formatting commands twice if you decide to duplicate a document format as a style-sheet entry. You can create as many style-sheet entries as you want using this technique, and you need not record the style right after applying the formats.

The Style-Sheet–Outline Connection

This section describes an extremely nifty point about key-coding the headings in your document. In the last section's tutorial, you created a centered, boldfaced heading. When you selected a variant, you chose *Heading level 1*. This variant, and the other heading level variants listed when you press F1 from the **variant** field in Paragraph usage, have a most beguiling characteristic: any text formatted with a key code using a heading level variant automatically appears as an outline heading in the outline mode. Once you define the key code, it's automatic; you don't have to do another thing.

You can try this yourself by using the Alt-1 key code you created in the last section and then switching to the outline view (press Shift-F2). Presto! Your heading is a Level 1 heading in outline view (see fig. 20.13).

Fig. 20.13.

Heading key code in outline view.

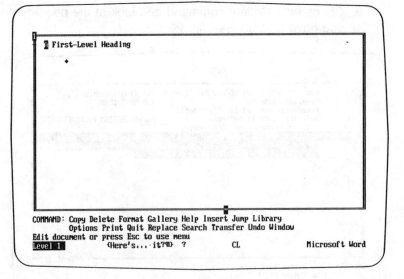

Try creating additional key codes (Alt-2, Alt-3, and so on) for second-level and third-level document and outline headings. Be sure to format each heading with space above and below (don't use paragraph returns for extra space), and remember to choose **Yes** in the **keep follow** field of the Format Paragraph menu (so that a heading is never positioned at the bottom of the page with no text under it).

Welcome to the ultimate in word processing!

More Style Sheet Facts

This isn't the place for everything there is to say about style-sheet formatting, but the following sections describe a few facts that you may find helpful when working with style sheets.

About Key Codes

As you have learned, you can create one-letter or two-letter key codes. If you use two-letter key codes for all style-sheet entries, you can create up to 125 distinct key codes. Wonderful, huh? Actually, it isn't. You are better off keeping your key codes to the minimum. You also should do your best to emulate the NORMAL.STY key codes as much as you can. Several reasons follow for this advice, and all of them are important.

❏ You're used to the NORMAL.STY key codes. Why compound the difficulties of learning and using Word by creating dozens of obscure commands, the meaning and function of which you will quickly forget? The key-code philosophy underlying this chapter is that it is much better to build on the NORMAL.STY key codes, modifying existing ones, and adding just a few of your own when necessary.

❏ Entering a one-letter key code is easier and faster than entering a two-letter key code.

❏ You will find it much easier to use Word if you develop a limited standard set of one-letter key codes used in every style sheet you create. That way, no matter which style sheet you use, you get bold when you press Alt-B, a hanging indentation when you press Alt-T, and a quotation environment when you press Alt-Q.

❑ If you use a limited standard set of key codes for every style sheet, you can take advantage of a unique and nifty feature: reformatting a document just by attaching a new style sheet. Suppose that I create a style sheet in which all the paragraph entries are formatted with double-line spacing and the Helvetica font. Then I create another version of the style sheet with the same entries and the same key codes, but the entries are formatted with single-spacing and the Times Roman font. First, I create the document and print it with double-spaced, Helvetica formats. Then, I use the Format Stylesheet Attach command to attach the other style sheet. Presto! With just one command, the whole document is completely reformatted.

This advice runs against the grain of most other books on Word's style sheets, which take delight in presenting dozens of pages of obscure style-sheet entries with dozens of two-letter key codes. I bet the people who dream up these things don't actually use them! In my estimation, the most advanced style sheet is the one that's easiest to use and makes sense in terms of knowledge you already possess.

To be sure, you can't create more than 36 one-letter (or one-number) key codes; and to keep them mnemonic, you may want to create some two-letter codes. If you do create two-letter key codes, you need to know about an important limitation on your freedom in choosing codes. Once you use a letter in a one-letter code, you cannot use it again as the first letter of a two-letter code. So if you create a code called Alt-Z, you cannot later create a code called Alt-ZA in the same style sheet. If you try, the message Key codes conflict appears. Label the code differently, beginning with a letter or number you haven't already used.

When you create a style-sheet entry using one of the NORMAL.STY key codes, your entry overrides the old NORMAL.STY key code. If you modify Alt-C, for example, Word uses your definition for Alt-C, not the default one. However, you can still access the old, default Alt-C. Just press X before the letter (press Alt-XC).

Note: In previous versions of Word, you had to press Alt-X to access any NORMAL.STY key code after attaching a style sheet. In Word 5, that is no longer true. Press Alt-X only if you have created a style-sheet entry with a key code conflicting with a NORMAL.STY key code.

Don't create key codes starting with X. If you do, you cannot access the old default key codes of NORMAL.STY by using the technique just described.

To summarize, keep your key codes simple. Use one-letter codes and build on the NORMAL.STY key-code nomenclature as much as possible. Develop a standard list of key codes and use them in every style sheet you create so that you can use the same commands no matter which style sheet you attach to a document.

Using the Style Bar

A nifty option in the Options menu displays the *style bar*, a column on the left side of the screen that automatically displays the key code of the paragraph formats chosen.

To see which key code you have assigned to a paragraph, choose **Yes** in the **show style bar** field of the Options menu. If you have formatted a paragraph using direct formatting techniques (that is, using the Format command in the edit command menu), you see an asterisk in the style bar.

Canceling Style-Sheet Formatting

To cancel a format you have applied with a style-sheet key code, select the desired text. Then press Alt-P to cancel paragraph formatting or Alt-space bar to cancel character formatting.

Viewing a List of Valid Key Codes

If you have forgotten the key codes you created, you can see a list of them (and apply them) with the Format Stylesheet commands (choose the Character, Paragraph, or Division command corresponding to the three style-sheet usages). When the command menu appears, press F1 to display a list of the key codes. If you choose a key code and carry out the command, Word applies the style to the selected text.

Another way to see a list of valid key codes is to choose the Gallery command and look at your style sheet. To help you remember your key codes, you can print the style sheet with the Gallery Print command.

Editing and Managing Style Sheets

Once you have created a style sheet, you may find that you will need to edit the entries you've created. And it pays to understand clearly how to attach style sheets to your documents.

Changing the Key Code, Variant, or Remark

If you want to change the key code, the variant, or the remark of a style-sheet entry, use the Name command by following these steps:

1. Highlight the entry by using the arrow keys or click the mouse on the entry you want to change.

2. Choose the **N**ame command in the Gallery menu.

3. When the Name command menu appears, change the key code, the variant, or the remark you want to change.

4. Carry out the command by clicking the command name or pressing Enter.

Changing the Formatting of a Style Sheet Entry

After you create a style-sheet entry, you can change the formats you have applied to it. Use the following procedure to change the formats:

1. Highlight the entry by using the arrow keys or click the mouse on the entry you want to change.

2. Choose the **F**ormat command. If the entry employs a character or division usage, Word displays the Format Character or Format Division menu. If the entry employs a paragraph usage, you may assign character, paragraph, division, and tab formats.

3. Carry out the command by pressing Enter or clicking the command name.

Repeat the Format command to assign additional formats to the entry, if you want.

You can select more than one entry when you change formats. To select more than one entry, use one of the variable-unit selection techniques discussed in Chapter 3, "Word 5 Editing Strategies." To select the entire style sheet, press Shift-F10.

Recording Changes to a Style Sheet

While using a style-sheet entry in your document, you may find that it doesn't do the job correctly. Suppose, for instance, that you create a heading entry and assign the Alt-H1 key code to it. When you press Alt-H1 in your document, however, you find that the format leaves insufficient blank space below the heading you type. You can quickly alter the entry by recording the changes you make to the format while you're in the edit mode. You need not use the Gallery at all. To record these changes, follow these steps:

1. Type the text, and apply the style using the key code you have created or modified.

2. Choose the **F**ormat command in the edit command menu to add additional formats to the style.

3. Choose the **F**ormat **S**tylesheet **R**ecord command. When the command menu appears, type the same key code, choose the same usage and variant, and type the remark. (You can change the remark, if you want.)

4. Carry out the command by clicking the command name or pressing Enter. When the prompt appears warning you that you're about to overwrite the existing entry, press Y.

5. When you quit Word, press Y to save the changes you've made to the style sheet.

Managing Style Sheet Files

Like glossary files, style sheets are nondocument files; you can't load them as you load a Word document. Every style sheet has the extension .STY, and the only way you can view and edit a style sheet is to use the Gallery.

To manage style sheets effectively, you must understand the difference between *attaching* a style sheet to your document and *loading* a style sheet with the Glossary Transfer Load command. The following are the distinctions between attaching and loading style sheets:

❏ *Attaching a style sheet*. You attach a style sheet to the document by using the Format Stylesheet Attach command in the edit command menu. After you attach the style sheet, the style sheet's automatic style definitions apply to your document, and you can use the key codes you have defined or modified. You also can continue to use the default speed keys, unless you have created style-sheet entries that use the same key codes. If you create a format with the key code Alt-N, for example, the default Alt-N speed key will be overridden. (You still can use the default Alt-N speed key, however, by pressing Alt-X before pressing N.)

❏ *Loading a style sheet*. In the Gallery, you can use the Gallery command menu's Transfer Load command to load a style sheet you have created and saved to disk. After loading the style sheet and choosing Exit, you will be shown a prompt asking whether you want to attach the style sheet to the document currently displayed in the active window.

When you start Word, the program looks for a style sheet called NORMAL.STY in the default directory (the directory from which you started Word or, if you saved your options in the Transfer Options menu, the directory named in that command's **setup** field). If Word finds a style sheet called NORMAL.STY, the program automatically attaches it to all the documents you open or create. You can make use of these facts to set up an automatic formatting system for your hard disk (see "Style Sheet Tips for Hard Disk Users").

If Word cannot find a style sheet file called NORMAL.STY, it uses the default formats. (The default version of NORMAL.STY is part of the Word program, and if you haven't modified the style sheet, it doesn't appear on the list of files stored on disk).

Style Sheet Tips for Hard Disk Users

If you have a hard disk and have followed the suggestions in the appendix, you have created several subdirectories for your documents, such as \LETTERS, \MEMOS, and \REPORTS. Following is a wonderful trick that Word users use every day. You can create a special version of NORMAL.STY for each directory. For the \LETTERS directory, for instance, create a version of NORMAL.STY appropriate for letters (single-line spacing, no page numbers, no justification, and so on). When you want to write a letter, start Word from that directory. Word automatically loads the letter version of NORMAL.STY.

You can change default directories in the middle of a Word session by using the Transfer Options command. When you finish writing a letter and want to start a report, for example, choose the Transfer Options command and make the \REPORT directory the new default. Word then uses the report version of NORMAL.STY.

The Format Stylesheet Attach command gives you a way to create a permanent link between a document and a style sheet, no matter where the style sheet is stored. If you want to use the letter style sheet for a document in the \REPORT subdirectory, for instance, use Format Stylesheet Attach, type the full path name and file name of the style sheet (such as C:\LETTER\NORMAL.STY), and press Enter to carry out the command.

Creating a Standard Character Format

If your system is equipped with a laser printer and font cartridges, you doubtless have discovered—to your dismay and anger—that the default font (usually Courier) tends to pop up here and there in your work. The reason: Whenever you press Alt-space bar to cancel character emphasis, Word restores all the default character styles, including the default font for your printer. Happily, you can define a new standard character format by using style sheets. In fact, if you use multiple fonts in your document, style sheets aren't a luxury; they're virtually a necessity.

You can avoid the "unwanted font" problem by creating a style sheet with a standard paragraph (Alt-P) entry (for instructions, refer to "Creating Standard Paragraph and Division Formats" earlier in this chapter). Format this entry and the rest of the style sheet with the character font and size you want. Once you format the standard paragraph entry with a font and size, Word uses that entry as the new default for all formats in your document. The following procedure steps you through this process:

≥ **Caution:** If you have already selected fonts and font sizes for some of the entries, the following procedure will change them. Be sure to reformat these entries after completing this procedure.

---

1. Create a modified NORMAL.STY style sheet that includes an entry for the standard paragraph usage.

2. Press Shift-F10 to select the entire style sheet.

3. Press Alt-F8 to access the **font name** field of the Format Character menu. Type the font name you want or press F1 and select the font name from the list (see fig. 20.14).

Fig. 20.14.

Attaching a font and font size to an entire style sheet.

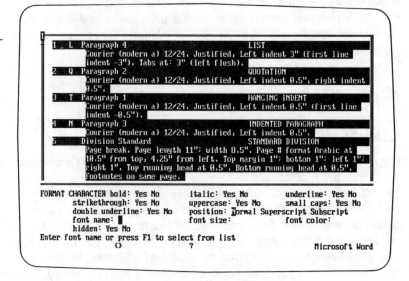

4. Press Enter to carry out the command.

Although you create a new default character format in this way, you still can override it for specific style-sheet entries. You can set up your style sheet, for example, so that Level 1 headings (Alt-1) print in 14-point Helvetica bold and Level 2 headings (Alt-2) print in 12-point Helvetica italic. Standard paragraph text can print in 10-point Times Roman and footnotes and the index appear in 8-point Times Roman. To assign fonts and font sizes to a style-sheet entry, select the entry. Then use the Gallery menu Format Character command.

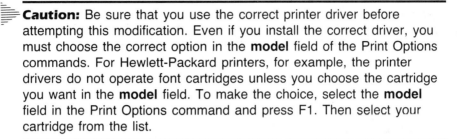

Caution: Be sure that you use the correct printer driver before attempting this modification. Even if you install the correct driver, you must choose the correct option in the **model** field of the Print Options commands. For Hewlett-Packard printers, for example, the printer drivers do not operate font cartridges unless you choose the cartridge you want in the **model** field. To make the choice, select the **model** field in the Print Options command and press F1. Then select your cartridge from the list.

Common Style Sheet Errors, Hazards, and Pitfalls

Following is a quick guide to some of the error messages you may see when creating and using style sheets.

Key code already defined. Enter a different key code. You are creating a style-sheet entry with Format Stylesheet Record or Gallery Insert, but you have already used this key code (or its first letter). Type a new key code.

Key code does not exist. See style sheet for valid key codes. You are formatting your document, but Word doesn't recognize the key code used. Check your style sheet and make sure that the style sheet is attached to your document with the Format Stylesheet Attach command.

Style already defined. You have just used the Insert command, but the variant you chose is already in use. Use the Insert command again and choose a different variant. To let Word choose a variant for you, just tab over the field.

Style already exists. Press Y to replace or Esc to cancel. When you use Format Stylesheet Record, you must choose a key code and variant different from those already used in the style sheet. Pick a new key code and variant.

When you move a document from one disk or computer to another, be sure to copy the document's style sheet, too. If you don't have the style sheet you used to format a document, you see an error message when you load the document and many formats are lost.

Use the **L**ibrary **D**ocument-retrieval **C**opy command to back up your work to floppy disks or to make copies of a file to take to another machine. This command copies all the necessary style sheets; all you have to do is choose **Yes** in the **copy style sheets** field.

Chapter Summary

Style sheets are the keys to mastery of Word 5 formatting. With the wonderful and sensible—if long overdue—modifications to style sheets in Version 5, most users are best off modifying NORMAL.STY so that it meets their needs. Begin by modifying some of the automatic styles, such as footnote reference marks or page numbers. Continue by creating new standard paragraph and division formats. Then modify existing NORMAL.STY Alt-key formatting commands and add a few new key codes of your own. When you want to add your own key codes, experiment with Format Stylesheet Record, which gives you a super-fast way to create style-sheet entries out of formats already created in your documents.

Now that you have learned one way to give several commands at once, I hope you are hooked on the idea of automating Word—especially because, in the next chapter, you learn how to get started with Word 5's most powerful feature: its elegant macro programming language. If the "programming" part sounds scary, don't worry. You already have done some programming as you worked through the tutorials in this chapter! (You just didn't realize it.) Anyone can learn to create Word 5 macros and put them to work. After all, why punch key after key when Word can do it for you?

21

Creating and Using
Word 5 Macros

Sometimes you find yourself pressing key after key to carry out a
series of commands with Word and wishing you had a little pet
robot to do the job for you. The wish becomes fervent if the operation
is one you repeat frequently. For example, although I'm a devoted
Word user, I miss the good old WordStar key that deletes the word
right (Ctrl-T). With Word, you have to press F8 to select it and Del to
do the job. And in the meantime, your fingers wander off the keyboard,
and you have to look down and place them correctly to resume typing.

Here's some good news. You already have your pet robot! It's Word
5's wonderful macro feature. A *macro* is a stored list of keystrokes that
you set in motion with just one keystroke. With Word 5's macros, you
can store the commands F8 (select word right) and Del (delete
selected text) in a macro assigned to Ctrl-T, that handy WordStar key.
Then whenever you want to delete the word right, you just press
Ctrl-T. Word enters the appropriate commands for you automatically!

You can create much more complicated macros than this one. In fact,
Word 5's macro capabilities amount to a superb programming
language for text-processing applications. (If you have some
experience with programming, you will find that Word 5 is one of the
most aesthetically pleasing macro languages ever seen in a personal
computer program. Word 5 is well structured, simple, elegant, and
powerful. But what else would you expect from the programming
language wizards at Microsoft?) You don't need a master's degree in
computer science, however, to use Word 5's macros. In fact, anyone
can create and run simple Word macros.

493

This chapter introduces Word 5's macro capabilities for beginning users. It's not intended to teach you *everything* about macro programming with Word. That subject is reserved for intermediate and advanced books on the program, such as *Microsoft Word 5 Tips, Tricks, and Traps: IBM Version*, by Bryan Pfaffenberger. But you can find in this chapter all the information you need in order to create and use simple Word macros. And if this chapter whets your taste for more, you can examine the advanced macro at the end of the chapter. The macro illustrates many of Word's advanced macro-programming features. Every line is explained in simple nontechnical language so that you can understand how the macro works. And you can copy and modify it for your own purposes.

In this chapter, you learn how to do the following:

❑ Use Word 5's supplied macros, the ones Microsoft wrote for you

❑ Turn on the record macro mode, which "captures" your keystrokes so that you can play them back at your command

❑ Expand the macros you have recorded so that they pause for user input and display messages on the screen

❑ Edit macros to fix mistakes

❑ Test macros, using the step mode and other helpful testing features

❑ Create a menu-based shell for Word that starts automatically every time you load the program and presents you with a choice of documents to load

Word 5's macro capabilities include a few important additions to earlier versions, but these features are beyond the scope of this introductory-level book.

You should be aware of one more point before you get started: Word stores macros as glossary entries, and you start macros by retrieving them from glossaries. Before using macros, then, you need to understand how to copy text to glossaries, how to load and save glossary files, and how to edit and delete glossary entries. If you haven't read Chapter 12 ("Using Glossaries and Bookmarks") yet, do so now.

Using the Supplied Macros

The easiest way to get started with Word's macros is to use one of the prewritten macros that come with the program. Table 21.1 presents a selective list of the macros included with Word 5 at this writing.

Table 21.1
Some of the Macros Supplied with Word 5

Macro Name	Description
annot_collect.mac	Compiles a formatted list of all the annotations included in a document (For information on annotations, see Chapter 15, "Enhancing Group Productivity: Using Annotations and Redlining.")
annot_merge.mac	Merges annotations from several different versions of a document into a single, authoritative version of the file
annot_remove.mac	Removes all the annotations from a document
authority_entry.mac	Formats a legal citation for inclusion in a table of authorities (For information on tables of authorities, see Chapter 14, "The Legal and Scholarly Word.")
authority_table.mac	Compiles a table of authorities from legal citations formatted with authority_entry.mac
chainprint.mac	Links documents for printing in a continuous chain with continuous pagination
character_test.mac	Prints all the characters available in a selected font
copy_text.mac	Copies text to a new location
freeze_style.mac	Converts all style sheet formats to direct formats (For more information on style sheets, see Chapter 20, "Using Style Sheets.")
index_entry.mac	Formats a concordance entry for indexing (For more information on indexing, see Chapter 13, "Creating Indexes and Tables of Contents.")

Table 21.1—Continued

Macro Name	Description
index.mac	Creates an index, using words drawn from a concordance file
memo_header.mac	Enters a memorandum header in a blank document
move_text.mac	Moves text to a new location
next_page.mac	Moves cursor to the beginning of the next page (document must be paginated)
prev_page.mac	Moves cursor to the beginning of the preceding page (document must be paginated)
save_selection.mac	Saves the selected text to a file you specify
side_by_side.mac	Formats text as side-by-side paragraphs (For information on side-by-side paragraphs, see Chapter 19, "Creating Multiple-Column Text and Newsletters.")
table.mac	Creates a tab format with the first tab positioned at a location you specify, then tabs at specified intervals across the screen
tabs.mac	Sets tabs from left to right and allows you to specify the type of tab
tabs2.mac	Prompts you for the number of columns you want in a table, the kind of tabs you want, and (if you select decimal tabs) the number of decimal places you need, and sets up a tab format for tables
3_delete.mac	Deletes text to glossaries (You can recover up to three deletions.)
3_undelete.mac	Recovers deletions from glossaries
toc_entry.mac	Formats table of contents entries (For more information on tables of contents, see Chapter 13, "Creating Indexes and Tables of Contents.")

To use one of the macros supplied with Word 5, use the following procedure:

1. Open a new, blank document that you can use to experiment with Word's supplied macros. (Don't experiment with a valuable file.)

2. Choose the **T**ransfer **G**lossary **L**oad command and load the glossary called MACRO.GLY.

   If you installed Word 5 on a hard disk with SETUP, MACRO.GLY is in Word's directory. If you're using a two-floppy system, insert Utilities Disk #2 into drive A and load the file from this disk.

3. Choose the **I**nsert command and press F1. When the list of glossary entries and macros appears, choose the macro you want from the list. Then press Enter or click the command name to carry out the command. Alternatively, use the macro's appropriate Ctrl-key code instead of using the Insert command.

As you will discover when you choose one of Word's supplied macros, they aren't like ordinary glossary entries. When you insert a glossary entry into your document, Word copies the text from the glossary to your file. When you insert a macro, however, Word doesn't insert it into your file. Instead, the program treats the macro's contents as if they were keyboard commands.

To stop a macro while it is running, just press Esc.

Recording Macros

Now that you have practiced with one or two of Word 5's supplied macros, you can see how convenient they are for performing complicated operations for you. You surely will think of many steps you take repeatedly that you would like to automate with macros. Although you can't include mouse actions in a Word macro, you can automate anything you can type at the keyboard, and that includes commands as well as text.

You can create macros in two different ways: by recording them or writing them. Of the two methods, recording macros is by far the easier. You use Word's record macro mode, which you can toggle on and off with Shift-F3. After you turn on the record macro mode, Word records all your keystrokes. When you turn off the mode, Word prompts you to name the recording and then copies it to the glossary. You can insert the recording from the glossary whenever you want, and Word plays back the recording you made.

Creating a Word-Deleting Macro

In the following tutorial, you learn how to create the Ctrl-T (delete word right) macro mentioned at the beginning of this chapter.

1. Start Word or choose **T**ransfer **C**lear **A**ll.

2. Type a sentence or two in the document so that you have some text with which to experiment. Place the cursor in the middle of a sentence, within a word.

3. Press Shift-F3 to start recording the macro. The code RM appears in the key status indicator, as shown in figure 21.1.

Fig. 21.1.

Using the record macro mode.

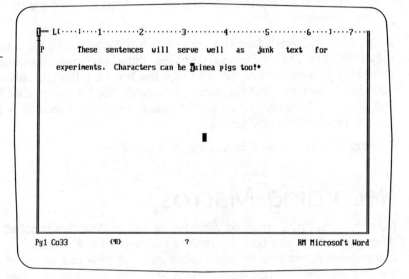

4. Press F8 twice.

5. Press Del.

6. Press Shift-F3 again to stop recording.

7. When the Copy menu appears, type

    wordright.mac^<ctrl t>

and carry out the command. If you made a mistake and don't want to record the macro, just press Esc.

The period and extension (.mac) aren't necessary, but they help you to differentiate macros from glossary entries when you're choosing them from F1 lists. The caret (ˆ), together with the Ctrl T contained in the less-than and greater-than symbols, tells Word that you want to be able to retrieve this macro by pressing Ctrl-T. (For more information on naming macros, see this chapter's section entitled "A Note about Naming Macros.")

8. Choose the **T**ransfer **G**lossary **S**ave command. Save the glossary (and the macro you have just created) to a glossary file called MYMACS.GLY.

   Don't try to save this macro to MACRO.GLY, the glossary file that contains Word's supplied macros. The key code Ctrl-T conflicts with key codes used for two of the supplied macros.

Creating a Macro To Toggle the Ruler

Here's another tutorial, which illustrates how you can use commands and command menus in a recorded macro. This example creates a macro that toggles the ruler on and off.

1. Use the MYMACS.GLY glossary file you created in the preceding tutorial, or clear Word's glossary by choosing the **T**ransfer **G**lossary **C**lear command.

2. Press Shift-F3 to start the record macro mode.

3. Because you cannot include mouse actions in a macro, you must choose the command by using keyboard techniques. Press Esc.

4. Type *o*.

   Another way to accomplish the same objective (choosing the **O**ptions command) is to press the down-arrow key and Enter.

5. When the Options menu appears, press the down-arrow key to select the **show ruler** field.

6. Press the space bar.

7. Press Enter to carry out the command.

8. Press Shift-F3 to toggle off the record macro mode.

9. When the Copy menu appears, type

   toggle_ruler.macˆ<ctrl r>

   and press Enter.

Note that this macro does the job it's supposed to do, toggling the ruler on and off, because of the crucial step 6. Suppose, in step 6, that you had typed *y* rather than pressed the space bar. If you had, the macro would choose the **Y**es option in the **show ruler** field every time you used the macro. The macro wouldn't succeed, therefore, in toggling the ruler on and off. But because you pressed the space bar, the macro changes the current setting in the command whenever you run the macro. (Try pressing the space bar in the **show menu** command field, and you can see that the highlight moves back and forth between the Yes and No options.)

In a macro, you can use the first letter of a command name or command field option only if it's capitalized (such as the Yes and No options in many command menus). You cannot, however, use the first letter to select many command fields, such as **show ruler**, because the first letters of most command fields aren't capitalized. You must use the arrow keys or the Tab key to guide the cursor to the command field in such cases. Keep this rule in mind when you're creating macros that use commands.

As you can see, recording macros successfully requires care and planning. Don't be surprised if the macros you record don't work correctly the first time. In this chapter's section on "Testing and Editing Recorded Macros," you learn how to test and edit your macros so that they work the way you intended.

Using a Recorded Macro

Once you have recorded a macro, you can retrieve it in three ways. First, you can type the glossary's name (such as *WordRight.mac*) and press F3. Second, you can choose the Insert command, press F1, and then choose the macro from the list. Third, if you saved the macro with the Ctrl-key code, you can press the Ctrl-key code to start the macro. You can see an obvious advantage to assigning a macro to a Ctrl key code. The first two techniques require more keystrokes to enter the macro than would be required to delete the word by using ordinary techniques.

Understanding How Glossary Files Work with Macros

Because macros are stored in glossary files, you need to remember these facts about glossary files when you save and retrieve macros:

- ❏ If you want your macros to be available in every Word session, save them to Word's default glossary file, NORMAL.GLY.

- ❏ If you save your macros to a file other than NORMAL.GLY, you have to load the glossary file, using Transfer Glossary Load, before you can use your macros. If you haven't loaded the file, the macros don't work. Word just beeps.

For more information on glossaries and glossary files, be sure to read Chapter 12, "Using Glossaries and Bookmarks."

A Note about Naming Macros

You can use up to 31 characters when naming macros, but the name must be a continuous string of characters. You can use underscore characters, hyphens, numbers, and periods, but you can't use spaces or any other punctuation.

You can assign your macro a one-letter or two-letter Ctrl-key code. Sticking to one-letter codes is best, however, because they're quicker and easier to enter. If you can, make the macro names mnemonic, or easy to remember, by assigning each macro to a letter that suggests the macro's function. For example, if you create a macro to add a closing to a letter, assign the code Ctrl-C (for Closing).

If you want to create many macros, however, you may want to use two-letter codes. To create a two-letter key code, put the second letter outside the > symbol when you use the Copy command to copy the macro to the glossary file. Here's a correctly typed macro name that creates a two-letter key code:

```
move_text.mac^<ctrl m>t
```

You can use either upper- or lowercase letters; Word converts lowercase to uppercase.

Caution: You can use any key on the keyboard when you create Ctrl-key combinations to retrieve your macros. You should avoid, however, using function keys such as Ctrl-F10 or Ctrl-F3. If you do, you disable the functions currently assigned to these keys. (If you accidentally use these keys in a macro name, just delete the macro from the glossary to restore the function.)

Testing and Editing Macros

As you will discover quickly when you experiment with recorded macros, it's easy to make mistakes. Frequently, when you run a new macro, it behaves in ways you didn't anticipate. At the extreme, you could inadvertently record a macro that would wipe out your work for the day. For this reason, you should always test your macros on a document that contains nothing of value.

Even if your macro's problem is less dramatic, however, you are still faced with the problem of tracking down and fixing the error. To help you do so, Word supplies a step mode (toggled on and off with Ctrl-F3). You also can insert the macro instructions themselves into your document, where you can inspect them to see what's wrong.

Note: The techniques discussed here can be used on the macros you write as well as on the ones you record.

Testing a Macro with the Step Mode

Ordinarily, Word runs macros as fast as it can—too fast, in most cases, for you to keep track of what's happening. The step mode "slows down" a macro so that you can see how it proceeds through each step. Word pauses at the conclusion of every action and waits for you to press Enter before it moves on to the next step. To use the step mode,

1. Press Ctrl-F3 to toggle on the step mode. The code ST appears in the key status indicator.

2. Run the macro that's giving you problems. Press Enter if nothing happens.

3. Press Enter to move through each step of the macro, one-by-one.

4. When the macro finishes, press Ctrl-F3 to toggle off the step mode.

As you step your macro through its paces, you will probably see where you went wrong in recording it. Often, you will find that you left out a crucial step or selected the wrong option in a menu.

To fix your macro, you have two options. You can record the whole macro again, which can be tedious if the macro is lengthy, or you can edit the macro and type the corrections. The next section shows you how to edit the macro.

Editing a Macro

To edit a macro you have recorded, you must move the macro's instructions from the glossary file to your document so that Word inserts the instructions into your document as if they were text. Here's how:

1. Choose the **Insert** command.

2. When the **from** command field appears, type the name of the macro. Then type a caret (ˆ) symbol immediately after the macro's name (see fig. 21.2).

3. Carry out the command.

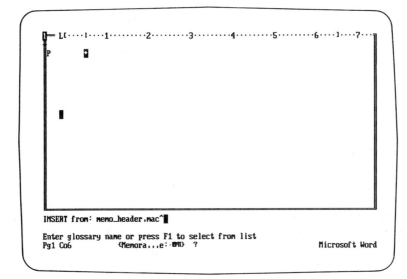

Fig. 21.2.

Inserting a macro into the document for editing.

When you add the caret to the macro's name, Word enters the macro as if it were text. You can edit or change this text and copy it back to the glossary. As you can see in figure 21.3, Word has recorded your keystrokes in the macro, using keynames enclosed in < and > symbols. For more information on keynames, see this chapter's section on "Using Keynames."

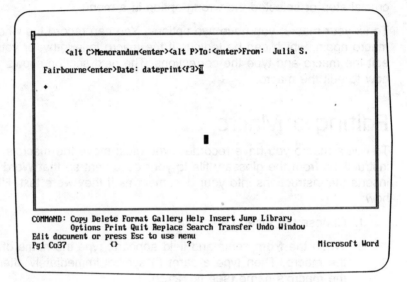

Suppose that you record a macro that creates a memorandum header, but when you use the macro, you discover that you misspelled "memorandum." To correct the error, follow the previous steps to insert the macro's text into your document. Then fix the spelling error. Select the whole macro, and use the **C**opy command to copy it back to its glossary (see fig. 21.4). When you see the message Enter Y to replace glossary entry, N to retype name, or Esc to cancel, press Y.

Writing Macros

Of the two techniques for creating macros, the second—writing them—is by far the more powerful. When you record macros, you are limited to the sequence of keystrokes you enter directly at the keyboard. When you write macros, however, you can include special macro instructions, which greatly increase your options. For example,

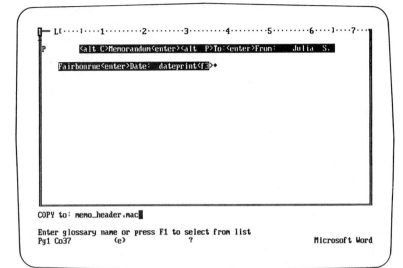

Fig. 21.4.

Copying the corrected macro back to the glossary file.

using these special macro instructions, you can force a macro to pause while the user does something, such as selects text (PAUSE). You can ask the user to type a response, which becomes the contents of a variable (ASK). You can set up conditional instructions that cause the macro to branch this way or that depending on whether a test condition is met (IF...ENDIF). You can create a set of instructions that continue executing until a condition is fulfilled (WHILE...ENDWHILE). You can create instructions that repeat a certain number of times (REPEAT...ENDREPEAT). And you can perform complex calculations and logical comparisons on the data stored in the macro's variables. In short, you can write macros with a sophisticated, but simple and elegant, programming language.

Word's macro programming language is beyond the scope of this book, but you can study and modify an extended application in the section called "Studying an Advanced Example: An Autoexec Menu System," which concludes this chapter.

Writing a Macro To Move Text

Many of you will want to make your macros pause so that a user can perform an operation. In the following tutorial, which includes the PAUSE instruction, you learn how to write a macro that moves text safely by cutting it to a glossary. (This method is safer than cutting to the scrap, where you can accidentally lose the text by performing another deletion before you insert the moved text.)

1. In a new, blank document, type the following text. Press Ctrl-[and Ctrl-] to enter the chevrons. The chevrons are essential; without them, Word would not distinguish between a macro instruction's name (such as PAUSE) and other elements of a macro.

   «SET promptmode = "ignore"»
   «PAUSE Select the text you want to move; press
     Enter when done.»
   <esc>dMOVE<enter>
   «PAUSE Select the text's destination; press Enter
     when done.»
   <esc>iMOVE<enter>

2. Carefully proofread what you have typed. Make sure that you have included one right chevron for each left one, and one less-than symbol for each greater-than symbol.

3. Select the macro and choose the **C**opy command. When the **to** field appears, type

   move.mac^<ctrl m>

   and press Enter.

This macro contains two macro instructions, SET and PAUSE. The SET instruction is needed because the first time you use this macro, a glossary entry named MOVE is created. Therefore, when the macro tries to delete new text to the glossary, a message appears (Enter Y to replace glossary entry, N to retype name, or Esc to cancel). This SET instruction tells Word to ignore such error messages while the macro is running. The PAUSE instructions stop the macro's execution so that you can select text and move the cursor. A message appears on-screen instructing you to select the text to be moved. After you select the text you want to move, you press Enter to resume the macro. Next, the macro "presses" Esc to bring up the command menu, and selects the Delete command by "typing" the letter "d". In the Delete command's **to** field, the macro "types" a glossary name, MOVE. Then it carries out the command by pressing Enter. Another PAUSE instruction displays a message telling you to move the cursor to the text's destination. Finally, the macro "presses" Esc, selects the Insert command, "types" MOVE in the **from** field, and carries out the command.

This macro couldn't be recorded—with recording techniques, you couldn't include the PAUSE instruction. Obviously, written macros are well worth investigating in detail. Although you will need practice (and documentation) to write complex macros, you can get started right away by emulating, and altering, macros that someone else has already written. The section to follow contains one such macro; you will find more in Que Corporation's *Microsoft Word 5 Tips, Tricks, and Traps*, by Bryan Pfaffenberger.

Using Keynames

Table 21.2 lists the keyname codes you should use when referring to keys in written macros.

Note: When you're writing keynames with the Ctrl, Alt, or Shift key, include the second key within the less-than and greater-than symbols, as in <ctrl f10>, <alt b>, and <shift f10>. Note, too, that you can have the cursor-control keys repeat a specified number of times. Typing <*right 5*>, for instance, is the same as typing <*right*> five times.

Table 21.2
Keyname Codes for Writing Macros

<alt>	<keypad + >
<backspace>	<keypad – >
<capslock>	<left>
<ctrl>	<numlock>
<del>	<pgdn>
<down>	<pgup>
<end>	<right>
<enter>	<scrolllock>
<esc>	<shift>
<f1>	<space>
<home>	<tab>
<ins>	<up>
<keypad*>	

Studying an Advanced Example: An Autoexec Menu System

One of the best ways to learn programming techniques is to study a working program, understand how it works, and modify it to suit your needs. This section contains an advanced Word macro that uses many of the language's features. Even if you don't understand everything in the macro, you can still type it into a Word document, define it as a macro using the Copy command, and experiment with it. And as you do, your grasp of Word's macros will grow by leaps and bounds. The macro creates a *shell* that starts every time Word is started. A shell is a program that displays menus to help users cope with complex command procedures. Users can choose options from the menus. From these menus, a user can load one of three document templates or edit an existing document.

Document templates contain everything you need in order to get started creating a letter, report, or memo. A *letter template*, for instance, would include the return address and the dateprint glossary entry. Moreover, the template would be linked (with the Format Stylesheet Attach command) to a style sheet containing key codes and character formats appropriate to letter writing. Similarly, the *memo template* would contain a memo header and be linked to a different style sheet.

The macro described in this section is an autoexec macro. If you create a macro and name it AUTOEXEC, Word runs it automatically every time the program loads the glossary in which the macro is stored. And if you store the AUTOEXEC macro in NORMAL.GLY, Word's default glossary file, the macro runs every time you start Word.

Preparing To Use the AUTOEXEC Macro

If you want to try running this macro, you need to make the following preparations:

1. Create (as subdirectories of the root directory) directories called MEMOS, REPORTS, and LETTERS on your hard disk. (If you don't have a hard disk, you still can use this macro, but you need to change the disk drive designators in the macro instructions from C:\ to B:\.)

2. Use Word to create a document called GREETING.DOC in Word's directory. See figure 21.5 for sample GREETING.DOC file.

3. Use Word to create a letter template called LETTER.DOC (see fig. 21.6). Create a style sheet (named LETTER.STY) for this document, and attach the style sheet to LETTER.DOC, using the **F**ormat **S**tylesheet **A**ttach

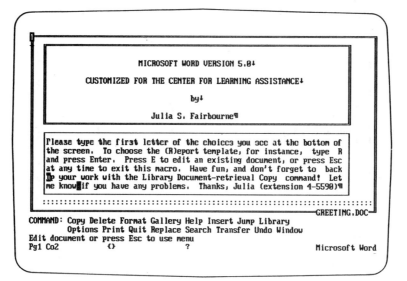

Fig. 21.5.

The file
GREETING.DOC.

command. Then save the document in the LETTERS
directory.

4. Use Word to create a memo template called MEMO.DOC
(see fig. 21.7). Create a style sheet (named MEMO.STY) for
this document, and attach the style sheet to MEMO.DOC,
using the **Format Stylesheet Attach** command. Then save
the document in the MEMOS directory.

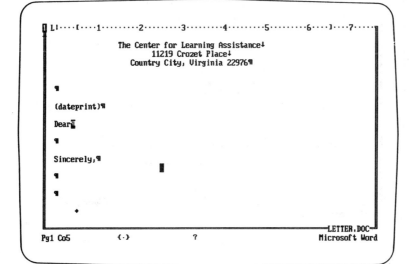

Fig. 21.6.

The file
LETTER.DOC.

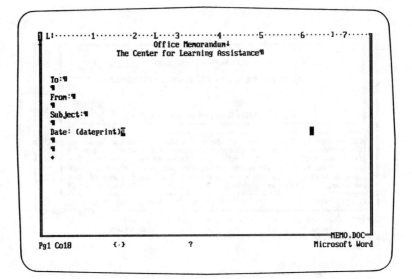

Fig. 21.7.

The file
MEMO.DOC.

5. Use Word to create a report template called REPORT.DOC (see fig. 21.8). Create a style sheet (named REPORT.STY) for this document, and attach the style sheet to REPORT.DOC, using the **F**ormat **S**tylesheet **A**ttach command. Then save the document in the REPORTS directory.

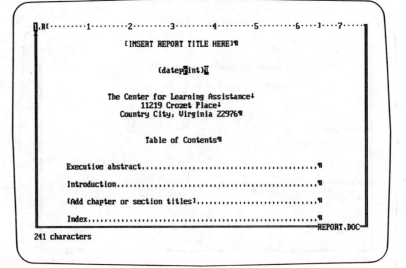

Fig. 21.8.

The file
REPORT.DOC.

Typing and Using the Macro

1. Clear Word and type this macro (see the next section for a line-by-line explanation):

```
<esc>tlGREETING.DOC<enter>
«SET response="false"»
«WHILE response="false"»
        «ASK document=?Write (L)etter, (M)emo, or (R)eport,
        or (E)dit an existing document?»
        «IF document="L" or "M" or "R" or "E"»
            «SET response="true"»«ENDIF»
«ENDWHILE»
«IF document="L"»
        <esc>tlC:\LETTERS\LETTER.DOC<enter>
«ENDIF»
«IF document="M"»
        <esc>tlC:\MEMOS\MEMO.DOC<enter>
«ENDIF»
«IF document="R"»
        <esc>tlC:\REPORTS\REPORT.DOC<enter>
«ENDIF»
«IF document="E"»
        «SET response="false"»
        «WHILE response="false"»
            «ASK known=?Do you know the name and
            location of the file ([Y]es or [N]o)?»
                «IF known="Y" or "N"»
                    «SET response="true"»
                «ENDIF»
        «ENDWHILE»
        «IF known="Y"»
            «ASK filename=?Please type the complete path and filename
            (i.e., c:\memos\memo1.doc).»
            <esc>tl«filename»<enter>
        «ENDIF»
        «IF known="N"»
            «PAUSE Please use Document-retrieval. Press  Enter to continue.»
            <esc>ld<enter>
        «ENDIF»
«ENDIF»
```

Be careful to accompany each opening chevron with a closing chevron, and don't forget to include the ENDWHILE and ENDIF instructions.

2. When you have finished typing the macro and have double-checked it for errors, select it. Then use the **C**opy command and type *test* in the **to** field. Carry out the command.

3. Choose the **T**ransfer **C**lear **W**indow command.

4. Type *test* and press F3. The macro will run. Watch for error messages!

Almost certainly, the macro won't work correctly the first time you try it. You can easily omit a closing chevron, mistype a file or directory name, or forget an ENDIF instruction. If Word displays an error message, examine it carefully to see which line contains the error, and then correct your macro. (See "Testing and Editing Macros" in this chapter for information on displaying and editing the macro.) Be sure that you have created and named the directories properly. Follow all possible paths through the macro. To run it repeatedly, incidentally, you don't need to restart Word over and over; just type *test* and press F3.

5. When the macro is working correctly, select it and copy it to NORMAL.GLY, using the name *autoexec*. Use the **T**ransfer **G**lossary **S**ave command to save the glossary, and quit Word.

6. Restart Word. The macro should carry out automatically.

A Line-by-Line Explanation of the Macro

    <esc>tlGREETING.DOC<enter>

This instruction loads the file called GREETING.DOC, which displays the screen shown in figure 21.5. This screen tells the user how to respond to the prompts presented by the RESPONSE queries in the command area.

    «SET response="false"»

This instruction displays a menu and keeps it on-screen until the user presses one of the correct response keys. The SET instruction creates a variable, a named storage space in Word's memory, called *response*. The instruction places the text "false" in this space. SET is frequently used in this way to set up a variable and assign text or numbers to it. The text or numbers can change later.

«WHILE response = "false"»
[. . .]
«ENDWHILE»

This instruction begins a WHILE...ENDWHILE instruction. Every WHILE instruction must be followed by an ENDWHILE instruction. As long as a test condition holds, Word continues executing the instructions between WHILE and ENDWHILE. The test condition here is that the variable called *response* continues to contain the text "false." It does now, because the preceding instruction, the SET instruction, assigned the text "false" to this variable. When the variable's contents change, however, Word stops executing these instructions.

«ASK document = ?Write (L)etter, (M)emo, or (R)eport, or (E)dit an existing document?»

This instruction is the first to be carried out while the variable *response* contains "false." The statement says, in effect, "Create a variable called *document*, and prompt the user to press a key. The key the user presses becomes the variable's contents." Word displays the text that comes after the question mark in a RESPONSE command menu (see fig. 21.9).

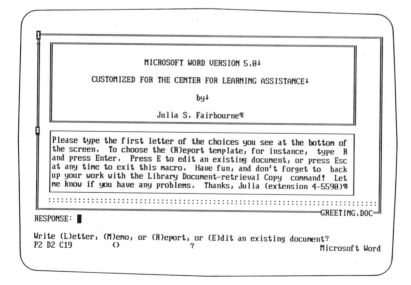

Fig. 21.9.

The Response command menu created by the ASK instruction

An important note here is that without creating the *response* variable and the WHILE...ENDWHILE instruction, Word would be satisfied with any response the user would make to the ASK instruction. ASK merely creates a variable and accepts any keyboard input as the variable's contents. The text that comes after the question mark is just text to be displayed on the screen, so far as Word is concerned. The text doesn't limit the range of responses the ASK instruction accepts as legal input. The user could thus type *X* or *Zanzibar* in response to this prompt, and ASK would dutifully accept it and define the *document* variable to contain whatever the user has typed.

```
«IF document = "L" or "M" or "R" or "E"»
«SET response = "true"»
«ENDIF»
```

This series of instructions keeps the ASK menu on-screen until the user has pressed one of the legal input keys (L, M, R, or E). The instruction is a conditional one, meaning that it's carried out only if a condition is met. And the condition is that the *document* variable must contain one of these four letters (lower- or uppercase). If the variable does contain one of these letters, a new SET instruction is carried out. This SET instruction places the text "true" in the variable *response*.

This SET instruction has big implications for the WHILE...ENDWHILE instruction. As you recall, the instructions within WHILE and ENDWHILE continue to carry out only as long as the variable *response* contains "false." But this SET instruction changes the text in *response* from "false" to "true." Word therefore stops executing the instructions between WHILE and ENDWHILE and goes on to the instruction that follows ENDWHILE.

Note: Just as every WHILE instruction must end with ENDWHILE, every IF instruction must end with ENDIF.

```
«IF document = "L"»
<esc>tlC:\LETTERS\LETTER.DOC<enter>
«ENDIF»
```

Here's another conditional instruction. Word carries it out only if the variable *document* contains the text "L." If it does, Word uses the Transfer Load command to load a template called LETTER.DOC.

```
«IF document = "M"»
<esc>tlC:\MEMOS\MEMO.DOC<enter>
«ENDIF»
```

```
«IF document = "R"»
<esc>tlC:\REPORTS\REPORT.DOC<enter>
«ENDIF»
```

These instructions, like the series that precede them, are conditional instructions. If the user presses M in response to the ASK prompt, Word loads MEMO.DOC. If the user presses R, Word loads REPORT.DOC.

```
«IF document = "E"»
[ . . . ]
«ENDIF»
```

This conditional instruction, which contains many lines between the IF and ENDIF statements, is designed to cope with the situations that may arise if the user wants to edit an existing document. The instructions between IF and ENDIF carry out only if the variable called document contains the text "E."

```
«SET response = "false"»
```

If the variable document contains "E," the first instruction to be carried out is a SET instruction just like the one near the beginning of the program. This instruction places the text "false" in the *response* variable again.

You can probably guess why this instruction is here: to display another menu and keep it on the screen until the user presses one of the legal input keys.

```
«WHILE response = "false"»
[. . .]
«ENDWHILE»
```

Here's the WHILE...ENDWHILE instruction that keeps the menu displayed as long as the variable called response contains "false."

```
«ASK known = ?Do you know the name and location of the file
([Y]es or [N]o)?»
```

And here's the menu. This instruction creates a variable called *known* and displays the message that comes after the question mark.

```
«IF known = "Y" or "N"»
«SET response = "true"»
```

This instruction carries out only if the test condition is met: the variable called *known* must contain the text "Y" or "N" (case doesn't matter). If the variable contains the proper response, the macro carries out the next line, the SET instruction. This instruction changes the text in the variable called *response* from "false" to "true." And as a result, the instructions placed within WHILE and ENDWHILE stop executing, and Word proceeds to the next instruction.

```
«IF known="Y"»
[. . .]
«ENDIF»
```

This instruction is carried out only if a test condition is met. The test condition here is that the variable *known* contains "Y" (in other words, the user knows the file's name and location, and has pressed Y in response to the ASK prompt).

```
«ASK filename=?Please type the complete path and filename
(i.e., c:\memos\memo1.doc).»
```

Word carries out this instruction only if the user has pressed Y. The instruction creates a variable called *filename* and displays the message that comes after the question mark.

```
<esc>tl«filename»<enter>
```

This instruction is the second one that Word carries out if the variable called *known* contains the text "Y." The instruction chooses the Transfer Load command, types in the command's first field the text contained in the *filename* variable, and presses Enter to carry out the command.

```
«IF known="N"»
[. . .]
«ENDIF»
```

The instructions placed within this IF and ENDIF are carried out only if the test condition is met. The test condition here is that the variable *known* contains the text "N." (In other words, the user doesn't know the file's name or location.)

```
«PAUSE Please use Document-retrieval. Press Enter to
continue»
```

This instruction warns the user that the macro is about to start document retrieval. After the user reads the message, pressing Enter continues the macro.

<esc>ld<enter>

This instruction chooses the Library Document-retrieval command and leaves the user to carry out the search and retrieval operations manually.

Modifying the Macro

Once you have been able to get AUTOEXEC to work, you can modify it for your own purposes. Here's how:

1. Consider the documents you normally create, and add additional options to the ASK menu. If you're a research scholar, for instance, you might want to add *(J)ournal article* or *research (N)otes* to the menu.

2. Add the first letter of each of your new choices to the IF instruction that immediately follows the ASK menu. Be sure to place an *or* between each letter, and quotation marks around each letter.

3. Add IF instructions that load the new document templates. If you added "J" to the menu, for instance, you would need this instruction:

   «IF document="J"»
   <esc>tlc:\JOURNART\JOURNART.DOC<enter>

   This instruction doesn't work until you have created a directory named JOURNART and a template named JOURNART.DOC.

Expanding Macro Horizons

Now that you have learned how easily you can make Word 5 jump through hoops, you may want to explore Word 5 macros in more detail. If you're anxious to learn more, you can find all the information you need in *Microsoft Word 5 Tips, Tricks, and Traps*, published by Que Corporation.

Chapter Summary

Anyone can create and use Word 5 macros to automate complicated, repetitive tasks. To record macros, you use the record macro mode to record your keystrokes. You can create more sophisticated macros by writing them with keynames and the PAUSE instruction. To get fancier still, you can learn to use more of Word's powerful macro instructions.

With this chapter, you have come to the end of *Using Microsoft Word 5*. I have enjoyed helping you explore this significant new version of Word, a version that incorporates all the suggestions and addresses the complaints users have been making. In a sense, Word is now truly a user-shaped product; much that's good about Version 5 is attributable to user input. (In my opinion, that's what personal computing is all about—or at least, it should be.) For this reason, I encourage you to let Microsoft know what you want to see in Version 6 and beyond. I have my own list already!

Appendix

Word and Your Computer: Configuring Your System for Word 5 and Using SETUP

You can use Word 5 on virtually any IBM-compatible computer system, even a very basic one. To get maximum performance from Word 5, however, you may want to choose certain advanced components. This appendix briefly surveys ways to optimize your system for Word and covers the installation procedure you will use when you run SETUP, Word's installation utility.

Word 5 and Your Computer System

An IBM-format computer system for word processing with Word includes, at the minimum, two disk drives, 384K of internal memory, a monochrome video adapter and monitor, and a printer. To get the most from Word 5, however, you should consider upgrading your system to include a hard disk, at least 640K of memory (more memory, using an expanded memory board), a graphics adapter, a color monitor, and a laser printer.

Disk Drives

At the minimum, you will need an IBM-compatible computer with two 360K disk drives. Although Word 5 will run on such a system, you will discover that it isn't much fun. Word goes to disk frequently, and you will often find yourself waiting while Word looks for information it needs. With 360K drives, moreover, you must frequently swap disks in and out of the computer. The program performs much better with two 720K drives, a configuration common among laptop computers. But Word 5 is at its best on hard disk systems.

You should, therefore, consider adding a hard disk to your system (if you haven't already). Like its predecessors, Word 5 doesn't maintain your whole file in memory; it goes to disk frequently to store and retrieve sections of your file and to obtain program information from a variety of files. On floppy drive systems, all this disk activity adds up to frequent interruptions of your work. Moreover, if you're using a hard disk, you can install Spell and Thesaurus with Word so that both are available at a keystroke. To get maximum performance with Word, add a hard disk to your system.

System Speed and Memory

Word runs at an acceptable pace even on 4.77-MHz systems equipped with the 8088 microprocessor chip. In fact, this book was written on such a system. Unlike its early predecessors, such as Version 2.0, Word 5 is a fast program—indeed, it's even faster than Word 4, which was designed specifically to beat WordPerfect in several key areas. On faster machines, such as 20-MHz systems equipped with the 80286 or 80386 microprocessors, the program's performance is breathtaking.

As Word has grown over the years, it has consumed more and more free memory space. With Word 5, the program has become large enough to reduce free memory space to the bare minimum, even on systems with 640K. To be sure, the program will run on computers equipped with only 384K, but not very well. Word needs large amounts of free memory to perform operations such as Search and Replace (see table A.1 for a list of such operations). On a 384K system, you may not be able to use these commands for any but the most trivial sorting or searching operations.

Indeed, even with 640K, Word 5 may not be able to complete lengthy replace, sort, or indexing operations. If there is insufficient memory to complete an operation, you will see the Insufficient memory message. You can save your work, clear Word, reload your document, and try again; but even so, you may not have enough memory to carry out the command. Even if Word can complete the operation, you will probably see the SAVE indicator on the status line after using one of the commands listed in table A.1. At this point, you must save your document. Sometimes you must clear Word's memory completely by using Transfer Clear All in order to make the SAVE indicator disappear. In such cases, you must reload your file to continue working. These interruptions are frustrating and detrimental to concentration.

Fortunately, Word 5 can use expanded memory conforming to the LIM (Lotus-Intel-Microsoft) expanded memory specification 3.2 or above. You can add expanded memory to your system by installing an optional memory board. Your computer may already be equipped with expanded memory on the main circuit board, so consult your computer's documentation for details. If you plan to create lengthy documents, use Word for all-day writing and editing sessions, or compile indexes from lengthy documents, consider adding expanded memory to your system. Add expanded memory, too, if you want to get maximum performance from Word. The more memory you have, the faster Word runs.

If you are running Word 5 under OS/2 on an 80286 or 80386 machine, Word automatically uses all the available memory beyond the 640K barrier. This fact alone makes OS/2 and additional memory very wise purchases for anyone designing a system around Word 5.

Caution: When you run Word 5 under MS-DOS on 640K systems, avoid loading memory-resident programs like SideKick. You will need all the free memory space you can get to run Word 5 efficiently. Most memory-resident programs include a command that removes the program from memory. Use this command before starting Word.

Table A.1
Operations Requiring Free Memory

Complex macros
Complex math operations
Extended editing sessions
Library Autosort
Library Index
Library Table
Paginate (auto or manual)
Replace
Search

Mouse

Word 5 fully supports the Microsoft mouse, a hand-held input device that is used to move the cursor, highlight text for editing purposes, and give commands. As you slide the mouse around on the tabletop next to the keyboard, a pointer on-screen parallels its moves.

Many word processing programs claim to be compatible with the mouse, but on closer inspection, the mouse capability these programs provide turns out to be little more than an afterthought, added on to the program to increase its marketability. With such programs, you will quickly find that it is difficult to control the cursor with the mouse, and editing operations take far longer with the mouse than they do with the keyboard. Word is virtually alone among IBM-format word processing programs in having been designed around the mouse from the beginning. With Word, the mouse provides precision cursor control, super-fast text highlighting, and convenient command capabilities. It is truly a pleasure to use a mouse with Word, and most people who try it feel handicapped when they must use a computer that lacks a mouse. In this way, Word 5 provides much of the convenience and feel of Apple's Macintosh computers, which—like Word—were designed around the use of the mouse.

Still, you can use Word 5 without a mouse without suffering any penalty. Almost every command can be given using the mouse or the keyboard. If you are an expert typist and prefer not to take your hands away from the keyboard, you can omit the mouse from your system. In this respect, Word is unlike most Macintosh software (and even the Macintosh version of Word), which frequently fail to provide keyboard alternatives to mouse commands. Word 5's keyboard commands are exceptionally well conceived, and as you will learn in this book, you can reconfigure the keyboard to your heart's content.

Video Adapters and Display Monitors

Laptops aside, most IBM-compatible computers can be equipped with a variety of video adapters (a circuit board that controls the screen display) and display monitors. Generally, you can choose from monochrome (green, yellow, or white text and black background) or color adapters and monitors. Adapters and monitors differ also in their resolution, or their ability to display fine-detailed images on the screen. Resolution is usually expressed by the number of distinct dots the adapter and monitor can display, measured horizontally and vertically. The IBM Color Graphics Adapter, a low-resolution adapter, can display

640 dots horizontally but only 200 vertically. Some adapters and monitors can display only the characters built into IBM-compatible computers, while others can display graphics. Word 5 is designed to work with all these video displays and monitors, and you can use the program even with very basic display systems (such as the Color Graphics Adapter or IBM Monochrome Adapter).

If you want to use a mouse or display graphic images, Word 5 is at its best with a high-resolution graphics display adapter and monitor, such as the Hercules Graphics Card, Hercules Graphics Card Plus, the Enhanced Graphics Adapter (EGA), or the Video Graphics Array (VGA) adapter. To understand why, it is helpful to understand the difference between Word's two display modes. As explained in Chapter 1, Word operates in two basic video display modes: the text mode and the graphics mode.

❑ In the text mode, Word displays only the 254 characters built into your computer. The text mode cannot display graphics or character emphases other than underline and boldface, but text mode is significantly faster than the graphics mode.

❑ In the graphics mode, Word displays all the character emphases, such as italic, double underline, strikethrough, and superscripts. Moreover, with the new Print preView mode, you can see the graphics you have integrated into Word 5's text. The graphics mode is superior for mouse users because it displays the mouse pointer's many shape changes with more detail. (These shape changes tell you when the mouse is ready to accept a command.) The graphics mode, unfortunately, comes with a penalty: it is slower than the text mode. Since Version 4.0 it has been possible to switch between the text mode and graphics mode at a keystroke (Alt-F9). This capability enables you to scroll through your document in text mode, switching to graphics mode only when you need to view graphic images. If you are in text mode, Word 5 automatically switches to graphics mode when you choose the Print preView command. If you plan to use a mouse or integrate text and graphics, equip your system with a graphics adapter and monitor.

New Word 5 features make a good case for adding a color monitor to your system. A new command field in the Options command menu, for instance, enables you to code font sizes and character emphases with distinctive colors. Compared to previous versions, moreover, you have far more control over the colors of menu items, borders, and backgrounds. With EGA and VGA color monitors, you can display color without sacrificing text resolution. The EGA adapter and monitor can display 640 dots horizontally and 350 vertically, while the VGA can display 640 horizontally and 480 vertically.

If you are a professional writer, editor, or publisher, consider adding a Genius full-page display and monitor to your system. In graphics mode, Word will display 66 lines with a resolution of 1,024 by 768 lines, an exceptionally high figure.

Printers

Like all word processing programs, Word 5 is at its best when used with a supported printer. A supported printer is one for which the program includes a printer driver, which is a special file that contains information about the printer. This information allows the program to "translate" its printing and formatting commands so that the printer can respond to them. For this reason, you don't have to worry about all those complicated control codes you see in your printer's manual. Just hook up and prepare your printer as the manual suggests, and install Word, using the SETUP program. Word automatically translates your formatting commands so that your printer prints your work properly.

If Your Printer Is Not Supported by Word 5

Microsoft Word is famous for supporting many printers, and more than 100 printer drivers come with Word 5. Even if your printer isn't on the list of supported printers, however, you still may be able to use it with Word. Many printers are compatible with a better-known brand's command set. Dot-matrix printers, for instance, frequently respond to EPSON commands, and laser printers frequently respond to Hewlett-Packard commands. Check your printer's manual to find out whether your printer responds to another brand's commands. If it does, try using your printer with the better-known brand's printer driver. For more information on installing printer drivers, see "Using SETUP," elsewhere in this appendix.

Word and Laser Printers

Today's laser printers are increasingly affordable, and if you want to get maximum performance from Word 5, you should consider adding one to your system. Laser printers fall into the following two categories:

❑ Hewlett-Packard LaserJet Printers and Compatibles. These printers construct text by drawing characters from complete character sets, one for each typestyle (font) and size. Usually, these printers come with one built-in font (Courier), a typewriter-style font that is not proportionally spaced. To use additional fonts, you must purchase font cartridges. Alternatively, you can purchase additional memory for the computer, and use downloadable fonts. Downloadable fonts are provided on disk. For most printers in this category, Word 5 will download fonts automatically when you print your document. Many fonts are available in both cartridge and disk form from the printer manufacturers, as well as from third-party suppliers. *Note:* Printer cartridges have a limited life.

❑ Apple LaserWriter Printers and Compatibles (PostScript printers). These printers construct text by using a mathematical formula written with an advanced printer control language called PostScript. Usually, these printers come with 10 or more such formulas built into the printer's memory. You do not need to purchase a cartridge, and you do not need to download the fonts built into the printer. If you want, you can choose among approximately 200 downloadable fonts available on disk. You can set up Word to download fonts automatically.

Hewlett-Packard printers and compatibles are significantly cheaper than Apple LaserWriters and compatibles, and they have an advantage with Word 5. As you will learn in this book, you can integrate text and graphics with Word 5. If you are using a PostScript printer, however, you cannot see the graphic image on-screen in the Print preView mode. (The reason is that PostScript printers construct graphic images from mathematical representations, the same way they construct text. Hewlett-Packard LaserJet printers and compatibles, in contrast, print bit-mapped graphic images, which are made up of tiny dots. Your computer's screen can display the dots, but it cannot construct an image from a formula.) You therefore can see the image in Print preView. Choose a PostScript-compatible printer only if you are interested in pursuing professional layout and document design.

If your budget is limited, note that Word 5 fully supports the Hewlett-Packard DeskJet, which is priced at the level of a good impact printer. The DeskJet is a sophisticated ink jet printer that produces output virtually indistinguishable from that produced by the same company's LaserJet, but at substantially slower speeds (2 pages per minute). You can use font cartridges and downloadable fonts to supplement the printer's built-in Courier font. The ink used in a DeskJet is water-soluble, however, and will smear if you get it wet.

Most laser printers cannot print on the perimeter of the page. In previous versions of Word, the margin settings you chose in the Format Division Margins command menu did not take these unprintable regions into account, so you had to adjust your margins to get them to print correctly. The printer drivers supplied with Word 5, however, automatically compensate for these regions.

Another welcome feature of Word 5 is its support for downloadable fonts. If you are using a printer driver that supports downloadable fonts, Word 5 will automatically download the fonts you need when you print your document. It's as simple as that! Among the drivers that support automatic downloading are the ones for the Hewlett-Packard DeskJet and the Apple LaserWriter.

If you are using downloadable fonts, note that you may have to send in a coupon to receive the Supplemental Printers Disk, which gives you full support for these fonts. The coupon for this disk comes with your Word package. Microsoft does not charge for the disk.

Using SETUP

The best way to install Word 5 is to use the SETUP program provided on Utilities Disk #1. You can install Word 5 without SETUP, but you should do so only if you are an intermediate or advanced user and fully understand all the system modifications you must make.

Preparing to use SETUP

Before you run SETUP, you need to gather some information. You need to know your printer's make and model, as well as the output port to which it is connected (such as LPT1 or COM1). You also need to know the make and model of the video adapter you are using. If you are using a two floppy drive system, you need several blank, formatted disks and your DOS disk to install the program.

Using SETUP with Two Floppy Systems

SETUP modifies your DOS disk and copies the Word programs to a blank, formatted disk. If you are using 360K disks, you cannot fit all the Word programs on a single disk. SETUP creates two program disks, called Program Disk #1 and Program Disk #2. You start Word with Program Disk #1 and after Word appears, you remove Program Disk #1 and place Program Disk #2 into the same disk drive (drive A). Your document disk, the disk you use in drive B for your documents, must also contain information Word needs. SETUP creates for you a document disk that contains the necessary information. After running SETUP, make many copies of this document disk so that you always have properly prepared document disks available. Keep one copy just as SETUP prepared it so that you can make additional copies in the future.

If you are using a two floppy system, you still can use Thesaurus and Spell. However, you must insert these disks when directed to do so by Word. Do not use the original copies of these disks; make and use backup copies. SETUP does not make these copies for you. Use the DOS DISKCOPY program to make backup copies of these disks.

 Caution: When you install Word on a two floppy system, SETUP makes modifications to your DOS disk. You always must start your computer with this copy of your DOS disk, and no other, if you want to use Word. If you use some other copy of your DOS disk that SETUP has not modified, Word may not run. If Word does not run, restart your system with the DOS disk that SETUP modified.

Installing Word on a Hard Disk System

You can create your own directory for Word 5. If you do not, SETUP creates one for you. SETUP copies all the Word programs and information to this directory, including Spell, Thesaurus, and Learning Word, if you want them.

Caution: SETUP creates or makes modifications to two files on your hard disk, called AUTOEXEC.BAT and CONFIG.SYS. If you erase or change these files, Word may not run. If Word does not run, use SETUP again or modify these files as indicated in the section called "Installing Word without SETUP," elsewhere in this appendix. Incidentally, be careful when you use the installation software provided with some programs. Sometimes these installation utilities wipe out existing AUTOEXEC.BAT and CONFIG.SYS files without asking your permission, and then write their own. (SETUP does not erase these files; if they exist, it just modifies them.) If one of these utilities wipes out the files SETUP created, Word may not run. Before installing a new program, make copies of these files so that you can restore them if the installation utility wipes them out.

Starting SETUP

To use SETUP, follow these steps:

1. Place the Word Utilities Disk #1 in drive A.

2. If the A› prompt is not visible, type *a:* and press Enter.

3. Type *setup* and press Enter.

4. Follow the SETUP program's instructions to install Word 5 on your computer.

5. After running SETUP, restart your computer by pressing Ctrl-Alt-Del.

   The changes SETUP makes do not take effect until you restart your system.

Hard Disk Tips

By far the best way to use Word on a hard disk is to create separate directories for your documents, such as \LETTERS and \REPORTS. If you have installed Word using SETUP, your AUTOEXEC.BAT file contains an instruction that tells DOS where to find Word, even if you start Word from another directory. This instruction enables you to start Word from \LETTERS, for instance. When you do, the \LETTERS directory becomes the default directory for the entire operating session. You need not supply any additional path information to save files to \LETTERS; Word automatically saves files to the default directory.

Starting Word from document directories has another significant advantage with Word 5. When you start Word from a document directory, Word looks in that directory for a style sheet called NORMAL.STY. If it finds this file, Word uses the style definitions recorded in it as the default styles for the entire operating session (unless you deliberately attach another style sheet or load a document to which another style sheet has been attached).

As explained in Chapter 20, "Using Style Sheets," you now can much more easily modify Word's default style sheet, NORMAL.STY, which defines the default formatting settings. You can modify NORMAL.STY if you want to change these default settings. For instance, you can set up a version of NORMAL.STY that automatically uses your printer's Helvetica fonts. See Chapter 20 for information on modifying NORMAL.STY.

Because NORMAL.STY is now so easy to modify, you can place a version of NORMAL.STY appropriate to single-spaced business letters in the \LETTERS directory you created. You can place another version of NORMAL.STY, this one suitable for double-spaced reports, in the directory called \REPORTS. If you start Word in \LETTERS, the blank document that appears on-screen automatically will have all the formats you need for business letters. If you start Word in \REPORTS, the blank document will have all the formats you need for reports.

If you need help with topics such as subdirectories and AUTOEXEC.BAT files, I recommend Que's *MS-DOS User's Guide,* 3rd Edition, and especially Que's *Managing Your Hard Disk*, 2nd Edition, both by Chris DeVoney.

Word Start-Up Options

Word 5 can be started by several methods. The one you choose may depend on what you want to accomplish in the new work session (begin a new document, open an existing document, or continue where you left off during your last editing session). Table A.2 lists start-up options with Word 5.

Table A.2
Word Start-Up Options

Command	Result
Word	Starts Word and loads a new, blank document
Word filename	Starts Word and loads the document you name. If you are loading a Word document, you need not type the period and extension (.DOC).
Word/l	Starts Word and loads the document you were working on when you last saved your work and quit Word; moves the cursor to its last location in the document

Caution: If you have used previous versions of Word, you may be accustomed to starting Word with the /c, /g, and /k switches to control graphics modes. These switches no longer work. To choose a graphics mode, after starting Word use Alt-F9 to toggle between text and graphics. Use the **display mode** field of the Options command to choose 43- and 60-line displays, if your graphics adapter supports these high-resolution modes.

Index

531

N

More Computer Knowledge from Que

Lotus Software Titles

1-2-3 Database Techniques	24.95
1-2-3 Release 2.2 Business Applications	39.95
1-2-3 Release 2.2 Quick Reference	7.95
1-2-3 Release 2.2 QuickStart	19.95
1-2-3 Release 2.2 Workbook and Disk	29.95
1-2-3 Release 3 Business Applications	39.95
1-2-3 Release 3 Quick Reference	7.95
1-2-3 Release 3 QuickStart	19.95
1-2-3 Release 3 Workbook and Disk	29.95
1-2-3 Tips, Tricks, and Traps, 3rd Edition	22.95
Upgrading to 1-2-3 Release 3	14.95
Using 1-2-3, Special Edition	24.95
Using 1-2-3 Release 2.2, Special Edition	24.95
Using 1-2-3 Release 3	24.95
Using Lotus Magellan	21.95
Using Symphony, 2nd Edition	26.95

Database Titles

dBASE III Plus Applications Library	24.95
dBASE III Plus Handbook, 2nd Edition	24.95
dBASE III Plus Tips, Tricks, and Traps	21.95
dBASE III Plus Workbook and Disk	29.95
dBASE IV Applications Library, 2nd Edition	39.95
dBASE IV Handbook, 3rd Edition	23.95
dBASE IV Programming Techniques	24.95
dBASE IV QueCards	21.95
dBASE IV Quick Reference	7.95
dBASE IV QuickStart	19.95
dBASE IV Tips, Tricks, and Traps, 2nd Edition	21.95
dBASE IV Workbook and Disk	29.95
dBXL and Quicksilver Programming: Beyond dBASE	24.95
R:BASE User's Guide, 3rd Edition	22.95
Using Clipper	24.95
Using DataEase	22.95
Using Reflex	19.95
Using Paradox 3	24.95

Applications Software Titles

AutoCAD Advanced Techniques	34.95
AutoCAD Quick Reference	7.95
AutoCAD Sourcebook	24.95
Excel Business Applications: IBM Version	39.95
Introduction to Business Software	14.95
PC Tools Quick Reference	7.95
Smart Tips, Tricks, and Traps	24.95
Using AutoCAD, 2nd Edition	29.95
Using Computers in Business	24.95
Using DacEasy	21.95

Using Dollars and Sense: IBM Version, 2nd Edition	19.95
Using Enable/OA	23.95
Using Excel: IBM Version	24.95
Using Generic CADD	24.95
Using Harvard Project Manager	24.95
Using Managing Your Money, 2nd Edition	19.95
Using Microsoft Works: IBM Version	21.95
Using PROCOMM PLUS	19.95
Using Q&A, 2nd Edition	21.95
Using Quattro	21.95
Using Quicken	19.95
Using Smart	22.95
Using SmartWare II	24.95
Using SuperCalc5, 2nd Edition	22.95

Word Processing and Desktop Publishing Titles

DisplayWrite QuickStart	19.95
Harvard Graphics Quick Reference	7.95
Microsoft Word 5 Quick Reference	7.95
Microsoft Word 5 Tips, Tricks, and Traps: IBM Version	19.95
Using DisplayWrite 4, 2nd Edition	19.95
Using Freelance Plus	24.95
Using Harvard Graphics	24.95
Using Microsoft Word 5: IBM Version	21.95
Using MultiMate Advantage, 2nd Edition	19.95
Using PageMaker: IBM Version, 2nd Edition	24.95
Using PFS: First Choice	22.95
Using PFS: First Publisher	22.95
Using Professional Write	19.95
Using Sprint	21.95
Using Ventura Publisher, 2nd Edition	24.95
Using WordPerfect, 3rd Edition	21.95
Using WordPerfect 5	24.95
Using WordStar, 2nd Edition	21.95
Ventura Publisher Techniques and Applications	22.95
Ventura Publisher Tips, Tricks, and Traps	24.95
WordPerfect Macro Library	21.95
WordPerfect Power Techniques	21.95
WordPerfect QueCards	21.95
WordPerfect Quick Reference	7.95
WordPerfect QuickStart	21.95
WordPerfect Tips, Tricks, and Traps, 2nd Edition	21.95
WordPerfect 5 Workbook and Disk	29.95

Macintosh/Apple II Titles

The Big Mac Book	27.95
Excel QuickStart	19.95
Excel Tips, Tricks, and Traps	22.95
Using AppleWorks, 3rd Edition	21.95
Using AppleWorks GS	21.95
Using dBASE Mac	19.95
Using Dollars and Sense: Macintosh Version	19.95
Using Excel: Macintosh Verson	22.95
Using FullWrite Professional	21.95

Using HyperCard:	24.95
Using Microsoft Word 4: Macintosh Version	21.95
Using Microsoft Works: Macintosh Version, 2nd Edition	21.95
Using PageMaker: Macintosh Version	24.95
Using WordPerfect: Macintosh Version	19.95

Hardware and Systems Titles

DOS Tips, Tricks, and Traps	22.95
DOS Workbook and Disk	29.95
Hard Disk Quick Reference	7.95
IBM PS/2 Handbook	21.95
Managing Your Hard Disk, 2nd Edition	22.95
MS-DOS Quick Reference	7.95
MS-DOS QuickStart	21.95
MS-DOS User's Guide, Special Edition	29.95
Networking Personal Computers, 3rd Edition	22.95
Norton Utilities Quick Reference	7.95
The Printer Bible	24.95
Understanding UNIX: A Conceptual Guide, 2nd Edition	21.95
Upgrading and Repairing PCs	27.95
Using DOS	22.95
Using Microsoft Windows	19.95
Using Novell NetWare	24.95
Using OS/2	23.95
Using PC DOS, 3rd Edition	22.95

Programming and Technical Titles

Assembly Language Quick Reference	7.95
C Programmer's Toolkit	39.95
C Programming Guide, 3rd Edition	24.95
C Quick Reference	7.95
DOS and BIOS Functions Quick Reference	7.95
DOS Programmer's Reference, 2nd Edition	27.95
Power Graphics Programming	24.95
QuickBASIC Advanced Techniques	21.95
QuickBASIC Programmer's Toolkit	39.95
QuickBASIC Quick Reference	7.95
SQL Programmer's Guide	29.95
Turbo C Programming	22.95
Turbo Pascal Advanced Techniques	22.95
Turbo Pascal Programmer's Toolkit	39.95
Turbo Pascal Quick Reference	7.95
Using Assembly Language	24.95
Using QuickBASIC 4	19.95
Using Turbo Pascal	21.95

For more information, call

1-800-428-5331

All prices subject to change without notice. Prices and charges are for domestic orders only. Non-U.S. prices might be higher.

SELECT QUE BOOKS TO INCREASE
YOUR PERSONAL COMPUTER PRODUCTIVITY

Microsoft Word 5 Tips, Trips, and Traps: IBM Version

by Bryan Pfaffenberger

Microsoft Word expert Bryan Pfaffenberger brings you this comprehensive collection of important tips and techniques to get the most from the newest version of the popular IBM-compatible word processing program. Included is information on macros, style sheets, indirect formatting, and on-screen windows.

Using Microsoft Windows

by Ron Person

Using Microsoft Windows is an easy-to-follow guide to Windows 2.0 and Windows/386. Incorporating a series of hands-on practice sessions, this well-written text helps you get up and running with Windows and Windows applications. Both an in-depth tutorial and a lasting reference, this book shows you how to manage the Windows interface; control the MS-DOS Executive; customize Windows; and use Windows Write, Windows Paint, and the desktop applications. Open the world of Windows with Que's *Using Microsoft Windows*!

Using PageMaker on the IBM, 2nd Edition

by Diane Burns and S. Venit

Updated for the IBM-compatible version of PageMaker 3.0, this popular text now covers the cover separations capabilities of the program. An ideal introductory text, *Using PageMaker* presents both program basics and basic design concepts. Soon you'll be producing professional publications—just like the dozens of detailed examples presented in this book!

Using Excel: IBM Version

by Ron Person and Mary Campbell

Excel is one of the most advanced spreadsheets available for IBM and compatible personal computers. Que's *Using Excel: IBM Version* helps you master this powerful program. If you are a spreadsheet novice, the Quick Start tutorials will help you get up and running with the program. More experienced users will appreciate the tips and tricks that help you improve your efficiency and troubleshoot Excel problems. This well-written text also includes a special section for 1-2-3 users making the switch to Excel. *Using Excel* will help you excel with Excel!